UK FISHING VESSF'^

Welcome to the first edition of our
seen around our coastline. Because
longest running occupations we hav
our fishermen going out in all weath
'food on the table'. The vessels the
ships. Some date from the nineteentl .... _ built right up to
the present day, admittedly in smaller .....n in earlier years. The advances
in design means faster, more efficient vessels and due to many countries overfishing
the waters that surround us, the advances in electronic gadgetry, such as fish finding
radar, have become essential to the modern day fisherman. The industry is one of
the most regulated of all, with quotas for numbers, types of fish, size etc. Even so,
the principle remains the same – find the fish, catch them, and market them. This
oversimplified picture of present day fishing does not do the men and women who
risk life and limb, justice. They have our sincere thanks and admiration.

Every registered fishing boat has to be licensed by an administrative port and have
annual checks regarding safety and sea-worthiness. I have included this port in our
database. Each vessel carries her name and port code. This code consists of an
abbreviated port name, usually, though not always, in the form of first and last
letters (e.g. BM = Brixham), and the purpose of this book is to be able to identify a
vessel from either piece of information. The remaining details shown are the overall
length in metres, gross tonnage and the year that the vessel was built. The first part
of the book shows an alphabetical listing, with full details known. The second part is
a port id/name index.

We hope you will find our publication useful, and to that end, we would be very
grateful to receive any comments, additional information or corrections by email or
snail mail to our address below. Thank you.

Photos by the author.
Front cover: 'Girl Rona' (TH117) entering her home port, Teignmouth
Rear cover: 'Harvest Queen' (SE116) seen after her overhaul and fresh paintjob, on
the River Exe

EGGWords Publications (eggwords@gmail.com)
Trescombe, Third Drive, Teignmouth, Devon TQ14 9JT

FISHING PORT REGISTRATION CODES

A	Aberdeen	DA	Drogheda	LK	Lerwick	SC	Scilly
AA	Alloa	DE	Dundee	LL	Liverpool	SD	Sunderland
AB	Aberystwyth	DH	Dartmouth	LN	King's Lynn	SE	Salcombe
AD	Ardrossan	DK	Dundalk	LO	London	SH	Scarborough
AH	Arbroath	DO	Douglas	LR	Lancaster	SM	Shoreham
AR	Ayr	DR	Dover	LT	Lowestoft	SN	North Shields
B	Belfast	DS	Dumfries	LY	Londonderry	SO	Sligo
BA	Ballantrae	E	Exeter	M	Milford Haven	SR	Stranraer
BCK	Buckie	F	Faversham	ME	Montrose	SS	St Ives
BD	Bideford	FD	Fleetwood	MH	Middlesbrough	SSS	South Shields
BE	Barnstaple	FE	Folkestone	ML	Methil	ST	Stockton
BF	Banff	FH	Falmouth	MN	Maldon	SU	Southampton
BH	Blyth	FR	Fraserburgh	MR	Manchester	SY	Stornoway
BK	Berwick-on-Tweed	FY	Fowey	MT	Maryport	T	Tralee
BL	Bristol	G	Galway	N	Newry	TH	Teignmouth
BM	Brixham	GE	Goole	NE	Newcastle	TN	Troon
BN	Boston	GH	Grangemouth	NN	Newhaven	TO	Truro
BO	Bo'ness	GK	Greenock	NT	Newport, Gwent	TT	Tarbert, Loch Fyne
BR	Bridgwater	GN	Granton	OB	Oban	UL	Ullapool
BRD	Broadford	GR	Gloucester	P	Portsmouth	W	Waterford
BS	Beaumaris	GU	Guernsey	PD	Peterhead	WA	Whitehaven
BU	Burntisland	GW	Glasgow	PE	Poole	WD	Wexford
BW	Barrow	GY	Grimsby	PH	Plymouth	WH	Weymouth
C	Cork	H	Hull	PL	Peel	WI	Wisbech
CA	Cardigan	HH	Harwich	PN	Preston	WK	Wick
CE	Coleraine	HL	Hartlepool	PT	Port Talbot	WN	Wigtown
CF	Cardiff	IE	Irvine	PW	Padstow	WO	Workington
CH	Chester	IH	Ipswich	PZ	Penzance	WT	Westport
CK	Colchester	INS	Inverness	R	Ramsgate	WY	Whitby
CL	Carlisle	J	Jersey	RN	Runcorn	YH	Great Yarmouth
CN	Campbeltown	K	Kirkwall	RO	Rothesay		
CO	Caernarfon	KY	Kirkcaldy	RR	Rochester		
CS	Cowes	L	Limerick	RX	Rye		
CT	Castletown	LA	Llanelli	RY	Ramsey		
CY	Castlebay	LH	Leith	S	Skibbereen		
D	Arklow/Dublin	LI	Littlehampton	SA	Swansea		

UK Fishing Vessels 2015

Vessel Name	Code	Port Name	Loa	Ton Gt	Year	Construction Place
007 II	GU119	GUERNSEY	5.06	0.79	1995	ARUNDEL WEST SUSSEX
3 STROKES	B906	BELFAST	5.12	0.84	1972	BANGOR
4-EVER	SM26	SHOREHAM	4.40	0.74	1980	NEWHAVEN
A MAIREACH	CN7	CAMPBELTOWN	6.20	1.50	2005	GBR
AALSKERE	K373	KIRKWALL	33.89	532.00	1997	POLAND
AALTJE ADRIAANTJE	PZ198	PENZANCE	28.60	125.00	1967	HOLLAND
AARON	N370	NEWRY	9.10	7.00	1974	RYE SUSSEX
AARVEY JO	RX450	RYE	5.20	0.79	1995	HAVANT HAMPSHIRE
ABBA II	J407	JERSEY	5.78	1.11	2000	GBR
ABBA-CAT	AB170	ABERYSTWYTH	7.50	1.15	2003	NORTHUMBERLAND
ABBACY ANNIE	B351	BELFAST	4.60	0.50	1979	PORTAVOGIE
ABBI	PE81	POOLE	7.68	3.96	1978	UNKNOWN
ABBIE JAYNE	LN454	KINGS LYNN	13.94	20.65	1997	ABERYSTWYTH
ABBIE LOU	LO574	LONDON	9.95	10.88	2005	ENGLAND
ABBIE SHANAY	LA38	LLANELLI	4.22	0.62	1997	LLANELLI
ABBYJACK	WK856	WICK	7.95	7.03	2007	BRIGHTON
ABE	P946	PORTSMOUTH	5.73	1.21	1996	PLYMOUTH
ABIGAIL	B969	BELFAST	5.45	0.93	2005	NOT KNOWN
ABIGAIL	BN24	BOSTON	9.88	8.91	1984	HULL
ABIGAIL III	B28	BELFAST	6.05	2.00	2014	IRL
ABIGALE	M1041	MILFORD HAVEN	5.90	1.48	1982	GBR
ABILITY	M372	MILFORD HAVEN	5.79	1.57	1996	ARUNDEL
ABILITY	N294	NEWRY	23.06	111.00	1980	ABERDEEN
ABOUT TIME	GK8	GREENOCK	11.90	16.24	1987	POOLE
ACADEMUS	BA817	BALLANTRAE	16.11	66.00	1998	PAULL NR HULL
ACADIA	PD365	PETERHEAD	8.10	4.20	2012	EDINBURGH
ACCORD	BCK262	BUCKIE	21.03	126.00	1979	UNK
ACCORD	LK31	LERWICK	8.15	3.88	1973	NORWAY
ACCORD	M90	MILFORD HAVEN	9.90	8.34	1999	LEWES
ACCORD III	CN67	CAMPBELTOWN	11.47	21.03	1967	ARBROATH

1

UK Fishing Vessels 2015

Vessel Name	Code	Port Name	Loa	Ton Gt	Year	Construction Place
ACES HIGH	PH11	PLYMOUTH	9.10	3.21	2011	ENGLAND
ACHATES	LH232	LEITH	7.00	1.58	2006	ISLAND PLASTICS
ACHIEVABLE	YH15	YARMOUTH	10.82	4.27	1957	COWES ISLE OF WIGHT
ACHIEVE	BF223	BANFF	24.80	309.00	2001	ABERDEENSHIRE
ACHIEVE	FR100	FRASERBURGH	19.36	129.00	1984	BUCKIE
ACHIEVE	HL257	HARTLEPOOL	9.93	14.61	1997	POLRUAN
ACHIEVE	K16	KIRKWALL	6.74	5.57	1978	STROMNESS
ACHIEVE	SY75	STORNOWAY	10.24	12.33	1979	MEVAGISSEY CORNWALL
ACHILLES	N109	NEWRY	21.20	154.00	2004	DENMARK
ACORN	INS237	INVERNESS	25.94	177.00	1980	DENMARK
ACTIVE	LK3369	LERWICK	6.30	1.31	1983	PENRYN
ADAM THOMAS	PN8	PRESTON	5.64	0.24	2008	GBR
ADAMS JOY	M36	MILFORD HAVEN	5.87	0.99	2007	CORNWALL
ADAPTABLE	HL41	HARTLEPOOL	14.04	17.09	1971	MIDDLESBOROUGH
ADBRENAT	E282	EXETER	7.32	2.41	1980	EXMOUTH
ADELA	BM79	BRIXHAM	9.15	9.93	1981	FRANCE
ADELE II	B209	BELFAST	6.01	1.73	1990	GBR
ADELPHI	FR280	FRASERBURGH	7.93	2.37	2007	GBR
ADEN-Y-DON	M34	MILFORD HAVEN	5.85	1.04	2013	DEVON
ADENIA	LK193	LERWICK	61.90	1776.00	2003	NORWAY
ADMIRAL BLAKE	PH440	PLYMOUTH	22.20	136.00	1989	HOLLAND
ADMIRAL GORDON	PH330	PLYMOUTH	22.21	137.00	1988	HOLLAND
ADMIRAL GRENVILLE	PH550	PLYMOUTH	23.97	152.00	2001	BRUINISSE
ADORATION II	CN78	CAMPBELTOWN	12.24	19.74	1964	FAIRLIE
ADORN	LK54	LERWICK	7.08	3.77	1989	GBR
ADORNE II	FR220	FRASERBURGH	27.00	269.00	1987	GREAT YARMOUTH
ADRENALINE	NN768	NEWHAVEN	5.55	1.31	2003	U K
ADRIENNE	M3	MILFORD HAVEN	5.35	1.20	2002	NEYLAND
ADVANCE	FR171	FRASERBURGH	7.20	2.66	1989	POOLE
ADVANCE	WY77	WHITBY	26.54	251.00	1987	CAMPBELTOWN
ADVENTURE	BH2	BLYTH	9.86	6.74	1980	FALMOUTH

UK Fishing Vessels 2015

Vessel Name	Code	Port Name	Loa	Ton Gt	Year	Construction Place
ADVENTURE	LH546	LEITH	9.90	9.86	1998	BARTON UPON HUMBER
ADVENTURER II	INS8	INVERNESS	23.95	337.00	2001	NAVIA
AEOLUS	BA808	BALLANTRAE	13.67	34.27	1997	TROON
AEOLUS	LH560	LEITH	5.15	0.75	2009	GBR
AEOLUS	LK102	LERWICK	6.70	2.73	1984	SCALLOWAY
AERON BELLE	AB128	ABERYSTWYTH	9.43	5.69	1962	APPLEDORE DEVON
AFONDALE	CA103	CARDIGAN	7.15	3.43	1989	HAVANT
AGAINST ALL ODDS	CF1	CARDIFF	6.10	0.83	1999	Unk
AGAN BORLOWEN	SS229	ST IVES	6.88	1.67	2013	PORTUGAL
AGAN DEVEDHEK	SS227	ST IVES	5.12	0.80	1993	PENZANCE
AGAN PROVIYAS	SS225	ST IVES	5.61	1.56	1977	NANCLEDRA
AGNES	PD991	PETERHEAD	5.10	0.95	2001	GBR
AHAB	DH399	DARTMOUTH	4.69	0.60	1984	DEVON
AIGRETTE	J114	JERSEY	6.60	1.79	1996	UK
AILSA JANE	K24	KIRKWALL	8.45	2.84	1972	ANSTRUTHER
AIMEE J	WK832	WICK	6.95	2.21	1986	GBR
AIMEE S	K998	KIRKWALL	5.75	1.26	1985	GBR
AJ	BA844	BALLANTRAE	7.00	2.34	2005	SOUTH AYRSHIRE
AJAX	TO32	TRURO	16.98	74.00	1972	BUCKIE
AKELA	KY1021	KIRKCALDY	5.83	1.12	2006	FIFE
AKELA	RX30	RYE	12.19	22.93	1966	SANDWICH
ALAN C	BM6	BRIXHAM	4.30	0.46	1980	GBR
ALANA JANE	LK983	LERWICK	8.00	3.86	1989	PENRYN
ALANDA	WH20	WEYMOUTH	8.70	4.24	2011	ENGLAND
ALASKA	CE707	COLERAINE	11.99	24.63	1990	BERWICK-UPON-TWEED
ALAUNA	MT55	MARYPORT	14.98	47.72	1973	ARBROATH
ALBA	LH487	LEITH	6.40	1.40	1972	GBR
ALBANNACH	ME55	MONTROSE	9.20	5.51	1985	TYNESIDE
ALBATROS II	GU472	GUERNSEY	9.99	8.97	1977	ENGLAND
ALBATROSS	CS154	COWES	5.74	0.99	1985	YAPTON ARUNDEL WEST SUSSEX

UK Fishing Vessels 2015

Vessel Name	Code	Port Name	Loa	Ton Gt	Year	Construction Place
ALBATROSS	M6	MILFORD HAVEN	5.35	1.16	1998	PEMBS
ALBATROSS	PD184	PETERHEAD	7.81	3.12	1968	MONTROSE
ALBATROSS	PH5546	PLYMOUTH	9.20	2.81	1960	ENGLAND
ALBATROSS	UL256	ULLAPOOL	9.27	5.35	1985	RYE
ALBION	DS10	DUMFRIES	34.90	375.00	1986	ZEEBRUGGE - BELGIUM
ALBION	FD170	FLEETWOOD	12.17	19.90	1955	BUCKIE
ALENA	CT145	CASTLETOWN	13.82	29.06	2004	NEWBURY ENGINEERING
ALERT	FR777	FRASERBURGH	9.65	6.09	2010	FALMOUTH CORNWALL
ALERT	LK124	LERWICK	7.62	3.95	1969	BALTASOUND
ALERT	SM163	SHOREHAM	6.83	1.23	2013	UK
ALERT II	LK375	LERWICK	9.97	6.77	1992	FALMOUTH
ALEX	SH319	SCARBOROUGH	5.07	0.71	1987	UK
ALEX C	BRD18	BROADFORD	11.80	22.11	1988	CORNWALL
ALEXANDRA JANE	PO4	PORTLAND	6.10	1.28	2007	GBR
ALEXI ROSE	YH4	YARMOUTH	5.55	1.13	2009	NORWICH
ALFIE ELLIOT	RX60	RYE	9.20	7.75	1969	TANKERTON KENT
ALGRIE	PZ199	PENZANCE	26.20	121.00	1968	HOLLAND
ALI B	PO19	PORTLAND	4.95	0.78	1992	ORKNEY BOATS
ALI T	MN6	MALDON	6.35	2.13	2001	SHETLAND
ALIBI	E516	EXETER	9.99	3.27	1991	FRANCE
ALICE	B113	BELFAST	6.02	2.06	2003	FALMOUTH
ALICE	BS9	BEAUMARIS	9.95	6.89	2005	ANGLESEY
ALICE	TH37	TEIGNMOUTH	5.80	1.76	1989	TEIGNMOUTH
ALICE LOUISE	PZ592	PENZANCE	7.94	3.53	1978	CORNWALL
ALICEAMELIA	HL8	HARTLEPOOL	9.73	4.66	1976	PENRYN
ALICIA	YH294	YARMOUTH	6.45	1.58	2003	GBR
ALINE	SY854	STORNOWAY	4.85	0.70	1992	GBR
ALISA	B260	BELFAST	16.61	41.00	1969	ST MONANCE
ALISA	BCK362	BUCKIE	7.56	4.11	1992	PORTKNOCKIE
ALISA M	LA639	LLANELLI	6.90	1.31	2006	ISLE OF WIGHT

UK Fishing Vessels 2015

Vessel Name	Code	Port Name	Loa	Ton Gt	Year	Construction Place
ALISHA	GY563	GRIMSBY	6.20	1.85	1995	VENTNOR
ALISON	CY236	CASTLEBAY	7.92	5.41	1978	STORNAWAY
ALISON	HH988	HARWICH	6.70	2.37	1982	HARWICH
ALISON CHRISTINE	LN179	KINGS LYNN	8.98	5.79	1982	COLTISHALL NORFOLK
ALISON KATHERINE	YH845	YARMOUTH	5.72	1.25	1992	YAPTON ARUNDEL SUSSEX
ALISON KAY	LK57	LERWICK	23.95	246.00	2001	DENMARK
ALISON LYNN	LI209	LITTLEHAMPTON	6.30	1.46	1984	BOGNOR REGIS
ALISON MARIE	K420	KIRKWALL	11.14	11.17	1999	WICK
ALISON MARY	N308	NEWRY	12.19	25.70	1985	GUERNSEY
ALK II	LI535	LITTLEHAMPTON	4.94	1.02	1980	NEWHAVEN
ALL JS	LA46	LLANELLI	4.93	1.03	2009	GBE
ALLEGIANCE	FY449	FOWEY	9.27	6.11	1976	CORNWALL
ALLEGIANCE	SH90	SCARBOROUGH	25.89	206.00	1987	GOOLE
ALLEY CAT	OB992	OBAN	5.90	1.09	1998	GBR
ALLIANCE	B144	BELFAST	9.99	10.91	1998	LINCOLNSHIRE
ALLIANCE	CN207	CAMPBELTOWN	16.76	51.00	1975	ST MONANCE
ALLOETTE	J525	JERSEY	5.85	1.17	1989	GBR
ALLORA	SE7	SALCOMBE	5.60	1.98	1972	WALDRINGFIELD SUFFOLK
ALLOUETTE	SA402	SWANSEA	7.28	3.70	1985	PLYMOUTH
ALLYCAT	WH66	WEYMOUTH	7.17	1.52	2005	GUERNSEY
ALMORAH	WH684	WEYMOUTH	7.50	1.61	1960	SOUTHAMPTON
ALMORAH TOO	WH695	WEYMOUTH	7.05	1.90	1967	SOUTHAMPTON
ALONA	P725	PORTSMOUTH	6.55	1.75	1979	FALMOUTH
ALPHA	B409	BELFAST	16.52	41.00	1967	FORKES SANDHAVEN
ALPHA	GU69	GUERNSEY	4.88	1.02	1988	PLYMOUTH DEVON
ALRESCHA	DS9	DUMFRIES	7.00	2.35	2007	CAMBORNE
ALTAIR	LK3412	LERWICK	8.95	5.74	1989	BERWICK ON TWEED
ALTAIRE	LK429	LERWICK	76.43	2809.00	2004	TOMREFJOFD
ALVIC	CK934	COLCHESTER	5.24	0.69	1992	ESSEX
ALVIC	PZ810	PENZANCE	5.64	1.55	1994	UNK

UK Fishing Vessels 2015

Vessel Name	Code	Port Name	Loa	Ton Gt	Year	Construction Place
ALWAYS OUT	CT151	CASTLETOWN	5.75	1.30	2002	AUGUSTOW
ALYSON CATHERINE	LI551	LITTLEHAMPTON	5.80	0.59	2005	WEST SUSSEX
AMADEUS	FE270	FOLKESTONE	9.98	5.87	1996	CANVEY ISLAND
AMADEUS	TH7	TEIGNMOUTH	24.50	258.00	1992	MACDUFF
AMANDA J	B291	BELFAST	6.49	1.05	2002	BRIDALINGTON EAST YORKSHIRE
AMANDA J	FH9	FALMOUTH	5.90	1.59	1999	CORNWALL
AMANDA JANE	M100	MILFORD HAVEN	9.98	12.79	1988	UNKNOWN
AMANDA JANE	TH420	TEIGNMOUTH	11.25	19.24	1984	CORNWALL
AMANDA M	K904	KIRKWALL	6.20	1.21	1998	GBR
AMARYLIS	ME11	MONTROSE	6.70	2.83	1983	ORKNEY
AMATHUS	BK522	BERWICK ON TWEED	8.90	4.92	1999	NORTHUMBERLAND
AMAZING GRACE	LK406	LERWICK	6.55	1.74	1992	WALES
AMAZING GRACE II	B77	BELFAST	6.98	2.16	2012	ANNALONG CO.DOWN
AMBER J	BM224	BRIXHAM	23.98	89.00	1962	HOLLAND
AMBER-DAWN	GU98	GUERNSEY	7.40	3.03	1979	ITCHENOR
AMBITION	LI287	LITTLEHAMPTON	6.31	1.11	1992	BOGNOR REGIS
AMBITIOUS	B420	BELFAST	21.00	68.00	1964	BUCKIE
AMBUSH	AB30	ABERYSTWYTH	5.80	2.00	1980	PENRHYN CORNWALL
AMELIA	CY3	CASTLEBAY	8.00	4.21	1985	LOWESTOFT
AMELIA	N120	NEWRY	17.48	70.00	1978	PAULL
AMELIA GRACE	DO159	DOUGLAS	5.96	1.62	2001	CAMBOURNE
AMELIA JO	PE1105	POOLE	6.85	0.95	2006	POOLE
AMETHYST	B456	BELFAST	9.48	8.80	1960	FRASERBURGH
AMETHYST	BF19	BANFF	19.05	167.00	2008	GBS
AMETHYST	DR171	DOVER	5.90	1.97	1995	CORNWALL
AMETHYST	FH664	FALMOUTH	9.90	11.46	1998	FALMOUTH
AMETHYST	N123	NEWRY	14.76	31.01	1975	MACDUFF
AMETHYST	SY305	STORNOWAY	10.97	12.08	1980	WORCESTER
AMETHYST	WO668	WORKINGTON	4.34	0.52	1992	CUMBRIA
AMIE ELLEN	GU479	GUERNSEY	7.20	4.00	1971	GBR

UK Fishing Vessels 2015

Vessel Name	Code	Port Name	Loa	Ton Gt	Year	Construction Place
AMIGO	FH51	FALMOUTH	7.62	2.75	1979	CORNWALL
AMIGO	LI27	LITTLEHAMPTON	5.04	0.61	1978	BOGNOR REGIS
AMITY	BRD185	BROADFORD	9.75	7.06	1979	PENRYN CORNWALL
AMITY	N444	NEWRY	10.57	13.02	1989	PORTAVOGIE
AMITY II	PD177	PETERHEAD	21.23	132.00	1989	NOT KNOWN
AMMO	SS261	ST IVES	5.45	0.58	2001	WADEBRIDGE
AMOUR II	LA279	LLANELLI	4.80	1.04	1992	ENGLAND
AMPHITRITE II	KY783	KIRKCALDY	7.85	2.73	1987	FALMOUTH
AMPS	BRD212	BROADFORD	8.94	4.70	1974	NEW MILTON
AMSER	CO118	CAERNARVON	4.07	0.43	1999	PWLLHELI
AMY	K56	KIRKWALL	5.93	1.80	1990	UNK
AMY BLUE	GU116	GUERNSEY	14.33	32.13	1993	CARRIGALINE
AMY HARRIS IV	CN35	CAMPBELTOWN	18.50	93.00	1979	SANDHAVEN
AMY J II	K1143	KIRKWALL	5.80	1.49	2008	SUFFOLK
AMY JANE	LR73	LANCASTER	5.98	1.33	1987	ARUNDEL SUSSEX
AMY KATE	BW262	BARROW	4.56	0.53	1995	UK
AMY M	BS526	BEAUMARIS	5.62	1.21	2002	ARUNDEL SUSSEX
AMY O	PW37	PADSTOW	4.85	0.73	2002	FINLAND
AMY R	E495	EXETER	14.97	39.02	1999	FALMOUTH
AN CUANTACH	SY829	STORNOWAY	8.60	7.30	1984	LOOE
ANA - MOSKEEN	CN213	CAMPBELTOWN	5.09	0.78	1972	HAYLING ISLAND
ANA MARIA	LN478	KINGS LYNN	13.28	27.30	2008	GRIMSBY
ANASTASIA II	CO807	CAERNARVON	4.88	0.77	1988	SUSSEX
ANDERIDA	NN769	NEWHAVEN	7.95	7.09	2010	ENGLAND
ANDERS	LK12	LERWICK	6.40	1.85	1986	DUBLIN IRELAND
ANDIGEE	WY372	WHITBY	9.95	11.93	1992	WHITBY NORTH YORKSHIRE
ANDORAY OF LOOE	FY528	FOWEY	7.74	4.66	1979	LOOE
ANDRIAS	N470	NEWRY	18.30	66.00	1967	BANFF
ANDURIL	GU336	GUERNSEY	4.61	0.76	1975	ENGLAND

UK Fishing Vessels 2015

Vessel Name	Code	Port Name	Loa	Ton Gt	Year	Construction Place
ANERITA	CA63	CARDIGAN	5.79	1.74	1986	PLYMOUTH
ANGEL EMIEL	BM55	BRIXHAM	23.99	159.00	1999	HOLLAND
ANGEL J	GU489	GUERNSEY	5.94	1.97	1992	GUERNSEY
ANGELA	WK26	WICK	5.03	0.84	1988	UK
ANGELA MARY	AB206	ABERYSTWYTH	9.00	3.97	1979	HULL
ANGELENA	BM271	BRIXHAM	13.99	29.61	1988	UNKNOWN
ANGELENA	BN77	BOSTON	11.86	21.00	1981	BOSTON
ANGELENE	RO18	ROTHESAY	9.96	5.23	1978	HAMBLESIDE
ANGELINA	F172	FAVERSHAM	8.50	5.37	1985	KENT
ANGELLE MARIE	SU233	SOUTHAMPTON	10.42	6.20	1974	KIRKWALL
ANGELUS	SA140	SWANSEA	5.86	1.77	1986	FALMOUTH
ANGIE	CS79	COWES	7.20	3.70	1986	COWES
ANGIE M	J37	JERSEY	6.05	1.07	1995	UK
ANGLO DAWN	SE9	SALCOMBE	9.68	5.02	2012	UK
ANGUS ROSE III	ME19	MONTROSE	15.18	36.00	1969	ARBROATH
ANGUSINA	LH25	LEITH	9.16	4.86	1983	WEST MERSEA
ANITA	BS219	BEAUMARIS	5.60	0.84	1989	BRITAIN
ANITRA	PD67	PETERHEAD	11.29	12.95	1980	ORKNEY
ANJUR	J628	JERSEY	5.53	1.06	1981	UK
ANN	CO75	CAERNARVON	5.80	1.80	1940	TREFOR CAERNARVON
ANN	SE14	SALCOMBE	6.98	3.91	1924	BRIXHAM
ANN ISABELLA	LO61	LONDON	9.91	3.19	1937	COWES I O W
ANN KATHLEEN	PW479	PADSTOW	8.20	4.50	2002	NOT KNOWN
ANN LOUISE	BD22	BIDEFORD	9.95	16.32	2012	BUCCANEER BOATS LTD
ANN LOUISE	LT266	LOWESTOFT	9.82	11.97	2008	MIDDLESBOROUGH
ANN MARIE	YH119	YARMOUTH	6.48	1.22	1998	NORTH WALSHAM
ANN MARIE II	CY20	CASTLEBAY	10.26	14.56	1978	RYE SUSSEX
ANN ROSA	PZ80	PENZANCE	4.54	0.77	1995	CORNWALL
ANN VIRGINIA	J204	JERSEY	10.73	16.07	1978	N/K
ANNA	BD9	BIDEFORD	7.60	6.05	1983	LEIGH ON SEA
ANNA	N727	NEWRY	5.56	1.56	1986	DEVON

UK Fishing Vessels 2015

Vessel Name	Code	Port Name	Loa	Ton Gt	Year	Construction Place
ANNA BELL	LA620	LLANELLI	4.89	1.04	1996	SELF BUILD
ANNA BHAN	B981	BELFAST	6.54	1.44	1972	CO.DOWN
ANNA CATHERINE	PZ146	PENZANCE	4.44	0.67	1978	ST JUST
ANNA D	LA9	LLANELLI	9.95	11.14	2007	ESSEX
ANNA GAIL	YH2413	YARMOUTH	6.60	2.19	1988	BLAKENEY
ANNA II	J405	JERSEY	9.76	6.45	1974	GUERNSEY
ANNA J	GU114	GUERNSEY	5.57	1.48	2014	GBR
ANNA LOUISE	HH56	HARWICH	9.82	8.18	1982	CORNWALL
ANNA MAIRI	UL564	ULLAPOOL	5.87	1.14	2003	WEST SUSSEX
ANNA MARIA	SS262	ST IVES	6.45	2.21	1993	ENGLAND
ANNA MARIE	WK835	WICK	4.90	0.55	1985	GBR
ANNA MARIE II	WK875	WICK	6.20	1.28	2012	CHICHESTER
ANNA ROSE	CY62	CASTLEBAY	7.35	1.94	2002	PLYMOUTH
ANNABEL	SN349	NORTH SHIELDS	9.95	9.36	1997	PENRYN
ANNALOUSION	FE382	FOLKESTONE	9.83	8.38	2010	COLCHESTER ESSEX
ANNE	CO519	CAERNARVON	6.18	2.56	1994	UNK
ANNE CAMERON	P1027	PORTSMOUTH	5.76	0.92	1998	LITTLEHAMPTON
ANNE LOUISE	J321	JERSEY	4.98	1.11	1989	UK
ANNE MARIE	BW106	BARROW	7.98	2.06	1984	POOLE
ANNE MARY B	M33	MILFORD HAVEN	13.39	26.73	1989	PENRHYN DOCK BANGOR GWYNEDD
ANNE SCOTT	GY150	GRIMSBY	18.03	71.00	1969	DENMARK
ANNE THIERRY	M199	MILFORD HAVEN	17.07	46.00	1975	GBR
ANNEGINA	PD43	PETERHEAD	42.00	477.00	1984	STELLANDAM HOLLAND
ANNETTE	GY5	GRIMSBY	16.20	38.00	1982	DENMARK
ANNIE	B988	BELFAST	14.84	57.48	2006	BERWICKSHIRE
ANNIE	WY100	WHITBY	5.46	0.98	1982	WHITBY
ANNIE B	LK20	LERWICK	5.26	0.48	1998	SHETLAND
ANNIE BAINBRIDGE	WY50	WHITBY	9.40	4.51	2008	NORTHUMBERLAND
ANNIE JANE	CY177	CASTLEBAY	7.90	4.34	1973	ARUNDEL
ANNIE JAYNE	E83	EXETER	6.48	1.18	1988	DEVON

UK Fishing Vessels 2015

Vessel Name	Code	Port Name	Loa	Ton Gt	Year	Construction Place
ANNIE T	CY1	CASTLEBAY	9.15	5.88	2006	UNKNOWN
ANNIES SONG	SU463	SOUTHAMPTON	8.84	3.49	1977	NEW MILTON
ANNITA	CY156	CASTLEBAY	8.00	2.97	1988	PENRYN
ANSGAR	E104	EXETER	36.60	435.00	2002	SPAIN
ANT IASGAIR	INS94	INVERNESS	5.60	0.79	1992	GBR
ANTARCTIC II	LK145	LERWICK	61.90	1771.00	2004	FLEKKEFJORD
ANTARES	B407	BELFAST	22.80	151.00	1976	NEWRY
ANTARES	K268	KIRKWALL	12.77	28.25	1987	HULL
ANTARES	KY23	KIRKCALDY	10.05	5.54	1972	WEYMOUTH
ANTARES	LK419	LERWICK	72.80	2060.00	1996	NORWAY
ANTARIES	BF27	BANFF	16.70	106.00	2001	ST PETETSBURG
ANTELMA	E201	EXETER	6.50	2.33	1989	HULL
ANTON SCOTT	LO406	LONDON	8.70	12.60	1975	APPLEDORE
ANTONIO	FR296	FRASERBURGH	5.01	1.01	1989	WALLSEND ON TYNE
ANTURUS	FD20	FLEETWOOD	9.96	10.52	1958	CONWAY
ANYA JAIDYN	NN182	NEWHAVEN	6.23	1.09	2013	WEST SUSSEX
ANZAC	RY56	RAMSEY	9.99	14.67	1996	GBR
AOIFE OG	CN21	CAMPBELTOWN	6.30	1.52	2007	GBR
AOIFE ROSE	RY210	RAMSEY	9.95	11.67	2005	GBR
APOLLO	INS179	INVERNESS	23.95	246.00	2001	VESTRE STRANDVES
APOLLO	LA644	LLANELLI	4.64	0.78	2004	UNKNOWN
APOMORPH	GU449	GUERNSEY	5.65	1.09	1992	ENGLAND
APRYL LOUISE	HH182	HARWICH	9.90	15.44	1988	MIDDLESBROUGH
AQUA	AB201	ABERYSTWYTH	9.00	4.20	1999	ABERYSTWYTH
AQUA C	B924	BELFAST	5.87	1.23	2001	CAMBORNE
AQUAGEM	H59	HULL	6.20	1.46	1988	BARMSTON NORTH HUMBERSIDE
AQUAMANDA	FY96	FOWEY	8.12	5.07	1980	HAYLE CORNWALL
AQUARIA	K232	KIRKWALL	15.52	42.00	1991	STROMNESS
AQUARIAN	SM244	SHOREHAM	4.91	1.20	1987	BOGNOR REGIS
AQUARIUS	BF89	BANFF	20.80	189.00	1994	BUCKIE

UK Fishing Vessels 2015

Vessel Name	Code	Port Name	Loa	Ton Gt	Year	Construction Place
AQUARIUS	CA306	CARDIGAN	4.36	0.91	1976	NEWHAVEN
AQUARIUS	CY34	CASTLEBAY	19.84	92.00	1974	ARBROATH
AQUARIUS	FY74	FOWEY	8.74	6.87	1966	PORTLOE
AQUARIUS	LK35	LERWICK	8.71	4.94	1983	WORCESTER
AQUARIUS	SM236	SHOREHAM	7.01	1.44	1980	ISLE OF WIGHT
AQUARIUS	UL343	ULLAPOOL	5.87	1.27	2010	GAMRIE
AQUARIUS	WK22	WICK	6.56	1.96	2004	CAMBORNE
AQUARIUS II	BH456	BLYTH	14.94	51.91	2001	WHITBY
AQUARIUS II	J307	JERSEY	9.10	4.40	1983	GUERNSEY
AQUASPORT	J657	JERSEY	4.88	0.82	1983	UK
AQUILA	BA379	BALLANTRAE	13.41	36.20	1988	HULL
AQUILA	DH10	DARTMOUTH	14.95	59.29	2006	NORTH YORKSHIRE
AQUILA	FY324	FOWEY	9.35	7.93	1974	FALMOUTH
AQUILA	PZ580	PENZANCE	4.75	1.01	1978	HAYLE
AQUILA ROI	AR89	AYR	6.10	1.82	1990	EMSWORTH HANTS
AQUINIS	BA500	BALLANTRAE	18.27	96.00	1992	HEPWORTHS OF HULL
ARA	K238	KIRKWALL	6.35	1.38	2009	NORTHERN IRELAND
ARANATHA	LK318	LERWICK	9.99	9.81	1985	FALMOUTH
ARANDORA STAR	E44	EXETER	8.53	4.91	1976	EXMOUTH
ARANDORA STAR II OF EXE	E477	EXETER	7.30	2.90	1997	EXMOUTH
ARCANE	N907	NEWRY	24.45	158.00	1981	CAMPBELTOWN
ARCTIC MOON	BA847	BALLANTRAE	12.41	18.59	1974	INVERGORDON BOAT YARD
ARCTIC SOLITAIRE	LK40	LERWICK	9.95	13.85	1997	ISLE OF SHEPPEY
ARCTIC STAR	LH592	LEITH	7.35	4.15	1980	POOLE
ARCTIC TERN	KY6	KIRKCALDY	6.46	3.20	1992	ANSTRUTHER SCOTLAND
ARCTIC WARRIOR	H176	HULL	55.50	1621.00	1987	SOVIKNES
ARCTURUS	INS167	INVERNESS	24.56	192.00	1984	CAMPBELTOWN
ARCTURUS	LK59	LERWICK	26.00	302.00	2000	EYEMOUTH
ARCTURUS	UL300	ULLAPOOL	13.10	26.50	1985	EYEMOUTH
ARDENT	LK472	LERWICK	22.80	136.00	1981	SWEDEN

UK Fishing Vessels 2015

Vessel Name	Code	Port Name	Loa	Ton Gt	Year	Construction Place
ARDENT II	INS127	INVERNESS	26.70	251.00	1986	CAMPBELTOWN
ARDYNE	OB972	OBAN	7.11	2.65	2002	MACDUFF
ARETHUSA	WH48	WEYMOUTH	8.11	6.31	2010	EDINBURGH
ARGO	BA809	BALLANTRAE	13.00	21.69	1997	ABERYSWYTH
ARGO	MT3	MARYPORT	6.46	1.72	1999	ENGLAND
ARGONAUT	BA858	BALLANTRAE	23.96	150.00	1992	NETHERLANDS
ARGONAUT	BD228	BIDEFORD	8.22	3.68	1979	NEWHAVEN
ARGOSY	BA804	BALLANTRAE	18.25	96.00	1995	HULL
ARGOSY	FR128	FRASERBURGH	7.18	3.16	1984	ST. COMBS
ARGOSY II	INS296	INVERNESS	6.40	1.44	2007	CORNWALL
ARGUS	BA391	BALLANTRAE	5.63	1.23	1989	YAPTON SUSSEX
ARIANNA	KY180	KIRKCALDY	6.03	0.88	1999	MACDUFF
ARIEL II	LI518	LITTLEHAMPTON	7.02	2.35	1988	ISLE OF WIGHT
ARIES	ME220	MONTROSE	5.91	1.06	1997	MONTROSE
ARKTOS	WA32	WHITEHAVEN	8.01	3.84	1981	KIRKCUDBRIGHT
ARLANDA	N306	NEWRY	18.43	68.00	1976	DENMARK
ARMAVEN UNO	M1170	MILFORD HAVEN	31.65	268.00	1995	SPAIN
ARNBORG	LK172	LERWICK	16.20	46.00	1974	BUCKIE SCOTLAND
ARRIVAL	N754	NEWRY	4.99	0.37	1970	NEWHAVEN
ARTEMIS	INS564	INVERNESS	27.69	399.00	1995	MACDUFF
ARTEMIS	KY35	KIRKCALDY	5.78	1.28	1992	ORKNEY BOATS
ARTEMIS	WY809	WHITBY	23.13	131.00	1978	ABERDEEN
ARTFUL DODGER III	SE156	SALCOMBE	8.19	3.38	1989	IPSWICH
ARTICUS	K826	KIRKWALL	8.40	5.98	1987	UNK
ARTISAN	SM243	SHOREHAM	5.49	1.22	1979	BOGNOR REGIS
ARUM	FY60	FOWEY	9.50	12.20	1981	GUERNSEY
ARUN DIVER II	WK73	WICK	10.40	5.21	1988	CORNWALL
ASGARD	HL787	HARTLEPOOL	9.81	8.23	1989	LYMINGTON
ASHALEY	M59	MILFORD HAVEN	9.95	4.56	2010	ISLE OF WIGHT
ASHLEIGH JANE	OB81	OBAN	9.91	9.54	1984	CORNWALL
ASHLEIGH M	RO88	ROTHESAY	9.30	3.16	1972	RYE

UK Fishing Vessels 2015

Vessel Name	Code	Port Name	Loa	Ton Gt	Year	Construction Place
ASHLEIGH-LEAH	GU84	GUERNSEY	5.56	1.08	1990	ARUNDEL WEST SUSSEX
ASHLYN	PD342	PETERHEAD	4.70	0.51	1973	NOT KNOWN
ASILE SUR	GU127	GUERNSEY	6.22	0.91	1979	VALE GUERNSEY
ASK ME	P11	PORTSMOUTH	9.95	13.01	1997	NEWHAVEN
ASKARI	BA17	BALLANTRAE	13.27	21.81	1994	HULL
ASPER	SS8	ST IVES	5.15	1.35	2000	ISLE OF WIGHT
ASPIRE	AH24	ARBROATH	8.54	4.92	1980	CORNWALL
ASPIRE	B903	BELFAST	22.66	138.00	1976	MACDUFF
ASPIRE	P921	PORTSMOUTH	9.32	2.92	1974	GBR
ASPIRE II	CN16	CAMPBELTOWN	12.18	24.13	1975	INVERGORDAN
ASPIRE II	KY1000	KIRKCALDY	8.31	6.87	1999	CORNWALL
ASPIRE III	KY91	KIRKCALDY	7.95	2.66	2010	ESSEX
ASTERIA	B185	BELFAST	16.04	108.00	1995	SANDHAVEN
ASTERIA	BRD250	BROADFORD	18.27	133.00	2000	WHITBY
ASTERIAS	PE503	POOLE	11.99	21.53	1994	FORT WILLIAM
ASTERIX	CK6	COLCHESTER	8.00	3.83	1991	TOLLESBURY
ASTHORE	PZ182	PENZANCE	13.92	31.95	2010	UK
ASTRA III	SY153	STORNOWAY	22.44	134.94	1981	MACDUFF
AT LAST	SU3	SOUTHAMPTON	8.10	1.66	1995	COLVIC ESSEX
ATHENA	GU124	GUERNSEY	5.03	0.79	2013	GBR
ATHENA	WH181	WEYMOUTH	9.00	3.76	1986	WEYMOUTH
ATHENA FAY	PZ49	PENZANCE	6.00	1.27	2008	PORTUGAL
ATHENA M	SY201	STORNOWAY	14.10	42.63	1988	CORNWALL
ATLANTA II	PW82	PADSTOW	11.75	23.34	1987	MEVAGISSEY CORNWALL
ATLANTIA	UL62	ULLAPOOL	9.98	10.83	1985	PENRYN CORNWALL
ATLANTIA II	LK502	LERWICK	12.19	20.55	1999	CORNWALL
ATLANTIC	N258	NEWRY	20.40	112.00	1983	FRANCE
ATLANTIC BELLE	PZ90	PENZANCE	5.80	1.16	1999	ORKNEY BOATS
ATLANTIC CHALLENGE	PD197	PETERHEAD	40.00	611.00	1999	TROON
ATLANTIC LASS	PZ93	PENZANCE	5.60	1.06	2008	PORTUGAL

UK Fishing Vessels 2015

Vessel Name	Code	Port Name	Loa	Ton Gt	Year	Construction Place
ATLANTIC SPIRIT	DH18	DARTMOUTH	6.70	1.66	2010	PORTUGAL
ATLANTIS	FY830	FOWEY	9.90	11.79	2000	CORNWALL
ATLANTIS	OB991	OBAN	9.50	9.70	2008	GBR
ATLANTIS BELLE	DS3	DUMFRIES	18.27	72.00	1989	PAULL HUMBERSIDE
ATLANTIS II	BM499	BRIXHAM	9.97	3.03	1997	CORNWALL
ATLAS	BF182	BANFF	7.13	1.44	1996	SCOTLAND
ATLAS	CN258	CAMPBELTOWN	16.79	66.00	1973	MACDUFF
ATLAS	FR101	FRASERBURGH	20.80	173.00	1992	MACDUFF
ATTAIN II	PD332	PETERHEAD	26.00	172.00	1979	CAMPBELTOWN
ATTITUDE	E534	EXETER	9.02	5.93	1985	LITTLEHAMPTON
AUBRETIA	BCK32	BUCKIE	18.23	116.00	1986	BUCKIE
AUBRIETIA	B58	BELFAST	21.33	126.00	1986	SANDHAVEN
AUDACIOUS	BF83	BANFF	27.40	286.00	1989	ST. MONANS
AUDACITY	SU156	SOUTHAMPTON	8.00	3.78	1989	WOOLSTON SOUTHAMPTON
AUDREY	OB597	OBAN	8.30	2.25	1961	PORTHLEVEN
AUDREY	WH401	WEYMOUTH	7.45	3.84	1964	SOUTHAMPTON
AUDREY M	IH5	IPSWICH	9.70	10.60	2011	FALMOUTH CORNWALL
AUDREY PATRICIA	LN486	KINGS LYNN	13.94	30.31	2008	BARTON ON HUMBER
AUDRINA	LN483	KINGS LYNN	13.65	29.95	2009	GBR
AUGUST MIST	PE19	POOLE	7.89	2.55	2005	UK
AUK	CT25	CASTLETOWN	3.85	0.31	1975	GBR
AUK	UL554	ULLAPOOL	11.02	8.03	1980	CHANNEL ISLES
AURELIA	B336	BELFAST	19.00	179.00	2003	MACDUFF
AURELIA	WY319	WHITBY	19.45	86.00	1980	KYRKSAETERORA NORWAY
AURIGA	J8	JERSEY	5.68	1.25	1995	UK
AURORA	A73	ABERDEEN	8.71	2.69	1968	POOLE
AURORA	B515	BELFAST	9.73	6.57	1980	WICK
AURORA	BS15	BEAUMARIS	9.63	8.66	1998	POLRUAN
AURORA	NN759	NEWHAVEN	5.30	1.18	1992	EAST SUSSEX
AURORA	PD16	PETERHEAD	6.44	3.19	1992	ANSTRUTHER

14

UK Fishing Vessels 2015

Vessel Name	Code	Port Name	Loa	Ton Gt	Year	Construction Place
AURORA	PE37	POOLE	6.66	1.17	2002	TRALEE
AURORA	SD395	SUNDERLAND	6.20	1.38	2005	ORKNEY
AURORA	YH33	YARMOUTH	6.68	2.44	2003	NORFOLK
AUTUMN DAWN	SA73	SWANSEA	8.29	5.57	2002	CORNWALL
AUTUMN ROSE	FH30	FALMOUTH	6.55	1.90	2002	CAMBORNE
AUTUMN SILVER	SS739	ST IVES	5.97	1.54	2007	BRITAIN
AUTUMN SILVER II	DH47	DARTMOUTH	5.50	1.11	1994	SCOTLAND
AUTUMN TIDE	SD407	SUNDERLAND	3.80	0.45	1985	Unk
AVA	E24	EXETER	5.58	1.38	1988	WEYMOUTH
AVALETTE	J132	JERSEY	5.95	0.78	1983	UK
AVALON	M361	MILFORD HAVEN	8.84	7.24	1995	SEATON DEVON
AVALON II	CN690	CAMPBELTOWN	13.77	25.36	1997	CAMPBELTOWN
AVANTI	NN85	NEWHAVEN	7.60	2.70	1988	ISLE OF WIGHT
AVISTA	INS4	INVERNESS	5.90	0.98	2006	NOT KNOWN
AVIT	A272	ABERDEEN	9.62	5.34	1978	GBR
AVOCET	FD518	FLEETWOOD	4.44	1.00	1998	CHORLEY
AVOCET	FR162	FRASERBURGH	17.31	100.00	1988	ARBROATH
AVOCET	FY886	FOWEY	4.60	0.32	1980	UNKNOWN
AVOCET	UL348	ULLAPOOL	4.81	0.68	1992	UNK
AVRIL ROSE	LT16	LOWESTOFT	8.53	4.92	2008	CAMBORNE CORNWALL
AWA	INS9	INVERNESS	4.58	0.79	1992	SCOTLAND
AWAKE	LT413	LOWESTOFT	7.34	5.01	1978	OULTON BROAD
AWEL-Y-MOR	CA182	CARDIGAN	6.55	1.15	1989	PENRYN CORNWALL
AYEGANTY	KY269	KIRKCALDY	6.83	2.65	2004	GBR
AYR DAWN	FD522	FLEETWOOD	31.26	226.00	1966	LOWESTOFT
AYR QUEEN	AR94	AYR	32.31	290.00	1961	ABERDEEN
AZALEA	CY11	CASTLEBAY	9.73	6.55	1985	WHITBY
AZALEA	LH37	LEITH	11.49	15.06	1968	BANFF
AZTEC	BA224	BALLANTRAE	16.15	59.00	1986	PAULL
AZULA	BA70	BALLANTRAE	17.13	66.00	1990	HULL
AZURE	WK668	WICK	10.55	8.09	1992	CADBOLL FACTORY TAIN

UK Fishing Vessels 2015

Vessel Name	Code	Port Name	Loa	Ton Gt	Year	Construction Place
AZZURRO	E566	EXETER	4.60	0.65	1999	SCOTLAND
B ALERT	FR776	FRASERBURGH	7.60	2.19	2005	NORTHUMBERLAND
B G	WY71	WHITBY	5.00	0.59	1985	YORKSHIRE
B J	PE31	POOLE	5.28	0.73	1992	RINGWOOD
BAARAGUTT II	AB8	ABERYSTWYTH	8.84	4.26	1989	MOSTYN
BAFFIN BAY	M1033	MILFORD HAVEN	60.82	1871.00	1989	VIGO SPAIN
BAGPUSS	LI44	LITTLEHAMPTON	5.50	0.88	1988	YAPTON SUSSEX
BAHATI	KY4	KIRKCALDY	16.48	53.00	1978	BUCKIE
BAHR NAGASH	B358	BELFAST	6.50	1.66	1969	CHICHESTER
BAJIN	BA777	BALLANTRAE	7.55	1.67	2000	ENGLAND
BAKERBOY	P27	PORTSMOUTH	5.65	0.43	2001	CARNFORD
BALCARY	MT120	MARYPORT	13.95	26.91	1967	FRANCE
BALLAST	BW1	BARROW	5.60	1.41	1991	ORKNEY
BALLISTIC	J171	JERSEY	8.23	4.86	1996	UK
BALTIC	BK411	BERWICK ON TWEED	8.53	3.34	1991	BERWICK-UPON-TWEED
BANANA SPLIT	J357	JERSEY	6.86	1.55	2003	ISLE OF WIGHT
BANANA SPLIT	LO540	LONDON	6.20	1.62	1997	ISLE OF WIGHT
BANDIT	P908	PORTSMOUTH	5.05	0.56	1985	COWES I.O.W.
BANTAC	J268	JERSEY	7.50	4.87	1990	UK
BARBARA	WK1	WICK	6.10	1.99	1913	STROMA
BARBARA ANNE	WA38	WHITEHAVEN	11.92	30.75	1988	NEWHAVEN
BARBARA JONES	CA373	CARDIGAN	5.63	1.62	1984	PLYMOUTH
BARBARA L	BL57	BRISTOL	6.58	1.85	1996	CAMBOURNE
BARBOSSA	AB3	ABERYSTWYTH	4.57	0.53	1992	PORTSMOUTH
BARBRA ANN	BS418	BEAUMARIS	5.30	0.85	1991	HOLYHEAD
BARENTSZEE	BM361	BRIXHAM	30.55	249.00	1984	OOSTENDE BELGIUM
BARNACLE III	CY97	CASTLEBAY	11.35	12.69	1985	PENRYN CORNWALL
BARNEY C	KY10	KIRKCALDY	5.45	1.17	2001	NORTHUMBERLAND
BARRACUDA	K1104	KIRKWALL	4.85	1.03	1985	REDGRAVE
BARRACUDA	PZ815	PENZANCE	5.60	0.51	1985	ISLE OF MAN
BARRAMUNDI	CY453	CASTLEBAY	4.90	0.75	1998	GBR

UK Fishing Vessels 2015

Vessel Name	Code	Port Name	Loa	Ton Gt	Year	Construction Place
BARRY ANN	PZ490	PENZANCE	4.99	0.82	1989	HAYLE
BARRY JEAN	A344	ABERDEEN	6.93	1.28	2009	ISLE OF WIGHT
BASS BOY	PZ527	PENZANCE	5.14	1.09	1981	THE LIZARD
BASS HUNTER	J125	JERSEY	5.79	1.16	1990	UK
BASS VILLIAN	CK23	COLCHESTER	5.23	0.73	2002	BECCLES SUFFOLK
BASSET	CK948	COLCHESTER	5.15	0.89	2006	NOT KNOWN
BAY HUNTER	KY434	KIRKCALDY	7.00	0.99	1986	UNKNOWN
BAY JOE	WY810	WHITBY	6.85	1.36	2001	NORTH YORKS
BAY OF PLENTY	UL28	ULLAPOOL	6.50	1.64	1977	PENRYN
BAY VENTURE	FD399	FLEETWOOD	9.90	16.07	1991	HAYLING ISLAND
BE ON TIME	LT11	LOWESTOFT	4.88	0.78	1989	UNK
BE READY	LK973	LERWICK	6.30	1.45	1996	MACDUFF
BE READY	N99	NEWRY	8.23	3.36	2010	KILKEEL CO.DOWN
BE READY	PD902	PETERHEAD	6.85	3.31	2013	COUNTY DOWN
BEACHCOMBER	CT88	CASTLETOWN	8.13	2.66	1995	GBR
BEACHY HEAD	NN748	NEWHAVEN	11.83	16.29	2006	ESSEX
BEADNAL	BCK630	BUCKIE	5.45	1.00	1973	ISLE OF WIGHT
BEADY EYE	PH1001	PLYMOUTH	6.65	1.75	2010	PORTUGAL
BEARS WATCHING	BM126	BRIXHAM	7.90	3.47	1989	CORNWALL
BEBLOWE	SH313	SCARBOROUGH	8.48	3.89	1992	COLCHESTER
BECCI	E73	EXETER	5.00	0.64	1991	EXMOUTH
BECCI OF LADRAM	E508	EXETER	9.79	6.31	2001	EXETER
BECKY JANE	FE379	FOLKESTONE	7.80	4.16	2007	KENT
BEE	K70	KIRKWALL	5.55	1.62	1905	ORKNEY
BEENY	PW494	PADSTOW	9.23	6.30	2013	UK
BELINDA BEE	BM276	BRIXHAM	7.74	2.42	1970	BARROW
BELINDA II	K7	KIRKWALL	11.60	13.92	1981	CORNWALL
BELIVIA	WH16	WEYMOUTH	4.70	0.38	1990	CORNWALL
BELLA	DH9	DARTMOUTH	5.85	0.95	2009	GBR
BELLDOREY	LI565	LITTLEHAMPTON	6.90	1.06	2007	ISLE OF WIGHT

UK Fishing Vessels 2015

Vessel Name	Code	Port Name	Loa	Ton Gt	Year	Construction Place
BELLE BETTINA	SS266	ST IVES	5.58	1.94	1978	HAYLE
BELLE BIRD	J33	JERSEY	8.66	7.09	1973	FRANCE
BELLE ISLE II	OB33	OBAN	9.14	5.84	1978	HULL
BELTANE	M1039	MILFORD HAVEN	9.60	6.77	1972	BRISTOL
BEN LOYAL	TO23	TRURO	21.22	66.00	1960	PETERHEAD
BEN MANZ	NN784	NEWHAVEN	6.60	1.14	1999	CORNWALL
BEN THOMAS	N310	NEWRY	9.90	8.59	1986	POOLE
BENAIAH IV	B350	BELFAST	20.34	104.00	1987	FRANCE
BENARKLE	PD400	PETERHEAD	17.99	171.00	2001	MACDUFF
BENBECULA	J227	JERSEY	4.90	1.10	1990	SCOTLAND
BENBOW 11	LA27	LLANELLI	5.90	0.51	1984	ESSEX
BENEDICTION	FH623	FALMOUTH	5.85	1.84	1993	PORTLOE CORNWALL
BENJAMIN GUY	SU177	SOUTHAMPTON	9.94	6.96	1989	WADEBRIDGE
BENOLAS	PL11	PEEL	13.20	35.24	1974	GBR
BERLEWEN	OB156	OBAN	6.50	1.39	1987	BAKERS YARD STARCROSS DEVON
BERLEWEN	PW1	PADSTOW	14.97	45.73	2002	YORKSHIRE
BERNADET	LR66	LANCASTER	7.32	3.32	1974	HEYSHAM
BERYL	BF440	BANFF	27.85	331.00	1998	NAVIA SPAIN
BERYL	SM12	SHOREHAM	4.95	0.72	1974	NEWHAVEN
BERYL II	FR558	FRASERBURGH	5.75	1.12	1984	UK
BERYL M	SH271	SCARBOROUGH	9.95	4.81	2013	UK
BESS	FH32	FALMOUTH	6.46	1.71	1989	PENRYN FALMOUTH
BESSIE ANNE	OB844	OBAN	10.00	5.39	1978	FALMOUTH
BESSIE BELL	LI577	LITTLEHAMPTON	6.23	1.09	2013	SIDLESHAM
BEST EVER	FH18	FALMOUTH	5.92	1.49	2008	GBR
BETHAN LOUISE	RX389	RYE	9.95	16.12	1997	NEWHAVEN
BETHANY J	WH111	WEYMOUTH	8.40	2.69	1994	DORSET
BETHANY MILLICENT	WH769	WEYMOUTH	5.75	1.33	1976	GBR
BETHSHAN	SS252	ST IVES	7.98	5.13	2010	NORTHUMBERLAND
BETTY G II	E316	EXETER	11.95	28.70	2008	CORNWALL

UK Fishing Vessels 2015

Vessel Name	Code	Port Name	Loa	Ton Gt	Year	Construction Place
BETTY PEERLEY	LI188	LITTLEHAMPTON	7.37	2.94	1988	GBR
BETTY SMITH	KY207	KIRKCALDY	6.40	2.82	1990	CELLARDYKE FIFE
BETTY'S BOYS	E487	EXETER	6.52	1.61	1980	FOWEY
BEVERLY ANN	SN363	NORTH SHIELDS	9.83	16.67	2004	COLCHESTER
BIBIEN	CO585	CAERNARVON	6.59	2.10	1993	FRECKLETON
BIG BEAR	TH156	TEIGNMOUTH	6.80	1.87	2013	COLCHESTER
BILLEN	BS79	BEAUMARIS	5.76	1.77	1972	CHICHESTER
BILLERIC	FH58	FALMOUTH	5.56	1.57	1978	MULLION CORNWALL
BILLIRIS	MT119	MARYPORT	8.87	6.03	2007	COLCHESTER
BILLY B	BS501	BEAUMARIS	5.14	0.96	1983	CHICHESTER
BILLY JOE	SA524	SWANSEA	9.91	11.17	1997	CORNWALL
BILLY ROWNEY	PZ532	PENZANCE	31.86	187.00	1973	HOLLAND
BILLY THOMAS OF PORTHGAIN	M149	MILFORD HAVEN	8.35	7.49	2000	CORNWALL
BIRLING GAP	NN267	NEWHAVEN	8.50	5.34	2005	ESSEX
BIRSAY BOY	K17	KIRKWALL	9.97	9.64	1980	HULL
BIT LATE	PE20	POOLE	6.20	1.77	2000	GBR
BIT ON THE SIDE	WH17	WEYMOUTH	4.90	1.07	2009	CORNWALL
BLACK KNIGHT	J531	JERSEY	6.90	1.54	1997	GBR
BLACK KNIGHT	TT280	TARBERT	6.80	1.59	1998	ARUNDEL WEST SUSSEX
BLACK PEARL	IH325	IPSWICH	3.30	0.34	1990	NOT KNOWN
BLACK PEARL	PH1010	PLYMOUTH	5.65	0.97	2000	ORKNEY
BLACK PEARL	PW41	PADSTOW	4.90	0.96	1985	ENGLAND
BLACK PEARL	WH13	WEYMOUTH	6.80	1.83	2010	PORTUGAL
BLACK PEARL II	CE6	COLERAINE	5.06	0.77	1991	ARUNDAL SUSSEX
BLACK TOM	B1003	BELFAST	5.67	1.03	1984	1984
BLACK VELVET	LA643	LLANELLI	5.25	1.12	2008	UNKNOWN
BLAIDD	M5	MILFORD HAVEN	11.98	15.68	1978	MILFORD HAVEN
BLOODAXE	RX37	RYE	6.75	2.11	1985	NEWHAVEN
BLOOM	FR604	FRASERBURGH	7.25	1.61	1989	FINDHOEN
BLOSSOM	LK424	LERWICK	7.72	2.21	1962	SCALLOWAY SHETLAND ISLANDS

UK Fishing Vessels 2015

Vessel Name	Code	Port Name	Loa	Ton Gt	Year	Construction Place
BLOSSOM	WK827	WICK	6.20	1.54	2012	WEST SUSSEX
BLU EYE D	SN94	NORTH SHIELDS	9.90	10.21	1990	SANDHAVEN
BLUCHER	LN8	KINGS LYNN	9.15	5.66	2000	NORFOLK
BLUE ANGEL	OB595	OBAN	8.24	4.00	1996	FALMOUTH
BLUE ARC	OB593	OBAN	8.87	8.90	1995	TOBERMORAY ISLE OF MULL
BLUE BELLE	GU43	GUERNSEY	6.54	1.53	2013	Unk
BLUE BELLE	SS2	ST IVES	5.48	1.68	2008	PLYMOUTH
BLUE BOY	CF319	CARDIFF	4.80	0.69	1990	SOUTH WALES
BLUE BOY	YH363	YARMOUTH	6.50	1.96	1989	SHERINGHAM
BLUE DART III	WH736	WEYMOUTH	6.15	1.57	2004	GBR
BLUE DIAMOND	PW10	PADSTOW	6.44	1.63	2000	FIFE
BLUE FIN	P15	PORTSMOUTH	7.90	3.14	1989	FALMOUTH
BLUE FOX	PW460	PADSTOW	8.20	2.14	1991	NORWICH
BLUE GATE	BM254	BRIXHAM	38.59	324.00	1975	PASAJES
BLUE GRACE	P1033	PORTSMOUTH	6.23	1.09	2011	WEST SUSSEX
BLUE JAY	K1008	KIRKWALL	6.40	1.34	1995	ORKNEY
BLUE LADY	E249	EXETER	6.79	3.69	1979	SEATON
BLUE LADY	GU70	GUERNSEY	6.98	0.94	1986	VALE GUERNSEY
BLUE LAGOON	CN73	CAMPBELTOWN	4.90	0.57	1989	UNKNOWN
BLUE MARLIN	CE526	COLERAINE	5.02	0.70	1991	GBR
BLUE MARLIN	FY399	FOWEY	9.45	9.45	1975	GOLANT
BLUE MARLIN	N950	NEWRY	6.01	2.05	1989	PENRYN
BLUE MIST	FY917	FOWEY	6.52	1.61	2002	ESSEX
BLUE MIST	M201	MILFORD HAVEN	5.35	1.01	1997	UK
BLUE MOON	B790	BELFAST	7.68	3.66	1979	PENRYN CORNWALL
BLUE MOON	GU36	GUERNSEY	5.02	0.94	1996	GUERNSEY
BLUE MOON	PE1042	POOLE	5.16	0.83	1992	UNK
BLUE OSPREY	LK3423	LERWICK	6.06	0.85	2001	SHETLAND
BLUE PEARL	J163	JERSEY	6.25	1.27	2013	Unk
BLUE PLOVER	SE10	SALCOMBE	6.50	3.47	1983	PENRYN

UK Fishing Vessels 2015

Vessel Name	Code	Port Name	Loa	Ton Gt	Year	Construction Place
BLUE SHARK	ME1	MONTROSE	5.90	0.88	1983	ENGLAND
BLUE SKY	BCK215	BUCKIE	13.40	27.66	1985	DUNSTON
BLUE SUE	M141	MILFORD HAVEN	5.00	0.88	1992	YAPTON WEST SUSSEX
BLUE THUNDER	BM557	BRIXHAM	8.78	2.64	2008	CORNWALL
BLUE TINNY	BM558	BRIXHAM	5.48	1.37	1991	ALUMACRAFT ALDRIDGE
BLUE WATER	E19	EXETER	8.10	2.28	2010	I.O.W
BLUEBELL	TT278	TARBERT	7.57	2.05	2002	WEST SUSSEX
BLUEBELLE	J150	JERSEY	5.75	1.03	2000	UK
BLUEFIN	INS31	INVERNESS	5.49	1.13	1998	GBR
BLUEFIN	ME7	MONTROSE	7.60	1.79	2003	ISLE OF WIGHT
BLUEJAY	FY906	FOWEY	5.52	2.20	2010	CORNWALL
BLUEMIST	P284	PORTSMOUTH	6.92	1.62	1985	SOUTHAMPTON
BLUEY	J20	JERSEY	5.22	0.94	2008	UK
BO PEEP	PH91	PLYMOUTH	5.85	1.44	2005	DEVON
BOA PESCADORA	DO166	DOUGLAS	8.10	4.62	1972	YEALM
BOA PESCADORA	DO166	DOUGLAS	8.10	4.62	1972	YEALM
BOB	SM816	SHOREHAM	5.30	1.33	2009	SHOREHAM BY SEA
BOB WINNIE	FH691	FALMOUTH	5.94	1.99	2002	CAMBOURNE
BOBBIE DEE II	FH322	FALMOUTH	10.82	11.94	1975	AXMINSTER
BOBENA	FR403	FRASERBURGH	8.24	4.63	1981	FRASERBURGH
BOLD ENDEAVOUR	BH45	BLYTH	7.32	1.89	2005	CORNWALL
BOLD VENTURE	B338	BELFAST	9.45	3.57	1998	GBR
BOLD VENTURE	BH450	BLYTH	6.26	1.19	2000	CORNWALL
BOLD VENTURE	BM529	BRIXHAM	5.62	1.21	1991	SCOTLAND
BOLD VENTURE	KY1036	KIRKCALDY	9.94	3.46	1976	FALMOUTH
BOLD VENTURE	SN34	NORTH SHIELDS	5.91	1.01	1990	FALMOUTH
BOLD VENTURE II	BH188	BLYTH	6.10	1.62	1982	BERWICK UPON TWEED
BOLT HEAD QUEEN	SE27	SALCOMBE	11.71	9.90	1970	EXMOUTH DEVON
BOLTON GIRL	BRD9	BROADFORD	5.92	2.68	1988	GRIMSAY
BON ACCORD	BM367	BRIXHAM	14.93	29.41	1968	TWICKENHAM

21

UK Fishing Vessels 2015

Vessel Name	Code	Port Name	Loa	Ton Gt	Year	Construction Place
BON AMY	DH176	DARTMOUTH	9.80	3.21	1987	CAMELFORD
BON AMY	TN104	TROON	8.25	4.45	2005	CORNWALL
BONA FIDE	N189	NEWRY	25.41	155.00	1968	URK NETHERLANDS
BONAVENTURE	BH453	BLYTH	9.98	13.31	1999	WALES
BONAVENTURE	LH111	LEITH	21.78	154.00	1987	BUCKIE
BONAVENTURE	N325	NEWRY	19.88	62.00	1969	BUCKIE
BOND GIRLS	FD7	FLEETWOOD	6.90	1.07	2013	ENGLAND
BONITO	SS711	ST IVES	7.17	1.75	2003	CORNWALL
BONNE PECHE	J41	JERSEY	6.85	1.53	2003	Unk
BONNIE	KY14	KIRKCALDY	4.73	0.91	1984	CORNWALL
BONNIE GRACE	PZ27	PENZANCE	7.74	2.17	1984	CORNWALL
BONNIE LASS	AH59	ARBROATH	8.51	6.66	2007	CAMBORNE
BONNIE LASS	INS11	INVERNESS	7.52	3.14	1976	ST MONANCE FIFE
BONNIE LASS	WK191	WICK	7.15	1.82	1990	STONEHAVEN
BONNIE LASS II	AH4	ARBROATH	10.40	2.74	2012	UK
BONNIE LASS II	HH154	HARWICH	8.27	3.67	1989	HARWICH
BONNIE LASS II	LH26	LEITH	7.70	5.28	1983	ISLE OF WIGHT
BONNIE LASS III	MT126	MARYPORT	16.45	37.00	1971	ARBROATH
BONNY & KELLY	N98	NEWRY	25.42	123.00	1990	BORTH DYFED
BONNY LASS	HL125	HARTLEPOOL	6.40	2.73	1992	FALMOUTH CORNWALL
BONXIE	OB541	OBAN	6.83	1.56	1975	RYDE ISLE OF WIGHT
BORDER LASSIE	BH44	BLYTH	13.41	25.85	1958	GIRVAN
BORDER QUEEN	BH155	BLYTH	11.03	6.91	1979	AMBLE
BORE DA	SA47	SWANSEA	9.87	11.50	1990	SOUTHAMPTON/SOUTHGATE
BORERAY ISLE	UL105	ULLAPOOL	9.23	7.88	1972	STROMENESS
BOSCASTLE PEGANINA	PW289	PADSTOW	10.05	12.07	1979	RYE
BOSLOE	PH122	PLYMOUTH	14.39	23.59	1966	PLYMOUTH
BOSUN	PE3	POOLE	6.88	0.89	2012	DORSET
BOTE	SS120	ST IVES	4.27	0.46	1963	SOUTHAMPTON
BOUDICCA	WH760	WEYMOUTH	5.30	0.74	2008	YEOVIL

UK Fishing Vessels 2015

Vessel Name	Code	Port Name	Loa	Ton Gt	Year	Construction Place
BOUNTEOUS	N942	NEWRY	19.79	88.00	1976	NORTHSHIELDS
BOUNTIFUL	BF79	BANFF	21.10	112.00	1987	GIRVAN
BOUNTIFUL	LK280	LERWICK	7.77	2.66	1930	CUNNINGSBURGH
BOUNTIFULL	UL193	ULLAPOOL	11.70	23.63	1996	PENRYN
BOUNTY	WO148	WORKINGTON	5.64	1.52	1975	PLYMOUTH
BOUNTY HUNTER	RX448	RYE	9.97	4.73	2009	WADEBRIDGE CORNWALL
BOUT TIME	NN763	NEWHAVEN	6.70	1.80	2008	USA
BOX-A-DAY	WY369	WHITBY	7.05	2.25	1989	LIVERPOOL / WHITBY
BOY ADAM	PZ302	PENZANCE	5.86	2.04	1992	NEWLYN
BOY ADAM	SC168	SCILLY	4.73	0.70	1997	NOT KNOWN
BOY ADRIAN	LK115	LERWICK	7.73	3.67	1985	BURRA ISLE SHETLAND
BOY ALAN	WK803	WICK	9.80	7.70	2007	GBR
BOY ANDREW	CY96	CASTLEBAY	7.22	3.12	1977	MACDUFF
BOY ANDREW	FR988	FRASERBURGH	7.40	4.62	1982	DEVON
BOY ANDREW	HH40	HARWICH	7.47	3.88	1984	BRIGHTLINGSEA
BOY ANDREW	LH316	LEITH	12.17	19.63	1958	ST MONANS
BOY ANDREW	N179	NEWRY	16.27	63.00	1973	ARBROATH ANGUS
BOY ANDREW	SY868	STORNOWAY	6.51	1.28	1999	FIFE
BOY ANDREW	UL12	ULLAPOOL	7.46	3.19	1990	SOUTHGATE MIDDLESBROUGH
BOY ANDREW	WK170	WICK	26.61	235.00	1986	CAMPBELTOWN
BOY ANDREW	WY177	WHITBY	7.10	4.74	1992	NORTHUMBRIA MARINE
BOY ANGUS	SY15	STORNOWAY	5.79	1.12	1987	CORNWALL
BOY ARRAN	SY882	STORNOWAY	5.66	0.93	2009	NORFOLK
BOY BEAU	FE60	FOLKESTONE	9.95	12.48	1995	NEWHAVEN
BOY BLUE	LL12	LIVERPOOL	9.60	7.73	1982	FALMOUTH CORNWALL
BOY BRAD	M597	MILFORD HAVEN	4.80	0.96	1989	HAYLE
BOY BRAX	WH578	WEYMOUTH	5.59	1.53	1980	UNK
BOY BRIAN	BA823	BALLANTRAE	6.40	1.40	2000	GBR
BOY BRYAN	INS5	INVERNESS	11.35	6.12	1987	SOUTH SHIELDS
BOY CALLUM	WO4	WORKINGTON	9.98	13.66	1989	HULL/WORKINGTON

UK Fishing Vessels 2015

Vessel Name	Code	Port Name	Loa	Ton Gt	Year	Construction Place
BOY CHARLIE	YH11	YARMOUTH	8.02	1.62	2007	UNITED KINGDOM
BOY CHRIS	SS276	ST IVES	4.74	1.01	1978	HAYLE CORNWALL
BOY CLIVE	YH2447	YARMOUTH	5.18	0.88	1988	CAISTER ENGLAND
BOY CODY	PZ95	PENZANCE	5.59	1.48	1992	PLYMOUTH
BOY COLIN	LH292	LEITH	7.90	1.79	1972	WALSSEND
BOY CORRIN	BRD694	BROADFORD	9.00	3.24	1991	KINNEFF
BOY CRAIG	LN237	KINGS LYNN	8.03	3.44	1992	PENRYN CORNWALL
BOY DANE	ME56	MONTROSE	7.60	2.42	1980	PENRYN CORNWALL
BOY DANIEL	FH614	FALMOUTH	4.40	0.40	1982	HELFORD
BOY DANIEL	SD4	SUNDERLAND	9.96	12.00	1998	TYNE & WEAR
BOY DANIEL	SS717	ST IVES	5.50	1.43	1979	TEIGNMOUTH
BOY DANIEL	YH438	YARMOUTH	7.50	3.04	1992	GREAT YARMOUTH
BOY DARREN	CY190	CASTLEBAY	17.02	54.00	1974	IRVIN SCOTLAND
BOY DARREN	PW422	PADSTOW	6.40	1.43	1991	AMLWCH
BOY DAVID	INS64	INVERNESS	10.70	6.87	1989	HULL/LOWESTOFT
BOY DAVID	ML121	METHIL	7.33	1.81	2000	ISLAND PLASTICS
BOY DAVID	RY148	RAMSEY	9.27	8.73	1976	FALMOUTH
BOY DAVID	SU302	SOUTHAMPTON	3.10	0.24	1990	GREAT BRITAIN
BOY DOUGLAS	LI386	LITTLEHAMPTON	8.16	8.19	1982	WORCESTER
BOY DYLAN	ME242	MONTROSE	4.82	0.64	1977	GBR
BOY DYLAN	PZ11	PENZANCE	5.80	1.27	1985	WEST SUSSEX
BOY EOIN	N963	NEWRY	6.83	1.87	1998	KENT
BOY ETHAN	PH215	PLYMOUTH	14.45	37.16	1977	FRANCE
BOY FRAZER	LK137	LERWICK	7.25	2.09	1989	MORVAL LOOE
BOY GABRIEL	PZ824	PENZANCE	7.90	2.33	2000	GBR
BOY GARY	CY37	CASTLEBAY	9.84	10.47	1963	BANFF
BOY GORDON	K114	KIRKWALL	8.00	3.89	1989	CORNWALL
BOY GORDON V	A441	ABERDEEN	11.28	28.06	1989	MONTROSE ABERDEENSHIRE
BOY GRANT II	B9	BELFAST	9.65	6.90	1998	MACDUFF

UK Fishing Vessels 2015

Vessel Name	Code	Port Name	Loa	Ton Gt	Year	Construction Place
BOY GRANT III	SY969	STORNOWAY	9.98	5.29	1997	CORNWALL
BOY HARRY	FR37	FRASERBURGH	9.50	7.93	1996	PENRYN
BOY HARVEY	PZ379	PENZANCE	7.65	4.24	1973	NEWLYN
BOY JACK	N18	NEWRY	6.15	1.69	1989	FALMOUTH
BOY JACK 11	PH1190	PLYMOUTH	4.52	0.49	1993	FALMOUTH CORNWALL
BOY JAKE	SS1	ST IVES	4.83	1.12	1989	UK
BOY JAMES	BA846	BALLANTRAE	8.44	2.30	1986	Unk
BOY JAMES	PZ1197	PENZANCE	5.38	1.21	1989	PLYMOUTH
BOY JAMES	WK479	WICK	8.95	4.27	1975	KIRKWALL
BOY JASON	CO34	CAERNARVON	6.73	1.93	1989	YAPTON W. SUSSEX
BOY JEFF	GU50	GUERNSEY	4.25	0.69	1991	GUERNSEY
BOY JOE II	FY588	FOWEY	4.75	1.27	1978	HAYLE
BOY JOHN	CY147	CASTLEBAY	6.65	1.84	1975	STORNOWAY
BOY JOHN	INS110	INVERNESS	20.84	174.00	1996	MACDUFF
BOY JOHN	PD48	PETERHEAD	7.49	3.83	1972	WHITBY
BOY JOHN	WK859	WICK	8.00	2.66	2007	GBR
BOY JOHN B	PD996	PETERHEAD	9.32	4.96	1979	RYE
BOY JOHN III	PW235	PADSTOW	5.25	1.24	2003	CORNWALL
BOY JONATHAN	TT2	TARBERT	5.06	0.83	2005	ORKNEY
BOY JORDON	WK826	WICK	5.55	1.03	2001	UK
BOY JOSEPH	N793	NEWRY	9.18	8.29	1978	POOLE
BOY JOSHUA	R480	RAMSGATE	9.96	14.47	1982	PENRYN
BOY JUAN	DO1	DOUGLAS	9.12	6.13	1975	UNK
BOY KIAN	WK29	WICK	8.08	4.46	1984	HULL
BOY KOBEN	FH34	FALMOUTH	4.95	0.58	1995	SURREY
BOY LEE	BD76	BIDEFORD	9.75	10.13	1986	FALMOUTH
BOY LEVI	LT1	LOWESTOFT	6.50	1.60	2012	ENGLAND
BOY LEW	CK945	COLCHESTER	4.88	0.79	1986	NANTWICH CHESHIRE
BOY LIAM	LH2	LEITH	8.07	4.57	1980	WEYMOUTH
BOY LIAM	WH457	WEYMOUTH	9.75	6.20	1980	FALMOUTH

UK Fishing Vessels 2015

Vessel Name	Code	Port Name	Loa	Ton Gt	Year	Construction Place
BOY LIAM	WK914	WICK	6.50	1.34	1995	GBR
BOY LUKE	DR122	DOVER	7.54	2.16	1990	RYE
BOY LUKE B	HH32	HARWICH	7.87	4.86	1979	RYE
BOY LUKIE	LO89	LONDON	13.97	22.52	2005	ENGLAND
BOY MARK	FR44	FRASERBURGH	5.96	1.08	2006	SCOTLAND
BOY MATT	PZ699	PENZANCE	4.88	1.04	1967	PENZANCE
BOY MATTHEW	CE510	COLERAINE	8.35	5.69	1997	CO.DONEGAL
BOY MICHAEL	CK109	COLCHESTER	9.98	12.67	1986	UNKNOWN
BOY MICHAEL	LO92	LONDON	9.95	10.68	2005	HUMBERSIDE
BOY MICHAEL II	MN1	MALDON	9.98	12.92	2006	SOUTH HUMBERSIDE.
BOY MITCHELL	WY819	WHITBY	8.79	3.23	1963	GBR
BOY NEIL	LN126	KINGS LYNN	11.92	20.59	1981	KINGS LYNN
BOY NIALL	OB316	OBAN	4.93	0.80	1987	SUSSEX
BOY OWEN	LH439	LEITH	7.16	3.46	1974	EXMOUTH
BOY PAUL	CE12	COLERAINE	11.90	25.30	1992	STROMNESS
BOY PAUL II	N922	NEWRY	4.79	0.56	1999	GBR
BOY PETER	WK874	WICK	9.26	6.51	2005	GLASGOW
BOY PHILLIP	BM40	BRIXHAM	6.65	1.75	2011	PORTUGAL
BOY REGGIE	PW72	PADSTOW	4.17	0.57	2010	FIBRAMAR
BOY RICHIE II	WK810	WICK	13.00	19.21	1998	WICK
BOY ROBERT	PZ764	PENZANCE	4.70	1.06	1983	PLYMOUTH
BOY RYAN	BRD38	BROADFORD	9.95	4.79	1989	CORNWALL
BOY RYAN	TO41	TRURO	4.78	0.89	1997	TREEVE
BOY SAM	BW260	BARROW	6.16	1.34	2004	LANCARSHIRE
BOY SCOTT	AB104	ABERYSTWYTH	8.04	3.46	1979	LULWORTH
BOY SEAN II	CE538	COLERAINE	6.94	4.00	2008	IRL
BOY SHANE	WK673	WICK	18.20	150.00	1996	YNYSLAS BORTH DYFED
BOY SHAYNE	PL777	PEEL	7.95	7.09	2011	East Quay
BOY STAN	LK97	LERWICK	7.57	3.05	1968	UK
BOY STEVEN	LN129	KINGS LYNN	11.83	16.19	1978	KINGS LYNN
BOY STEVEN 11	CK896	COLCHESTER	7.97	2.30	1992	HAYLING ISLAND

UK Fishing Vessels 2015

Vessel Name	Code	Port Name	Loa	Ton Gt	Year	Construction Place
BOY STUART	B920	BELFAST	19.11	101.00	1974	MACDUFF
BOY STUART	LH491	LEITH	4.20	0.45	1992	NOT KNOWN
BOY TIM	LN271	KINGS LYNN	9.92	8.71	1978	KINGS LYNN
BOY WILL	B993	BELFAST	5.54	1.61	2000	GBR
BOY WILLIAM	FY764	FOWEY	6.32	2.18	1989	PENRYN CORNWALL
BOY'S OWN II	FY838	FOWEY	5.85	1.90	2001	CORNWALL
BOYS OWN	LH536	LEITH	6.52	1.60	1999	GBR
BOYS OWN	SD36	SUNDERLAND	11.25	6.91	1989	AMBLE
BOYS OWN	TH4	TEIGNMOUTH	9.99	4.85	1978	NOT KNOWN
BOYS PRIDE	BD217	BIDEFORD	9.83	13.40	2008	GBR
BRACODEN	BF37	BANFF	20.75	171.00	1991	MACDUFF
BRADAUR	DE131	DUNDEE	4.99	1.20	1970	NOT KNOWN
BRAMA	J13	JERSEY	7.01	2.15	1986	UK
BRANDON I	GU133	GUERNSEY	7.81	3.75	1984	FALMOUTH
BRANDON JOHN	N1043	NEWRY	16.17	34.00	1962	MACDUFF
BRANDY'S THUNDER	GU118	GUERNSEY	4.70	1.24	1990	UNKNOWN
BRANSCOMBE PEARL II	E293	EXETER	6.52	2.04	1981	SEATON
BRANTIA	BCK2	BUCKIE	6.95	3.19	2013	ANNALONG
BRAVEHEART	LK946	LERWICK	9.75	12.44	1998	WIGTOWN
BRAVEHEART	RX189	RYE	9.90	11.91	1991	ISLE OF WIGHT
BRAVEHEART II	SR91	STRANRAER	9.90	12.49	2004	WIGTOWN
BRAW LASS	LH6	LEITH	7.01	4.43	1983	PORT SETON
BRAWLASS II	LH572	LEITH	7.94	2.53	2002	Unk
BREADWINNER	LI564	LITTLEHAMPTON	5.55	1.48	1963	UNKNOWN
BREAKING DAWN	NN135	NEWHAVEN	9.60	7.25	1988	NEWHAVEN
BREEZE	FY9	FOWEY	5.20	0.73	2002	CORNWALL
BREJON	R76	RAMSGATE	8.37	5.87	1989	GUERNSEY
BREN JEAN	PD776	PETERHEAD	6.02	2.49	1993	FALMOUTH
BRENDA	SM263	SHOREHAM	4.91	1.00	1978	NEWHAVEN
BRENDA C	PH254	PLYMOUTH	9.30	3.04	1973	RYE AND NEWQUAY
BRETTANE	J214	JERSEY	5.80	1.24	1990	UK

UK Fishing Vessels 2015

Vessel Name	Code	Port Name	Loa	Ton Gt	Year	Construction Place
BRIAN ARTHUR	M50	MILFORD HAVEN	5.94	0.99	2007	NOT KNOWN
BRIGHT HORIZON	BA850	BALLANTRAE	12.14	13.99	2008	CANVEY ISLAND
BRIGHT HORIZON	UL98	ULLAPOOL	9.76	11.45	1990	HAVANT HAMPSHIRE
BRIGHT RAY	LH163	LEITH	16.61	52.00	1971	ST MONANS FIFE
BRIGHT RAY 11	LK16	LERWICK	8.77	6.89	1982	DIGLIS BASIN
BRIGHTER HOPE	WY224	WHITBY	9.96	6.97	1965	WHITBY
BRIGHTER MORN	CY77	CASTLEBAY	17.07	52.00	1976	STROMENESS/FRASERBURGH
BRIGHTER MORN	N396	NEWRY	25.15	152.00	1970	RENFREW
BRILLIANT	LK1	LERWICK	11.00	30.86	1990	ORKNEY
BRISAN	FD9	FLEETWOOD	35.70	286.00	1961	ABERDEEN
BRISCA	UL37	ULLAPOOL	26.75	302.00	1987	ST MONANS
BRISSONS	SS665	ST IVES	4.75	1.23	1990	NEWLYN
BRITANNIA	BA130	BALLANTRAE	4.30	0.40	1975	AYR
BRITANNIA	GU31	GUERNSEY	9.15	8.90	1975	PORT MELLON
BRITANNIA II	BH314	BLYTH	9.30	12.25	2004	CORNWALL
BRITANNIA IV OF FALMOUTH	FH508	FALMOUTH	10.00	10.95	1980	MEVAGISSEY
BRITANNIA OF BEESANDS	DH141	DARTMOUTH	9.83	11.81	2004	ESSEX
BRITANNIA V	FH121	FALMOUTH	15.15	66.00	1986	GIRVAN
BRITTANY JAMES	PD965	PETERHEAD	4.73	0.77	2005	GBR
BROADSWORD	M120	MILFORD HAVEN	9.50	4.05	1989	ESSEX
BRODI SEA	SS324	ST IVES	9.20	4.02	1979	RYE
BROGAN	SS15	ST IVES	5.36	0.68	2009	GBR
BRONCO	TH74	TEIGNMOUTH	6.80	1.70	2011	PORTUGAL
BROSME	UL576	ULLAPOOL	37.66	299.23	1974	ERANDIO SPAIN
BROTHERS	BH479	BLYTH	4.90	0.69	2001	NORTHUMBERLAND
BROTHERS	LK96	LERWICK	6.23	2.55	1988	IRELAND
BROTHERS	N2	NEWRY	6.10	1.29	2010	KILKEEL COUNTY DOWN
BROTHERS K	CN1	CAMPBELTOWN	5.77	1.00	2007	GBR
BRUISER	WH729	WEYMOUTH	4.20	0.58	1990	GBR
BRUNO OF SUTTON	PH58	PLYMOUTH	14.98	34.70	1973	CREMYLL

UK Fishing Vessels 2015

Vessel Name	Code	Port Name	Loa	Ton Gt	Year	Construction Place
BRYONY	WY4	WHITBY	5.17	0.79	2005	WHITBY
BUBBLES TOO	GU71	GUERNSEY	6.54	1.53	2009	NEYLAND PEMBROKESHIRE
BUCCANEER	FY88	FOWEY	8.38	6.04	1970	LOOE
BUCCANEER	PD34	PETERHEAD	7.92	4.55	2008	CORNWALL
BUDDING ROSE	PD418	PETERHEAD	24.54	192.00	1990	CAMPBELTOWN
BUDDING ROSE	SH156	SCARBOROUGH	16.76	42.00	1972	MACDUFF
BULLDOG	GU56	GUERNSEY	3.55	0.37	1982	ST SAMPSONS
BUMBLE	R1	RAMSGATE	6.50	1.09	1991	RAMSGATE
BUMBLE B	R84	RAMSGATE	5.85	0.56	1989	RAMSGATE
BUNG II	SA154	SWANSEA	4.42	0.55	2004	CORNWALL
BUSTER BEN	LI103	LITTLEHAMPTON	6.20	1.21	2012	ENGLAND
BUTTS	PZ584	PENZANCE	5.73	1.20	1977	FALMOUTH
C AND C	N6	NEWRY	6.35	1.38	2010	KILKEEL CO DOWN
C J LEWIS	RX408	RYE	9.95	7.13	2000	CORNWALL
C LADY	WY79	WHITBY	9.95	6.15	2013	NORTHUMBERLAND
C LOUISE	WK16	WICK	6.20	1.54	2013	WEST SUSSEX
C SHARP	BS446	BEAUMARIS	5.75	0.98	1998	ORKNEY
C.J.	FY52	FOWEY	6.50	2.90	1987	PENRYN
CAAREEN	N964	NEWRY	18.41	94.00	1979	DONEGAL
CABERFEIDH	OB368	OBAN	7.67	3.93	1975	BRIDPORT
CABIN BOY	LA11	LLANELLI	4.90	0.85	2001	GBR
CABO ORTEGAL	AR865	AYR	28.13	203.00	1991	ASTURIAS SPAIN
CACHE-CACHE	GU23	GUERNSEY	6.64	2.31	1980	CREDITON DEVON
CADENZA	BRD695	BROADFORD	6.65	1.72	2007	GBR
CADOR	SS9	ST IVES	4.40	0.46	1978	PENRYN
CAIR VIE	RY3	RAMSEY	12.79	28.60	1986	GBR
CAITLIN BEE	CK8	COLCHESTER	3.97	0.37	1999	NORWAY
CAITLYN	BS125	BEAUMARIS	5.64	0.91	2006	NOT KNOWN
CALAMARI	BS16	BEAUMARIS	4.56	0.54	1987	GBR
CALEDONIA	TT34	TARBERT	16.04	62.20	1973	WHITBY

UK Fishing Vessels 2015

Vessel Name	Code	Port Name	Loa	Ton Gt	Year	Construction Place
CALEDONIA II	BCK35	BUCKIE	16.70	106.00	2001	BUCKIE
CALIOPE	CA44	CARDIGAN	4.50	0.64	1980	NOT KNOWN
CALISHA	PD235	PETERHEAD	26.24	121.00	1968	HOLLAND
CALLY SERANNE	BN430	BOSTON	9.95	10.48	2000	HUMBERSIDE
CALON MOR	K91	KIRKWALL	11.80	11.64	1983	POOLE DORSET
CALYPSO	BM78	BRIXHAM	6.95	1.82	1974	PLYMOUTH
CALYPSO	BS541	BEAUMARIS	4.75	1.27	2011	ENGLAND
CALYPSO	OB9	OBAN	6.12	0.35	2008	HERTS
CALYPSO	WK15	WICK	9.43	12.46	1987	FALMOUTH
CAMANNA	BF16	BANFF	6.46	1.91	2012	CRAIL
CANDY	YH2476	YARMOUTH	6.37	1.58	2002	GBR
CANNY BOY	M191	MILFORD HAVEN	5.95	2.05	1987	FALMOUTH
CAOL MUILE	OB482	OBAN	7.07	2.58	1989	STONEHAVEN
CAPELLA	LH503	LEITH	9.98	11.25	1996	FRASERBURGH
CAPELLA	LK86	LERWICK	9.95	8.23	1956	SCALLOWAY
CAPERNAUM	SH4	SCARBOROUGH	9.30	5.23	1992	RYE SUSSEX
CAPRICE	GU310	GUERNSEY	7.40	2.76	1986	GUERNSEY
CAPRIOLE	PZ15	PENZANCE	10.35	3.94	1989	GBR
CARA LEE	FY33	FOWEY	10.00	12.57	1992	UNK
CARA MARIE	YH2470	YARMOUTH	6.00	0.87	1999	ENGLAND
CARA MOR	FY773	FOWEY	5.60	1.64	1994	PLYMOUTH
CARALAN	PE1087	POOLE	6.90	1.19	1998	VENTNOR
CARALISA	OB956	OBAN	17.60	70.00	1975	ST MONANS
CARASUE	AB2	ABERYSTWYTH	8.10	4.04	1990	PENRYN
CARDIUM II	F165	FAVERSHAM	13.95	23.28	1993	NEWHAVEN
CARELLIN	CE52	COLERAINE	5.70	1.17	1996	ORKNEY BOATS
CARES LEL	PZ715	PENZANCE	5.58	1.52	1979	HAYLE
CARHELMAR	BM23	BRIXHAM	23.80	128.00	1989	ZONTCAMP HOLLAND
CARIAD	CO137	CAERNARVON	7.01	3.73	1972	PWLLHELI

UK Fishing Vessels 2015

Vessel Name	Code	Port Name	Loa	Ton Gt	Year	Construction Place
CARIAD	FH89	FALMOUTH	7.30	2.56	1989	REDRUTH
CARINA	BF803	BANFF	25.93	335.00	1996	MACDUFF
CARINA	WK4	WICK	8.27	5.63	2003	CORNWALL
CARISMA	INS1037	INVERNESS	8.27	5.72	2003	MACDUFF
CARISSA ANN	PZ17	PENZANCE	6.36	2.50	1997	GORRAN HAVEN
CARLA JANE	BE13	BARNSTAPLE	4.54	0.30	1982	BIDEFORD
CARLA MAY	PH12	PLYMOUTH	7.17	4.98	1972	LAWSAND
CARLEE	FY847	FOWEY	7.00	1.57	2003	ESSEX
CARLEEN	P935	PORTSMOUTH	5.80	1.91	1993	UNITED KINGDOM
CARLEEN FRANCES	LT1039	LOWESTOFT	5.90	2.30	1970	GBR
CARLIAN	LA39	LLANELLI	5.20	0.74	1986	LLANELLI
CARLOTTA	SU507	SOUTHAMPTON	5.45	0.77	1970	SOUTHAMPTON
CARLSBAY	SY873	STORNOWAY	9.95	7.40	2005	CORNWALL
CARLY ANNE	PH799	PLYMOUTH	7.70	4.46	1991	CORNWALL
CARLY BETH	PE1170	POOLE	5.88	1.08	2005	NOT KNOWN
CARLY D	P600	PORTSMOUTH	5.76	1.29	1990	GBR
CARLY ROSE	LA618	LLANELLI	5.36	1.15	2001	SOUTHAMPTON
CARMISA II	CY820	CASTLEBAY	9.21	5.81	2001	PENRYN
CAROL	CE226	COLERAINE	4.88	0.58	1978	SURREY
CAROL	LL174	LIVERPOOL	4.88	1.00	1980	LIVERPOOL
CAROL & DAVID	PZ620	PENZANCE	4.75	0.86	1978	HAYLE
CAROL ANN	B758	BELFAST	10.97	12.51	1981	WORCESTER
CAROL ANN	J559	JERSEY	5.49	1.33	1977	JERSEY
CAROL ANN	KY1009	KIRKCALDY	9.65	11.58	2002	GBR
CAROL ANN	PD175	PETERHEAD	8.36	3.67	2013	PETERHEAD
CAROL ANN	SH265	SCARBOROUGH	7.49	1.61	1995	SEATON NR HULL
CAROL ANNE	WK54	WICK	6.70	4.67	1993	SCARFSKERRY
CAROL JUNE	GU107	GUERNSEY	4.56	0.75	1980	UNKNOWN
CAROLE ANNE	LN88	KINGS LYNN	13.91	26.02	1988	WICK
CAROLE G	J49	JERSEY	9.55	8.26	1989	FRANCE

UK Fishing Vessels 2015

Vessel Name	Code	Port Name	Loa	Ton Gt	Year	Construction Place
CAROLI-JEN	CE3	COLERAINE	8.03	3.87	1983	NOT KNOWN
CAROLINA	LA30	LLANELLI	6.98	3.79	2000	CORNWALL
CAROLINA	SU413	SOUTHAMPTON	6.09	0.44	1978	LYMINGTON
CAROLINE	P3	PORTSMOUTH	5.26	1.13	2002	Unk
CAROLINE DIANE	LR22	LANCASTER	7.38	4.07	1976	MORECOMBE
CAROLINE DOLL	LH600	LEITH	6.92	1.83	1956	EYEMOUTH
CAROLYN	HL4	HARTLEPOOL	9.96	12.02	2004	ENGLAND
CARONA	BCK9	BUCKIE	9.80	7.94	1982	HULL
CAROUSEL	SH298	SCARBOROUGH	14.52	41.67	2005	HARRIS & GARROD
CARPE DIEM	M70	MILFORD HAVEN	33.10	134.00	1983	GERMANY
CARPE DIEM	SE322	SALCOMBE	5.90	0.98	1989	PENRYN
CARRIE ANNE	OB990	OBAN	7.57	3.49	2004	SCOTLAND
CARRIE B	LH29	LEITH	8.30	3.93	1988	PENRYN
CARRIE R	NN790	NEWHAVEN	4.83	0.97	2000	UK
CARYS	SA347	SWANSEA	9.95	5.35	1999	GBR
CASHFLO	SY839	STORNOWAY	3.80	0.30	1999	HUMBER INFLATABLES
CASIE H	DH19	DARTMOUTH	4.84	1.02	2001	WALLASEY
CASPIAN	K994	KIRKWALL	8.00	4.75	1997	STROMNESS
CASPIAN III	UL63	ULLAPOOL	6.90	3.62	2012	COUNTY DOWN NORTHERN IRELAND
CASTANET	P687	PORTSMOUTH	9.50	5.27	1989	EMSWORTH
CASTLE LIGHTS	J67	JERSEY	9.10	5.23	1983	Unk
CASTLEBAY	BCK612	BUCKIE	4.93	0.79	2001	GBR
CASTLEWOOD	FR216	FRASERBURGH	25.91	195.00	1978	CAMPBELTOWN
CASTRIES	NN725	NEWHAVEN	9.88	11.28	2001	CANVEY ISLAND
CAT 'A' TAC	J10	JERSEY	6.93	1.19	2005	ISLE OF WIGHT
CAT FISH	BS474	BEAUMARIS	7.40	2.98	2002	ISLE OF WIGHT
CATALINA	INS383	INVERNESS	6.00	0.93	1999	UK
CATATONIA	BW256	BARROW	6.87	2.67	2002	UNITED KINGDOM
CATCH 22	FE381	FOLKESTONE	5.10	0.73	1999	GBR
CATCH 22	M432	MILFORD HAVEN	6.00	1.00	1994	ISLE OF WIGHT

UK Fishing Vessels 2015

Vessel Name	Code	Port Name	Loa	Ton Gt	Year	Construction Place
CATCH 22	OB287	OBAN	8.10	5.85	1992	MONTROSE SCOTLAND
CATCH 23	GU317	GUERNSEY	6.80	1.42	2001	UNKNOWN
CATHARINA	BM111	BRIXHAM	23.97	160.00	1992	HOLLAND
CATHERINE	RO11	ROTHESAY	8.00	1.66	1989	CLYDE
CATHERINE ANN	SY276	STORNOWAY	9.60	3.89	1952	CLYNDER
CATHERINE ANNE	CY43	CASTLEBAY	6.46	2.95	1985	KALLIN GRIMSAY
CATHERINE ANNE	FY902	FOWEY	4.24	0.66	2009	PEMBROKESHIRE
CATHERINE ANNE	LN476	KINGS LYNN	11.88	15.71	2006	ENGLAND
CATHERINE ANNE	SM700	SHOREHAM	9.92	8.02	1996	CANVEY ISLAND
CATHERINE ANNE II	SM820	SHOREHAM	9.98	9.24	2010	SUSSEX
CATHERINE JANE	SD412	SUNDERLAND	9.60	3.90	1975	UNK
CATHRYN	PZ32	PENZANCE	12.16	16.25	1955	BRIXHAM
CATHY ANN	N368	NEWRY	9.75	5.68	1983	PORTAVOGIE
CATHY ANNE	CK922	COLCHESTER	9.99	4.47	1981	LIVERPOOL
CATRIONA	BRD180	BROADFORD	11.61	21.29	1967	STROMNESS ORKNEY
CATRIONA	MH83	MIDDLESBROUGH	5.49	1.01	1967	SANDSEND
CATRIONA ANNE	KY1019	KIRKCALDY	5.63	1.43	1980	GLENROTHES
CATRIONA I	SY26	STORNOWAY	8.81	6.51	1976	ORKNEY
CATRIONA M	INS354	INVERNESS	9.14	8.41	1983	ANNALONG
CAWSAND BAY	PH601	PLYMOUTH	5.89	2.01	1991	MEVAGISSEY
CAYLA DORA	SN566	NORTH SHIELDS	5.35	1.45	2001	NOT KNOWN
CAZADORA	FY614	FOWEY	10.77	12.89	1985	MORVAL
CAZEE D	PH82	PLYMOUTH	5.01	0.79	1989	ARUNDEL WEST SUSSEX
CEANOTHUS	UL72	ULLAPOOL	11.00	15.47	1971	LERWICK
CEE J	FY25	FOWEY	3.88	0.40	1985	UK
CEINWEN	CO77	CAERNARVON	4.87	0.98	1982	UK
CELESTIAL DAWN	BF109	BANFF	19.90	195.00	2000	ABERDEENSHIRE
CELESTIAL DAWN	FH6	FALMOUTH	11.39	11.35	1988	PENRYN
CELIA CRAIG	ME218	MONTROSE	4.80	0.69	1996	UNKNOWN
CELT	CO798	CAERNARVON	4.85	0.76	1980	BURNESS

UK Fishing Vessels 2015

Vessel Name	Code	Port Name	Loa	Ton Gt	Year	Construction Place
CELTIC	M509	MILFORD HAVEN	11.44	27.30	1988	FRANCE
CELTIC BREEZE	PW21	PADSTOW	6.24	1.29	2003	CORNWALL
CELTIC BREEZE	PZ557	PENZANCE	7.31	4.04	1976	PENZANCE
CELTIC DAWN	FY10	FOWEY	13.45	27.84	1983	PENRYN CORNWALL
CELTIC DAWN II	K76	KIRKWALL	16.95	105.00	2004	WHITBY
CELTIC HARVESTER	N978	NEWRY	40.08	142.00	1957	HOLLAND
CELTIC LADY	CO22	CAERNARVON	7.70	2.07	1990	Unk
CELTIC MOR	M29	MILFORD HAVEN	7.95	5.83	2004	CORNWALL
CELTIC MOR OF NEWQUAY	PW31	PADSTOW	10.67	13.92	1984	HAYLE
CELTIC PRIDE	UL574	ULLAPOOL	7.98	7.06	2007	BRIGHTON
CELTIC SPIRIT	AB14	ABERYSTWYTH	8.90	7.27	2010	ESSEX
CELTIC STAR	CO365	CAERNARVON	11.95	23.41	1982	BIRKENHEAD
CELTIC STAR	WK338	WICK	7.99	3.68	1978	UNKNOWN
CELTIC SUNRISE	PZ1200	PENZANCE	5.94	1.54	2002	GBR
CEOL NA MARA	CN699	CAMPBELTOWN	8.30	6.40	2000	GBR
CEOL NA MARA	OB5	OBAN	8.84	6.59	1975	BURRAY ORKNEY
CEOL NA MARA	SY400	STORNOWAY	5.65	1.26	1988	SUSSEX
CEOL NA MARA B	BD11	BIDEFORD	11.00	14.75	1988	RAMSGATE
CERALIA	GU29	GUERNSEY	7.30	2.99	1990	JERSEY
CERALIA	J188	JERSEY	6.91	2.06	1990	UK
CERI	BS457	BEAUMARIS	5.75	0.99	1999	GBR
CERI	MN200	MALDON	5.31	0.68	1959	GBR
CERI-LEE	BD279	BIDEFORD	4.45	0.70	1989	LIZARD
CERULEAN	NN722	NEWHAVEN	13.43	28.35	2001	SUSSEX
CESCA	SY4	STORNOWAY	14.99	36.16	1968	SANDHAVEN BY FRASERBURGH
CHALE BAY	BD87	BIDEFORD	11.98	19.83	1990	BIDEFORD
CHALICE II	UL251	ULLAPOOL	7.30	2.40	1989	STONEHAVEN
CHALLENGE	FR226	FRASERBURGH	65.00	1676.00	2004	VIZCAYA
CHALLENGE	FY32	FOWEY	9.63	9.78	1999	YORK
CHALLENGE	PH5568	PLYMOUTH	8.13	4.51	1986	PENRYN CORNWALL

UK Fishing Vessels 2015

Vessel Name	Code	Port Name	Loa	Ton Gt	Year	Construction Place
CHALLENGE	SU513	SOUTHAMPTON	9.98	14.29	1997	CORNWALL
CHALLENGE A	WY133	WHITBY	10.67	10.53	1974	SANDSEND
CHALLENGER	FR90	FRASERBURGH	19.07	166.00	2010	YORKSHIRE
CHALLENGER	GK6	GREENOCK	10.27	7.32	1996	WADEBRIDGE
CHALLENGER	KY985	KIRKCALDY	9.86	12.01	1998	FIFE
CHALLENGER	LH499	LEITH	7.92	4.41	1972	UK
CHALLENGER	LI543	LITTLEHAMPTON	4.65	0.88	2003	SUSSEX
CHALLENGER	UL27	ULLAPOOL	12.50	18.25	1985	SCRABSTER
CHALLENGER	WO370	WORKINGTON	7.80	4.03	1975	WORKINGTON
CHAMELEON	N72	NEWRY	6.67	1.66	1985	ENGLAND
CHAMP	OB88	OBAN	5.57	1.74	1970	GOSPORT HANTS
CHANCE	BF324	BANFF	7.65	2.48	1974	GBR
CHANCE	K831	KIRKWALL	4.90	0.80	1975	UNKNOWN
CHANCER II	OB397	OBAN	6.45	2.11	1992	LOCHGILPHEAD
CHANNEL FISHER	CA33	CARDIGAN	9.85	8.19	1975	WEYMOUTH
CHANNEL HOUND	OB761	OBAN	9.80	6.24	1992	CORNWALL
CHANNEL SURVEYOR	SA46	SWANSEA	10.00	2.05	1984	ISLE OF WIGHT
CHANNEL SURVEYOR II	SA67	SWANSEA	11.55	9.78	1990	RYE
CHANNEL VENTURE II	SN360	NORTH SHIELDS	13.44	28.81	1982	CORNWALL
CHARELLA OF SHOREHAM	SM799	SHOREHAM	11.86	21.42	1983	BIRKENHEAD
CHARISMA	BF296	BANFF	14.11	32.25	1981	ARBROATH
CHARISMA	BH27	BLYTH	9.98	15.14	2000	BERWICKSHIRE
CHARISMA	LK362	LERWICK	70.70	2424.00	2003	NORWAY
CHARISMA	NN111	NEWHAVEN	9.99	11.90	1989	PENRYN
CHARISMA	PW45	PADSTOW	16.60	159.00	1988	EYEMOUTH
CHARISMA	SS11	ST IVES	5.10	1.14	1989	ST. IVES
CHARISMA A	SN24	NORTH SHIELDS	9.96	6.17	1989	WHITBY
CHARITY & LIBERTY	DS4	DUMFRIES	14.95	40.10	2005	CORNWALL
CHARLES EDWARD	FE385	FOLKESTONE	14.95	23.40	2013	Unk
CHARLES WILLIAM	YH2442	YARMOUTH	9.90	9.16	1991	OULTON BROAD

UK Fishing Vessels 2015

Vessel Name	Code	Port Name	Loa	Ton Gt	Year	Construction Place
CHARLIE BOY	F111	FAVERSHAM	9.99	12.84	1988	ENGLAND
CHARLIE BOY	LH531	LEITH	8.58	7.28	2001	WEST SUSSEX
CHARLIE GIRL	LI546	LITTLEHAMPTON	5.60	1.40	2005	UNKNOWN
CHARLIE JACK	WK862	WICK	4.95	0.65	1989	Unk
CHARLIE JOHN	YH776	YARMOUTH	10.10	8.11	2013	ENGLAND
CHARLOTTA	PW362	PADSTOW	7.98	3.87	1979	PORTHLEVEN
CHARLOTTE	LN466	KINGS LYNN	13.60	28.29	2001	BARTON UPON HUMBER
CHARLOTTE	WY210	WHITBY	5.10	0.92	1979	WHITBY
CHARLOTTE	YH966	YARMOUTH	6.94	1.58	1994	UNK
CHARLOTTE ANN	SE99	SALCOMBE	5.95	1.49	1998	PLYMOUTH
CHARLOTTE B	FD449	FLEETWOOD	4.75	0.76	1992	BRISTOL ENGLAND
CHARLOTTE JOAN	LO1	LONDON	13.95	24.11	2006	SUSSEX
CHARLOTTE LILY	WH75	WEYMOUTH	7.00	1.64	1999	YEOVIL
CHARLOTTE LOUISE	PW25	PADSTOW	7.32	2.08	2013	PETERHEAD
CHARLOTTE MARIE	YH350	YARMOUTH	5.12	0.72	1992	GREAT YARMOUTH
CHARMEL	OB22	OBAN	17.07	88.00	1980	BUCKIE
CHARTREUSE	SE4	SALCOMBE	5.80	0.85	2007	BECCLES
CHATERS	KY31	KIRKCALDY	9.95	5.99	2009	ASHINGTON
CHE SARA	DR178	DOVER	6.20	0.91	1987	UK
CHEEKY BOY	PL7	PEEL	6.00	1.00	2001	UNIED KINGDOM
CHEERFULL	CY254	CASTLEBAY	16.46	88.00	1985	ARBROATH
CHEETAH	GU222	GUERNSEY	6.20	1.29	1996	VENTNOR
CHEETAH	OB993	OBAN	6.94	1.76	2004	ISLE OF WIGHT
CHEETAH IV	LA65	LLANELLI	6.20	1.02	2002	ISLE OF WIGHT
CHELARIS	MT23	MARYPORT	14.98	32.89	1970	SCOTLAND
CHELSEA	WH741	WEYMOUTH	4.02	0.49	2005	UNKNOWN
CHERENA	K54	KIRKWALL	6.20	1.67	1993	ORKNEY
CHERYL ANN	NT5	NEWPORT	5.72	1.65	1998	CORNWALL
CHERYL SARAH	CK78	COLCHESTER	8.82	3.13	1979	BOTLEY HAMPSHIRE
CHEVERTON	GU81	GUERNSEY	5.52	1.38	1965	COWES ISLE OF WIGHT
CHICADEE	PZ82	PENZANCE	7.01	2.38	1935	LOOE

UK Fishing Vessels 2015

Vessel Name	Code	Port Name	Loa	Ton Gt	Year	Construction Place
CHIEFTAIN	SY861	STORNOWAY	10.60	6.92	1990	SCOTLAND
CHIPS	R264	RAMSGATE	6.07	0.84	1982	MALDEN
CHLOE B	PN64	PRESTON	5.08	0.82	2009	Unk
CHLOE BETH	CO829	CAERNARVON	5.43	1.46	2003	UK
CHLOE MAY	FR983	FRASERBURGH	9.95	10.29	2006	SEAWAY MARINE
CHLOE MAY	PL150	PEEL	6.02	2.62	2001	SAINT HILAIRE DE REIZ
CHLOE ROSE	LH15	LEITH	6.90	1.68	2009	I.O.W
CHOTI	WK699	WICK	6.86	2.26	1995	UNK
CHRIS ANDRA	FR228	FRASERBURGH	71.20	2247.00	2006	NORWAY
CHRIS-TACHA	PL26	PEEL	16.19	73.60	2002	Unk
CHRISDIAN R	R61	RAMSGATE	5.06	0.83	2000	WEST SUSSEX
CHRISLIN	BA582	BALLANTRAE	4.93	0.82	1980	MACKAY'S OF AYR
CHRISSIE B	SM1	SHOREHAM	9.95	9.54	2008	GBR
CHRISSIE JEAN	WH775	WEYMOUTH	5.90	0.96	1984	GBR
CHRISTEL STAR	H56	HULL	13.07	30.26	1983	HULL
CHRISTELLE	B5	BELFAST	7.98	2.67	1986	FELIXSTOWE
CHRISTIAN M	UL578	ULLAPOOL	35.40	322.00	1972	CHERBOURG
CHRISTINA	FD100	FLEETWOOD	28.00	188.00	1973	HOLLAND
CHRISTINA CARA	CK168	COLCHESTER	9.50	8.58	1979	SHEERNESS
CHRISTINA S	FR224	FRASERBURGH	71.96	2411.00	2007	NORWAY
CHRISTINE	BRD2	BROADFORD	10.60	8.23	1982	HAYLE
CHRISTINE	FY19	FOWEY	6.70	3.41	1948	MEVAGISSEY
CHRISTINE	M9	MILFORD HAVEN	5.80	0.88	2006	SUFFOLK
CHRISTINE	N32	NEWRY	9.79	5.22	1981	ABERYSTWYTH
CHRISTINE	RX11	RYE	7.10	3.49	2010	SHOREHAM BY SEA WEST SUSSEX
CHRISTINE	WH717	WEYMOUTH	4.65	0.73	1985	GBR
CHRISTINE ANN	CA387	CARDIGAN	6.90	0.88	2009	ISLE OF WIGHT
CHRISTINE ANN	CY103	CASTLEBAY	4.90	0.69	2014	ENGLAND
CHRISTINE ANNE	P26	PORTSMOUTH	7.41	3.83	1984	PORTSMOUTH
CHRISTINE CLAIRE	H25	HULL	9.80	9.70	1977	GOSPORT

UK Fishing Vessels 2015

Vessel Name	Code	Port Name	Loa	Ton Gt	Year	Construction Place
CHRISTINE MARIE	M8	MILFORD HAVEN	9.87	10.51	1992	HULL
CHRISTOPHER	BH477	BLYTH	9.80	7.19	2004	ANSTRUTHER
CHUAN	SM808	SHOREHAM	4.93	1.06	2006	UNKNOWN
CHUSAN	WK52	WICK	4.79	0.98	1970	WICK
CHUTNEY	WY830	WHITBY	5.10	0.74	1999	SUSSEX
CHWARAE TEG	M28	MILFORD HAVEN	6.66	1.67	2006	CHANNEL ISLANDS
CIAN	CO810	CAERNARVON	5.10	0.87	2006	HAMPSHIRE
CIARA NAOIMH	CE539	COLERAINE	7.60	3.39	1990	NORTHERN IRELAND
CIMWCH 2	BS475	BEAUMARIS	6.00	1.14	1980	CONWAY
CINTRA	TT7	TARBERT	4.90	0.68	1985	GBR
CINTRA	TT7	TARBERT	6.82	1.20	2012	YEOVIL
CJ1	E35	EXETER	5.60	0.87	1986	YORKSHIRE
CKS	BS425	BEAUMARIS	16.73	58.00	1973	ANSTRUTHER
CLAIR	PZ91	PENZANCE	4.33	0.64	1969	SOUTHAMPTON
CLAIRE	AB210	ABERYSTWYTH	4.60	0.60	1982	GBR
CLAIRE	FR64	FRASERBURGH	5.18	0.99	1985	ABERDEEN
CLAIRE ANN	YH239	YARMOUTH	7.06	3.68	1989	STIFFKEY
CLAIRE JAYNE II	BRD259	BROADFORD	7.01	2.01	1976	PORT TALBOT
CLAIRE L	A857	ABERDEEN	4.80	0.68	1988	ARUNDEL
CLAIRE LOUISE	R39	RAMSGATE	8.60	7.02	1985	CORNWALL
CLAIRE LOUISE	SE150	SALCOMBE	11.90	17.62	1978	GUERNSEY
CLAIRE LOUISE	WK860	WICK	4.90	0.88	2009	GBR
CLAIRE MADISON	BH441	BLYTH	9.81	5.96	1985	SANDSEND
CLAIRE MARIE	YH78	YARMOUTH	5.98	1.31	2009	UNITED KINGDON
CLAIRVOYANT	PZ1184	PENZANCE	8.96	4.12	1974	MEVAGESSEY
CLANSMAN	CN96	CAMPBELTOWN	11.50	12.37	1988	CORNWALL
CLANSMAN	LT74	LOWESTOFT	12.47	21.03	1972	EYEMOUTH
CLAR INNIS	NN732	NEWHAVEN	9.83	11.81	2003	COLCHESTER
CLARE LOUISE	SH93	SCARBOROUGH	9.84	6.84	1992	SANSEND
CLARICE	CA372	CARDIGAN	8.26	5.57	2002	FALMOUTH

UK Fishing Vessels 2015

Vessel Name	Code	Port Name	Loa	Ton Gt	Year	Construction Place
CLARIN	N906	NEWRY	8.20	3.19	2009	KILKEEL
CLARISSA	PH60	PLYMOUTH	9.95	8.37	2010	ENGLAND
CLASINA	DS15	DUMFRIES	28.04	165.00	1968	HOLLAND
CLAYMORE	OB552	OBAN	5.55	1.01	1987	MALLAIG
CLAYTONIA	OB24	OBAN	6.85	1.78	2012	COLCHESTER
CLEAR HORIZON	WH786	WEYMOUTH	7.60	1.32	2012	ISLE OF WIGHT
CLIFFORD NOEL	CN357	CAMPBELTOWN	9.99	7.02	1986	PENRYN CORNWALL
CLOCAROL	RO107	ROTHESAY	6.97	1.46	1989	NORTH QUEENSFERRY
CLOUDY	BS33	BEAUMARIS	9.85	15.33	1992	BEVERLEY
CLYDE	M1075	MILFORD HAVEN	4.92	0.65	1989	PEMBROKESHIRE
COASTAL FLYER	SU20	SOUTHAMPTON	6.20	1.18	1991	I.O.W
COASTAL QUEEN	BF111	BANFF	5.70	1.58	2006	CULLEN BUCKIE
COBBER	LI532	LITTLEHAMPTON	4.93	0.87	1980	GBR
COBO MAID	GU44	GUERNSEY	5.58	1.61	1979	GUERNSEY
COBRA	LA607	LLANELLI	5.26	0.83	2004	CARMS
COD FATHER	DE132	DUNDEE	6.21	1.52	2006	GBR
CODONGER TOO	FE21	FOLKESTONE	10.68	12.08	1986	ROCHESTER
COELLEIRA	OB93	OBAN	30.00	210.00	1970	HOLLAND
COLINNE	FD160	FLEETWOOD	21.21	81.00	1958	BUCKIE
COLL	BA838	BALLANTRAE	5.10	0.79	2000	GBR
COLLEEN	CO30	CAERNARVON	7.80	2.83	1983	HAILE CORNWALL
COMELY III	KY455	KIRKCALDY	9.90	8.41	1979	PENRYN
COMET	LK326	LERWICK	5.72	1.23	1988	WEST SUSSEX
COMET	YH238	YARMOUTH	5.70	0.96	1987	SUSSEX
COMMODORE	SN108	NORTH SHIELDS	10.00	7.92	1986	TYNE AND WEAR
COMPANION	WK66	WICK	6.86	1.84	1983	CAITHNESS
COMPASS ROSE	CE546	COLERAINE	9.38	5.02	1970	GBR
COMPASS ROSE	E3	EXETER	9.99	5.79	1964	CORNWALL
COMPASS ROSE	FR84	FRASERBURGH	6.17	1.53	2007	NOT KNOWN
COMPASS ROSE	GU38	GUERNSEY	5.60	1.61	1982	GUERNSEY
COMPASS ROSE	PD707	PETERHEAD	6.02	1.26	2008	GBR

UK Fishing Vessels 2015

Vessel Name	Code	Port Name	Loa	Ton Gt	Year	Construction Place
COMPASS ROSE	PH160	PLYMOUTH	8.24	4.51	1956	UNKNOWN
COMPASS ROSE	SH314	SCARBOROUGH	8.40	1.98	2000	GBR
COMPASS ROSE II	BD78	BIDEFORD	10.98	11.34	1974	CARDIFF
COMRADE	LN69	KINGS LYNN	9.50	7.74	1999	ORKNEY
COMRADE	SY337	STORNOWAY	16.65	64.00	1972	FRASERBURGH
COMRADES	LK325	LERWICK	16.30	41.00	1958	BANFF
COMRADES	WK181	WICK	6.80	3.07	1887	HUNA
CONCHRA	TN18	TROON	7.90	2.00	1982	PENRYN
CONCORD	KY99	KIRKCALDY	8.80	4.60	1981	COLVIC ESSEX
CONCORD	LK657	LERWICK	7.35	3.50	1970	BURRAY ORKNEY
CONCORD	ML114	METHIL	7.00	1.84	1962	ANSTRUTHER
CONCORDE	N268	NEWRY	16.52	47.00	1970	MACDUFF
CONDOR	HH15	HARWICH	6.55	3.06	1973	WACTON
CONDOR	OB247	OBAN	7.32	2.52	1980	CLYDE
CONFIDENCE	BF600	BANFF	5.96	1.79	2001	UK
CONNOR BOY	BF11	BANFF	5.83	1.21	2012	BANFF
CONQUEST	BCK265	BUCKIE	22.86	167.00	1984	BUCKIE
CONSORT	PD901	PETERHEAD	6.35	3.20	1991	POOLE
CONSTANT FRIEND	BH212	BLYTH	11.29	8.21	1958	EYEMOUTH
CONSTANT FRIEND	BM484	BRIXHAM	14.99	40.75	1998	FALMOUTH
CONSTANT FRIEND	PD83	PETERHEAD	18.54	152.00	1994	MACDUFF
CONSTANT FRIEND	PL168	PEEL	12.13	24.25	1970	ARBROATH
CONSTELLATION	FR294	FRASERBURGH	8.20	4.82	2009	NORTHERN IRELAND
CONSTELLATION	K42	KIRKWALL	5.86	1.63	2010	UK
CONTENDER	J4	JERSEY	7.50	1.33	2003	GBR
CONTEST	LK70	LERWICK	18.40	127.00	1985	SANDHAVEN
CONWAY	FY823	FOWEY	4.70	1.07	1989	PENRYN
COOL BREEZE	SH64	SCARBOROUGH	8.01	1.83	1986	WHITBY
COOL DAWN	P1008	PORTSMOUTH	7.00	1.23	2005	GBR
COPESAITIC	J88	JERSEY	5.43	0.93	2003	SOUTH AFRICA

UK Fishing Vessels 2015

Vessel Name	Code	Port Name	Loa	Ton Gt	Year	Construction Place
COPIOUS	FH145	FALMOUTH	13.99	28.89	1990	GBR
COPIOUS	LK985	LERWICK	18.98	145.00	2006	WHITBY
COPIOUS	WY170	WHITBY	18.25	106.00	1982	CAMPELTOWN
COPTIC	FE370	FOLKESTONE	8.01	2.73	2000	SUSSEX
COQUET LIGHT II	OB446	OBAN	11.58	8.66	1979	DEVORAN
COQUET QUEEN	MH222	MIDDLESBROUGH	9.91	5.22	1976	AMBLE
CORAL	LK696	LERWICK	8.30	4.60	1994	CORNWALL
CORAL MARIE	PH1012	PLYMOUTH	4.90	0.54	1980	UK
CORAL REEF	FY167	FOWEY	5.70	1.70	1951	PORTHLEVEN
CORAL SEA	BRD629	BROADFORD	7.49	2.13	1976	UNKNOWN
CORAL STRAND II	PL80	PEEL	16.52	46.91	1969	UNITED KINGDOM
CORALIE DAWN	LI6	LITTLEHAMPTON	7.42	3.06	1989	GBR
CORDELIA	KY70	KIRKCALDY	6.53	2.87	1981	FALMOUTH
CORDELIA K	INS151	INVERNESS	40.27	336.00	1983	THE NETHERLANDS
CORENTINE	J154	JERSEY	19.12	78.35	1955	FRANCE
CORINA II	NN57	NEWHAVEN	13.94	40.24	1986	NEWHAVEN
CORMORAN	PZ4	PENZANCE	6.19	2.87	1999	CORNWALL
CORMORANT	GU148	GUERNSEY	7.72	3.96	1963	WEYMOUTH
CORMORANT	MT79	MARYPORT	5.00	0.70	1979	ORKNEY
CORMORANT	SM655	SHOREHAM	4.88	0.83	1978	BOGNOR
CORMORANT	WK377	WICK	6.04	1.46	1880	STROMA
CORNELIS GERT JAN	DS18	DUMFRIES	35.77	328.00	1985	ZEEBRUGGE
CORNELIS VROLIJK FZN	H171	HULL	113.97	5579.00	1988	NETHERLANDS
CORNISH GEM	PH819	PLYMOUTH	9.50	16.17	1996	NEWHAVEN
CORNISH GEM	PW32	PADSTOW	8.35	4.78	1984	TONBRIDGE
CORNISH LASS	FH702	FALMOUTH	8.25	3.64	1989	CORNWALL
CORNISH LASS	FY860	FOWEY	9.97	10.24	2010	SOUTHAMPTON
CORNISH LASS	PZ339	PENZANCE	7.98	4.18	1950	LOOE
CORNISH LASS IV OF COVERACK	FH717	FALMOUTH	4.89	0.92	2003	HELSTON

UK Fishing Vessels 2015

Vessel Name	Code	Port Name	Loa	Ton Gt	Year	Construction Place
CORNISH MAID OF LOOE	FY242	FOWEY	5.85	1.36	1973	LOOE
CORNISH ROSE	PW11	PADSTOW	4.72	1.14	2000	CORNWALL
CORNISHMAN	FY868	FOWEY	5.85	0.65	2003	CORNWALL
CORNISHMAN	PZ512	PENZANCE	32.82	208.20	1971	NETHERLANDS
CORNUCOPIA	K4	KIRKWALL	4.69	0.78	1970	UK
CORNUCOPIA	LK372	LERWICK	9.98	15.15	1992	WHITBY
CORNUCOPIA	SH17	SCARBOROUGH	9.92	5.52	1981	MACDUFF
CORNUCOPIA I	K175	KIRKWALL	6.90	1.51	2005	ISLE OF WIGHT
CORONA	K226	KIRKWALL	9.29	7.96	1971	STROMNESS ORKNEY
CORVINA	BS448	BEAUMARIS	4.58	0.35	1998	DEVON
CORVUS	LK219	LERWICK	7.55	1.86	1993	UNKNOWN
COSMOS MARINER	TO7	TRURO	6.95	2.23	2008	CAMBORNE
COURAGE	UL595	ULLAPOOL	12.90	18.86	1980	SWEDEN
COURAGE	WY151	WHITBY	9.97	6.16	1986	SANDSEND
COURAGE II	BCK50	BUCKIE	8.02	3.82	1980	BUCKIEN
COURAGEOUS III	H292	HULL	25.94	177.00	1980	DENMARK
COURTNEY REBECCA	LA26	LLANELLI	5.24	1.09	1988	SWANSEA
COWRIE BAY	N911	NEWRY	15.71	48.00	1973	STONE STAFFORDSHIRE
CRABSTER	BRD686	BROADFORD	5.65	1.23	1985	ENGLAND
CRACK O DAWN	LN244	KINGS LYNN	9.86	4.32	1989	LOWESTOFT
CRAIGNAIR	LK331	LERWICK	10.00	9.63	1974	PORTLEVEN CORNWALL
CRAWPEEL	A53	ABERDEEN	5.05	0.63	2004	COVE BAY
CRAZY CAT	H1121	HULL	6.90	1.16	2005	ISLE OF WIGHT
CRAZY HORSE	M1110	MILFORD HAVEN	5.35	1.12	1992	SUFFOLK
CREACHAN MHOR	OB26	OBAN	9.98	12.53	1989	CARDIFF
CREST	CO60	CAERNARVON	4.90	0.58	1990	GBR
CREST	OB187	OBAN	11.03	11.54	1975	STROMNESS
CRIMOND	WY157	WHITBY	9.02	5.05	1988	SANDSEND
CRIMSON ARROW	CN43	CAMPBELTOWN	13.47	25.69	1985	SUNDERLAND
CRIMSON ARROW IV	OB128	OBAN	16.69	40.00	1963	FRASERBURGH

UK Fishing Vessels 2015

Vessel Name	Code	Port Name	Loa	Ton Gt	Year	Construction Place
CRIMSON TIDE	FY875	FOWEY	5.94	0.95	2006	CORNWALL
CRISTAL WATERS	B95	BELFAST	9.99	10.56	1969	PORTREUX FRANCE
CROFTER	SH304	SCARBOROUGH	8.25	10.17	2006	CORNWALL
CROWDED HOUR	N66	NEWRY	9.15	4.03	2004	CORNWALL
CRUSADER	DE25	DUNDEE	6.60	1.60	1979	ESSEX
CRUSADER	FD71	FLEETWOOD	17.29	43.00	1976	APPLEDORE
CRUSADER	KY995	KIRKCALDY	9.79	16.26	1999	FIFE
CRUSADER	SA16	SWANSEA	6.80	1.45	1990	HAVANT HANTS
CRUSADER	SY720	STORNOWAY	6.20	1.82	1988	TEIGNMOUTH DEVON
CRYSTAL ANN	LK836	LERWICK	7.38	1.53	1980	WHALSAY
CRYSTAL DAWN	CN20	CAMPBELTOWN	14.95	60.28	2011	ABERDEENSHIRE
CRYSTAL DAWN	H116	HULL	9.98	7.58	1981	BRIDLINGTON
CRYSTAL RIVER	FR178	FRASERBURGH	25.91	208.00	1985	DENMARK
CRYSTAL RIVER A	BH476	BLYTH	9.92	16.34	1999	FIFE
CRYSTAL SEA	BH95	BLYTH	9.60	3.89	1964	AMBLE
CRYSTAL SEA	HL106	HARTLEPOOL	9.15	10.57	1988	LIVERPOOL
CRYSTAL SEA	K18	KIRKWALL	7.93	4.58	1972	HAMNAVOE
CRYSTAL SEA	SS118	ST IVES	20.94	158.00	1989	MACDUFF
CRYSTAL STAR	WA85	WHITEHAVEN	9.05	6.87	1988	POOLE
CRYSTAL STREAM	LH147	LEITH	17.78	112.34	1984	BUCKIE
CRYSTAL TIDE	CE135	COLERAINE	18.47	74.56	1971	MACDUFF
CRYSTAL WATERS	YH585	YARMOUTH	5.12	0.99	1994	NORFOLK
CUDDY SHARK	FR14	FRASERBURGH	4.85	0.85	1985	ARUNDEL SUSSEX
CULANE	BCK619	BUCKIE	5.49	1.55	1965	NORWAY
CURLEW	LK73	LERWICK	7.45	2.51	1983	SHETLAND
CURLEW	OB108	OBAN	8.90	8.84	1985	INVERNESS
CURLEW	P121	PORTSMOUTH	5.71	1.64	1964	PORTSMOUTH
CURLEW	PZ585	PENZANCE	4.78	1.07	1991	SENNEN PENZANCE
CURLEW	SC70	SCILLY	8.23	4.05	1948	LOOE
CUSHLIN	B972	BELFAST	7.94	4.29	1980	GBR

UK Fishing Vessels 2015

Vessel Name	Code	Port Name	Loa	Ton Gt	Year	Construction Place
CUSHLIN II	PL5	PEEL	4.15	0.36	1987	UNK
CWIN MERI	CO791	CAERNARVON	4.85	1.16	1998	UNKNOWN
CYCLONE	HL1059	HARTLEPOOL	8.09	3.99	1995	CORNWALL
CYGNET	GU90	GUERNSEY	6.65	0.58	2008	PENICHE
CYGNET	TT89	TARBERT	7.69	2.79	1979	TARBERT ARGYLL
CYNTH	PZ734	PENZANCE	4.50	0.67	1981	MARAZION
CYNTHIA	PZ663	PENZANCE	5.60	1.55	1980	NEWLYN
CYNTHIA	SS136	ST IVES	5.59	1.45	1974	NEWLYN
CYNTHIA MARY	J38	JERSEY	10.20	10.54	2012	JERSEY
CZAR	LH588	LEITH	9.64	3.96	2011	NORTHUMBERLAND
D-IMMP	GU219	GUERNSEY	10.73	6.73	1972	WEYMOUTH
D.H.S.	AB29	ABERYSTWYTH	7.49	1.68	1981	BORTH
D.J.P.	CA9	CARDIGAN	10.67	12.48	1988	LYMINGTON
DA CALYPSO	FR515	FRASERBURGH	8.60	2.85	1988	CAICKERELL WEYMOUTH
DAG DAN	A5	ABERDEEN	4.97	0.64	1978	SCOTLAND
DAISY	E227	EXETER	5.06	0.94	2008	GBR
DAISY	ME6	MONTROSE	4.87	0.74	1990	CELLARDYKE
DAISY	WK301	WICK	6.65	1.61	1912	STROMA
DAISY II	PD245	PETERHEAD	21.20	95.00	1988	COURSEULLES
DAISY MAE	M43	MILFORD HAVEN	5.85	2.02	1981	HAYLE CORNWALL
DAISY T	WH6	WEYMOUTH	6.89	2.27	2008	UK
DALRIADA	FE76	FOLKESTONE	11.28	8.94	1974	INVERGORDON
DALWHINNIE	A913	ABERDEEN	12.48	9.28	2011	ICELAND
DAN-JOHN	J658	JERSEY	5.10	0.96	1992	UK
DANDA	PZ609	PENZANCE	8.23	4.41	1978	PORTHLEVEN
DANIELLE	BM478	BRIXHAM	31.99	250.00	1973	SLUISKIL
DANIELLE	YH488	YARMOUTH	10.39	11.17	1980	WORCESTER
DANMARK M8	SC8	SCILLY	9.77	8.42	1979	GOODWICK
DANNY BOY	LA44	LLANELLI	4.80	0.72	1992	ORKNEY
DANNY BOY	NN736	NEWHAVEN	6.80	1.62	2003	KENT
DANNY BOY	OB162	OBAN	8.05	3.73	1981	CORNWALL

UK Fishing Vessels 2015

Vessel Name	Code	Port Name	Loa	Ton Gt	Year	Construction Place
DANNY BOY	PD6	PETERHEAD	7.40	2.47	1973	CORNWALL
DANNY BOY II	R60	RAMSGATE	8.25	9.47	1989	RAMSGATE ENGLAND
DANNY BUOY	SA1	SWANSEA	9.99	8.01	2000	UK
DANNY J	BRD639	BROADFORD	9.40	3.99	1990	RYE SUSSEX
DAPHNE ROSE	SS226	ST IVES	4.75	0.93	1977	HAYLE CORNWALL
DARAMORE	INS19	INVERNESS	7.36	2.14	1999	HAVANT
DARCIE GIRL	N209	NEWRY	8.01	2.61	2008	ICELAND
DARIEN	BRD652	BROADFORD	6.10	1.17	2001	SUSSEX
DARING	PW56	PADSTOW	5.15	0.89	1984	HAMPSHIRE
DARK HARVESTER	BS505	BEAUMARIS	5.80	0.70	2006	SUFFOLK
DARK STAR	CH257	CHESTER	7.95	3.49	1991	HOYLAKE
DARTANGLER	DH4	DARTMOUTH	9.98	4.90	2007	ISLE OF WIGHT
DARTER	PH316	PLYMOUTH	9.75	7.48	1974	FALMOUTH
DAS BOAT	J368	JERSEY	4.87	0.74	1985	GBR
DASU	UL577	ULLAPOOL	26.60	169.00	1987	GIJON SPAIN
DAVANLIN	FR890	FRASERBURGH	20.89	157.00	1995	MACDUFF
DAVE	NN50	NEWHAVEN	5.18	0.66	1984	HAVANT
DAVELLE	SM399	SHOREHAM	5.03	0.63	1977	BOGNOR REGIS
DAVRIK I	SE16	SALCOMBE	9.75	7.19	1981	WEYMOUTH
DAWN	DH77	DARTMOUTH	4.30	0.59	1978	KINGSBRIDGE
DAWN	SY203	STORNOWAY	6.71	1.45	1980	SUFFOLK
DAWN DIVER	DR104	DOVER	8.10	5.26	1985	DEAL KENT
DAWN FISHER	PE521	POOLE	6.55	1.62	2007	PORTUGAL
DAWN HARVEST	K1155	KIRKWALL	9.95	16.20	2004	ESSEX
DAWN HUNTER	J252	JERSEY	5.73	1.06	1994	UK
DAWN HUNTER II	TH155	TEIGNMOUTH	6.50	1.16	2000	BJR WESTRAL CHIEF
DAWN LADY	J308	JERSEY	5.00	0.83	1991	UK
DAWN LIGHT	BA811	BALLANTRAE	5.20	1.05	1988	WHITHORN
DAWN LIGHT	J148	JERSEY	7.10	1.30	1979	ISLE OF WIGHT
DAWN MAID	TN102	TROON	16.51	37.00	1969	GIRVAN

UK Fishing Vessels 2015

Vessel Name	Code	Port Name	Loa	Ton Gt	Year	Construction Place
DAWN MIST	WH9	WEYMOUTH	6.40	1.59	1983	CARDIGAN
DAWN MIST 11	WK27	WICK	8.20	2.70	1982	FALMOUTH
DAWN QUEST	CN324	CAMPBELTOWN	11.00	11.96	1981	WORCESTER
DAWN RAIDER	P940	PORTSMOUTH	9.90	10.97	2002	ESSEX
DAWN RISE	GK76	GREENOCK	9.48	7.00	1967	PORTAVOGIE
DAWN STAR	WK833	WICK	6.10	1.51	1965	SCOTLAND
DAWN TIDE	NN727	NEWHAVEN	4.34	0.54	1999	SUSSEX
DAWN TILL DUSK	GU94	GUERNSEY	5.55	1.52	1985	GUERNSEY
DAWN TREADER	BA835	BALLANTRAE	6.70	1.51	2003	HAMPSHIRE
DAWN TREADER	OB461	OBAN	11.10	16.09	1988	GBR
DAWN WATCH II	BA120	BALLANTRAE	15.69	41.00	1962	MCDUFF
DAWNLIGHT	B230	BELFAST	6.30	1.09	1970	STROMNESS
DAY DAWN	AH95	ARBROATH	8.72	5.67	1947	ROVE
DAY DAWN	BF285	BANFF	5.63	1.30	1989	GARDENSTOWN
DAY DAWN	N182	NEWRY	19.17	57.00	1965	BANFF
DAY DREAMER	TH6	TEIGNMOUTH	4.85	0.58	1980	ARUNDEL WEST SUSSEX
DAYBREAK	INS329	INVERNESS	6.20	2.44	1979	HAYLING ISLAND HANTS
DAYBREAK	PD3	PETERHEAD	7.95	2.41	2005	ISLE OF WIGHT
DAYBREAK	WA1	WHITEHAVEN	10.01	9.98	2012	NEWHAVEN
DAYDA B	BH20	BLYTH	5.07	1.12	1990	ENGLAND
DAYDA II	BH26	BLYTH	6.56	3.37	1992	WALES
DAYMER BAY	PW333	PADSTOW	8.00	6.33	1982	PLYMOUTH
DAYSTAR	BF151	BANFF	18.60	167.00	2008	SCOTLAND
DDRAIG GOCH	M657	MILFORD HAVEN	7.90	2.74	1952	UNK
DEALAN-DE	BRD669	BROADFORD	9.96	10.42	2003	CANVEY ISLAND
DEANO II	PH996	PLYMOUTH	4.09	0.47	1997	GBR
DEBBIE G	P824	PORTSMOUTH	9.83	8.63	1968	CORNWALL
DEBORAH JANE	DH3	DARTMOUTH	6.95	3.57	2007	ESSEX
DEBORAH JAYNE	SM790	SHOREHAM	4.76	1.06	1979	BOGNOR WEST SUSSEX
DEBRA JAYNE	H1128	HULL	7.59	1.34	2007	ISLE OF WIGHT

UK Fishing Vessels 2015

Vessel Name	Code	Port Name	Loa	Ton Gt	Year	Construction Place
DEBRA LOUISE	SN30	NORTH SHIELDS	9.55	4.00	1976	BEAUMARIS ANGLESEY
DEE J	BM5	BRIXHAM	9.96	13.71	1998	DARTMOUTH
DEEP BLUE III	M567	MILFORD HAVEN	4.87	0.75	2007	CORNWALL
DEEP HARMONY	K375	KIRKWALL	9.95	6.47	1997	PENRYN
DEEP HARMONY IV	INS135	INVERNESS	8.00	4.90	1996	CORNWALL
DEEP MARINER	B893	BELFAST	9.74	2.70	1985	LYMINGTON
DEEP SEA ONE	GK52	GREENOCK	7.13	1.45	1985	UK
DEESIDE	BCK595	BUCKIE	24.35	216.00	1989	CAMPBELTOWN
DEFIANCE	FR385	FRASERBURGH	26.21	187.00	1975	BERWICK
DEFIANCE	GU168	GUERNSEY	11.90	24.71	2013	GBG
DEFIANCE IV	CN5	CAMPBELTOWN	5.62	0.97	1985	HAMPSHIRE
DEFIANT	FY848	FOWEY	13.97	41.50	2004	CORNWALL
DEFIANT	K337	KIRKWALL	11.50	16.66	1980	FALMOUTH
DEFIANT	KY221	KIRKCALDY	6.10	1.40	1981	WORCESTER
DEFIANT	LK371	LERWICK	26.61	241.00	1987	CAMPBLETOWN
DEFIANT	R467	RAMSGATE	9.80	7.91	1997	RAMSGATE
DEJA VU	CT122	CASTLETOWN	6.97	1.70	2001	UNK
DEJA VU	SU21	SOUTHAMPTON	7.46	2.98	2004	ISLE OF WIGHT
DEJAVU	M11	MILFORD HAVEN	5.40	1.24	1980	SUFFOLK
DEL-PHIL	SA322	SWANSEA	5.20	1.00	2001	GBR
DELIA MAY	GU302	GUERNSEY	7.02	2.09	1989	UNKNOWN
DELIVERANCE	CN8	CAMPBELTOWN	5.60	1.16	1989	UNKNOWN
DELIVERANCE	FR254	FRASERBURGH	20.60	172.00	1989	MACDUFF
DELLA	LR116	LANCASTER	5.92	1.26	1977	OVERTON
DELLA M	WH326	WEYMOUTH	4.27	0.56	1982	POOLE DORSET
DELTA BARBARA	WH103	WEYMOUTH	8.00	4.86	1986	PENRYN
DELTA DAWN	LK23	LERWICK	7.62	3.74	1969	NORWAY
DELTA DAWN A	SY309	STORNOWAY	8.22	7.72	2006	GBR
DELTA DAWN III	SY788	STORNOWAY	12.23	26.43	1992	GIRVAN
DELTA LADY	LH99	LEITH	7.30	4.92	1978	CHESTER

UK Fishing Vessels 2015

Vessel Name	Code	Port Name	Loa	Ton Gt	Year	Construction Place
DELTA STAR	R31	RAMSGATE	9.98	8.80	1999	COUNTY CORK
DEMARUS	FR173	FRASERBURGH	25.90	217.00	1984	ST MONANS
DEMELZA	FY53	FOWEY	8.23	5.59	1970	LOOE
DEMPER	FY841	FOWEY	4.88	0.62	2000	GBR
DEN MAR	J76	JERSEY	8.03	4.11	1983	GUERNSEY
DENISE	FE371	FOLKESTONE	5.06	1.31	1966	SANDWICH
DESTINY	MT421	MARYPORT	12.14	22.19	1963	ARGYLLSHIRE
DESTINY	TT279	TARBERT	16.31	50.00	1974	ARBROATH
DETERMINATION	N39	NEWRY	9.90	7.56	1989	GBR
DEVOTION	LK801	LERWICK	22.85	206.00	1993	MACDUFF
DIAMOND	LK6	LERWICK	12.20	19.90	1962	ST MONANS FIFE
DIAMOND D	SN100	NORTH SHIELDS	16.77	48.00	1973	FRASERBURGH
DIANA	K471	KIRKWALL	6.04	1.17	1981	SHAPINSAY
DIANA	SS7	ST IVES	4.85	0.70	1979	YAPTON
DIANA MARION	PW33	PADSTOW	6.50	1.24	1984	PENRYN CORNWALL
DIANA MAY	M92	MILFORD HAVEN	9.15	8.83	1987	PEMBROKE DOCK DYFED
DIANE MARIE	PD323	PETERHEAD	6.09	1.38	1992	STONEHAVEN
DIANE MAXWELL	LK152	LERWICK	11.30	11.79	1989	SOUTH SHIELDS
DIEU TE GARDE	GU315	GUERNSEY	9.33	4.61	1972	GUERNSEY
DIGNITY	DO167	DOUGLAS	6.02	1.18	2005	CORNWALL
DIGNITY	PH666	PLYMOUTH	7.90	8.11	1985	PLYMOUTH
DIGNITY	SS161	ST IVES	7.95	6.17	2005	NOT KNOWN
DIGNITY JAY	CN140	CAMPBELTOWN	11.70	11.70	1989	POOLE DORSET
DILEAS	AD7	ARDROSSAN	6.33	1.34	1988	BRANSBURTON
DILIGENCE	PW240	PADSTOW	8.65	3.83	1975	CHARLESTOWN
DILIGENT	B772	BELFAST	9.75	6.32	2001	MACDUFF
DILIGENT	KY1	KIRKCALDY	8.00	4.57	1988	DEAL
DING	PE639	POOLE	6.11	0.88	1997	HAMWORTHY
DINGENIS JAN	N936	NEWRY	31.73	98.00	1987	HOLLAND
DIONNE	CN25	CAMPBELTOWN	7.80	4.11	1980	PLYMOUTH
DIPPER	WK126	WICK	4.83	0.72	2004	GBR

UK Fishing Vessels 2015

Vessel Name	Code	Port Name	Loa	Ton Gt	Year	Construction Place
DIRE STRAITS	TH90	TEIGNMOUTH	5.26	1.10	1986	POOLE
DISCOVERY	BF268	BANFF	23.38	145.00	1981	CAMPBELTOWN
DISCOVERY	GU41	GUERNSEY	9.97	6.23	1994	PENRYN
DISPATCHER	FY303	FOWEY	6.14	2.36	1984	HAYLE
DISTANT SHORES	B979	BELFAST	5.62	0.99	2006	N.IRELAND
DIVINE STAR	LK624	LERWICK	7.07	2.48	1964	SCALLOWAY SHETLAND
DIVINE WIND	N52	NEWRY	9.49	3.40	1980	KINGSLYNN
DO MAR	FH609	FALMOUTH	4.24	0.48	1991	ST KEVERNE
DOBHRAN	OB516	OBAN	8.29	3.19	1976	MALLAIG SCOTLAND
DODGER	OB211	OBAN	8.00	2.15	1999	GRUNDISBURGH
DODGER TOO	PO3	PORTLAND	4.60	0.67	1985	WEYMOUTH
DOGFISH	LO78	LONDON	4.90	0.73	1998	UNKNOWN
DOLLY ANNE	M119	MILFORD HAVEN	11.90	13.29	1979	CORNWALL
DOLPHIN	LI502	LITTLEHAMPTON	5.53	1.41	1996	NOT KNOWN
DOLPHIN	LK755	LERWICK	6.40	3.06	1986	DUBLIN
DOLPHIN	OB262	OBAN	5.64	1.19	1976	FINDHORN
DOLPHIN	SD397	SUNDERLAND	6.33	1.46	1960	UNKNOWN
DOLPHIN	SE5	SALCOMBE	5.54	1.63	2005	PORTUGAL
DOLPHIN	SH286	SCARBOROUGH	6.32	1.52	1992	GBR
DOLPHIN	TT1	TARBERT	5.80	1.51	1989	YAPTON SUSSEX
DOLPHIN	WK98	WICK	5.02	0.88	1983	GILLS CANISBAY
DOMINATOR A	WY333	WHITBY	10.29	11.36	1981	WORCESTER
DON VALLEY	N53	NEWRY	9.80	15.03	1992	SUNDERLAND & SILLOTH ENGLAND
DON-ALL-D	OB930	OBAN	6.46	3.16	1981	PENRYN
DONALD JOHN	RX18	RYE	8.38	6.64	1982	HULL CORNWALL
DONNA	CA84	CARDIGAN	5.79	1.08	1971	CHEVERTON
DONNA	CY830	CASTLEBAY	4.86	0.72	2004	GBR
DONNA DEE	SM7	SHOREHAM	9.80	4.66	2009	FALMOUTH CORNWALL
DONNA J	AB125	ABERYSTWYTH	5.54	0.50	1990	PLYMOUTH PILOT
DONNA MARIE	INS17	INVERNESS	9.70	5.47	1992	FALMOUTH

UK Fishing Vessels 2015

Vessel Name	Code	Port Name	Loa	Ton Gt	Year	Construction Place
DONNA ROSE	LK72	LERWICK	9.90	5.97	1968	FRANCE
DONT KNOW	YH2466	YARMOUTH	5.75	1.04	1999	NORTH WALSHAM
DOO DA DAY	PW453	PADSTOW	7.10	1.38	1999	ISLE OF WIGHT
DOODLE BUG	LI579	LITTLEHAMPTON	6.83	1.23	2013	UK
DORA MARY	DH407	DARTMOUTH	5.13	0.83	1989	ARUNDEL
DORADO	E146	EXETER	7.57	5.25	1983	POOLE
DORADO	GU151	GUERNSEY	7.72	4.16	1999	CORNWALL
DOREEN T	FE4	FOLKESTONE	9.95	2.91	2011	SUSSEX
DORIS ANNE	WK876	WICK	4.56	0.71	1990	GBR
DORIS LIZZIE	IH234	IPSWICH	9.34	5.78	1977	TUDDENHAM IPSWICH
DOROTHY ANN	FH35	FALMOUTH	6.45	1.54	2011	PORTUGAL
DOROTHY ANN	UL18	ULLAPOOL	9.29	4.56	2002	ISLE OF LEWIS
DOROTHY B	K39	KIRKWALL	5.90	1.12	2003	GUERNSEY
DOROTHY ELLEN	HH120	HARWICH	7.01	2.31	1980	CORNWALL
DOT	NN747	NEWHAVEN	4.50	0.71	1980	GBR
DOUBLE OR NOTHING	CS2	COWES	9.66	7.33	2006	ISLE OF WIGHT
DOUBLE TROUBLE	LI569	LITTLEHAMPTON	5.10	0.75	2006	ARUNDEL WEST SUSSEX
DOVE	CS30	COWES	5.20	0.67	1982	GURNARD I.O.W.
DOVEY BELLE	AB33	ABERYSTWYTH	8.00	1.49	1976	WALLSEND ON TYNE
DOWNDERRY MAID	FY6	FOWEY	6.30	1.74	2010	WADEBRIDGE CORNWALL
DRAGUN-AN-MOAR	WH97	WEYMOUTH	6.60	3.32	1982	PENRYN CORNWALL
DREAM CATCHER	J99	JERSEY	6.07	1.33	2010	PORTUGAL
DREAM CATCHER	ST5	STOCKTON	5.40	1.42	1990	GBR
DREAM CATCHER	WH8	WEYMOUTH	6.00	1.20	2010	PORTUGAL
DRIE GEBROEDERS	B927	BELFAST	30.98	78.00	1922	NLD
DRIFT FISHER	WK91	WICK	5.00	1.88	1973	LYBSTER
DRIFT FISHER 11	WK5	WICK	10.50	13.93	1988	SHAPINSAY
DRIFTER	CK9	COLCHESTER	4.60	0.85	1985	TEPCO
DRIFTER	LA462	LLANELLI	5.18	1.28	1988	ISLE OF WIGHT
DRIFTER	NN491	NEWHAVEN	6.25	1.33	1996	NEWHAVEN

UK Fishing Vessels 2015

Vessel Name	Code	Port Name	Loa	Ton Gt	Year	Construction Place
DRIFTER	R493	RAMSGATE	6.07	2.50	1980	PORTSMOUTH
DRIFTER I	M1085	MILFORD HAVEN	3.90	0.26	1998	DEVON
DRIFTWOOD	GU453	GUERNSEY	5.75	1.18	1992	SARK
DUCHESS	PH1013	PLYMOUTH	7.40	2.69	1992	HOLTON
DUN LIR	N40	NEWRY	9.85	8.35	1981	PENRYN CORNWALL
DUNAN	SY10	STORNOWAY	9.15	4.98	2004	PENRYN
DUNAN STAR	CY26	CASTLEBAY	11.19	13.64	1979	ORKNEY
DUNAN STAR II	BRD123	BROADFORD	13.41	30.32	1987	PENRYN CORNWALL
DUNBYIN	UL298	ULLAPOOL	7.27	2.42	1991	PORT STEWART
DUNLIN	SE25	SALCOMBE	6.17	2.46	1981	HAYLE CORNWALL
DUNMARICK	OB918	OBAN	11.01	12.32	1979	KYLE
DUSTY	WH118	WEYMOUTH	4.14	0.51	1982	WEST LULWORTH
DUSTY BIN	J135	JERSEY	9.13	5.47	1999	UK
DUTHIES	FR287	FRASERBURGH	5.00	1.00	1986	STAFFORDSHIRE
DWYFOR	CO394	CAERNARVON	5.55	1.45	1979	PLYMOUTH
DYLAN	M1116	MILFORD HAVEN	6.47	1.39	2008	PEMBS
EARLY DAWN	LL307	LIVERPOOL	8.20	4.88	1981	TOLLEYS
EARLY ON	HL5	HARTLEPOOL	9.84	4.20	1965	WEYMOUTH
EARLY ROSE	YH46	YARMOUTH	5.78	1.32	2005	NORFOLK
EARLY ROSE II	YH48	YARMOUTH	6.90	1.15	2010	I O W
EAST BAR	LL1	LIVERPOOL	6.19	2.50	1987	CONWAY WEST WALES
EASTER MORN	WY820	WHITBY	6.42	1.48	1947	GBR
EASTERN STAR	N804	NEWRY	6.55	1.53	1989	MALAHIDE
EASTERN TIDE	N104	NEWRY	6.90	2.79	2010	UK
EBEN HAEZER	GY57	GRIMSBY	40.00	418.00	1983	GDYNIA
EBONNIE	BM176	BRIXHAM	14.95	69.45	2005	YORKS
EBONY MAY	SA387	SWANSEA	7.85	9.14	2007	SOMERSET
EBONY ROSE	DH397	DARTMOUTH	4.27	0.58	1990	SUSSEX
ECHO	PE771	POOLE	5.50	0.88	1990	DORSET
ECLIPSE	LK287	LERWICK	6.89	2.09	2004	ENGLAND

UK Fishing Vessels 2015

Vessel Name	Code	Port Name	Loa	Ton Gt	Year	Construction Place
ECLIPSE	SC6	SCILLY	7.92	2.77	1976	FALMOUTH
EDER SANDS	UL257	ULLAPOOL	38.20	307.00	1974	ZUMAYA SPAIN
EDGE ON	PE1049	POOLE	6.20	1.18	1997	ISLE OF WIGHT
EDITH MARY	LR57	LANCASTER	8.54	5.98	1977	MORECAMBE
EDLEI	GY455	GRIMSBY	20.18	64.00	1975	BUCKIE
EDWARD HENRY	DH100	DARTMOUTH	25.50	279.00	2002	NAVIA
EDWARD J	OB120	OBAN	6.45	2.72	1997	CORNWALL
EEL DO	E21	EXETER	6.00	1.89	1990	Unk
EENDRACHT	B935	BELFAST	37.99	150.00	1962	ZOLLE
EHEDYDD	CO818	CAERNARVON	4.60	1.03	1980	UNITED KINGDON
EIDER	LN134	KINGS LYNN	12.99	12.89	1989	UNKNOWN
EILANE	BRD518	BROADFORD	6.20	3.17	1978	NORWAY
EILEAN BAN	OB998	OBAN	9.77	10.69	2004	SCOTLAND
EILEAN FREYER	K10	KIRKWALL	4.85	0.61	1997	UK
EILEEN ROSE	N813	NEWRY	8.37	8.10	1991	FALMOUTH
EILEENA ANNE	LT317	LOWESTOFT	10.82	4.27	1948	ISLE OF WIGHT
EILIDH	BRD149	BROADFORD	12.73	27.39	2001	CORNWALL
EILIDH	CY16	CASTLEBAY	5.60	1.29	1979	PLYMOUTH
EILIDH	FR97	FRASERBURGH	5.54	1.17	1982	SANDHAVEN
EILIDH ANNE	GK2	GREENOCK	9.95	13.55	2003	ENGLAND
EILIDH BHAN	GU106	GUERNSEY	8.65	4.19	1998	FOWEY
EIYEEN	SU412	SOUTHAMPTON	8.38	6.59	1971	ST PETER PORT GUERNSEY
EKEDE	YH2450	YARMOUTH	5.70	1.08	1987	UNKNOWN
EKI	P590	PORTSMOUTH	5.18	0.57	1977	CHICHESTER
EL BARCO	P936	PORTSMOUTH	8.90	8.17	1980	UNK
EL-SHADDAI	FR285	FRASERBURGH	16.00	90.00	1987	ARBROATH
ELA-J	FH638	FALMOUTH	6.81	2.40	1996	FALMOUTH
ELAINALEE	BW23	BARROW	11.00	10.61	1987	BARROW IN FURNESS
ELEANOR B	LR76	LANCASTER	5.84	0.78	2008	LANCS

UK Fishing Vessels 2015

Vessel Name	Code	Port Name	Loa	Ton Gt	Year	Construction Place
ELEANOR MAY	HL1082	HARTLEPOOL	5.63	1.05	1983	WHITBY
ELEGANCE	PD33	PETERHEAD	19.90	163.00	1989	MACDUFF
ELEGANT II	B907	BELFAST	20.03	99.00	1971	BUCKIE
ELENA	OB14	OBAN	6.95	2.10	2011	Unk
ELENA LOUISA	KY1042	KIRKCALDY	5.55	0.65	2011	ORKNEY
ELENOR	N1030	NEWRY	4.87	0.72	1990	UNITED KINGDOM
ELINOR ROGET	PW95	PADSTOW	10.12	5.80	1979	APPLEDORE NORTH DEVON
ELISABETH VERONIQUE	FY83	FOWEY	14.98	51.89	1984	FRA
ELISE	CK110	COLCHESTER	9.09	7.78	1990	WIVENHOE
ELISHIA	SS92	ST IVES	5.55	1.61	1975	PLYMOUTH
ELIZA DOT	WK86	WICK	8.10	2.17	1979	HAYLE CORNWALL
ELIZABETH B	K168	KIRKWALL	9.74	10.23	1992	SCARFSKERRY CAITHNESS
ELIZABETH II	SD254	SUNDERLAND	9.94	5.96	1942	AMBLE
ELIZABETH JADE	BH462	BLYTH	9.00	3.06	1980	GBR
ELIZABETH JANE	N69	NEWRY	5.77	1.18	1972	LIVERPOOL
ELIZABETH JAYNE	M79	MILFORD HAVEN	9.85	13.53	1982	FALMOUTH
ELIZABETH M	SY307	STORNOWAY	7.20	2.94	1996	POOLE
ELIZABETH MARY	LN84	KINGS LYNN	10.55	5.01	1974	GERMANY
ELIZABETH N	PZ100	PENZANCE	22.82	100.00	1984	HOOGEZAND
ELIZABETH SHAUN	PW159	PADSTOW	8.38	3.17	1971	FOWEY CORNWALL
ELKIE B	CF7	CARDIFF	9.30	4.00	1990	KENT
ELLA	FY24	FOWEY	11.30	17.89	1989	LOOE
ELLA	NN781	NEWHAVEN	4.65	0.73	2001	GBR
ELLA	SM826	SHOREHAM	5.48	1.92	2003	SHOREHAM BY SEA
ELLA	WK129	WICK	5.36	0.87	1987	THURSO
ELLA B	M542	MILFORD HAVEN	9.95	5.99	2008	ASHINGTON
ELLA GRACE	PE17	POOLE	8.23	5.19	2010	SCOTLAND
ELLA M	TT277	TARBERT	12.17	19.50	1964	PORTINCAPLE
ELLANORAH	SH321	SCARBOROUGH	9.17	3.35	1999	HAYLE

UK Fishing Vessels 2015

Vessel Name	Code	Port Name	Loa	Ton Gt	Year	Construction Place
ELLE C	B652	BELFAST	7.01	4.04	1979	ISLE OF WHITE
ELLE JAY	PE1176	POOLE	6.43	0.91	2003	DORSET
ELLE V	SS697	ST IVES	6.90	0.96	2001	ISLE OF WIGHT
ELLEN	B22	BELFAST	20.66	58.00	1969	DENMARK
ELLEN	PZ439	PENZANCE	4.48	0.66	2003	GBR
ELLEN	WY209	WHITBY	5.70	1.18	1980	YAPTON SUSSEX
ELLEN K	KY25	KIRKCALDY	7.25	2.09	1989	CORNWALL
ELLEN M	N929	NEWRY	9.90	14.72	2000	GBR
ELLEN MAC	LH272	LEITH	11.80	23.48	1991	BARROW IN FURNESS
ELLEN MARY	PW44	PADSTOW	5.40	1.41	1968	COWES
ELLEN P	DH25	DARTMOUTH	5.92	1.17	2012	PORTUGAL
ELLIE A	KY1003	KIRKCALDY	6.60	3.13	1984	FALMOUTH
ELLIE B	K55	KIRKWALL	4.76	0.59	1995	SCOTLAND
ELLIE JANE	YH10	YARMOUTH	5.90	1.40	2013	NORFOLK
ELLIE JEAN	PE4	POOLE	5.97	0.77	1996	POOLE
ELLIE JOY	BH467	BLYTH	5.05	0.95	1999	NORTHUMBERLAND
ELLIE TESSA	BF10	BANFF	5.83	1.21	2011	GBR
ELLORAH	BF12	BANFF	18.95	174.00	2009	SCOTLAND
ELM	DH392	DARTMOUTH	3.73	0.47	1999	KINGSBRIDGE
ELMA ANNE	K335	KIRKWALL	6.38	2.44	1949	WESTRAY ORKNEY
ELMAY	PE1218	POOLE	6.65	0.83	2005	GBR
ELOISE	BM192	BRIXHAM	8.60	9.48	1997	LINCOLNSHIRE
ELOISE	M247	MILFORD HAVEN	5.33	0.97	1987	SHETLAND
ELONA	PD11	PETERHEAD	6.16	0.55	1985	HAMPSHIRE ENGLAND
ELOS	HH107	HARWICH	6.53	2.29	1984	LANGHAM
ELSA	K30	KIRKWALL	4.03	0.55	1968	EDAY ORKNEY
ELSHEDAWN	SH22	SCARBOROUGH	7.95	5.21	2007	FAREHAM
ELSIE B	BM65	BRIXHAM	9.83	10.81	1992	FALMOUTH
ELSIE LEIGH	PH8	PLYMOUTH	7.53	6.60	2011	NEWHAVEN SUSSEX
ELSIE M	LK126	LERWICK	7.75	3.61	1984	PENRYN CORNWALL

UK Fishing Vessels 2015

Vessel Name	Code	Port Name	Loa	Ton Gt	Year	Construction Place
ELSIE MAY	LT320	LOWESTOFT	7.74	4.98	1978	HAYLE CORNWALL
ELVEN HUNTER	LO324	LONDON	10.70	10.77	1983	SOUTHEND ON SEA
ELVINA	SH129	SCARBOROUGH	9.99	19.17	1988	POOLE
ELYSIAN	PD416	PETERHEAD	6.55	2.96	1979	PORTSMOUTH
EMBLEM	FY174	FOWEY	4.61	0.66	1989	UNKNOWN
EMBRACE	BH229	BLYTH	4.60	0.60	1989	CULLERCOATS
EMERALD DAWN	BCK303	BUCKIE	23.00	164.00	1999	SPAIN
EMERALD DAWN	SC35	SCILLY	7.77	1.29	1979	HAYLE CORNWALL
EMERALD ISLE II	CE525	COLERAINE	5.81	1.18	2002	CO ANTRIM
EMERALD STAR	DO90	DOUGLAS	19.90	86.55	1984	NLD
EMERITUS	LK989	LERWICK	6.17	1.23	1992	NEWLYN
EMI LOU	FY4	FOWEY	5.15	0.79	2011	UNKNOWN
EMILIA JAYNE	BM10	BRIXHAM	23.00	125.00	1991	HOLLAND
EMILY	B971	BELFAST	5.78	1.52	2000	UK
EMILY	PE1135	POOLE	7.65	3.80	2001	HAMPSHIRE
EMILY ANN	SE330	SALCOMBE	4.50	0.59	1985	DEVON
EMILY B	E14	EXETER	5.40	1.07	1991	ORKNEY
EMILY B	LH458	LEITH	6.40	1.53	1994	TEIGNMOUTH
EMILY GRACE	DH2	DARTMOUTH	5.70	1.46	1991	ORKNEY
EMILY J	E123	EXETER	11.93	26.53	2004	AYRSHIRE
EMILY JAYNE	BS485	BEAUMARIS	8.55	6.64	1984	ISLE OF WHITE
EMILY JAYNE	FH756	FALMOUTH	9.15	4.72	1999	HORTON
EMILY JAYNE	M45	MILFORD HAVEN	5.50	1.42	2014	UK
EMILY MAY	BS515	BEAUMARIS	7.26	1.77	2001	GBR
EMILY MAY	J216	JERSEY	4.65	0.70	2013	UK
EMILY MAY	M57	MILFORD HAVEN	6.40	1.36	2005	CORNWALL
EMILY ROSE	BM28	BRIXHAM	26.15	105.00	1967	DEN HOLDER HOLLAND
EMILY ROSE	M701	MILFORD HAVEN	9.93	9.54	1989	BRUNDAL NORFOLK
EMMA	CH537	CHESTER	5.88	1.03	2006	NOT KNOWN
EMMA	PE10	POOLE	6.79	0.98	1997	POOLE

UK Fishing Vessels 2015

Vessel Name	Code	Port Name	Loa	Ton Gt	Year	Construction Place
EMMA	SY843	STORNOWAY	5.05	0.85	1986	GBR
EMMA DEE	LA15	LLANELLI	4.76	0.99	1992	POOLE
EMMA JANE	BF405	BANFF	9.85	10.50	1982	GBR
EMMA JANE	SE101	SALCOMBE	18.35	122.00	1989	DEN HELDER NETHERLANDS
EMMA JANE	WY173	WHITBY	11.28	9.57	1987	SANDSEND
EMMA JANE 2	FY916	FOWEY	6.40	1.18	1985	DEVON
EMMA JANE N	BH108	BLYTH	7.77	3.74	1978	PENRYN
EMMA KATE	B96	BELFAST	7.09	2.01	1972	DEVON
EMMA KATHLEEN	ME87	MONTROSE	14.33	42.92	1988	ARBROATH
EMMA LOU	MH30	MIDDLESBROUGH	5.89	1.69	2001	CORNWALL
EMMA LOUISE	LA591	LLANELLI	4.27	0.71	2000	LLANELLI
EMMA LOUISE	PH5557	PLYMOUTH	9.90	11.46	1998	FALMOUTH
EMMA LOUISE	TO60	TRURO	16.42	106.00	2012	UK
EMMA LOUISE II	FY101	FOWEY	6.25	1.54	2013	UK
EMMA MARIE	BS66	BEAUMARIS	5.45	0.68	1987	BODEDERN
EMMA MAY	FH416	FALMOUTH	7.28	2.88	1977	CADGWITH
EMMA R	LA281	LLANELLI	5.05	0.80	1982	PLYMOUTH
EMMA RAITCH	LT442	LOWESTOFT	9.00	3.96	1973	LOOE
EMMA ROSE	PZ69	PENZANCE	7.47	4.20	1967	PORTLOE MEVAGISSEY
EMMA T	N968	NEWRY	4.94	0.69	2000	FIFE
EMMA-JAY	CS645	COWES	5.59	1.50	2000	GBR
EMMA-MARIA	OB107	OBAN	6.41	1.93	2004	CAMBOURNE
EMMA-MAY	GU83	GUERNSEY	9.25	3.70	2013	Unk
EMMA'S TERN	LA1	LLANELLI	6.20	1.13	2006	GBR
EMMAJEN	J57	JERSEY	4.65	0.60	1996	UK
EMMALEY	BF777	BANFF	6.00	1.59	2010	GBR
EMMANUEL	SH25	SCARBOROUGH	9.90	10.68	1989	TARBERT ARGYLL
EMMY LEIGH	CN746	CAMPBELTOWN	7.09	1.84	1991	ISLE OF WIGHT
EMMY LOU	CE133	COLERAINE	6.20	1.31	1991	FALMOUTH
EMULATE	BM1	BRIXHAM	14.95	45.64	2004	GBR

UK Fishing Vessels 2015

Vessel Name	Code	Port Name	Loa	Ton Gt	Year	Construction Place
EMULATE A	BH18	BLYTH	9.96	10.65	2004	BARTON ON HUMBER
EMULATOR	SH83	SCARBOROUGH	18.25	110.00	1983	SANDHAVEN
ENA DOLAN	SSS680	SOUTH SHIELDS	7.00	2.37	1996	GBR
ENCHANTED	BRD74	BROADFORD	10.60	11.29	1988	RYE
ENDEAVOUR	BCK31	BUCKIE	8.02	4.01	1969	EDAY ORKNEY
ENDEAVOUR	BH36	BLYTH	5.85	1.69	1985	FALMOUTH
ENDEAVOUR	BK241	BERWICK ON TWEED	9.30	5.14	1978	WHITBY
ENDEAVOUR	BS519	BEAUMARIS	5.06	0.60	1972	SUSSEX
ENDEAVOUR	CK97	COLCHESTER	9.84	6.56	1988	HULL
ENDEAVOUR	CS73	COWES	6.20	1.29	1992	ISLE OF WIGHT ENGLAND
ENDEAVOUR	FR156	FRASERBURGH	16.77	116.00	2001	SCOTLAND
ENDEAVOUR	FY798	FOWEY	9.98	5.10	1997	PENRYN
ENDEAVOUR	LH169	LEITH	15.58	47.00	1972	PORTAVOGIE D342
ENDEAVOUR	LI14	LITTLEHAMPTON	6.83	1.23	2014	UK
ENDEAVOUR	LK11	LERWICK	7.98	3.82	2002	CORNWALL
ENDEAVOUR	PL160	PEEL	6.54	1.93	2005	CO ANTRIM
ENDEAVOUR IV	BF515	BANFF	28.96	478.00	2008	GBR
ENDLESS SUMMER	M1152	MILFORD HAVEN	6.20	1.15	1994	VENTNOR
ENDURANCE	AH136	ARBROATH	9.82	10.40	2013	PETERHEAD
ENDURANCE	B340	BELFAST	9.83	6.35	1995	FALMOUTH
ENDURANCE	FR111	FRASERBURGH	24.45	171.00	1984	BUCKIE
ENDURANCE	GW42	GLASGOW	8.20	4.14	1996	UK
ENDURANCE	HL3	HARTLEPOOL	9.07	3.91	1978	WHITBY
ENDURANCE	R80	RAMSGATE	9.32	9.85	1982	UNKNOWN
ENDURANCE II	BH1	BLYTH	9.83	16.39	2003	ESSEX
ENERGY	SH105	SCARBOROUGH	9.44	5.32	1987	WHITBY
ENERGY C	BA269	BALLANTRAE	9.91	6.00	1997	LINCOLNSHIRE
ENIGMA	FD507	FLEETWOOD	5.20	1.36	2002	SELSEY
ENIGMA 1	PL164	PEEL	9.96	9.53	2012	UNITED KINGDOM
ENNIS LADY	PZ50	PENZANCE	7.30	3.57	2004	CORNWALL

UK Fishing Vessels 2015

Vessel Name	Code	Port Name	Loa	Ton Gt	Year	Construction Place
ENSIS	INS3	INVERNESS	6.28	1.15	2006	ISLE OF WIGHT
ENSIS	OB1004	OBAN	10.65	11.61	1992	NOR
ENTERPRISE	IH320	IPSWICH	8.55	3.50	2008	ENGLAND
ENTERPRISE	LI321	LITTLEHAMPTON	8.00	2.48	1979	LITTLEHAMPTON
ENTERPRISE	LK686	LERWICK	7.25	2.76	1966	SCALLOWAY
ENTERPRISE	OB863	OBAN	9.92	9.93	1995	ALNWICK
ENTERPRISE	PD147	PETERHEAD	44.94	748.00	1995	ZAANDAM
ENTERPRISE	SH323	SCARBOROUGH	8.95	6.35	2007	ESSEX
ENTERPRISE	ST1	STOCKTON	7.15	1.61	1990	DORSET
ENTERPRISE A	K461	KIRKWALL	9.60	10.19	2001	CORNWALL
ENTERPRISE II	BF1	BANFF	26.00	421.00	1999	ABERDEENSHIRE
EOS	HH150	HARWICH	8.00	2.97	1980	PENRYN CORNWALL
EQUINOX	CN9	CAMPBELTOWN	7.30	2.90	1989	NOT KNOWN
EQUINOX	P29	PORTSMOUTH	11.85	14.71	1995	CORNWALL
EQUITY	TH377	TEIGNMOUTH	6.49	1.51	1983	HULL
ERIN	WK241	WICK	6.40	1.51	2012	SELSEY WEST SUSSEX
ERINDORS	PW392	PADSTOW	5.13	0.89	1993	GBR
ESCAPE	CN367	CAMPBELTOWN	5.65	1.20	1994	ARUNDUL
ESCARGOT	ME225	MONTROSE	7.00	1.98	1989	FALMOUTH
ESHCOL	M220	MILFORD HAVEN	9.95	12.48	2005	ENGLAND
ESME	E92	EXETER	4.26	0.68	1989	ENGLAND
ESPADON II	M214	MILFORD HAVEN	9.81	8.01	1978	RYE
ESPEMAR DOS	AR325	AYR	39.24	481.00	1975	GOOLE
ESPERANCE	GU275	GUERNSEY	7.42	3.20	1989	GUERNSEY
ESPERANCE	PE1127	POOLE	5.60	1.19	1974	ISLE OF WIGHT
ESTHER	RR2	ROCHESTER	6.18	1.61	2009	UK
ESTHER JAYNE	FY870	FOWEY	5.49	1.30	1976	SUSSEX
ETHANS WAY	LA593	LLANELLI	4.82	1.00	2001	GBR
EUPHEMIA	K92	KIRKWALL	14.95	30.43	1970	CAMPBELTOWN
EUROCLYDON	TH77	TEIGNMOUTH	18.20	108.00	1987	ST MONANS

UK Fishing Vessels 2015

Vessel Name	Code	Port Name	Loa	Ton Gt	Year	Construction Place
EV	KY250	KIRKCALDY	8.04	2.60	1978	ENGLAND
EVA-MAE	BA687	BALLANTRAE	4.92	1.01	1996	CORNWALL
EVAN GEORGE	M4	MILFORD HAVEN	7.90	1.62	2007	ISLE OF WIGHT
EVANDA	DE2	DUNDEE	4.89	0.92	1985	GBR
EVANDA	KY37	KIRKCALDY	5.54	1.45	1982	GBR
EVARA	N27	NEWRY	9.83	8.72	1977	CORNWALL
EVE	PE111	POOLE	6.60	0.55	2002	POOLE
EVE N SAN	SM805	SHOREHAM	5.40	1.76	2003	LANCASHIRE
EVELYN	BRD323	BROADFORD	4.97	0.83	1979	PORTREE
EVELYN	CO517	CAERNARVON	6.10	2.43	1991	WALES
EVELYN	E6	EXETER	7.90	1.01	2001	ISLE OF WIGHT
EVELYN JANE	YH2460	YARMOUTH	5.82	1.15	1998	NORTH WALSHAM
EVENING STAR	FH280	FALMOUTH	6.25	2.44	1973	PORTHOUSTOCK
EVENING STAR	PD1022	PETERHEAD	21.34	160.00	1991	PAULL
EVENING STAR	PZ92	PENZANCE	5.90	1.68	1991	PENRYN
EVENTIDE	B198	BELFAST	9.78	9.80	1988	MIDDLESBOROUGH
EVENTIDE	N112	NEWRY	5.60	1.30	1995	UNKNOWN
EVENTIDE	WH321	WEYMOUTH	4.60	0.83	1984	WEYMOUTH
EVENTUS	RX168	RYE	10.80	12.02	1983	GILLINGHAM PIER
EVER-AM	SE2	SALCOMBE	4.90	0.87	2012	PORTUGAL
EVIE MAE	MH8	MIDDLESBROUGH	5.86	1.44	2011	NORTH WALSHAM
EVIE MAE	SM74	SHOREHAM	9.95	9.32	2014	NEWHAVEN
EVIE ROSE	RX53	RYE	9.99	14.95	1995	BROADSTAIRS
EWYN	CO186	CAERNARVON	4.27	0.65	1983	UNKNOWN
EX MARE GRATIA	B182	BELFAST	33.53	186.00	1986	GBR
EXCALIBUR	J296	JERSEY	5.03	0.86	1991	UK
EXCALIBUR	LH8	LEITH	7.30	1.59	2007	ENGLAND
EXCALIBUR	LK889	LERWICK	9.70	7.50	1996	FALMOUTH
EXCEL	BF110	BANFF	18.95	174.00	2009	MACDUFF ABERDEENSHIRE

UK Fishing Vessels 2015

Vessel Name	Code	Port Name	Loa	Ton Gt	Year	Construction Place
EXCEL	CK898	COLCHESTER	6.10	0.89	1994	ISLE OF WIGHT
EXCEL	DH17	DARTMOUTH	16.04	31.00	1971	APPLEDORE
EXCELSIOR	H105	HULL	9.96	6.08	1990	PENRYN FALMOUTH
EXCELSIOR	UL33	ULLAPOOL	7.33	2.76	2008	CORNWALL
EXODUS	UL335	ULLAPOOL	11.19	9.97	1974	UNK
EXPLORER	BF21	BANFF	6.02	1.48	2011	PETERHEAD SCOTLAND
EXTOSEA	P182	PORTSMOUTH	9.98	6.49	1970	EXMOUTH DEVON
EXTREME	SU1	SOUTHAMPTON	9.98	12.09	2008	SOUTHAMPTON
EYECATCHER	TH21	TEIGNMOUTH	5.70	1.10	1990	ARUNDEL SUSSEX
FAE SILVIE	PE1211	POOLE	5.90	0.86	2000	UNKNOWN
FAIR BAY	P319	PORTSMOUTH	8.35	5.11	1972	PORTSMOUTH
FAIR DAWN	SM10	SHOREHAM	5.30	1.30	2008	SHOREHAM BY SEA WEST SUSSEX
FAIR FORTUNE	K96	KIRKWALL	8.75	6.61	1984	DEAL
FAIR HARVEST	BH85	BLYTH	9.91	4.85	1963	AMBLE
FAIR LASS	CY263	CASTLEBAY	11.09	10.46	1973	STROMENESS
FAIR MAIDEN	LA60	LLANELLI	6.93	1.19	2005	ISLE OF WIGHT
FAIR MORN	BA19	BALLANTRAE	17.10	24.24	1973	MACDUFF
FAIR MORN	CY85	CASTLEBAY	5.08	1.36	1973	KENERY GRIMSAY
FAIR MORN	K166	KIRKWALL	11.78	18.89	1979	DEVORAN CORNWALL
FAIR MORN	NN184	NEWHAVEN	8.20	8.66	1979	PENRYN CORNWALL
FAIR TRADE	PH5590	PLYMOUTH	6.50	1.50	1982	ISLAND PLASTIC
FAIR TRIAL	P358	PORTSMOUTH	5.50	1.30	1975	PORTSMOUTH
FAIR TRY	LK19	LERWICK	7.50	5.43	1985	SCALLOWAY
FAIR WIND	B918	BELFAST	11.53	15.29	2000	GBR
FAIR WIND	FY822	FOWEY	7.30	1.59	1999	FALMOUTH
FAIRNIES	LH142	LEITH	9.96	9.65	1997	CORNWALL
FAIRWAY	K19	KIRKWALL	9.09	6.81	1968	STROMNESS
FAIRWAY II	LK270	LERWICK	23.24	173.00	1989	FLEKKE FJORD (NORWAY)
FAIRWAY TWO	N862	NEWRY	10.19	11.18	1981	WORCESTER
FAIRWIND	R11	RAMSGATE	8.83	3.74	1983	RAMSGATE

UK Fishing Vessels 2015

Vessel Name	Code	Port Name	Loa	Ton Gt	Year	Construction Place
FAITH	SC84	SCILLY	6.15	1.40	1991	FALMOUTH
FAITH	SH111	SCARBOROUGH	7.26	2.00	2008	SCARBOROUGH
FAITH EMILY	LK244	LERWICK	8.60	3.84	1999	MACDUFF
FAITHFUL	AH67	ARBROATH	7.50	3.07	1991	DORSET
FAITHFUL	FR129	FRASERBURGH	23.50	198.00	1985	SANDHAVEN
FAITHFUL	INS38	INVERNESS	5.59	1.33	1996	ARUNDEL WEST SUSSEX
FAITHFUL	SY540	STORNOWAY	8.23	6.17	1990	PENRYN CORNWALL
FAITHFUL B	K741	KIRKWALL	6.40	2.65	1989	DUBLIN
FAITHFUL FRIEND V	B952	BELFAST	16.76	71.00	1971	MACDUFF
FAITHFULL STAR	LT1002	LOWESTOFT	7.75	4.06	1997	CORNWALL
FALCON	H119	HULL	25.90	213.00	1985	ST. MONANS
FALCON	INS12	INVERNESS	5.54	1.09	2007	ENGLAND
FALCON	PD1056	PETERHEAD	4.70	0.94	2008	GAMRIE
FAMILY AFFAIR II	DH7	DARTMOUTH	6.90	1.52	2005	UK
FAMILY FRIEND	SY148	STORNOWAY	7.31	4.23	1984	CORNWALL
FAMILYS PRIDE II	BRD687	BROADFORD	8.45	3.83	1998	ISLE OF SKYE
FANNY ADAMS	PE856	POOLE	8.50	5.66	1980	WEYMOUTH
FARAY	PE73	POOLE	3.24	0.34	1983	ISLE OF WIGHT
FARNELLA	H135	HULL	40.20	667.00	2000	DEVON
FARNOID FARNWORTH	IH330	IPSWICH	3.85	0.39	1997	UK
FAST LADY	PD1018	PETERHEAD	6.25	1.21	1980	NORFOLK
FASTLINE	GY34	GRIMSBY	5.77	1.28	1987	WEYMOUTH
FASTNET	J676	JERSEY	6.27	0.90	1987	UK
FASTNET	P623	PORTSMOUTH	8.50	3.40	1977	ISLE OF WIGHT
FAT CAT	F179	FAVERSHAM	8.25	2.70	2005	ENGLAND
FATHER BOB	PZ39	PENZANCE	4.60	1.09	1990	HAYLE CORNWALL
FAVONIUS	PD17	PETERHEAD	23.00	215.24	2009	SCOTLAND
FAYRO	PD38	PETERHEAD	4.95	0.87	2001	GBR
FEAR NOT	SH132	SCARBOROUGH	10.40	14.65	1989	STROMNESS ORKNEY

UK Fishing Vessels 2015

Vessel Name	Code	Port Name	Loa	Ton Gt	Year	Construction Place
FEAR NOT II	PD354	PETERHEAD	18.26	120.00	1986	ARBROATH
FEARLESS	WH36	WEYMOUTH	4.99	0.96	1968	CRICKRELL BOAT BUILDERS
FEITIZO	OB1015	OBAN	29.10	215.00	1970	VIGO SPAIN
FELICITY	DH26	DARTMOUTH	4.39	0.70	1985	KINGSBRIDGE S DEVON
FELICITY	RX58	RYE	9.63	8.93	1980	RYE
FERRIBY II	H1117	HULL	6.90	1.18	2005	ISLE OF WIGHT
FERRY TEN	B62	BELFAST	9.14	6.05	1960	PORTAVOGIE CO DOWN
FERTILITY	PD4	PETERHEAD	7.30	2.48	1990	STONEHAVEN
FFYON MARIE	PT9	PORT TALBOT	6.15	1.16	2005	GBR
FIADH OR	CN323	CAMPBELTOWN	8.13	4.67	1978	ORKNEY
FIDDLER'S GREEN	LH46	LEITH	9.78	9.51	1990	SCARBOROUGH
FIDELITAS	LK45	LERWICK	16.64	42.00	1972	ST MONANCE
FIDELITY	BH92	BLYTH	16.73	69.00	1975	MACDUFF
FIDWAY	LK5	LERWICK	7.00	2.79	1992	DUBLIN IRELAND
FILADELFIA	PZ542	PENZANCE	26.26	131.00	1969	HOLLAND
FINE PAIR	KY160	KIRKCALDY	4.85	0.58	2001	ANSTRUTHER
FINNISH GIRL	PW440	PADSTOW	5.98	0.58	1998	SUSSEX
FIONA	CE239	COLERAINE	4.65	0.70	1980	NEW MILTON
FIONA	SY670	STORNOWAY	6.32	2.88	1992	MALAHIDE CO DUBLIN
FIONA 11	SD144	SUNDERLAND	7.93	2.59	1982	BRITAIN
FIONA MARY	PW160	PADSTOW	9.99	10.04	1972	GRANVILLE FRANCE
FIONA ME	OB936	OBAN	9.33	4.12	1979	FALMOUTH
FIONA ROSE	TO62	TRURO	7.75	1.68	1992	FALMOUTH
FIONA S	KY981	KIRKCALDY	7.77	2.73	1991	HOYLAKE WIRRAL
FIONAGHAL	INS37	INVERNESS	9.82	8.90	1974	STROMNESS ORKNEY
FIONNAGHAL	TT104	TARBERT	13.84	12.49	1989	BERWICK UPON TWEED
FIRECREST	LN479	KINGS LYNN	11.07	7.85	1989	HESSLE
FIRECREST	OB46	OBAN	9.20	8.01	1985	PENRYN
FIREFLY	M14	MILFORD HAVEN	5.08	0.69	1986	POOLE
FIRST LIGHT	GU95	GUERNSEY	7.35	1.88	1978	ISLE OF WIGHT

UK Fishing Vessels 2015

Vessel Name	Code	Port Name	Loa	Ton Gt	Year	Construction Place
FIRST LIGHT	RX428	RYE	7.30	2.56	1979	NOT KNOWN
FIRST LIGHT	YH7	YARMOUTH	7.98	1.97	1999	ENGLAND
FIRST PRIORITY	GU37	GUERNSEY	6.54	0.86	2013	Unk
FISARAKAH	OB8	OBAN	8.37	5.23	1979	CORNWALL
FISH EAGLE	WH197	WEYMOUTH	8.49	2.81	1990	WEYMOUTH
FISH ON	DH14	DARTMOUTH	5.60	1.05	1990	GBR
FISH TAILS	J95	JERSEY	3.94	0.43	1992	UK
FISHER BOYS	FR54	FRASERBURGH	20.26	139.00	1986	MACDUFF
FISHER LASSIE	CK91	COLCHESTER	9.85	8.34	1961	FRASERBURGH
FISHER LASSIE	LH57	LEITH	9.92	5.29	1979	CORNWALL
FISHKEY	GU48	GUERNSEY	6.50	3.65	1983	CORNWALL
FISHY BUSINESS II	CO817	CAERNARVON	3.70	0.37	2006	SCANDINAVIA
FIVE BROTHERS	CE515	COLERAINE	9.93	5.98	1996	SANDWICH KENT
FIVE JS	BN435	BOSTON	9.53	8.72	2002	LINCOLNSHIRE
FIVE SISTERS	OB353	OBAN	11.00	13.19	1983	WORCESTER
FLASH HARRY	FH747	FALMOUTH	5.60	1.09	2009	CORNWALL
FLEUR DE BRAYE	GU79	GUERNSEY	7.47	3.08	1979	PENRYN
FLEUR DE FRANCE	J86	JERSEY	19.13	82.98	1976	FRANCE
FLINT PHOENIX	CN758	CAMPBELTOWN	6.40	1.10	1990	PATRINGTON
FLIPPER	OB268	OBAN	4.50	0.62	1977	DEVON
FLIXIE	LN73	KINGS LYNN	11.35	9.60	1981	PORTSMOUTH
FLO FAN	CS8	COWES	8.50	2.83	2010	ISLE OF WIGHT
FLORA	B443	BELFAST	9.14	6.59	1923	CARNLOUGH
FLORA	CY5	CASTLEBAY	4.60	0.57	2004	ISLE OF BARRA
FLORA JANE	WY251	WHITBY	7.41	3.16	1975	WHITBY
FLORENCE	SU949	SOUTHAMPTON	7.48	1.51	1998	HAMPSHIRE
FLOURISH	BF410	BANFF	5.89	1.58	1979	UNKNOWN
FLOURISH	E11	EXETER	9.70	16.94	1991	SUNDERLAND
FLOURISH N	BF340	BANFF	19.90	195.00	2001	ABERDEENSHIRE
FLOWER OF THE FAL II	FH733	FALMOUTH	5.49	1.45	1981	PLYMOUTH
FLOWING TIDE	PZ574	PENZANCE	5.55	1.51	1977	MULLION

UK Fishing Vessels 2015

Vessel Name	Code	Port Name	Loa	Ton Gt	Year	Construction Place
FLUKE	H1122	HULL	7.95	2.24	2005	ISLE OF WIGHT
FLYING BREEZE	FH106	FALMOUTH	6.19	1.77	1967	CORNWALL
FLYING FISH OF TARBERT	TT272	TARBERT	9.94	5.14	1978	GBR
FLYING FISHER	WH95	WEYMOUTH	7.35	2.42	2001	CORNWALL
FLYING SPRAY IV	FY777	FOWEY	8.13	6.27	1995	PENRYN
FOR A FEW DOLLARS MORE	PW469	PADSTOW	6.00	1.34	1991	ENGLAND
FORCE FOUR	J101	JERSEY	5.78	1.11	2000	UK
FOREVER GRATEFUL	FR249	FRASERBURGH	63.97	1464.00	2001	SANTURCE
FORGET-ME-NOT	PE534	POOLE	8.69	6.30	1976	WEYMOUTH
FORGET-ME-NOT	SC19	SCILLY	6.35	2.87	1981	HAYLE
FORTH HARVESTER	KY990	KIRKCALDY	7.50	2.40	1984	MARYPORT
FORTITUDE	UL48	ULLAPOOL	11.43	15.63	1984	WICK CAITHNESS
FORTUNA II	AH153	ARBROATH	7.62	2.49	1970	LOOE CORNWALL
FORTUNE BOUND	KY79	KIRKCALDY	6.25	1.53	1999	ITALY
FORTUNE II	BK108	BERWICK ON TWEED	10.67	11.23	1958	ST MONANS FIFE
FOU DE BASSAN	J35	JERSEY	7.90	2.09	2007	FRANCE
FOU DE BASSAN	SS685	ST IVES	5.46	0.73	1999	UNKNOWN
FOUR ACES II	M40	MILFORD HAVEN	9.90	4.22	2013	UK
FOUR BOYS	CE521	COLERAINE	5.63	1.24	2002	CO KERRY
FOUR BROTHERS	RX77	RYE	9.96	13.58	2002	SUSSEX
FOUR DAUGHTERS	LT601	LOWESTOFT	9.56	4.61	1996	LOWESTOFT
FOUR MAIDENS	FY15	FOWEY	4.30	0.63	1989	GBR
FOUR WINDS	N955	NEWRY	6.25	1.16	2003	GBR
FOUR WINDS	SM624	SHOREHAM	7.20	3.64	1976	UNKNOWN
FOWAN	RY18	RAMSEY	7.41	4.41	1975	GBR
FOX	CK20	COLCHESTER	4.25	0.54	1980	CLACTON ON SEA
FOX	PE1181	POOLE	4.43	0.56	1995	PORTSMOUTH
FOXY LADY	FH57	FALMOUTH	4.74	1.04	1990	HAYLE CORNWALL
FRAM III	BRD1	BROADFORD	11.70	11.27	1990	RYE
FRAM OF SHIELDAIG	BRD679	BROADFORD	9.83	11.63	2004	ESSEX

UK Fishing Vessels 2015

Vessel Name	Code	Port Name	Loa	Ton Gt	Year	Construction Place
FRANCES	CY445	CASTLEBAY	4.60	0.73	1980	UNKNOWN
FRANCES ANN D	BH37	BLYTH	9.40	2.83	2007	NORTHUMBERLAND
FRANCES B	FH714	FALMOUTH	7.29	4.79	1983	POOLE
FRANCES ROSE	N106	NEWRY	6.54	1.32	2011	KILKEEL
FRANCES ROSE	PZ437	PENZANCE	5.56	1.37	1994	CORNWALL
FRANCHISE	UL45	ULLAPOOL	14.95	43.77	1969	ARBROATH
FRANCIS ANNE	BD8	BIDEFORD	7.32	3.16	1993	BRIDPORT DORSET
FRANCIS JANE	E167	EXETER	7.30	3.66	1972	ST KEVERNE
FRAOCH GEAL	CY67	CASTLEBAY	6.20	1.61	1930	GBR
FRAOCH GEAL	SY46	STORNOWAY	10.93	11.65	1980	RYE SUSSEX
FREDA ANN	ME14	MONTROSE	7.25	2.33	2005	NORTHUMBERLAND
FREDERICK ROSE	NN201	NEWHAVEN	8.40	4.32	1987	NEWHAVEN
FREDWOOD	BA338	BALLANTRAE	19.35	45.17	1975	ST MONANCE FIFE
FREE N ARF	M1181	MILFORD HAVEN	4.56	0.62	2007	FINLAND
FREE SPIRIT	GU93	GUERNSEY	7.90	1.75	2009	FALMOUTH
FREE SPIRIT	N7	NEWRY	8.06	6.20	1996	GBR
FREE SPIRIT II	PW163	PADSTOW	9.95	6.95	2007	ESSEX
FREEBIRD	UL14	ULLAPOOL	7.95	2.28	2008	Unk
FREEDOM	B200	BELFAST	9.65	5.56	2004	CORNWALL
FREEDOM	BK536	BERWICK ON TWEED	8.36	5.75	1991	FALMOUTH
FREEDOM	FR11	FRASERBURGH	9.65	6.09	2010	CORNWALL
FREEDOM	NN753	NEWHAVEN	9.33	3.85	1998	RYE
FREEDOM	P105	PORTSMOUTH	8.20	4.07	1970	FRANCE
FREEDOM	SD383	SUNDERLAND	9.99	10.98	2000	BARTON ON HUMBER
FREEDOM II	BH56	BLYTH	10.40	7.06	1985	AMBLE
FREEDOM II	CN111	CAMPBELTOWN	16.79	74.00	1975	FRASERBURGH
FREEDOM III	BA280	BALLANTRAE	19.72	62.00	1967	BUCKIE
FREEDON	SM315	SHOREHAM	7.16	3.71	1980	HAVANT
FREELINER	WH757	WEYMOUTH	6.95	1.46	2008	GBR
FREEWARD	BCK264	BUCKIE	9.95	14.29	1981	FELIXSTOWE

UK Fishing Vessels 2015

Vessel Name	Code	Port Name	Loa	Ton Gt	Year	Construction Place
FREM	SN361	NORTH SHIELDS	9.90	4.28	1997	BARTON UPON HUMBER
FREM P.D.	SN5	NORTH SHIELDS	9.34	10.43	1997	WIGTOWNSHIRE
FREM W	SN1	NORTH SHIELDS	13.40	20.53	1981	DENMARK
FRENCHIE	WY836	WHITBY	5.01	0.70	1990	UK
FRESH START	PE1048	POOLE	6.73	1.34	1996	BEDHAMPTON
FREY	CT137	CASTLETOWN	15.94	42.74	1972	UNITED KINGDOM
FREYA	BH121	BLYTH	6.97	1.31	1976	NEWBIGGIN
FREYA	LH589	LEITH	8.89	4.84	1999	GBR
FREYA	UL81	ULLAPOOL	8.00	4.88	1981	GUERNSEY
FREYA	WH368	WEYMOUTH	5.59	1.51	1988	BRIDPORT
FREYA	WI3	WISBECH	10.75	6.95	1988	KINGSTON UPON HULL
FREYA JAE	FY5	FOWEY	5.85	2.10	2010	HUNTINGDON CAMBS
FREYA MAY	PO9	PORTLAND	6.50	1.33	1980	GBR
FREYJA	SM31	SHOREHAM	5.20	1.57	2002	SELSEY
FRIENDLY ISLE	TN98	TROON	10.00	9.32	1961	MACDUFF
FRIENDLY SHORE	CT20	CASTLETOWN	13.40	27.97	1970	GBR
FRIGATE BIRD	TT137	TARBERT	17.04	65.00	1977	MACDUFF
FRUITFUL	KY40	KIRKCALDY	9.26	3.03	1988	DUBLIN
FRUITFUL BOUGH	PD109	PETERHEAD	19.90	195.00	2004	MACDUFF
FRUITFUL HARVEST 111	GY991	GRIMSBY	19.81	113.00	1976	FRASERBURGH
FRUITFUL VINE	BF240	BANFF	21.22	191.00	2009	ABERDEENSHIRE
FRUITION	CY312	CASTLEBAY	7.86	4.28	1989	UNKNOWN
FULL MONTY	DH97	DARTMOUTH	9.90	4.10	2003	SUSSEX
FULLBORE II	J55	JERSEY	12.19	20.95	1995	UK
FULMAR	FR915	FRASERBURGH	9.00	4.56	1985	MORCAMBE
FULMAR	KY1035	KIRKCALDY	6.50	1.65	2008	FIFE
FULMAR	MH1034	MIDDLESBROUGH	6.04	1.36	2002	GBR
FULMAR	OB39	OBAN	11.33	12.99	1976	ORKNEY
FULMAR	P1009	PORTSMOUTH	5.75	0.70	1966	ARUNDEL

UK Fishing Vessels 2015

Vessel Name	Code	Port Name	Loa	Ton Gt	Year	Construction Place
FULMAR	PZ601	PENZANCE	5.85	1.47	2002	PENRYN
FULMAR	SA372	SWANSEA	7.73	3.68	1985	SWANSEA
FULMAR	SY41	STORNOWAY	4.87	0.82	2004	ENGLAND
FULMAR	UL176	ULLAPOOL	8.10	3.84	1988	FALMOUTH
FULMAR	WY191	WHITBY	8.70	4.19	1973	PLYMOUTH
FULMAR 2	BK533	BERWICK ON TWEED	9.92	8.51	2003	HAFNARFJORDUR
FULMAR OF COLERAINE	CE545	COLERAINE	5.65	1.61	1995	PLYMOUTH
G AND E	LT446	LOWESTOFT	11.61	12.33	1963	LOWESTOFT
GABRIELLA	LT104	LOWESTOFT	9.99	4.32	1990	WADEBRIDGE CORNWALL
GAIRM NA MARA II	CS646	COWES	6.88	1.80	2000	ISLE OF WIGHT
GAL CADORA	PW17	PADSTOW	10.40	9.27	1990	TARBERT ARGYLL
GALATEA	FY97	FOWEY	12.00	26.88	1984	FALMOUTH
GALENA	N59	NEWRY	10.90	9.55	1982	WORCESTER
GALLOPER	TT75	TARBERT	6.25	0.71	1993	VENTNOR I.O.W.
GALLOS	SC177	SCILLY	7.36	3.08	2005	CORNWALL
GALWAD Y MOR	BR116	BRIDGEWATER	14.88	63.23	2007	EAST YORKS
GALWAD-Y-MOR	FH76	FALMOUTH	11.89	24.23	1984	MEVAGISSEY
GALWAD-Y-MOR OF LYMINGTON	SU116	SOUTHAMPTON	11.95	29.75	1986	POLRUAN CORNWALL ENGLAND
GANGWARILY	OB284	OBAN	9.00	6.76	1975	ORKNEY
GANGWARILY OF TIREE	OB358	OBAN	5.62	1.08	1988	ORKNEY
GANNET	LK56	LERWICK	7.00	3.30	1981	TORPOINT CORNWALL
GANNET	LT711	LOWESTOFT	5.79	1.80	1962	SOUTHWOLD
GANNET	SY756	STORNOWAY	4.20	0.36	1997	HAMPSHIRE
GANNET II	CY110	CASTLEBAY	10.15	8.59	1974	STORNOWAY
GARDENIA 11	MH202	MIDDLESBROUGH	6.47	0.85	1966	SANDSEND
GARDENIA III	MH203	MIDDLESBROUGH	6.40	1.83	2010	ENGLAND
GARFISH	SM814	SHOREHAM	4.80	0.95	1992	UK
GARN	E4	EXETER	4.84	0.68	2000	SUSSEX
GARY M	PZ643	PENZANCE	11.87	25.44	1982	ARBROATH
GAYLE FORCE	M1131	MILFORD HAVEN	5.00	1.07	1997	GBR

UK Fishing Vessels 2015

Vessel Name	Code	Port Name	Loa	Ton Gt	Year	Construction Place
GAZELLE	PZ536	PENZANCE	4.69	0.94	1978	HAYLE
GEE WIZ	CO4	CAERNARVON	7.32	3.89	1970	STOKE
GEERTRUIDA	OB99	OBAN	23.97	152.00	2001	THE NETHERLANDS
GEESKE	BM140	BRIXHAM	30.40	171.00	1971	WEST GRAFTDIJK
GEM	CY832	CASTLEBAY	4.30	0.52	2004	GBR
GEM	K50	KIRKWALL	5.47	1.67	1983	ORKNEY
GEM	OB182	OBAN	7.81	2.10	1984	BUCKIE
GEM	PE1086	POOLE	7.04	0.68	1998	POOLE
GEMINI	AH709	ARBROATH	9.14	9.24	1978	PORTHLEVEN
GEMINI	BD18	BIDEFORD	7.13	2.36	1980	PLYMOUTH
GEMINI	J325	JERSEY	4.90	0.83	1987	UK
GEMINI	KY196	KIRKCALDY	7.90	2.15	1987	SHOTLEY
GEMINI	RX26	RYE	8.00	4.30	1989	PENRYN CORNWALL
GEMINI	SM643	SHOREHAM	5.49	0.99	1978	BOGNOR
GEMINI II	RX413	RYE	5.05	0.73	1997	SUSSEX
GEMINI TWO	PZ1202	PENZANCE	4.79	1.03	2002	CORNWALL
GEMMA	PZ40	PENZANCE	6.54	2.80	1979	PENRYN
GEN-B	M647	MILFORD HAVEN	8.23	2.91	2000	ISLE OF WIGHT
GENESIS	B11	BELFAST	7.30	2.83	1991	GBR
GENESIS	BCK19	BUCKIE	35.70	298.00	1977	NORWAY
GENESIS	BF505	BANFF	27.47	362.00	1993	MACDUFF
GENESIS	FR41	FRASERBURGH	8.45	2.77	2001	RYE
GENESIS	GU240	GUERNSEY	6.48	2.96	1977	PENRYN
GENESIS	HL1065	HARTLEPOOL	9.75	5.22	1977	FALMOUTH AND LITTLEHAMPTON
GENESIS	KY18	KIRKCALDY	6.52	3.07	1992	ANSTRUTHER
GENESIS	PL400	PEEL	15.98	56.34	1996	PADSTOW
GENESIS ROSE	SH37	SCARBOROUGH	14.99	53.86	2009	HULL
GENESIS T	KY20	KIRKCALDY	9.10	6.10	2010	COUNTY KERRY
GENEVIEVE	FH7	FALMOUTH	6.20	1.65	2006	PORTUGAL
GENTLE BARBARA II	WY17	WHITBY	9.10	4.48	1983	SANDSEND WHITBY

UK Fishing Vessels 2015

Vessel Name	Code	Port Name	Loa	Ton Gt	Year	Construction Place
GENTOO	CY452	CASTLEBAY	5.26	0.94	1987	DUMBARTON
GEORDAN	SN1043	NORTH SHIELDS	8.48	3.14	1988	PORT ISAAC
GEORGE EDWIN	SE58	SALCOMBE	10.50	11.21	1987	POLRUAN
GEORGE IAN ROSE	PO10	PORTLAND	9.76	7.49	1980	PENRYN
GEORGELOU - N	TN38	TROON	25.50	160.00	1978	BROMBOROUGH
GEORGIA	CS673	COWES	8.22	2.55	1980	CORNWALL
GEORGIA DAWN	INS140	INVERNESS	18.00	102.00	2005	GRAMPIAN
GEORGIE FISHER	LN474	KINGS LYNN	13.90	22.89	2005	KINGS LYNN
GEORGIE GIRL	LT1042	LOWESTOFT	9.99	11.14	2005	OFFSHORE STEEL BOATS
GERRY ANN	TH169	TEIGNMOUTH	11.74	21.95	1967	TEIGNMOUTH
GERRY ANN C	TH257	TEIGNMOUTH	14.96	33.88	1975	PORTHLEVEN SHIPYARD
GERT JAN	LT87	LOWESTOFT	36.50	312.00	1986	DEN HELDER HOLLAND
GERTRUDE	CO267	CAERNARVON	7.00	3.25	1992	ISLE OF WIGHT
GERTRUDE ANN	N75	NEWRY	24.78	156.00	1972	GERMANY
GET THIS	CS121	COWES	6.90	0.86	1997	ISLE OF WIGHT
GIBSONS CHOICE	WH282	WEYMOUTH	4.88	1.26	1978	HAYLE CORNWALL
GILLIAN S	WH166	WEYMOUTH	7.62	6.06	1986	CORNWALL
GIMMAGH	CT74	CASTLETOWN	5.90	1.40	1994	GBR
GINA C	LK570	LERWICK	7.32	3.48	2003	ST COMBS
GINA C	M56	MILFORD HAVEN	8.28	4.66	1997	MACDUFF
GINA LOUISE	GU110	GUERNSEY	12.47	22.03	2013	Unk
GINGER WAVE	PZ462	PENZANCE	4.70	0.62	1996	GBR
GINNY	LL503	LIVERPOOL	5.70	1.04	2005	GBR
GIRL ABBELL	WK867	WICK	7.10	3.06	1989	I.O.W
GIRL ALISON	OB913	OBAN	14.92	28.12	1981	BALTIMORE
GIRL AMANDA	FY755	FOWEY	6.16	1.91	1982	HELSTON CORNWALL
GIRL AMY	K1013	KIRKWALL	4.95	0.92	1986	ABERDEEN
GIRL ANDREA	P433	PORTSMOUTH	6.55	3.34	1974	HAYLING ISLAND ENGLAND
GIRL ANN III	B10	BELFAST	15.31	35.00	1968	ANSTRUTHER
GIRL BARBARA	MN46	MALDON	8.50	2.22	1925	MERSEA ESSEX

UK Fishing Vessels 2015

Vessel Name	Code	Port Name	Loa	Ton Gt	Year	Construction Place
GIRL BETH	WK674	WICK	6.90	4.32	1990	STONEHAVEN SCOTLAND
GIRL BETH II	N312	NEWRY	9.85	7.65	1990	POOLE DORSET
GIRL CATHERINE	CY29	CASTLEBAY	4.90	0.79	2009	GBR
GIRL CHERRY	SS10	ST IVES	5.60	0.96	1980	DEVON
GIRL DEBRA	E444	EXETER	14.98	55.51	2000	FALMOUTH
GIRL EILEEN II	LA21	LLANELLI	9.99	8.07	1989	LLANELLI
GIRL ELLIE	WK2	WICK	6.13	0.95	2010	CORNWALL
GIRL ELSIE	LH533	LEITH	6.80	1.41	1961	FIFE
GIRL EMMA	N4	NEWRY	6.43	2.85	1991	THE WIRRAL
GIRL ERICA	WK822	WICK	8.30	3.55	1990	CORNWALL
GIRL ERRIN	CN131	CAMPBELTOWN	11.56	15.00	1975	SEAHOUSES
GIRL EVIE	WK18	WICK	6.80	1.54	2012	BANFF
GIRL FIONA	CY100	CASTLEBAY	9.80	12.66	1974	WICK
GIRL FIONA	LT17	LOWESTOFT	8.30	2.85	1991	BOWER
GIRL GUCCI	YH2483	YARMOUTH	4.40	0.81	1996	UNKNOWN
GIRL HANNAH	SY123	STORNOWAY	5.66	1.32	2005	GBR
GIRL HELEN	CO68	CAERNARVON	9.47	7.20	1963	AMBLE
GIRL JACKIE	BK111	BERWICK ON TWEED	6.47	1.33	2009	CO.DOWN
GIRL JAN	FH468	FALMOUTH	6.30	2.39	1979	ST KEVERNE
GIRL JEAN	LH73	LEITH	12.23	19.02	1973	ST MONANS FIFE
GIRL JILL II	B238	BELFAST	7.14	2.40	1999	ABERDEEN
GIRL JOLENE	SM437	SHOREHAM	8.94	2.95	1983	SHOREHAM
GIRL JOSIE	CY131	CASTLEBAY	8.05	5.23	1973	ORKNEY
GIRL JULIE	BF4	BANFF	7.95	6.69	2000	MACDUFF
GIRL JUSTINE	WK24	WICK	5.85	0.99	1993	ORKNEY SCOTLAND
GIRL KAYLA	RX256	RYE	9.10	7.99	1999	PLYMOUTH
GIRL KERRY	RX28	RYE	7.25	2.06	1988	HOLTON
GIRL KILDA	K44	KIRKWALL	11.28	8.44	1983	CEMAES BAY
GIRL KIM	PZ85	PENZANCE	6.03	1.64	1968	PORTHLEVEN
GIRL LAUREN	LH17	LEITH	7.55	5.13	2010	BRISTOL

UK Fishing Vessels 2015

Vessel Name	Code	Port Name	Loa	Ton Gt	Year	Construction Place
GIRL LINDA	CN104	CAMPBELTOWN	4.92	0.69	1986	ORKNEY
GIRL LIZZIE	LK537	LERWICK	5.91	0.98	1933	SHETLAND
GIRL LUCY	FH20	FALMOUTH	5.55	1.29	1971	WOODBRIDGE
GIRL LUCY	LT4	LOWESTOFT	5.73	1.33	1992	HAPPISPURGH
GIRL LYNNE	LK301	LERWICK	8.72	4.39	1952	FRASERBURGH
GIRL LYNSEY	LK10	LERWICK	8.21	3.35	1996	SUFFOLK
GIRL MARGARET	BRD16	BROADFORD	8.58	4.16	2008	ASHINGTON
GIRL MARY	B236	BELFAST	19.96	56.00	1956	SANDHAVEN SCOTLAND
GIRL MILLIE	WK820	WICK	4.72	0.81	2000	CORNWALL
GIRL MOIRA	B977	BELFAST	5.40	1.05	2000	NOT KNOWN
GIRL MORAG	PD181	PETERHEAD	5.96	1.67	2001	CORNWALL
GIRL NICOLA	CE500	COLERAINE	7.95	4.47	1999	IRELAND
GIRL PAMELA	PZ6	PENZANCE	11.48	17.04	1968	PENRYN
GIRL PAT	DO4	DOUGLAS	8.10	3.82	1991	GBR
GIRL PAULINE	FH293	FALMOUTH	5.28	1.18	1983	HAYLE CORNWALL
GIRL PENNY	PZ353	PENZANCE	9.91	7.50	1972	PORTHLEVEN
GIRL RACHAEL	FH598	FALMOUTH	9.91	10.37	1991	PENRYN
GIRL RACHEL	PW77	PADSTOW	9.95	4.36	1987	ROCK CORNWALL
GIRL RHEANNAN	OB467	OBAN	8.42	7.28	1982	BIRKENHEAD
GIRL RHIANNON	K500	KIRKWALL	7.55	2.93	1977	UNITED KINGDOM
GIRL RONA	TH117	TEIGNMOUTH	14.83	38.98	1980	DEVORAN
GIRL RONA II	SY50	STORNOWAY	7.30	5.20	2005	GBR
GIRL RUTH	PZ159	PENZANCE	7.13	2.33	1972	PORTHLEVEN
GIRL SANDRA	ME2	MONTROSE	6.42	1.30	1992	MACDUFF
GIRL SARAH	BRD682	BROADFORD	4.86	0.66	2001	GBR
GIRL SCOUT	TH436	TEIGNMOUTH	5.03	0.88	1998	SYSSEX
GIRL SHARON	BA61	BALLANTRAE	10.76	10.32	1970	ANSTRUTHER
GIRL SHARON	PW15	PADSTOW	6.39	1.56	2002	PAINGTON
GIRL STELLA	PZ1187	PENZANCE	6.38	0.71	1980	UNKNOWN
GIRL SUSAN	CY157	CASTLEBAY	7.76	3.96	1989	UNKNOWN

UK Fishing Vessels 2015

Vessel Name	Code	Port Name	Loa	Ton Gt	Year	Construction Place
GIRL TESS	PH10	PLYMOUTH	5.54	1.09	2007	PORTUGAL
GISELLE	DE1	DUNDEE	6.50	2.38	1987	SUSSEX
GIZZEN BRIGGS	INS1040	INVERNESS	13.15	24.40	2004	AYRSHIRE
GLAD TIDINGS	BH111	BLYTH	9.96	3.74	1976	AMBLE
GLAD TIDINGS II	BK226	BERWICK ON TWEED	9.88	7.91	1968	SOUTH SHIELDS
GLAD TIDINGS III	BK279	BERWICK ON TWEED	10.82	11.96	1971	SEAHOUSES
GLAD TIDINGS VII	BK10	BERWICK ON TWEED	11.60	7.19	2002	CORNWALL
GLADLY ANNE II	BRD676	BROADFORD	7.24	2.24	1986	ISLE OF WIGHT
GLADYS B	CO532	CAERNARVON	5.00	0.64	1985	ISLE OF WIGHT
GLAS-Y-DORLAN I	CA32	CARDIGAN	9.80	5.87	1988	NEVERN
GLEANER	CN444	CAMPBELTOWN	19.81	137.00	1986	BUCKIE
GLEANER II	CN777	CAMPBELTOWN	23.90	184.00	1985	FIFE
GLEN AMY	B917	BELFAST	8.08	2.95	1985	CORNWALL
GLEN BAY II	B999	BELFAST	6.35	1.76	2008	BALLYMARTIN CO.DOWN
GLEN COUL	UL78	ULLAPOOL	10.00	10.95	1997	CAITHNESS
GLEN ISLE	CE10	COLERAINE	5.03	0.86	1983	ENGLAND
GLENBAY	B714	BELFAST	5.45	1.35	1981	PLYMOUTH
GLENDEVERON	B63	BELFAST	16.51	42.00	1969	MACDUFF
GLENRAVEL	N191	NEWRY	26.25	153.00	1968	HOLLAND
GLENUGIE	PD347	PETERHEAD	26.00	252.00	2000	NAVIA
GLORIA VICTUS	AH711	ARBROATH	4.94	1.08	2000	CEMBORNE
GLORIOUS	BA90	BALLANTRAE	9.72	8.38	1978	N IRELAND
GO FOR IT	PZ903	PENZANCE	7.30	2.13	1998	CAMBORNE
GOEDE VERWACHTING	B931	BELFAST	33.26	76.00	1910	GBR
GOELAND	N23	NEWRY	9.39	6.98	1975	IRELAND
GOLDEN BELLS	SR28	STRANRAER	9.84	9.95	1973	WHITBY
GOLDEN BELLS 11	OB192	OBAN	16.92	56.00	1981	ST MONANS
GOLDEN BOW	N136	NEWRY	5.35	0.93	1985	GBR
GOLDEN CHANCE	BF91	BANFF	7.42	2.86	1988	RAMSGATE
GOLDEN DAWN	CY815	CASTLEBAY	7.90	2.64	1990	FARNDON NEWARK

UK Fishing Vessels 2015

Vessel Name	Code	Port Name	Loa	Ton Gt	Year	Construction Place
GOLDEN DAWN	FR8	FRASERBURGH	6.99	3.21	2013	CO DOWN
GOLDEN DAWN	SY819	STORNOWAY	8.08	6.07	1988	STARCROSS DEVON
GOLDEN DAWN	UL347	ULLAPOOL	4.89	0.72	1985	ORKNEY
GOLDEN DAYS	WY1	WHITBY	6.43	2.90	1980	FALMOUTH
GOLDEN EMBLEM	B908	BELFAST	19.63	123.00	1979	BUCKIE
GOLDEN FLEECE	B488	BELFAST	9.95	5.43	1982	UK
GOLDEN FLEECE	MT99	MARYPORT	13.90	31.00	1975	FRASERBURGH
GOLDEN FLEECE	PZ1198	PENZANCE	5.84	2.19	2000	CORNWALL
GOLDEN FLEECE II	FH207	FALMOUTH	14.95	42.24	2007	CORNWALL
GOLDEN GAIN V	FR59	FRASERBURGH	25.71	222.00	1989	ST. MONANCE SCOTLAND
GOLDEN GIRL	PE1130	POOLE	8.35	5.94	2001	CORNWALL
GOLDEN GRAIN	J485	JERSEY	11.58	19.05	1974	FRA
GOLDEN HARVEST	PZ63	PENZANCE	15.02	39.00	1972	STROMNESS
GOLDEN ISLES	UL214	ULLAPOOL	11.38	11.48	1980	FALMOUTH
GOLDEN JUBILEE	B235	BELFAST	9.45	4.90	1982	SOUTHAMPTON
GOLDEN LANCER	TH288	TEIGNMOUTH	9.90	8.34	1982	CORNWALL
GOLDEN LILY	BH115	BLYTH	9.56	6.85	1954	FRASERBURGH
GOLDEN OPPORTUNITY	SE67	SALCOMBE	9.70	10.03	1982	RAMSGATE
GOLDEN PROMISE	CY149	CASTLEBAY	7.10	3.72	1989	LOCHMADDY
GOLDEN PROMISE	FH401	FALMOUTH	14.20	35.40	1996	NEWHAVEN
GOLDEN RAY	B963	BELFAST	14.93	52.43	2005	CO DOWN
GOLDEN REAPER	B127	BELFAST	20.86	125.00	1973	SANDHAVEN
GOLDEN RULE	BRD109	BROADFORD	9.14	5.19	1979	CORNWALL
GOLDEN SCEPTRE	PD50	PETERHEAD	21.22	186.00	2010	ABERDEENSHIRE
GOLDEN SHADOW	LH551	LEITH	4.85	0.70	2001	SUSSEX
GOLDEN SHEAF	FR989	FRASERBURGH	4.83	1.02	1988	ENGLAND
GOLDEN SHORE	LK540	LERWICK	9.95	16.03	1999	EYEMOUTH
GOLDEN SHORE	N806	NEWRY	9.04	4.13	1983	LIVERPOOL
GOLDEN STAG	B746	BELFAST	8.83	6.08	1988	DRUMBO CO DOWN
GOLDEN STRAND III	BS100	BEAUMARIS	11.85	22.25	1967	UNKNOWN

UK Fishing Vessels 2015

Vessel Name	Code	Port Name	Loa	Ton Gt	Year	Construction Place
GOLDEN WEST	K101	KIRKWALL	9.76	5.48	1971	HAMPSHIRE
GOLDEN WEST	TT252	TARBERT	9.80	16.39	1989	UNK
GOLDFISH	BM4	BRIXHAM	9.99	7.16	2011	VENTNOR ISLE OF WIGHT
GONPEZ I	FH535	FALMOUTH	32.20	271.00	2003	PONTEVEDRA
GOOD DESIGN	A1	ABERDEEN	5.94	1.12	1967	PORTLETHEN
GOOD FELLOWSHIP	BK172	BERWICK ON TWEED	14.90	28.40	1960	ARBROATH
GOOD FORTUNE	TO48	TRURO	7.99	4.47	2003	ESSEX
GOOD FRIEND	AH39	ARBROATH	7.69	3.71	1981	BERWICK ON TWEED
GOOD HOPE	B116	BELFAST	16.31	58.00	1969	ARBROATH
GOOD HOPE	FR891	FRASERBURGH	20.40	170.00	1987	MACDUFF SCOTLAND
GOOD HOPE	H357	HULL	32.90	300.00	2007	SPAIN
GOOD HOPE	WK209	WICK	6.52	2.09	1991	ARDRISHAIG
GOOD INTENT	PW22	PADSTOW	7.96	3.50	2009	EDINBURGH
GOOD INTENT	SY79	STORNOWAY	18.21	86.00	1981	APPLEDORE
GOOD LIFE	E523	EXETER	5.50	2.07	2001	NOT KNOWN
GOOD LUCK	SM631	SHOREHAM	5.52	1.14	1989	BOGNOR REGIS
GOOD ONE	BS7	BEAUMARIS	6.85	0.76	2006	ISLE OF WIGHT
GOOD PROSPECT	CO106	CAERNARVON	9.58	8.03	1983	WEYMOUTH
GOOD VENTURE	GU47	GUERNSEY	8.95	1.52	2009	COLCHESTER ESSEX
GOODWILL	J609	JERSEY	9.39	6.49	1973	UK
GOODWILL	SC9	SCILLY	8.00	4.75	1996	FALMOUTH
GOOSANDER	OB421	OBAN	9.27	8.56	1975	FALMOUTH
GORDEANO STAR	WH763	WEYMOUTH	7.95	4.16	2009	BRIDGWATER SOMERSET
GOVENEK OF LADRAM	PZ51	PENZANCE	22.65	198.00	1986	MACDUFF
GOWER PRIDE	P65	PORTSMOUTH	7.40	1.83	1990	FALMOUTH
GRACE	BM14	BRIXHAM	6.50	1.99	2004	UK
GRACE	PN50	PRESTON	6.71	2.09	1962	FRECKLETON
GRACE ANN	BRD362	BROADFORD	7.96	7.12	2010	GBE
GRACE ELIZABETH	YH45	YARMOUTH	5.84	1.30	2003	NORFOLK
GRACE II	LL231	LIVERPOOL	6.55	3.04	1994	CHESTER

UK Fishing Vessels 2015

Vessel Name	Code	Port Name	Loa	Ton Gt	Year	Construction Place
GRACIE AVA	MH1041	MIDDLESBROUGH	12.66	18.90	2010	MIDDLESBOROUGH
GRACIE GEORGE	MT118	MARYPORT	7.68	3.87	1990	ISLE OF WIGHT
GRACIOUS	FR167	FRASERBURGH	7.30	1.90	1999	CORNWALL
GRACIOUS	K167	KIRKWALL	9.42	7.16	1977	FALMOUTH
GRADELY	OB42	OBAN	11.56	18.60	1986	CORNWALL
GRAMPIAN ADMIRAL	A40	ABERDEEN	39.15	368.00	1960	ABERDEEN
GRANDAD	FY787	FOWEY	5.48	1.92	1996	GBR
GRATITUDE	AB71	ABERYSTWYTH	9.91	11.12	1990	NEWHAVEN
GRATITUDE	BF103	BANFF	14.85	37.28	2003	EYEMOUTH
GRATITUDE	FR248	FRASERBURGH	8.15	4.87	2012	ROSYTH
GRATITUDE	N11	NEWRY	5.60	1.06	1986	PLYMOUTH
GRATITUDE	PD202	PETERHEAD	8.01	3.60	1978	CORNWALL
GRATITUDE II	SY303	STORNOWAY	5.79	1.50	1980	SOUTH UIST
GRAYLIN	SU432	SOUTHAMPTON	9.10	6.86	1979	POOLE
GREBE	P746	PORTSMOUTH	3.54	0.41	1960	FAREHAM
GREEN AND BUOYS	PE14	POOLE	6.74	1.72	2002	KENT
GREEN BRAE	CE208	COLERAINE	17.07	55.00	1973	GIRVAN
GREEN EYE	BD88	BIDEFORD	11.60	13.90	2013	UK
GREEN ISLE	BRD83	BROADFORD	8.09	4.08	1983	CUSHENDALL
GREEN ISLE III	BRD73	BROADFORD	9.90	7.59	1989	CORNWALL
GREEN ISLE V	CE509	COLERAINE	9.99	7.36	1997	HAYLE
GREEN PASTURES	BH156	BLYTH	16.89	56.00	1980	ST MONANS FIFE
GRETAS GIRL	AH714	ARBROATH	8.94	3.88	1999	FALMOUTH
GRETEL K	BM113	BRIXHAM	7.37	2.23	1986	UNKNOWN
GREY DAWN	GU64	GUERNSEY	8.03	3.39	1990	PENRYN
GREY DAWN	J208	JERSEY	8.05	3.95	2011	Unk
GREY GULL	IH225	IPSWICH	7.71	4.54	1958	IPSWICH
GREY HAZE	GU100	GUERNSEY	4.90	0.94	1995	GUERNSEY
GREY LADY	P287	PORTSMOUTH	6.12	1.00	1988	PORTSMOUTH
GREY MIST	E2	EXETER	8.09	6.74	1993	FALMOUTH

UK Fishing Vessels 2015

Vessel Name	Code	Port Name	Loa	Ton Gt	Year	Construction Place
GREY SEAL	PZ540	PENZANCE	4.63	1.04	1977	SENNEN COVE
GRIFFIN GIRL	M227	MILFORD HAVEN	5.16	0.90	2001	SUFFOLK
GRIMSAY ISLE	CY64	CASTLEBAY	8.67	7.35	1973	WICK
GRIZZLY	J200	JERSEY	4.98	0.82	1993	ORKNEY
GROUSE III	KY61	KIRKCALDY	7.87	2.35	1985	CORNWALL
GROWLER	WH764	WEYMOUTH	7.90	2.99	2003	DERBY
GUARDIAN	FY28	FOWEY	11.95	22.32	2013	CORNWALL
GUARDIAN ANGELL	LK272	LERWICK	26.56	257.00	1992	CAMPBELTOWN
GUESS AGAIN	KY58	KIRKCALDY	8.10	6.95	1983	PENRYN
GUESS AGAIN II	KY3	KIRKCALDY	9.74	11.07	1989	ANSTRUTHER
GUIDE ME	BK312	BERWICK ON TWEED	9.98	7.08	1974	LOOE CORNWALL
GUIDE ME	FR42	FRASERBURGH	7.32	3.74	1979	TARBERT
GUIDE ME	SS3	ST IVES	5.70	1.07	1975	DEVON
GUIDE ME 1	KY227	KIRKCALDY	10.98	14.20	1971	ST MONANCE
GUIDE US	FR4	FRASERBURGH	17.94	109.00	1982	DENMARK
GUIDE US	GK77	GREENOCK	9.86	12.50	2000	HUMBERSIDE
GUIDE US	SY340	STORNOWAY	16.82	46.00	1973	ST MONANS
GUIDING LIGHT	B1012	BELFAST	6.45	2.89	1980	CYGNUS MARINE
GUIDING LIGHT	CY127	CASTLEBAY	12.78	25.56	1988	BUCKIE
GUIDING LIGHT	LK84	LERWICK	23.02	168.00	1986	SANDHAVEN
GUIDING LIGHT	PD2	PETERHEAD	6.27	1.50	1985	UNK
GUIDING LIGHT III	BD1	BIDEFORD	14.98	48.02	2005	DEVON
GUIDING STAR	BF5	BANFF	7.11	1.89	1988	EYEMOUTH
GUIDING STAR	GU170	GUERNSEY	9.70	8.54	1987	ENGLAND
GUIDING STAR	H360	HULL	26.01	261.00	2013	WHITBY
GUIDING STAR	KY322	KIRKCALDY	16.15	39.00	1959	MACDUFF
GUIDING STAR	ME34	MONTROSE	9.60	8.96	1955	FRASERBURGH
GUIDING STAR	PZ61	PENZANCE	5.49	1.46	1997	UNKNOWN
GUIDING STAR	SSS7	SOUTH SHIELDS	8.00	4.77	1983	PENRYN
GUILLEMOT	B45	BELFAST	6.50	1.52	1986	BUCKIE
GUILLEMOT	SE122	SALCOMBE	6.43	1.49	1995	CORNWALL

UK Fishing Vessels 2015

Vessel Name	Code	Port Name	Loa	Ton Gt	Year	Construction Place
GUNGIR	FY903	FOWEY	5.70	1.08	2009	PORTUGAL
GUNNERS GLORY	UL548	ULLAPOOL	7.23	3.18	2000	ABERDEENSHIRE
GUNNERS GLORY II	SM561	SHOREHAM	9.69	5.58	2003	CORNWALL
GUNNHILDA	WK72	WICK	9.30	8.17	1967	STROMNESS
GUS	E460	EXETER	5.15	0.96	1994	ARUNDEL
GUSTO	GY2	GRIMSBY	9.28	2.19	2009	ISLE OF WIGHT
GUYONA	BM18	BRIXHAM	5.61	1.39	1979	NANCLEDRA CORNWALL
GUZBERT II	LA73	LLANELLI	5.13	0.76	1990	GBR
GWALARN	PH586	PLYMOUTH	9.95	15.91	1965	DOUARNENEZ
GWALCH Y MOR III	CA192	CARDIGAN	4.90	0.82	1994	WEST SUSSEX
GWALCH-Y-MOR	TT10	TARBERT	7.93	2.71	1983	CAMELFORD
GWEN PAUL M	BS115	BEAUMARIS	11.08	7.62	2011	FAREHAM
GWYLAN	N14	NEWRY	5.70	1.03	1979	SOUTHBOURNE HANTS
GYO	GY53	GRIMSBY	4.35	0.56	1973	ISLE OF WIGHT
GYPSY	BS456	BEAUMARIS	5.79	0.72	1980	GBR
GYPSY GIRL	HL1085	HARTLEPOOL	5.97	2.71	1980	GBR
GYPSY GIRL	LH559	LEITH	5.54	1.25	2002	GBR
H R K	CS177	COWES	4.25	0.66	1985	BLAKENEY NORFOLK
HAHNEN KAMM	NN48	NEWHAVEN	8.46	7.29	1985	NEWHAVEN
HALCYON	A94	ABERDEEN	4.80	0.67	2010	HUNTINGDON
HALCYON	B886	BELFAST	8.00	5.88	1992	FALMOUTH
HALCYON	BCK127	BUCKIE	5.90	1.18	2010	BANFFSHIRE
HALCYON	BF6	BANFF	6.45	0.98	1970	GBR
HALCYON	FY894	FOWEY	8.20	3.60	2008	CORNWALL
HALCYON	LK467	LERWICK	9.89	6.23	2011	EDINBURGH
HALCYON	NN114	NEWHAVEN	9.80	7.03	2001	CORNWALL
HALCYON II	BF500	BANFF	7.32	2.91	2011	UK
HALIMA	LA24	LLANELLI	5.20	1.03	1987	LLANELLI
HANDA ISLE	B210	BELFAST	12.00	18.29	1988	HULL
HANDY MAN	GU155	GUERNSEY	7.41	3.33	1993	GUERNSEY

UK Fishing Vessels 2015

Vessel Name	Code	Port Name	Loa	Ton Gt	Year	Construction Place
HANNA	LI56	LITTLEHAMPTON	4.99	0.62	1990	GBR
HANNAH BETH	DH23	DARTMOUTH	9.99	11.50	1996	CORNWALL
HANNAH COLLEEN	GU214	GUERNSEY	7.69	1.29	1989	COWES
HANNAH D	BM2	BRIXHAM	13.95	32.04	1991	NEWHAVEN
HANNAH JACK	PH5583	PLYMOUTH	9.83	13.49	2003	ESSEX
HANNAH KATE	SA36	SWANSEA	8.10	3.33	1988	PORTLAND
HANNAH LILY	SN4	NORTH SHIELDS	6.40	1.08	1990	UK
HANNAH LOUISE	J104	JERSEY	9.67	6.85	2001	UK
HANNAH LOUISE	YH281	YARMOUTH	10.70	11.27	1992	WEYBOURNE NORFOLK
HANNAH MARIE	BD33	BIDEFORD	9.94	16.86	2005	CORNWALL
HANNAH-CHARLOTTE	GY1428	GRIMSBY	5.61	1.23	1987	ENGLAND
HAPPISBURGH BUOY	YH2502	YARMOUTH	5.70	1.40	2009	EDINGTHORPE
HAPPY DAYS	PH41	PLYMOUTH	8.60	2.96	2012	COLCHESTER
HAPPY DAYS	YH2489	YARMOUTH	4.90	0.62	1974	GBR
HAPPY HOOKER	GU400	GUERNSEY	6.46	2.88	1978	ENGLAND
HAPPY HOOKER	PD1032	PETERHEAD	9.70	4.82	1980	GBR
HAPPY HOOKER	SC7	SCILLY	6.90	1.15	2005	ENGLAND
HAPPY HOOKER II	PE1157	POOLE	8.70	2.66	2009	ISLE OF WIGHT
HAPPY RETURN	CY90	CASTLEBAY	7.08	2.56	1973	ISLE OF WIGHT
HARD GRAFT	NN384	NEWHAVEN	6.16	1.58	1988	NEWHAVEN
HARINGVLIET	BM218	BRIXHAM	29.75	150.00	1968	DEN HELDER HOLLAND
HARM JOHANNES	BM51	BRIXHAM	25.40	83.00	1954	HOLLAND
HARMONI	M147	MILFORD HAVEN	14.96	59.48	2003	YORKSHIRE
HARMONY	AB1	ABERYSTWYTH	6.41	1.27	2007	Unk
HARMONY	AH708	ARBROATH	8.50	4.63	1980	BERWICK
HARMONY	CY777	CASTLEBAY	9.99	9.70	2011	SUSSEX
HARMONY	SY212	STORNOWAY	9.90	6.55	1987	HULL
HARMONY	UL137	ULLAPOOL	10.47	11.97	1974	STROMNESS ORKNEY
HARMONY J	SH262	SCARBOROUGH	6.40	1.98	1995	NORTH YORKSHIRE

UK Fishing Vessels 2015

Vessel Name	Code	Port Name	Loa	Ton Gt	Year	Construction Place
HARMONY JB	LK969	LERWICK	8.50	6.25	1984	POOLE
HAROLD FRANCIS WOODS	PH18	PLYMOUTH	5.74	1.38	1994	SUSSEX
HARRIER	PH5573	PLYMOUTH	6.50	2.73	1980	CORNWALL
HARRIET EVE	TO50	TRURO	14.15	26.82	1968	BUCKIE
HARRIET J	AH180	ARBROATH	7.19	2.64	1997	UNKNOWN
HARRY TOM	PE1184	POOLE	6.05	0.65	2007	NOT KNOWN
HARTLEY	BH174	BLYTH	11.22	9.40	1980	BRIDLINGTON
HARTLEY	PZ130	PENZANCE	8.92	7.27	1991	FALMOUTH
HARVEST DAWN	BH24	BLYTH	8.64	6.77	2002	KILKEEL
HARVEST HOME	BK224	BERWICK ON TWEED	8.72	5.71	1975	GBR
HARVEST HOPE	PD120	PETERHEAD	34.08	604.00	1999	EAST LOOE
HARVEST LIGHT	N808	NEWRY	7.18	3.98	1992	PLYMOUTH
HARVEST LILY	UL32	ULLAPOOL	9.75	8.34	1958	FRASERBURGH
HARVEST MOON	FR366	FRASERBURGH	21.34	165.42	1987	ARBROATH
HARVEST MOON	OB141	OBAN	12.88	32.57	1996	CORNWALL
HARVEST REAPER	ML4	METHIL	9.00	4.42	1982	HULL
HARVEST REAPER	PW177	PADSTOW	17.00	78.00	1975	FRASERBURGH
HARVEST REAPER	PZ329	PENZANCE	11.88	31.48	1988	BRISTOL
HARVEST REAPER II	BF177	BANFF	17.07	97.00	1980	LOSSIEMOUTH
HARVEST TRIUMPH	ME110	MONTROSE	7.52	3.14	1976	ST MONANCE
HARVESTER	A865	ABERDEEN	11.83	19.64	1973	MALLAIG
HARVESTER	BM127	BRIXHAM	14.96	39.17	1999	FALMOUTH
HARVESTER	CN200	CAMPBELTOWN	7.38	3.07	1974	SOUTH SHIELDS
HARVESTER	CY205	CASTLEBAY	9.00	5.23	1982	ORKNEY ISLES
HARVESTER	FH198	FALMOUTH	11.28	22.78	1974	FRASERBURGH
HARVESTER	LH597	LEITH	7.62	2.92	1960	PORTHLEVEN
HARVESTER	LK26	LERWICK	7.20	2.91	1982	TRONDRA SHETLAND
HARVESTER	PD98	PETERHEAD	28.35	349.00	2008	DNK
HARVESTER	SA328	SWANSEA	9.80	5.98	1997	WADESBRIDGE
HARVESTER II	FH723	FALMOUTH	11.83	16.29	2004	ESSEX

UK Fishing Vessels 2015

Vessel Name	Code	Port Name	Loa	Ton Gt	Year	Construction Place
HAUXLEY HAVEN	BH182	BLYTH	6.19	1.17	1981	HUMBERSIDE
HAVANA	NN749	NEWHAVEN	9.83	11.63	2006	ESSEX
HAVEN	WH588	WEYMOUTH	4.58	0.75	1992	ISLE OF WIGHT
HAVEN LAD	LO524	LONDON	7.40	2.00	1991	CANVEY ISLAND
HAWK	SS151	ST IVES	5.60	1.77	1989	UNK
HAYLEY B	GU355	GUERNSEY	10.78	16.78	1988	CORNWALL
HAYLEY GRACE	WH582	WEYMOUTH	3.80	0.37	2007	GBR
HAZEL ANN	CN373	CAMPBELTOWN	9.94	7.85	1996	CORNWALL
HAZEY DAWN	GU17	GUERNSEY	6.41	3.00	1993	GUERNSEY
HAZYMOL	CY111	CASTLEBAY	9.15	4.35	1981	CORNWALL
HEADWAY	WA8	WHITEHAVEN	18.22	107.00	1981	BUCKIE
HEATHER ANNE	FY126	FOWEY	11.00	11.54	1971	PORT MELLON
HEATHER BELLE	CY45	CASTLEBAY	8.20	5.22	1990	CRINAN
HEATHER BELLE	FR382	FRASERBURGH	20.87	127.00	1981	CAMPBELTOWN
HEATHER D	LA8	LLANELLI	11.60	25.77	1990	SUNDERLAND
HEATHER III	TT255	TARBERT	4.60	0.66	1995	ISLE OF IONA
HEATHER ISLE M	SY47	STORNOWAY	17.65	56.00	1966	SANDHAVEN BY FRASERBURGH
HEATHER JUNE	CO170	CAERNARVON	9.20	5.04	1980	HULL
HEATHER K	K77	KIRKWALL	16.95	132.00	2003	MACDUFF
HEATHER MAID	CT81	CASTLETOWN	16.65	46.32	1965	UNITED KINGDOM
HEATHER SPRIG	BCK181	BUCKIE	18.60	136.00	1989	MACDUFF
HEATHER VALLEY	N829	NEWRY	7.75	2.73	1993	CORNWALL
HEATSEEKER	DH76	DARTMOUTH	9.90	7.63	1989	PORT ISAAC
HECTOR	F140	FAVERSHAM	4.68	0.70	1988	HERNE BAY KENT
HECTORIA	K85	KIRKWALL	12.35	18.99	1972	COCKENZIE
HEIDI	YH497	YARMOUTH	4.78	0.74	1960	CAISTER
HELANDA	K159	KIRKWALL	9.75	7.52	1974	STROMNESS
HELEN	BH471	BLYTH	5.03	0.56	2002	NORTHUMBERLAND
HELEN	BK27	BERWICK ON TWEED	7.60	3.56	1984	CORNWALL
HELEN B	BM397	BRIXHAM	5.59	1.36	1989	BOGNOR REGIS

UK Fishing Vessels 2015

Vessel Name	Code	Port Name	Loa	Ton Gt	Year	Construction Place
HELEN BRUCE	BRD90	BROADFORD	10.40	5.36	1954	COCKENZIE
HELEN C	M1099	MILFORD HAVEN	6.37	1.71	1994	ENGALND
HELEN CLAIRE	BM258	BRIXHAM	14.39	26.82	1959	CAMERET FRANCE
HELEN CLARE	PW5	PADSTOW	9.66	7.99	2006	ISLE OF WIGHT
HELEN FREYA	OB1	OBAN	5.58	1.06	1981	BLYTH
HELEN JANE II	PW124	PADSTOW	9.83	16.86	2003	ESSEX
HELEN K	SD20	SUNDERLAND	7.00	3.04	2009	CORNWALL
HELEN REBECCA	LI33	LITTLEHAMPTON	5.70	0.89	1989	SUSSEX
HELENA	BF2	BANFF	7.92	1.77	1996	GBR
HELENA J	WH783	WEYMOUTH	5.50	0.88	2012	CORNWALL
HELENUS	BCK70	BUCKIE	11.48	16.44	1971	WICK
HELENUS	FR121	FRASERBURGH	26.61	235.00	1987	CAMPBELTOWN
HENDRIK BRANDS	LT162	LOWESTOFT	42.00	477.00	1983	HOLLAND
HENDRIKA JACOBA	GY127	GRIMSBY	40.20	454.00	1982	STELLENDAM
HENRI MUGE	DH191	DARTMOUTH	4.10	0.43	1997	HULL
HENRY	TH19	TEIGNMOUTH	5.50	1.38	1996	TEIGNMOUTH
HERITAGE	B786	BELFAST	21.31	88.00	1975	BUCKIE
HERITAGE	J73	JERSEY	9.98	12.72	1991	UK
HERON	P968	PORTSMOUTH	6.95	0.66	2005	DORSET
HEY JUDE	LI245	LITTLEHAMPTON	9.16	4.07	1972	SHOREHAM
HICCA	PZ654	PENZANCE	4.80	0.90	1988	HAYLE
HIGH-RIDER	GU248	GUERNSEY	6.70	2.91	1995	GALWAY
HIGHLAND QUEEN	N970	NEWRY	16.65	54.00	1972	DUNBAR
HIGHLAND SEABIRD	UL54	ULLAPOOL	7.20	2.14	2002	GBR
HIGHLANDER	CN717	CAMPBELTOWN	9.90	5.55	2003	HAFNARFJORDUR
HIGHLANDER	TT105	TARBERT	10.00	4.56	1990	WADEBRIDGE CORNWALL
HIGHLIGHT	YH563	YARMOUTH	4.91	0.90	1993	CATFIELD NORFOLK
HILDER	GU104	GUERNSEY	4.68	1.42	2000	GUERNSEY
HILDONA	K239	KIRKWALL	11.22	13.71	1971	ORKNEY
HOBBIT	FH705	FALMOUTH	5.88	1.96	1980	CORNWALL
HOBBIT	IH4	IPSWICH	5.56	2.38	1987	FELIXSTOWE

UK Fishing Vessels 2015

Vessel Name	Code	Port Name	Loa	Ton Gt	Year	Construction Place
HOBBY II	LI1	LITTLEHAMPTON	5.51	0.88	1981	BOGNOR REGIS
HOLLADAYS	R8	RAMSGATE	9.85	4.84	1977	FALMOUTH
HOLLIE J	H166	HULL	13.95	22.74	2004	LINCOLNSHIRE
HOLLIE ROSE	E563	EXETER	5.42	1.20	1993	GREAT BRITAIN
HOLLY ANNE	BM128	BRIXHAM	28.15	167.00	1968	HOLLAND
HOLLY J	SM804	SHOREHAM	6.63	4.01	1988	KENT
HOLLY JANE	WA265	WHITEHAVEN	3.83	0.34	2010	Unk
HOLLY JO	SU512	SOUTHAMPTON	6.90	1.72	2003	ISLE OF WHITE
HOLLY ROSE	OB158	OBAN	8.40	3.83	1979	SOUTH SHIELDS
HOLLYANNA	GU312	GUERNSEY	6.54	1.53	2002	PEMBROKESHIRE
HOMARD	J602	JERSEY	7.77	1.89	1979	JERSEY
HOMARUS	LH13	LEITH	11.18	10.86	1976	CARDIFF
HOMARUS	PL9	PEEL	7.90	1.89	1988	GBR
HOMARUS	PW132	PADSTOW	7.80	4.25	1979	HAYLE
HOMELAND	BCK225	BUCKIE	11.09	17.16	1981	POLRUAN
HOMELAND	BH120	BLYTH	9.98	9.41	1999	CORNWALL
HOMELAND	KY1015	KIRKCALDY	6.33	1.07	2003	SCOTLAND
HOMEWARD BOUND	CE277	COLERAINE	6.56	2.20	1983	PORTAVOGIE
HONEY-BEE	N971	NEWRY	6.51	1.42	2000	PENRYN
HONEYBOURNE III	PD905	PETERHEAD	29.16	215.00	1982	ZUIDBROEK HOLLAND
HONIE BEAU	CK958	COLCHESTER	5.79	0.86	2006	PRO ANGLER
HOOKER	PH477	PLYMOUTH	8.00	1.85	1982	GUERNSEY
HOOVER IT	B249	BELFAST	4.97	0.74	1972	ARUNDEL
HOPE	LK626	LERWICK	9.99	6.21	1952	UNK
HOPE	LR191	LANCASTER	9.15	7.49	1981	MORECOMBE
HOPE	RX71	RYE	5.20	0.83	1988	LONDON
HOPE	SS65	ST IVES	6.05	1.26	2010	PORTUGAL
HOPE	SU514	SOUTHAMPTON	11.99	16.43	2003	CORNWALL
HOPE	TH5	TEIGNMOUTH	4.86	1.08	2009	CAMBORNE CORNWALL
HOPE GAP	NN737	NEWHAVEN	9.83	11.35	2004	ESSEX

UK Fishing Vessels 2015

Vessel Name	Code	Port Name	Loa	Ton Gt	Year	Construction Place
HOPE III	WK118	WICK	9.91	7.95	1971	FALMOUTH
HOPE TOO	RX429	RYE	4.95	0.77	2006	GBR
HOPEFUL	BF55	BANFF	6.05	1.35	2010	GBR
HOPEFUL	K118	KIRKWALL	10.21	10.78	1959	FRASERBURGH
HOPEFUL	LK7	LERWICK	7.41	2.68	1933	BURRAY
HOPEFUL	LR209	LANCASTER	5.14	0.71	1982	LANCS
HOPEFUL	RR32	ROCHESTER	9.95	12.06	1985	ROCHESTER
HOPEFUL I	LL179	LIVERPOOL	11.18	14.99	1988	LYMINGTON
HORACE WRIGHT	WA14	WHITEHAVEN	10.95	13.92	1983	HARRINGTON IN CUMBRIA
HORIZON	CS658	COWES	9.45	7.77	2004	ESSEX
HORIZON	GY1492	GRIMSBY	6.88	2.74	2013	UK
HORIZON 11	FR24	FRASERBURGH	16.75	125.73	1987	HULL
HORNBLOWER	PE163	POOLE	9.24	3.33	1979	WEYMOUTH
HORNET	F167	FAVERSHAM	9.94	11.45	1998	NEWHAVEN
HOT PASTY	GU113	GUERNSEY	9.10	4.54	2006	PENRYN AND GUERNSEY
HOT SHOT	CK3	COLCHESTER	6.95	2.28	2011	ESSEX
HOUR OFF	PZ787	PENZANCE	6.75	1.73	2005	GUERNSEY
HOW ABOUT IT	HL1081	HARTLEPOOL	5.90	1.73	2007	ENGLAND
HOWNI	CA369	CARDIGAN	6.90	1.58	2004	ISLE OF WIGHT
HUERS	SS134	ST IVES	11.00	11.51	1970	PORT MELLON
HUMBLE	PE1164	POOLE	6.60	0.92	2000	GBR
HUNTER	GY368	GRIMSBY	11.30	15.78	1978	CORNWALL
HUNTER	ML445	METHIL	5.51	1.89	1967	GOSPORT
HUNTER II	SC56	SCILLY	8.20	6.60	1977	FALMOUTH
HUNTRESS	GU437	GUERNSEY	7.02	2.01	1971	GUERNSEY
HUNTRESS II	FR979	FRASERBURGH	7.65	2.73	2005	GBR
HUNTRESS OF GRIMSBY	GY15	GRIMSBY	10.80	10.76	2011	CANVEY ISLAND ESSEX
HURST TRADER	M71	MILFORD HAVEN	7.95	2.88	2000	ESSEX
HUSTLER	OB321	OBAN	5.49	0.29	1959	WESTBOURNE
HUSTLER	SE66	SALCOMBE	9.75	6.76	1975	FALMOUTH

UK Fishing Vessels 2015

Vessel Name	Code	Port Name	Loa	Ton Gt	Year	Construction Place
HYDROMYS	CO592	CAERNARVON	4.50	0.84	1997	SOUTHAMPTON
HYPNOS	GU128	GUERNSEY	6.11	1.28	2014	GBR
I DUNNO	SU465	SOUTHAMPTON	6.75	2.67	1969	LYMINGTON
IAIN OG	CN40	CAMPBELTOWN	5.74	1.21	1981	PLYMOUTH
IAN LLOYD	WH90	WEYMOUTH	4.90	1.00	1982	WEYMOUTH
IBIS	FY201	FOWEY	5.87	1.87	2007	LAMBOURNE
ICE	NN60	NEWHAVEN	5.60	2.08	1998	HAILSHAM
ICENE	LT175	LOWESTOFT	9.70	5.22	1991	GUERNSEY
ICHTHUS	TH177	TEIGNMOUTH	12.20	25.65	1990	PENRYN & GUERNSEY
IDA MAY	FH93	FALMOUTH	4.50	0.72	1990	LIZARD CORNWALL
IF ONLY II	YH1245	YARMOUTH	4.58	0.77	2001	GBR
ILAGLYN	K504	KIRKWALL	10.90	14.57	1978	ORKNEY
ILENE	B152	BELFAST	19.99	74.00	1968	BUCKIE
ILENE	OB580	OBAN	5.70	1.32	1991	INVERNESS
ILLUSION	PW2	PADSTOW	8.00	4.10	1990	CYGNUS PENRYN
ILLUSTRIOUS	K616	KIRKWALL	12.07	18.77	1956	FRASERBURGH
IMAGINE	GU237	GUERNSEY	5.10	0.86	1999	EYEMOUTH
IMELDA M	CE79	COLERAINE	5.65	1.23	1989	UNKNOWN
IMMANUEL VII	B78	BELFAST	16.40	44.00	1973	KYLE OF LOCHALSH
IMOAN	N987	NEWRY	5.66	1.09	2006	GBR
IMOGEN	FY470	FOWEY	10.40	24.00	1991	POLRUAN
IMOGEN III	PZ110	PENZANCE	14.50	39.04	1986	FRANCE
IMPALA	J136	JERSEY	4.30	0.53	2001	SPAIN
IMPULSE	OB547	OBAN	5.60	0.94	1989	CAMPBELTOWN
IMPULSIVE	YH2474	YARMOUTH	6.40	1.58	2001	NORFOLK
INCENTIVE	B89	BELFAST	6.50	1.72	1994	DEVON
INCENTIVE	BH243	BLYTH	9.90	11.96	1991	WHITBY
INCENTIVE	CE279	COLERAINE	9.70	7.38	1988	BRIDPORT
INCENTIVE	CN87	CAMPBELTOWN	4.95	1.04	1984	Unk
INCENTIVE I	WK242	WICK	5.60	0.76	1990	BURTON

UK Fishing Vessels 2015

Vessel Name	Code	Port Name	Loa	Ton Gt	Year	Construction Place
INCENTIVE II	B126	BELFAST	18.50	81.00	1973	EYEMOUTH
INDAVA	YH2	YARMOUTH	6.02	1.37	2006	CO.CORK
INDEPENDENCE	OB196	OBAN	17.90	96.00	1977	FRASERBURGH
INDEPENDENT	FD46	FLEETWOOD	10.59	10.56	1973	Unk
INDEPENDENT	FY851	FOWEY	5.70	1.91	2000	CORNWALL
INDIANNA	LO4	LONDON	13.98	29.14	2009	NEWHAVEN
INFINITY	FR993	FRASERBURGH	7.91	1.99	2007	NOT KNOWN
INGA NESS III	R501	RAMSGATE	11.78	22.09	2004	UK
INGER LIS	GY450	GRIMSBY	15.59	30.81	1974	DENMARK
INGRID MELISSA	HH35	HARWICH	7.62	5.26	1982	ROCHESTER KENT
INISFAIL	N954	NEWRY	4.92	0.70	2003	SUSSEX
INNISFALLEN	FY46	FOWEY	9.96	11.18	1986	CORNWALL
INNOVATOR	BA95	BALLANTRAE	8.98	8.50	1983	WORCESTER
INNOVATOR	MR1	MANCHESTER	13.98	30.36	1993	HULL
INSCHALLA	BCK626	BUCKIE	10.84	10.48	1979	UNKNOWN
INSHALLAH	BRD273	BROADFORD	8.13	3.21	1991	PENRYN CORNWALL
INSOMNIA	FD163	FLEETWOOD	5.51	1.74	2010	SHOREHAM BY SEA WEST SUSSEX
INSOMNIA	J51	JERSEY	8.05	4.05	1998	UK
INSPIRATION	GU338	GUERNSEY	7.02	1.68	1971	ISLE OF WIGHT
INSPIRATION	SS22	ST IVES	5.60	1.52	1966	GBR
INSPIRATION	SU10	SOUTHAMPTON	9.92	10.18	1997	PLYMOUTH
INTEGRITY	BCK39	BUCKIE	6.46	1.61	1997	ISLE OF LEWIS
INTEGRITY	BF420	BANFF	8.11	3.01	1982	GLASGOW
INTEGRITY	CO830	CAERNARVON	10.00	9.11	1962	FRASERBURGH
INTEGRITY	SY304	STORNOWAY	7.01	2.15	1979	CYGNUS HULL
INTEGRITY W	BF41	BANFF	5.98	1.08	1999	GBR
INTER-NOS II	K47	KIRKWALL	8.24	4.66	1981	UNKNOWN
INTREPID	BA100	BALLANTRAE	15.18	39.00	1970	BUCKIE
INTREPID	BCK608	BUCKIE	9.19	3.58	2000	CORNWALL

UK Fishing Vessels 2015

Vessel Name	Code	Port Name	Loa	Ton Gt	Year	Construction Place
INTREPID	BN67	BOSTON	11.20	12.08	1989	HULL
INTREPID	CE694	COLERAINE	9.95	10.59	2006	ENGLAND
INTREPID	E145	EXETER	7.33	3.74	1989	FALMOUTH
INTREPID	LK353	LERWICK	8.02	4.77	1978	ORKNEY
INTREPID	UL56	ULLAPOOL	8.36	4.18	2002	UNITED KINGDOM
INTUITION	TO40	TRURO	17.98	114.00	1995	HAYLE
INVADER	K14	KIRKWALL	10.40	6.35	1989	WADEBRIDGE
INVERDALE	INS29	INVERNESS	26.30	150.90	1992	SPAIN
INVESTOR	FY367	FOWEY	9.75	9.67	1989	BEVERLEY
INVESTOR	OB569	OBAN	9.95	10.87	2004	ENGLAND
IOLAIR	FR33	FRASERBURGH	7.37	3.47	1989	POOLE
IONA	BF849	BANFF	7.30	2.45	1998	MACDUFF
IONA	BRD664	BROADFORD	9.83	11.63	2003	COLCHESTER
IONA	FH23	FALMOUTH	4.50	0.65	1998	CORNWALL
IONA	INS74	INVERNESS	6.14	3.03	2001	MACDUFF
IONA	K1169	KIRKWALL	5.80	1.11	2007	GBR
IONA	OB909	OBAN	9.79	5.00	1997	FALMOUTH
IONA	WH347	WEYMOUTH	6.40	1.69	1972	UNKNOWN
IONA	WK42	WICK	4.58	0.60	1989	Unk
IONA EVE	OB64	OBAN	10.00	8.53	1983	FALMOUTH
IONA LOUISE	CY6	CASTLEBAY	8.20	5.08	1982	HAYLE CORNWALL
IRENE	SH292	SCARBOROUGH	8.53	3.21	1982	SANDSEND
IRENE	WY126	WHITBY	6.02	1.50	1970	WHITBY
IRENE D	YH2487	YARMOUTH	5.69	1.14	1992	ORKNEY BOATS
IRENE D II	YH212	YARMOUTH	6.20	1.63	2010	NORFOLK
IRENE K	A3	ABERDEEN	6.30	1.33	2004	GBR
IRENE M	GU141	GUERNSEY	7.56	4.78	1979	GUERNSEY
IRIS	AH28	ARBROATH	6.93	2.17	1988	POOLE
IRIS	SY18	STORNOWAY	7.80	3.01	1974	HOVE SUSSEX/EASDALE ARGYLL

UK Fishing Vessels 2015

Vessel Name	Code	Port Name	Loa	Ton Gt	Year	Construction Place
IRIS II	BRD19	BROADFORD	11.95	31.35	2004	MACDUFF SHIPYARDS LTD
IRIS.	ME8	MONTROSE	6.90	1.22	2008	ISLE OF WIGHT
IRISH ENTERPRISE	N300	NEWRY	19.81	79.00	1968	NORWAY
IRISH ROVER	CE235	COLERAINE	8.30	5.01	1977	BALLY CASTLE
ISA	BRD658	BROADFORD	5.80	1.15	1985	ORKNEY
ISA	SY14	STORNOWAY	6.10	2.50	1984	GRIMSAY NORTH UIST
ISAAC EDWARD	BK535	BERWICK ON TWEED	7.99	2.60	2004	ICELAND
ISABEL	SD21	SUNDERLAND	9.00	0.18	1947	AMBLE
ISABEL	SM5	SHOREHAM	8.10	4.27	1980	GUERNSEY
ISABEL	WK825	WICK	4.70	0.70	2002	GBR
ISABEL ANNE	SY564	STORNOWAY	4.80	0.69	1987	UNKNOWN
ISABEL MARY	BM26	BRIXHAM	6.80	1.55	2007	GBR
ISABELLA	CY464	CASTLEBAY	11.35	9.46	1995	SUFFOLK
ISABELLA	INS123	INVERNESS	9.96	11.37	1990	CANVEY ISLAND
ISABELLA	ML127	METHIL	4.07	0.41	1982	FIFE
ISABELLA	SD390	SUNDERLAND	9.98	9.63	1988	GBR
ISABELLA	UL8	ULLAPOOL	5.84	1.06	2008	GBR
ISABELLE	FH398	FALMOUTH	6.40	2.69	1968	PENRYN
ISABELLE KATHLEEN	LN74	KINGS LYNN	11.15	8.13	1975	KIRKWALL & WOLVERSTONE
ISADALE	FD177	FLEETWOOD	26.16	149.00	1971	ABERDEEN
ISIS	SC27	SCILLY	7.62	4.88	1980	HAYLE
ISIS	SH278	SCARBOROUGH	8.07	3.53	1998	SCARBOROUGH
ISLA S	DS1	DUMFRIES	40.11	396.00	1990	HOLLAND
ISLAND - PRINCESS	UL610	ULLAPOOL	6.20	2.70	1992	COWES
ISLAND FISHER	B882	BELFAST	4.73	0.70	1992	CUSHENDALL
ISLAND FISHER	CE311	COLERAINE	9.60	6.90	1984	CARDIFF
ISLAND LASS	B983	BELFAST	4.95	0.72	2007	NOT KNOWN
ISLAND LASS	SM272	SHOREHAM	7.32	2.46	1984	ISLE OF WIGHT
ISLAND LASS	SU950	SOUTHAMPTON	7.00	1.41	1980	ISLE OF WIGHT
ISLAND VENTURE	B104	BELFAST	7.50	3.90	1975	BANGOR

UK Fishing Vessels 2015

Vessel Name	Code	Port Name	Loa	Ton Gt	Year	Construction Place
ISLANDER	BA316	BALLANTRAE	16.66	35.00	1967	GIRVAN
ISLANDER	SC119	SCILLY	6.21	2.31	1988	MALAHIDE IRELAND
ISLE JERSEY	J59	JERSEY	4.62	0.58	1990	GBJ
ISLE RISTOL	UL34	ULLAPOOL	9.92	2.66	2001	Unk
ISOBEL KATE	SM685	SHOREHAM	7.10	1.83	1981	ISLE OF WIGHT
ITSIE BITSIE	BN428	BOSTON	10.55	9.53	2000	RIVERSIDE
IVY	PE113	POOLE	5.99	0.60	1934	POOLE
IVY DAWN	SA451	SWANSEA	6.90	1.30	1996	CHEETAH MARINE CATAMARANS
IVY LEAF	LK339	LERWICK	9.24	7.06	1973	STROMNESS
IVY ROSE	PD142	PETERHEAD	7.46	3.19	1992	SOUTH GARE TEESPORT
IVY ROSS	CO316	CAERNARVON	5.80	1.27	1997	ARUNDEL
IYSHA	GY341	GRIMSBY	18.91	60.00	1977	DENMARK
IZZY MAD	NN777	NEWHAVEN	8.47	2.32	1974	TREGATREATH
J & B	CS635	COWES	9.58	7.87	1998	COWES
J & N	SA1241	SWANSEA	4.04	0.34	2004	GBR
J AND A	OB149	OBAN	6.00	2.40	1992	SUFFOLK
J B	BS427	BEAUMARIS	5.05	0.84	1992	UK
J B P	GU103	GUERNSEY	8.07	4.05	1992	PENRYN CORNWALL
J C D	GU22	GUERNSEY	6.65	0.58	2008	MAIA PORTO DA LOBOS
J C L	WY57	WHITBY	5.74	1.08	1984	WHITBY
J KADASS II	H291	HULL	6.90	0.77	2010	VENTNOR ISLE OF WIGHT
J M T	M99	MILFORD HAVEN	10.00	9.11	1994	HULL
J O	BD169	BIDEFORD	3.69	0.33	1948	APPLEDORE NORTH DEVON
J R R	SA246	SWANSEA	7.72	2.73	1962	ACLE
J.J.	HL11	HARTLEPOOL	11.52	15.56	1998	GRIMSBY
J.T. GANNET	WY366	WHITBY	5.84	1.07	1986	LYTHE NR WHITBY
JAANA B	BN78	BOSTON	11.86	13.72	1982	FOSDYKE
JACAMAR	CN57	CAMPBELTOWN	8.57	3.07	1999	CORNWALL
JACAMAR II	SY16	STORNOWAY	9.66	7.16	2005	ISLE OF WIGHT

UK Fishing Vessels 2015

Vessel Name	Code	Port Name	Loa	Ton Gt	Year	Construction Place
JACINTH III	BF47	BANFF	4.80	0.74	1990	GBR
JACINTH W	BF272	BANFF	7.30	2.43	1990	STONEHAVEN
JACK	CK941	COLCHESTER	5.22	0.74	1980	NOT KNOWN
JACK HENRY	RX403	RYE	9.95	11.91	1999	NEWHAVEN
JACK OLLIE	LA10	LLANELLI	5.80	1.22	2014	UK
JACKALEE	SA5	SWANSEA	9.80	4.76	1979	PEMBROKE DOCK
JACKANNY	PZ779	PENZANCE	4.68	1.00	1988	UNK
JACKIE B	A15	ABERDEEN	5.57	1.12	1992	PLYMOUTH
JACKIE II	LI373	LITTLEHAMPTON	5.52	0.89	1980	BOGNOR
JACKIE M	OB908	OBAN	6.90	1.29	1998	BEDHAMPTON
JACKIE MARIE	PZ495	PENZANCE	5.60	1.51	1978	HAYLE
JACKO IV	F38	FAVERSHAM	5.00	1.41	1992	KINGSBRIDGE DEVON
JACKY J	OB2	OBAN	8.30	2.86	1979	PORT ISAC CORNWALL
JACKY-AN	LA47	LLANELLI	7.15	1.81	1981	BRIDGEND
JACLYN L	K391	KIRKWALL	4.94	1.34	2007	CAMBORNE
JACOB	FY842	FOWEY	3.86	0.61	1998	NOT KNOWN
JACOBA	BM77	BRIXHAM	22.18	126.00	1988	BROMBOROUGH
JACOBA	PZ307	PENZANCE	37.50	417.95	1975	HOLLAND
JACOBITE	OB560	OBAN	9.82	14.54	1992	GIRVAN SCOTLAND
JACOMINA	BM208	BRIXHAM	29.85	153.00	1968	ZAANDAM NETHERLANDS
JACQUELINE	A13	ABERDEEN	4.98	0.45	1982	ABERDEEN
JACQUELINE	BRD279	BROADFORD	6.50	1.74	1988	EXMOUTH
JACQUELINE	CO511	CAERNARVON	7.70	4.00	1991	CORNWALL
JACQUELINE	FE63	FOLKESTONE	9.00	4.66	1983	RAMSGATE
JACQUELINE	PW474	PADSTOW	6.78	2.73	1965	CORNWALL
JACQUELINE ANNE	CO555	CAERNARVON	9.90	19.11	1997	WHITBY
JACQUELINE ANNE	FE268	FOLKESTONE	8.25	4.06	1995	KENT
JACQUELINE ANNE	FH729	FALMOUTH	10.94	12.04	2005	CORNWALL
JACQUELINE ANNE	FR243	FRASERBURGH	23.00	227.00	2013	SCOTLAND
JACQUELINE STEPHENSON	BK155	BERWICK ON TWEED	9.45	4.27	1962	AMBLE

UK Fishing Vessels 2015

Vessel Name	Code	Port Name	Loa	Ton Gt	Year	Construction Place
JACQUI A	FH732	FALMOUTH	9.95	11.46	2000	GBR
JACQUI B	OB925	OBAN	8.37	5.98	1998	ARGYLL
JADE	PZ695	PENZANCE	5.90	1.33	1978	PENRYN CORNWALL
JADE ELIN	K1153	KIRKWALL	5.30	0.76	2003	SUFFOLK
JADE KATRICE	MH226	MIDDLESBROUGH	5.90	0.98	1988	LYTHE NR. WHITBY
JADE S	J401	JERSEY	8.05	4.31	1990	GBR
JAFA	SM17	SHOREHAM	5.54	1.14	1979	BOGNOR
JAFFA	PE741	POOLE	7.56	2.91	1980	POOLE
JAIME LOUISE	BN23	BOSTON	10.05	7.49	1992	HULL
JAKE	PE512	POOLE	6.00	1.04	1975	FAREHAM
JALETO	MT105	MARYPORT	9.88	10.34	1999	CORNWALL
JAMBO	NN51	NEWHAVEN	5.38	1.02	1992	SOUTH AFRICA
JAMES DENYER	SN7	NORTH SHIELDS	9.83	3.65	1969	AMBLE
JAMES GARY	CK351	COLCHESTER	9.15	5.20	1982	MORECAMBE
JAMES LEE	RY57	RAMSEY	13.15	17.46	1984	UNK
JAMES R.H. STEVENSON	PZ78	PENZANCE	29.80	153.00	1969	HOLLAND
JAMIAIN II	BRD120	BROADFORD	9.95	5.67	2007	SOMERSET
JAMIE	RX273	RYE	5.05	0.77	1993	HAVANT HAMPSHIRE
JAMIE LOUISE	PE1078	POOLE	5.85	0.72	1997	GBR
JAMIE M	LO583	LONDON	8.37	3.52	1976	CARDIFF
JAMISA	LK109	LERWICK	8.53	3.36	1971	SHETLAND
JAN	LH126	LEITH	6.19	2.47	1980	EYEMOUTH
JAN B	BE1	BARNSTAPLE	7.32	3.65	1971	PENZANCE
JAN FISHER	J6	JERSEY	6.52	1.69	1983	UK
JAN LE CLAIR	BS17	BEAUMARIS	6.40	1.59	1985	GLAN CONWY
JANALI	FR964	FRASERBURGH	6.90	1.74	1991	STONEHAVEN
JANE ANNE I	YH2454	YARMOUTH	4.50	0.66	1996	UNKNOWN
JANE ELIZABETH	SM75	SHOREHAM	11.47	23.01	1990	PADSTOW
JANE ELIZABETH	WY144	WHITBY	11.55	8.54	1960	WHITBY

UK Fishing Vessels 2015

Vessel Name	Code	Port Name	Loa	Ton Gt	Year	Construction Place
JANE I	KY458	KIRKCALDY	4.84	0.69	1996	UNK
JANE LOUISE	FH353	FALMOUTH	7.75	5.84	1985	GBR
JANEARL	B885	BELFAST	8.62	8.79	1983	WORCESTER
JANET	NN4	NEWHAVEN	4.88	0.71	1968	NEWHAVEN
JANET ANN	SC1	SCILLY	5.60	1.17	1977	PLYMOUTH
JANET V	GU39	GUERNSEY	8.64	2.58	2006	WADEBRIDGE
JANET V	GU39	GUERNSEY	6.89	2.43	2012	GUERNSEY
JANICE MARY	PW20	PADSTOW	6.00	0.68	2002	UNITED KINGDOM
JANILO	GU53	GUERNSEY	5.00	1.24	2006	GUERNSEY
JANINE	SY48	STORNOWAY	9.57	11.09	1971	WICK HIGHLAND REGION
JANMAR	LK980	LERWICK	8.15	2.40	1980	LONDON
JANN DENISE	FR80	FRASERBURGH	16.51	42.00	1971	FRASERBURGH
JANN DENISE III	SH293	SCARBOROUGH	6.70	1.82	1976	WHITBY
JANREEN	LH254	LEITH	11.90	16.83	1968	RAMSGATE
JANWAL II	SD277	SUNDERLAND	10.50	8.01	1990	BRIDLINGTON
JAS N	LH50	LEITH	10.01	6.20	2005	HAFNARFJOROUR
JASMINE	FH75	FALMOUTH	5.30	1.53	1982	CHARLESTOWN
JASMINE	PH457	PLYMOUTH	5.00	0.69	1993	W SUSSEX ENGLAND
JASON A	H106	HULL	6.97	2.43	1987	WHITBY
JASON II	J180	JERSEY	5.58	1.06	1984	Unk
JASPER	FH14	FALMOUTH	5.42	1.05	2003	PORTUGAL
JASPER	LK617	LERWICK	7.92	4.38	1998	ALDEBURGH
JASPER II	BF3	BANFF	10.93	15.29	1990	WHITBY
JASTLO C	OB145	OBAN	11.90	19.96	1990	BALMUCHY BY FEARN
JAWS	MN204	MALDON	5.36	0.76	1959	UNKNOWN
JAY	B27	BELFAST	8.11	5.72	1980	PENRYN
JAY C	E333	EXETER	11.95	25.23	2010	WALES
JAY-O	M174	MILFORD HAVEN	5.37	1.03	1981	NORFOLK
JAY-R	SU437	SOUTHAMPTON	6.20	0.65	1997	BONCHURCH VENTNOR
JAYDEE	WO270	WORKINGTON	4.64	0.64	1982	PORTSMOUTH
JAYLEE	NN84	NEWHAVEN	4.48	0.84	1970	NEWHAVEN

UK Fishing Vessels 2015

Vessel Name	Code	Port Name	Loa	Ton Gt	Year	Construction Place
JAYNE	LN110	KINGS LYNN	9.65	5.57	1973	KING'S LYNN
JAYNE	LR448	LANCASTER	5.92	1.00	1978	LANCASHIRE
JAYNE MARIE	YH909	YARMOUTH	6.40	1.79	1995	NOROLK
JBP	E17	EXETER	8.07	5.75	1992	ENGLAND
JEAN	LA579	LLANELLI	4.65	0.62	1992	LLANELLI
JEAN KELLY	CO1	CAERNARVON	5.40	1.06	2008	GBR
JEAN M	BS235	BEAUMARIS	6.57	1.25	2008	HOLYHEAD
JEAN YVONNE	GU21	GUERNSEY	6.75	2.91	1960	SOUTHAMPTON
JEAN-FRANCES	OB147	OBAN	9.60	9.31	1983	PENRYN
JEANNIE	A440	ABERDEEN	6.40	0.97	2008	SUFFOLK
JEANNIE	BRD15	BROADFORD	5.40	0.94	2005	GLASGOW
JEANNIE D	FR422	FRASERBURGH	6.05	1.97	1968	MONTROSE SCOTLAND
JEMET III	SY823	STORNOWAY	6.40	1.74	2000	IRELAND
JEMMA T	WH590	WEYMOUTH	7.39	2.26	1990	HAVANT HANTS
JEMONA	INS1035	INVERNESS	6.25	0.78	2001	GBR
JEN	SS170	ST IVES	4.87	1.05	1985	PLYMOUTH
JEN LOU II	FH200	FALMOUTH	5.00	0.77	1978	FALMOUTH
JENISKA	B916	BELFAST	16.68	42.00	1971	ST. MONANCE
JENNA	ME122	MONTROSE	7.88	1.82	1996	CYGNUS MARINE
JENNA H	BK69	BERWICK ON TWEED	9.60	6.14	2004	CORNWALL
JENNA LEA	LL272	LIVERPOOL	12.95	23.12	1992	HANSWEED
JENNA MAREE	BF73	BANFF	9.84	10.94	1998	PENRYN
JENNA-DEE	J90	JERSEY	10.90	14.88	1989	UK
JENNADORE	SM188	SHOREHAM	9.73	9.56	2007	COLCHESTER
JENNAH D	SM688	SHOREHAM	13.90	27.23	1995	EAST SUSSEX
JENNIFER ANNE	PE1167	POOLE	6.53	1.16	2005	LYMINGTON
JENNIFER ANNE II	PE13	POOLE	6.90	1.52	2009	POOLE
JENNIFER MARGARET	WY304	WHITBY	9.97	5.81	1979	WHITBY
JENNRHI K	CN11	CAMPBELTOWN	4.88	0.89	1995	ARRUNDEL
JENNY	PZ20	PENZANCE	4.69	0.78	1980	ST LEVAN

UK Fishing Vessels 2015

Vessel Name	Code	Port Name	Loa	Ton Gt	Year	Construction Place
JENNY A	M260	MILFORD HAVEN	5.49	1.03	1989	ENGLAND
JENNY D	GU78	GUERNSEY	5.00	0.83	1985	YAPTON ARUNDEL
JENNY G	P987	PORTSMOUTH	10.27	9.11	2001	PENRYN
JENNY JAMES	FY545	FOWEY	3.81	0.45	1972	KINGS LYNN
JENNY LASS	FR980	FRASERBURGH	6.40	1.75	2005	FIFE
JENNY M	SN57	NORTH SHIELDS	8.35	4.46	1982	GREECE
JESS	CK946	COLCHESTER	9.25	10.51	2005	BARTON UPON HUMBER
JESSICA	PD220	PETERHEAD	4.25	0.56	1980	GBR
JESSICA BETH	YH2484	YARMOUTH	5.21	1.08	1993	GBR
JESSICA GRACE	FY807	FOWEY	9.70	9.29	1997	POLRUAN
JESSICA IONE	AB22	ABERYSTWYTH	6.42	2.17	1999	PENZANCE
JESSICA LOUISE	OB237	OBAN	9.95	11.71	1990	PENRYN CORNWALL
JESSICA LYNN	PE1044	POOLE	8.07	4.88	1997	POOLE
JESSICA M	CK157	COLCHESTER	9.92	8.00	1988	HULL
JESSICA MAY	LH601	LEITH	8.02	4.28	1991	UK
JESSICA ROSE	PE767	POOLE	6.54	1.40	1978	POOLE
JESSIE	J292	JERSEY	4.50	0.75	1988	UK
JESSIE ALICE	HL81	HARTLEPOOL	9.97	8.15	1988	HARLTLEPOOL
JEST	PZ24	PENZANCE	6.95	1.87	2013	PORTUGAL
JEWEL	BF42	BANFF	5.90	1.13	2008	GBR
JIL	ME224	MONTROSE	4.77	0.50	2000	GBR
JILL	WO664	WORKINGTON	5.00	0.72	1998	BRITAIN
JILL ANNE	LT98	LOWESTOFT	6.10	2.53	1984	FELIXSTOWE
JILLMAR	J317	JERSEY	3.75	0.37	1978	SWEDEN
JILLY	PE416	POOLE	6.21	0.73	1968	MUDEFORD
JIM	CO281	CAERNARVON	4.41	0.64	1963	ABERDARON
JIMMY JOE	WH336	WEYMOUTH	5.62	1.51	1992	WEYMOUTH
JINGLING GEORDIE	BH138	BLYTH	4.65	0.91	1974	WHITLEY BAY
JINNY	M49	MILFORD HAVEN	5.35	1.01	1980	ENGLAND
JIZ WEAZLE	DH69	DARTMOUTH	4.35	0.53	1972	KINGSBRIDGE DEVON

UK Fishing Vessels 2015

Vessel Name	Code	Port Name	Loa	Ton Gt	Year	Construction Place
JJ	GU484	GUERNSEY	5.00	0.82	1992	ARUNDEL
JO ANNA	SM2	SHOREHAM	5.08	0.92	1980	BOGNOR REGIS
JO JO	CS670	COWES	7.80	2.13	2007	ISLE OF WIGHT
JO JO	GU334	GUERNSEY	5.53	1.53	1981	PLYMOUTH
JO JO LOUISE	GU154	GUERNSEY	5.53	1.53	1990	PLYMOUTH
JO-ANN	R5	RAMSGATE	6.10	1.36	1988	RYE
JOAN E	HH10	HARWICH	8.11	2.51	1987	HARWICH
JOANNA	CA57	CARDIGAN	5.57	1.09	1980	MOYLEGROVE
JOANNA	CY701	CASTLEBAY	17.16	76.00	1980	BUCKIE
JOANNA	NN137	NEWHAVEN	13.98	30.64	1989	NEWHAVEN
JOANNA C	BM265	BRIXHAM	13.94	38.07	1980	NEYLAND MILFORD HAVEN
JOANNE	BH15	BLYTH	5.15	1.22	2007	SCOTLAND
JOANNE CLAIRE	LK3376	LERWICK	8.10	4.31	1997	PENRYN
JOANNE LOISE	LI574	LITTLEHAMPTON	6.23	1.09	2012	SELSEY WEST SUSSEX
JOANNE T	H79	HULL	6.07	1.65	1991	DISS NORFOLK
JOBERT	LO243	LONDON	11.75	10.30	1979	ESSEX
JOCALINDA	RX1	RYE	9.93	11.10	1988	RYE
JOCELYN	WH445	WEYMOUTH	6.94	1.79	1970	ST SAMSONS GUERNSEY
JODA	SS24	ST IVES	6.00	1.28	2009	PORTUGAL
JODIE	GU114	GUERNSEY	3.58	0.47	2002	GUERNSEY
JODIE	PH4	PLYMOUTH	5.64	1.15	1997	YAPTON ARUNDEL WEST SUSSEX
JODIE ANN	DH300	DARTMOUTH	6.74	1.52	1992	BUDE CORNWALL
JODIE B	P977	PORTSMOUTH	9.80	7.90	1998	CORNWALL
JOE'S GIRL	CO53	CAERNARVON	6.97	4.00	1979	PORTSMOUTH
JOHANNA	NN56	NEWHAVEN	14.16	31.23	1985	NEWHAVEN
JOHN B	BM522	BRIXHAM	9.60	5.21	1998	PEMBROKE
JOHN BARRY	SH87	SCARBOROUGH	9.30	3.18	1972	RYE LYMINGTON
JOHN BOY	N1	NEWRY	8.33	5.37	1987	CLACTON ESSEX
JOHN BOY	SM469	SHOREHAM	5.50	1.43	1991	BOGNOR
JOHN DOE	LA636	LLANELLI	4.94	1.03	2007	PRESTON

UK Fishing Vessels 2015

Vessel Name	Code	Port Name	Loa	Ton Gt	Year	Construction Place
JOHN EDWARD	CS628	COWES	11.97	27.74	1996	FRESHWATER
JOHN EDWARD	P976	PORTSMOUTH	9.98	3.41	1999	HAYLING ISLAND
JOHN LOUISE	PZ689	PENZANCE	4.76	1.20	1980	HAYLE
JOHN WESLEY	SS284	ST IVES	11.95	32.82	1981	HAYLE
JOHN WILLY	LN465	KINGS LYNN	13.77	23.66	2001	BORTH
JOHNATHAN SEAGULL	PE112	POOLE	5.17	0.99	1985	HAMPSHIRE
JOHNY II	A955	ABERDEEN	6.02	1.26	2005	MONTROSE ANGUS
JOINT VENTURE	DH183	DARTMOUTH	7.95	3.41	1982	CORNWALL
JOKER OF NAVAX	WA22	WHITEHAVEN	7.83	4.32	1983	UNKNOWN
JOKERS WILD	P7	PORTSMOUTH	5.30	0.93	1981	BURY ST EDMONDS
JOLA	LI116	LITTLEHAMPTON	5.02	0.61	1975	BOGNOR REGIS SUSSEX
JOLA	OB12	OBAN	8.50	3.04	2010	ISLE OF WIGHT
JOLANDA	CL4	CARLISLE	11.50	22.16	1990	ALEXANDRA DOCK IN HULL
JOLENE	LN468	KINGS LYNN	11.92	22.97	2002	HUMBERSIDE
JOLENE	LT1020	LOWESTOFT	9.83	9.32	2005	SUFFOLK
JOLIE M	GU33	GUERNSEY	9.25	5.54	2000	PENRYN
JON BOY	CK14	COLCHESTER	5.16	0.84	2004	BECCLES SUFFOLK
JONATHAN JAMES	YH458	YARMOUTH	5.82	1.31	2002	NORTH WALSHAM
JORDAN A	BM225	BRIXHAM	27.53	139.00	1968	DEN OEVER
JORDAN I	H1094	HULL	8.20	2.94	2000	ISLE OF WIGHT
JORJA LOUISE	P2	PORTSMOUTH	9.30	4.29	1970	GBR
JORY	CO328	CAERNARVON	6.90	5.21	1978	UNITED KINGDOM
JOSA	BRD674	BROADFORD	4.86	0.66	1995	GBR
JOSEPH COOK II	BRD685	BROADFORD	7.20	1.43	1980	PLYMOUTH
JOSEPH WILLIAM	IH89	IPSWICH	6.90	2.89	2007	SUFFOLK
JOSEPH WILLIAM II	LT1001	LOWESTOFT	5.90	2.51	1989	ALDEBURGH SUFFOLK
JOSEPHINE	PZ111	PENZANCE	5.55	0.94	2007	ORKNEY
JOSH II	PZ79	PENZANCE	5.55	1.13	1980	UNKNOWN
JOSHUA B	LA106	LLANELLI	5.25	1.12	1986	ISLE OF WIGHT

UK Fishing Vessels 2015

Vessel Name	Code	Port Name	Loa	Ton Gt	Year	Construction Place
JOSIE AN	LA48	LLANELLI	7.38	1.57	2007	ANGLESEY
JOSIE ANNE	LK707	LERWICK	8.00	6.10	1994	CORNWALL
JOWEST	ME4	MONTROSE	5.95	1.96	1972	JOHNSHAVEN
JOY	CY150	CASTLEBAY	5.71	1.21	1988	SUSSEX
JOY OF LADRAM	E22	EXETER	20.40	109.00	1988	FRANCE
JP	OB6	OBAN	9.85	14.27	2009	ESSEX
JSW	PZ2	PENZANCE	4.45	0.68	1996	PENZANCE
JUBILEE	M16	MILFORD HAVEN	5.10	0.91	1985	GBR
JUBILEE BELLE	FY922	FOWEY	6.00	2.58	1984	Unk
JUBILEE GIRL	J27	JERSEY	5.02	0.63	2010	GBR
JUBILEE GIRL	LT987	LOWESTOFT	4.86	0.57	1984	UNKNOWN
JUBILEE JOY	IH290	IPSWICH	7.28	4.62	1977	WOODBRIDGE
JUBILEE PRIDE	GY903	GRIMSBY	17.76	47.00	1979	DENMARK
JUBILEE QUEST	GY900	GRIMSBY	21.67	195.00	2009	WHITBY NORTH YORKSHIRE
JUBILEE SPIRIT	GY25	GRIMSBY	21.20	178.00	1997	HULL
JUCLO	J350	JERSEY	4.26	0.56	1992	UK
JUDITH CLAIRE	B61	BELFAST	5.27	0.49	1985	CO FERMANAGH
JUDY JANE	OB546	OBAN	7.40	3.90	1981	COWES ISLE OF WIGHT
JUELAN	HL238	HARTLEPOOL	9.95	13.65	1991	GBR
JULIA ANN	BRD97	BROADFORD	9.08	7.71	1973	MEVAGISSEY
JULIA HELEN	LT546	LOWESTOFT	9.91	3.74	1951	UNK
JULIA P	GU109	GUERNSEY	6.94	1.37	2004	COLCHESTER
JULIA'S GIRL	PE26	POOLE	9.35	4.42	1974	KEYHAVEN
JULIE	CN50	CAMPBELTOWN	4.88	0.66	1981	SUSSEX
JULIE ANN	SD9	SUNDERLAND	8.70	4.19	1990	HARTLEPOOL
JULIE ANN	SM444	SHOREHAM	5.58	1.39	1983	BOGNOR
JULIE ANNE	PE1158	POOLE	7.00	0.94	2003	DORSET
JULIE D	SN365	NORTH SHIELDS	8.55	3.73	1990	CORNWALL
JULIE D	UL7	ULLAPOOL	9.75	5.65	1982	IRELAND
JULIE EM	LT10	LOWESTOFT	5.70	0.89	1983	CORNWALL

UK Fishing Vessels 2015

Vessel Name	Code	Port Name	Loa	Ton Gt	Year	Construction Place
JULIE GIRL	PW81	PADSTOW	8.15	2.44	1980	PORTHLEVEN CORNWALL
JULIE JEAN	FE380	FOLKESTONE	9.03	3.74	2008	GBR
JULIE KAREN	SN110	NORTH SHIELDS	9.88	5.43	1975	AMBLE
JULIE M	CT32	CASTLETOWN	8.40	4.32	1989	GBR
JULIE-ANN	LK292	LERWICK	8.25	4.80	1997	CORNWALL
JULUGA	RX303	RYE	9.20	5.74	1982	RYE
JUMBO I	LA588	LLANELLI	4.21	0.64	2000	GBR
JUNA	LK38	LERWICK	10.51	10.87	1970	SHETLAND ISLES
JUNE ROSE	K132	KIRKWALL	9.10	4.80	1967	SWEDEN
JUNE ROSE	LK779	LERWICK	8.89	5.05	1977	SOUTH SHIELDS
JUNE ROSE	PL4	PEEL	9.84	14.97	1995	UNITED KINGDOM
JUNE ROSE	SY99	STORNOWAY	7.94	6.45	1938	FRASERBURGH
JUNE-ANNE	SY38	STORNOWAY	7.78	3.89	1979	CORNWALL
JURA	SR100	STRANRAER	6.46	1.54	2001	ORKNEY
JURABLE	CN14	CAMPBELTOWN	7.12	2.17	1990	FALMOUTH
JURASELL	OB576	OBAN	9.15	5.48	1993	PENRYN CORNWALL
JUROMA	BA584	BALLANTRAE	5.90	0.94	1991	UNKNOWN
JUST JAYDA	LH30	LEITH	5.57	1.64	1948	TEIGNMOUTH
JUST MINE	CN397	CAMPBELTOWN	7.77	4.50	1981	CORNWALL
JUST REWARD	BF64	BANFF	14.00	31.97	1989	STROMNESS
JUST REWARD	KY198	KIRKCALDY	9.70	20.77	1991	SUNDERLAND
JUST REWARD	LH552	LEITH	6.40	1.33	2000	EAST LOTHIAN
JUST REWARD	SM161	SHOREHAM	5.43	0.84	1994	BOGNOR
JUST RIGHT	GU77	GUERNSEY	9.22	4.75	1982	COWES IOW
JUSTINE MARIE	LN119	KINGS LYNN	13.47	16.10	1988	KINGS LYNN
K C H	BD5	BIDEFORD	4.33	0.54	1980	ENGLAND
K G ONE	RX443	RYE	9.80	7.22	2008	ESSEX
K II	H5	HULL	9.99	10.11	2005	PEPE BOATYARD
K T J	M38	MILFORD HAVEN	11.55	15.20	1983	APPLEDORE
K-SANDS	BE29	BARNSTAPLE	3.80	0.28	1989	UNK
K2	E63	EXETER	9.27	7.85	1979	PENRYN

UK Fishing Vessels 2015

Vessel Name	Code	Port Name	Loa	Ton Gt	Year	Construction Place
K2	KY505	KIRKCALDY	6.46	3.33	1992	WIRRAL MERSEYSIDE
KAELLA ROSE	K67	KIRKWALL	9.15	3.88	1999	CORNWALL
KAIROS	BF36	BANFF	18.28	125.35	1988	ST MONANS
KAISA MARI	FH672	FALMOUTH	5.10	1.14	1998	CORNWALL
KALA	INS2	INVERNESS	4.98	0.79	1975	SCOTLAND
KALISTO	BF555	BANFF	9.45	6.01	1981	GARDENSTOWN
KALUGER	WH584	WEYMOUTH	9.85	20.12	1991	SUNDERLAND
KARA LOUISE	AD5	ARDROSSAN	5.99	1.15	2002	PENRYN
KARAN	FY566	FOWEY	7.77	3.93	1979	HAYLE
KARANNA	LK33	LERWICK	8.79	4.45	1973	WESTRAY
KAREN	B317	BELFAST	19.23	50.00	1975	DENMARK
KAREN	CK38	COLCHESTER	4.87	0.93	1984	SCOTLAND
KAREN JANE	WK36	WICK	8.12	4.40	1999	CORNWALL
KAREN LYNN	WH407	WEYMOUTH	7.30	3.52	1988	FALMOUTH
KAREN MARIE	PE474	POOLE	9.94	13.40	1989	SUNDERLAND
KAREN N	PZ10	PENZANCE	23.13	121.00	1990	POL
KAREN ROSE	PE755	POOLE	6.35	1.12	2002	LYTCHETT BAY MARINE
KARENANN II	FR559	FRASERBURGH	23.98	193.00	1981	ABERDEEN
KARENJO	LR9	LANCASTER	5.65	1.10	1990	ARUNDEL SUEEEX
KARENZA	RY5	RAMSEY	6.16	2.46	2014	GBR
KARENZA JAYNE	FH88	FALMOUTH	6.62	1.27	1986	FALMOUTH
KARIMA	N96	NEWRY	26.10	158.00	1978	ST. MALO BRITTANY
KARINYA	FR699	FRASERBURGH	18.26	120.00	1982	BUCKIE
KARLEE	CK230	COLCHESTER	6.30	0.89	1975	BRIGHTLINGSEA
KARMA	SD19	SUNDERLAND	6.50	3.23	1990	CELLARDYKE
KARMA BAY	CO734	CAERNARVON	4.87	0.99	2004	GBR
KARMALOR	H1123	HULL	9.00	4.03	2006	ISLE OF WIGHT
KASEY MARIE	BM517	BRIXHAM	13.40	35.56	1983	HEPWORTH
KASTEL PAOL	P1007	PORTSMOUTH	16.45	56.00	1962	FRANCE
KATE H	LA177	LLANELLI	9.82	6.63	1977	WESTON SUPER MARE
KATH B	PD26	PETERHEAD	4.90	1.11	2003	CORNWALL

UK Fishing Vessels 2015

Vessel Name	Code	Port Name	Loa	Ton Gt	Year	Construction Place
KATHANN	E30	EXETER	5.90	1.08	1996	STONEHAVEN
KATHERINE	LO58	LONDON	12.30	17.17	1987	LEIGH ON SEA
KATHLEEN	CH66	CHESTER	7.44	3.00	1989	UNK
KATHLEEN	LK64	LERWICK	9.82	7.32	1996	FALMOUTH
KATHLEEN	PZ86	PENZANCE	6.05	2.03	1979	FOWEY
KATHLEEN	SD107	SUNDERLAND	8.20	1.89	1949	SEAHOUSES
KATHLEEN	TT5	TARBERT	11.91	16.85	1991	HULL
KATHLEEN ELLEN	LO51	LONDON	9.87	2.70	1965	PORTSMOUTH
KATHLEEN II	WH758	WEYMOUTH	6.70	1.57	1980	GBR
KATHLEEN MAY	CA375	CARDIGAN	6.50	1.98	2002	CORNWALL
KATHRYN AND SARAH II	SH218	SCARBOROUGH	8.90	3.76	1970	WHITBY
KATHRYN JAMES	BN190	BOSTON	13.52	20.66	1996	SOUTH HUMBERSIDE
KATHRYN LOUISE II	FH629	FALMOUTH	4.50	0.68	1985	CORNWALL
KATIE	P176	PORTSMOUTH	9.14	7.24	1948	SHOREHAM
KATIE	UL16	ULLAPOOL	6.47	1.60	2007	SCOTLAND
KATIE	WK12	WICK	4.82	0.65	1977	ABERDEEN
KATIE BHEAG	OB986	OBAN	7.23	2.04	1979	UNKNOWN
KATIE C	GU74	GUERNSEY	9.95	11.99	2003	HUMBERSIDE
KATIE CLAIRE	CN4	CAMPBELTOWN	13.45	30.86	1996	FOWEY
KATIE H	WY150	WHITBY	6.47	1.71	1971	WHITBY
KATIE JANE	SD3	SUNDERLAND	5.86	1.48	2014	UK
KATIE LIL	FY180	FOWEY	5.90	2.01	1986	CORNWALL
KATIE LOU	CO538	CAERNARVON	4.94	0.82	1990	UNKNOWN
KATIE LOU	UL107	ULLAPOOL	9.76	4.55	1973	RYE
KATIE MAREE	WK680	WICK	4.77	0.67	1985	GBR
KATIE MAY	B7	BELFAST	6.32	1.07	1998	CO ANTRIM
KATIE NA MARA	KY9	KIRKCALDY	7.96	2.69	2007	CORNWALL
KATIES PRIDE	FY834	FOWEY	5.50	1.12	2001	CORNWALL
KATRINA	M18	MILFORD HAVEN	6.79	1.57	2000	KENT
KATRINA MAY	OB996	OBAN	9.99	7.04	1997	GBR
KATROSE	BA1	BALLANTRAE	5.64	1.45	1991	UNKNOWN

UK Fishing Vessels 2015

Vessel Name	Code	Port Name	Loa	Ton Gt	Year	Construction Place
KATY	B966	BELFAST	5.14	0.85	1993	IRELAND
KATY	CS295	COWES	4.40	0.51	1975	ISLE OF WIGHT
KATY	PZ18	PENZANCE	4.89	1.04	2005	CAMBORNE
KATY ANNE	H1063	HULL	4.93	0.85	1966	HULL
KATY B	SM47	SHOREHAM	9.96	9.43	1987	KENT
KATY JANE	BM487	BRIXHAM	11.70	21.04	1989	RIJNDIJK HOLLAND
KATYS PRIDE	N38	NEWRY	5.55	1.00	1980	GBR
KATYTU	FY124	FOWEY	6.01	1.85	1989	CORNWALL
KAVA	K999	KIRKWALL	4.63	0.52	1989	GBR
KAY LARIE	TH424	TEIGNMOUTH	6.58	3.28	1978	POOLE
KAY WYE	UL198	ULLAPOOL	9.80	8.31	1975	NEW MITTON
KAYA	P12	PORTSMOUTH	6.93	1.28	2006	ISLE OF WIGHT
KAYA	RX89	RYE	9.43	6.30	1974	CARDIFF
KAYLA DAWN	LH570	LEITH	7.40	0.67	1989	GBR
KAYLANA	SY21	STORNOWAY	17.26	64.00	1978	DEVON
KAYLEIGH	WK53	WICK	7.50	3.00	1997	UNKNOWN
KAYLEIGH ANN	BM42	BRIXHAM	6.60	2.48	2004	MACDUFF
KAYLEIGH C	BS218	BEAUMARIS	5.60	0.84	1988	SCOTLAND
KAYLEIGH M	K970	KIRKWALL	13.10	33.64	1991	STROMNESS
KAYLEIGH M	OB15	OBAN	13.08	28.53	1981	OLD KILPATRIC GLASGOW
KBJ	WA256	WHITEHAVEN	6.41	2.56	1980	CORNWALL
KEALINCHA DAWN	N973	NEWRY	11.95	10.93	1996	IRELAND
KEAVY	SR1	STRANRAER	4.73	0.62	1994	UK
KEELEY B	INS178	INVERNESS	5.07	0.81	1994	SUSSEX
KEILA	K121	KIRKWALL	27.36	279.00	1989	USKEDALEN NORWAY
KEIRA	LK3433	LERWICK	6.40	2.40	2000	GBR
KEIRA	SS61	ST IVES	5.75	1.14	2011	CORNWALL
KEIRAN TREFOR	BS494	BEAUMARIS	4.87	0.64	1995	ORKNEY BOATS
KELLIN STAR	A10	ABERDEEN	8.20	8.44	1987	WEYMOUTH
KELLIN STAR	BW10	BARROW	7.33	1.78	2008	SANDWICH KENT

UK Fishing Vessels 2015

Vessel Name	Code	Port Name	Loa	Ton Gt	Year	Construction Place
KELLY	BCK625	BUCKIE	18.17	84.00	1982	BUCKIE
KELLY	N12	NEWRY	6.45	1.83	1996	PENRYN
KELLY GAL	RX299	RYE	6.30	2.38	1980	NEWHAVEN
KELLY GIRL	SS25	ST IVES	5.82	1.95	1981	HAYLE
KELLY J	PH271	PLYMOUTH	7.32	3.22	1978	PLYMOUTH
KELLY MARENA II	BM454	BRIXHAM	9.99	13.09	1998	HUMBERSIDE
KELLY MARIE	SS762	ST IVES	6.10	1.20	2005	CORNWALL
KELSBIR	K1182	KIRKWALL	5.70	1.50	1985	GBR
KELSEY JANE	WH5	WEYMOUTH	8.05	2.41	2008	GBR
KELVIN STAR	WK32	WICK	7.29	3.62	1969	WICK
KELYN MOR	PZ480	PENZANCE	4.62	0.72	1974	PENZANCE
KEMARVIN	WK814	WICK	16.86	82.00	1975	BUCKIE
KENAVO	PZ244	PENZANCE	9.75	11.02	1983	PAIMPOL FRANCE
KENDORA	CY52	CASTLEBAY	4.88	0.86	1985	ANGLESEY
KENDORE	FH258	FALMOUTH	9.91	7.67	1978	FALMOUTH
KENMAUR	K64	KIRKWALL	9.95	12.62	2008	GBR
KERANY	FH613	FALMOUTH	4.75	0.89	1991	FALMOUTH
KERIOLET	CE695	COLERAINE	11.40	15.19	1994	CORNWALL
KERISTUM	SY76	STORNOWAY	17.76	101.00	1963	FRANCE
KERMELLY	RY157	RAMSEY	5.85	1.61	1990	GBR
KERRI	P181	PORTSMOUTH	5.10	0.56	1981	SCRATCH FACE LANE HAVANT
KERRIE MARIE	BM172	BRIXHAM	23.97	150.00	2000	HOLLAND
KERRY MARIA	WA261	WHITEHAVEN	9.98	4.26	2004	ISLE OF WIGHT
KESI G	M1163	MILFORD HAVEN	5.17	0.83	2000	SUSSEX
KESTEVEN	N277	NEWRY	16.84	53.00	1973	BUCKIE
KESTRAL	CN750	CAMPBELTOWN	6.58	1.70	1995	CORNWALL
KESTREL	BCK81	BUCKIE	30.20	180.00	1973	THE NETHERLANDS
KESTREL	BF365	BANFF	7.92	3.47	1980	GARDENSTOWN
KESTREL	FY10	FOWEY	6.55	1.06	1985	CORNWALL
KESTREL	GY388	GRIMSBY	18.25	80.00	1982	BRIGHTLING SEA

UK Fishing Vessels 2015

Vessel Name	Code	Port Name	Loa	Ton Gt	Year	Construction Place
KESTREL	LK268	LERWICK	13.76	26.16	2000	NEWHAVEN
KESTREL	SM360	SHOREHAM	5.25	0.91	1973	SHOREHAM
KESTREL	SN286	NORTH SHIELDS	8.84	3.27	1978	DORSET
KESTREL	SY73	STORNOWAY	7.95	3.88	2008	CORNWALL
KESTREL	WK41	WICK	6.18	1.24	2005	CORNWALL
KESTREL II	J273	JERSEY	4.85	0.81	1983	UK
KESTREL IV	CS81	COWES	5.54	1.10	1972	BEMBRIDGE
KEVALY	SD51	SUNDERLAND	8.45	6.87	1989	RYE
KEVI-TOR-RU	SE80	SALCOMBE	6.10	1.00	1980	PORTHLEVEN
KEVLOU	BD7	BIDEFORD	4.87	0.50	1999	ORKNEY
KEYTE	LH20	LEITH	5.70	1.23	2002	Unk
KEZZA	R19	RAMSGATE	4.40	0.82	1991	GBR
KHELORIN	K1117	KIRKWALL	7.92	2.46	1974	ORKNEY ISLES
KIA-ORA	LK3430	LERWICK	9.25	4.43	2000	UNK
KIEORRAN	INS384	INVERNESS	6.10	1.33	2012	NORTHERN IRELAND
KILDONAN	UL145	ULLAPOOL	16.52	44.00	1969	BUCKIE SCOTLAND
KIM	PE169	POOLE	5.13	0.59	1966	POOLE
KIMBERLEY	H131	HULL	12.15	8.39	1989	PENRYN
KIMBERLEY JO	FH715	FALMOUTH	6.53	3.14	2003	CORNWALL
KIMBERLY	OB345	OBAN	9.35	3.54	1988	HAYLE
KIMBERLY JAYNE	M10	MILFORD HAVEN	4.63	0.77	2008	SOLVA PEMROKESHIRE
KIND OF BLUE	PD1059	PETERHEAD	5.60	1.65	1980	PLYMOUTH
KINDLY LIGHT	B163	BELFAST	9.30	5.32	1973	PORTAVOGIE
KINDLY LIGHT	LK168	LERWICK	9.75	7.10	1963	FRASERBURGH
KINDLY LIGHT D	BK524	BERWICK ON TWEED	7.45	2.70	1990	DORSET
KINDRED SPIRIT	PE1193	POOLE	6.80	1.82	2008	PORTUGAL
KING CHALLENGER	BA87	BALLANTRAE	21.30	192.00	2005	SCOTLAND
KING EXPLORER	BA829	BALLANTRAE	23.66	202.00	2001	HULL
KING QUIDDLE	WH589	WEYMOUTH	4.10	0.58	1992	UNKNOWN
KINGFISHER	BA810	BALLANTRAE	22.94	163.00	1998	PAULL

UK Fishing Vessels 2015

Vessel Name	Code	Port Name	Loa	Ton Gt	Year	Construction Place
KINGFISHER	BCK617	BUCKIE	9.90	20.41	2003	GBR
KINGFISHER	DH110	DARTMOUTH	18.35	122.00	1989	DEN HELDER (HOLLAND)
KINGFISHER	E569	EXETER	8.10	1.90	1998	UK
KINGFISHER	FY17	FOWEY	10.30	11.56	1983	POLRUAN CORNWALL
KINGFISHER	GU308	GUERNSEY	6.70	2.89	1994	FALMOUTH
KINGFISHER	INS20	INVERNESS	6.40	2.66	1978	UK
KINGFISHER	K436	KIRKWALL	11.66	17.58	1991	GIRVAN
KINGFISHER	LT25	LOWESTOFT	6.20	2.25	2007	CORNWALL
KINGFISHER	M31	MILFORD HAVEN	4.90	0.60	1980	PLYMOUTH
KINGFISHER	MT72	MARYPORT	5.50	1.12	2005	UK
KINGFISHER	RX446	RYE	7.95	7.09	2008	NEWHAVEN
KINGFISHER	TT262	TARBERT	6.28	1.70	1989	SUFFOLK
KINGFISHER	WH99	WEYMOUTH	7.53	4.05	1967	WEYMOUTH
KINGFISHER	WK40	WICK	5.69	1.34	1988	SUSSEX
KINGFISHER II	FH529	FALMOUTH	7.62	2.72	2010	CORNWALL
KINGFISHER II	PD110	PETERHEAD	7.32	3.29	1998	LYME REGIS
KINGFISHER III	SA365	SWANSEA	5.20	0.73	1999	SUFFOLK
KINGHORN	LH137	LEITH	8.69	4.55	1981	HARTLEPOOL
KINGS CROSS	FR380	FRASERBURGH	70.00	2302.00	2003	NORWAY
KINLOCH	WA35	WHITEHAVEN	12.80	24.79	1969	SHOTTAN
KINSMAN	PH574	PLYMOUTH	9.98	17.80	1992	SHEPPEY KENT
KINTRA LASS	OB16	OBAN	7.91	5.16	1985	POOLE
KINWAIN	BF366	BANFF	8.69	7.99	1987	UNK
KIRK I	PO1	PORTLAND	4.93	1.11	1981	WEYMOUTH
KIROAN	AH45	ARBROATH	9.85	5.44	2002	HAFNARFJORDUR
KIROAN	PD23	PETERHEAD	23.10	148.00	1979	ABERDEEN
KIRSTY ANN	OB494	OBAN	6.60	2.24	1988	RAMSGATE KENT
KIRSTY GIRL	CS611	COWES	4.32	0.45	1990	FRESHWATER ISLE OF WIGHT
KIRSTY LEE	YH6	YARMOUTH	5.76	1.25	2002	UNITED KINGDOM
KIRSTY LIN	J64	JERSEY	9.99	9.44	1996	UK

UK Fishing Vessels 2015

Vessel Name	Code	Port Name	Loa	Ton Gt	Year	Construction Place
KIRSTY LOUISE	SH6	SCARBOROUGH	9.75	4.80	1974	FALMOUTH
KISMET	CS661	COWES	6.69	1.74	1985	ISLE OF WIGHT
KISS MY BASS	PW496	PADSTOW	6.00	1.46	2007	GUERNSEY
KIT KAT	A8	ABERDEEN	5.95	1.64	2008	PORTCHESTER
KITTIWAKE	RX439	RYE	7.98	7.13	2007	BRIGHTON
KITTIWAKE	SA22	SWANSEA	4.62	0.67	2002	FINLAND
KITTIWAKE	SU50	SOUTHAMPTON	6.41	1.57	1975	PORTSMOUTH
KITTIWAKE	SY532	STORNOWAY	5.84	1.09	1991	MACDUFF
KITTIWAKE	SY890	STORNOWAY	4.95	1.07	1990	DELL QUAY
KITTIWAKE	UL128	ULLAPOOL	9.49	8.29	1958	FRASERBURGH
KITTIWAKE	WK407	WICK	5.90	1.87	1930	SCOTLAND
KITTYFISHER	OB134	OBAN	6.17	0.44	1986	ISLE OF WIGHT
KITTYWAKE	CY8	CASTLEBAY	4.80	0.86	2001	Unk
KIWI	PD8	PETERHEAD	4.74	0.47	2011	UK
KJM	E1	EXETER	4.60	0.67	2007	UNKNOWN
KLONDYKE	SS5	ST IVES	5.45	0.72	1985	UNKNOWN
KON-TIKI	FH187	FALMOUTH	4.30	0.54	1980	FALMOUTH
KONI	J122	JERSEY	4.48	0.73	1970	UK
KOREYJO	M1122	MILFORD HAVEN	6.30	1.88	1980	GBR
KORNELIS JAN	FD281	FLEETWOOD	42.02	390.00	1998	HOLLAND
KRILL 3	CO217	CAERNARVON	6.50	2.28	1981	GWYNEDD
KRISTENBORG	GY199	GRIMSBY	19.01	70.00	1973	ESBJERG
KROSSFJORD	BF70	BANFF	57.60	1415.00	1996	NORWAY
KRYSTLE DAWN	LN26	KINGS LYNN	4.92	0.86	1989	UNK
KRYSTLE KAY	M55	MILFORD HAVEN	9.30	8.17	1989	FRANCE
KT SAM	E10	EXETER	6.25	1.35	1993	ORKNEY
KYDABRA	LA285	LLANELLI	5.30	0.80	1999	UNK
KYLIE S	KY449	KIRKCALDY	6.46	3.20	1993	ANSTRUTHER SCOTLAND
KYM	ML117	METHIL	4.87	0.68	2004	GBR
KYRA	OB469	OBAN	9.70	3.63	1989	CORNWALL
KYRENE	UL144	ULLAPOOL	11.91	17.17	1973	POLRUAN CORNWALL

UK Fishing Vessels 2015

Vessel Name	Code	Port Name	Loa	Ton Gt	Year	Construction Place
KYRENIA	CF167	CARDIFF	7.32	4.04	1980	BARROW IN FURNESS
L OGIEN	PZ28	PENZANCE	16.75	71.00	1979	FRANCE
L'AVENTURIER	SU438	SOUTHAMPTON	9.75	10.11	1971	CAMERET
L'ECUME II	J158	JERSEY	18.54	65.76	1968	FRANCE
L'ETOILE DU NORD	GU40	GUERNSEY	4.27	0.65	2008	SARK
LA COQUET	PH588	PLYMOUTH	7.45	2.89	1976	GUILVENEC
LA COQUILLE	J654	JERSEY	5.80	1.17	1996	IRELAND
LA CREOLE	BM177	BRIXHAM	12.72	21.73	1967	BRITTANY FRANCE
LA CRISE	J60	JERSEY	8.16	2.69	2009	FRANCE
LA ROUX	GU139	GUERNSEY	6.90	1.22	2009	VENTNOR IOW
LA SERIME	WH71	WEYMOUTH	9.23	6.22	1978	GUERNSEY
LA VAGABONDE DES MERS	J612	JERSEY	17.68	62.97	1969	DUDIERNE
LA ZENIA	HL208	HARTLEPOOL	6.40	2.09	2010	ENGLAND
LABRAXIA	J9	JERSEY	4.95	1.25	1990	UK
LACY GRACE	PW85	PADSTOW	4.80	1.07	1983	HAYLE CORNWALL
LADY ANGELA	OB980	OBAN	6.93	1.19	2002	GBR
LADY ANGELA	PE144	POOLE	7.93	2.99	1983	FISHBOURNE
LADY ANN III	BCK624	BUCKIE	6.00	1.31	2005	ABERDEENSHIRE
LADY ANNE	AH20	ARBROATH	9.20	6.77	1979	PENRHYN
LADY ANNE	B737	BELFAST	5.30	0.77	1989	COMBER
LADY B	RR45	ROCHESTER	5.60	1.61	1992	WEST MERSEA
LADY CHRISTINA	P960	PORTSMOUTH	5.10	0.56	1985	UNKNOWN
LADY CINDERELLA	NN243	NEWHAVEN	9.45	5.43	1974	RYE
LADY CLAIRE	AH728	ARBROATH	4.72	0.52	2014	UKNOWN
LADY CLARE	CE56	COLERAINE	6.65	0.81	1962	MOVILLE CO DONEGAL
LADY DI	FD61	FLEETWOOD	4.88	1.09	2011	LEYLAND
LADY DI	M1020	MILFORD HAVEN	9.91	4.90	1993	PORT ISAAC
LADY ELIZABETH	LA580	LLANELLI	4.62	0.54	1998	HARROWGATE
LADY FRANCES	BH4	BLYTH	9.94	7.24	1966	FRANCE
LADY GAIL	CN117	CAMPBELTOWN	10.00	15.53	1983	SWANSEA

UK Fishing Vessels 2015

Vessel Name	Code	Port Name	Loa	Ton Gt	Year	Construction Place
LADY HAMILTON OF HELFORD	FH214	FALMOUTH	8.53	6.32	1972	LOOE CORNWALL
LADY HELEN	GU111	GUERNSEY	7.94	6.58	1979	NEWHAVEN
LADY HELEN	PH891	PLYMOUTH	5.42	1.27	2008	Unk
LADY HELEN	PO15	PORTLAND	10.00	5.53	1979	WEYMOUTH
LADY HELEN - S	GU33	GUERNSEY	10.79	16.34	1990	PENRYN CORNWALL
LADY IRIS	YH79	YARMOUTH	6.60	2.33	2003	NORFOLK
LADY ISLE	N263	NEWRY	12.14	21.72	1968	EEL PIE ISLAND & CAMPBELLTOWN
LADY JACQUELINE	PZ1247	PENZANCE	6.75	1.81	2007	PORTUGAL
LADY JADE	BRD438	BROADFORD	9.95	8.85	1999	PENRYN
LADY JADE	CE531	COLERAINE	6.23	1.39	1998	CORNWALL
LADY JANE	OB349	OBAN	11.40	11.53	1978	PORTLAND
LADY JANET	M116	MILFORD HAVEN	9.71	8.76	1988	CORNWALL
LADY JAYNE	CA386	CARDIGAN	5.05	0.64	1997	UK
LADY JEAN	B986	BELFAST	9.83	13.27	1981	SOUTHAMPTON
LADY JEAN	BM9	BRIXHAM	11.52	26.47	1990	HULL
LADY JEN	BS234	BEAUMARIS	11.30	14.39	1989	DEGANWY DOCKS GWYNEDD
LADY JEN	PE219	POOLE	4.61	0.83	1976	SWANAGE
LADY JULIA	BW12	BARROW	6.71	3.30	1976	WORKINGTON
LADY K	BS14	BEAUMARIS	11.60	20.25	1984	TRURO
LADY K	IH3	IPSWICH	9.90	7.82	2006	NORTH LINCS
LADY K	K1	KIRKWALL	9.13	4.91	2002	CORNWALL
LADY L	BM63	BRIXHAM	13.97	37.25	2001	FALMOUTH
LADY LAURA	M451	MILFORD HAVEN	4.60	0.69	2006	SELSEY
LADY LAURA	YH86	YARMOUTH	6.40	1.75	2005	NORFOLK
LADY LINDA	SU450	SOUTHAMPTON	8.53	4.38	1960	SOUTHAMPTON
LADY LOU	BM110	BRIXHAM	23.98	159.00	1990	HOLLAND
LADY LOUISE	GU157	GUERNSEY	6.85	2.34	1981	ENGLAND
LADY LOUISE	SM300	SHOREHAM	7.00	4.64	1972	SHOREHAM
LADY LUCK	LI549	LITTLEHAMPTON	7.05	1.62	1992	CORNWALL

UK Fishing Vessels 2015

Vessel Name	Code	Port Name	Loa	Ton Gt	Year	Construction Place
LADY LYNDA	FH726	FALMOUTH	7.30	1.75	1975	Unk
LADY LYNNE	BRD678	BROADFORD	9.90	14.35	1988	FALMOUTH
LADY M	FY927	FOWEY	4.00	0.31	1991	UK
LADY MAGGIE	SE1	SALCOMBE	5.90	2.12	1986	PENRYN CORNWALL
LADY MARGARET	RX19	RYE	6.30	3.24	1987	NEWHAVEN
LADY MARGARET OF COVERACK	FH19	FALMOUTH	4.90	1.11	2010	GBR
LADY MAUREEN	BM7	BRIXHAM	23.97	151.00	2001	MACHINEFABRIEK PADMOS
LADY NICOLA	UL584	ULLAPOOL	11.39	15.33	1989	ENGLAND
LADY OF ENNIS	PZ21	PENZANCE	5.86	1.23	2012	PLYMOUTH
LADY OF LADRAM	E88	EXETER	28.00	186.00	1974	GRONINGEN
LADY OF LEISURE	GU27	GUERNSEY	7.37	3.21	1990	USA
LADY OF LUNDY	BD267	BIDEFORD	11.95	11.69	2007	ESSEX
LADY P	P1005	PORTSMOUTH	6.85	1.47	2003	GBR
LADY PATRICIA	GU168	GUERNSEY	11.10	11.04	1988	HESSELE HULL
LADY PATRICIA	HL16	HARTLEPOOL	9.94	8.41	1984	HARTLEPOOL
LADY PRIMROSE V.C.	MT113	MARYPORT	9.98	4.24	2002	ISLE OF WIGHT
LADY ROSE	FE142	FOLKESTONE	9.83	2.81	1974	WHITSTABLE
LADY ROSE	NN576	NEWHAVEN	5.06	0.85	1998	LLANELLI
LADY SARAH	R38	RAMSGATE	7.32	2.41	1986	RAMSGATE
LADY SHANNON	SA373	SWANSEA	5.00	1.03	1997	GBR
LADY SOVEREIGN	NN5	NEWHAVEN	5.40	0.45	1978	BOGNOR
LADY T EMIEL	BM100	BRIXHAM	30.30	232.00	1980	HOLLAND
LADY TRACY	J98	JERSEY	4.90	0.77	1985	UK
LADY VAL II	UL240	ULLAPOOL	8.20	5.24	1982	WORCESTER
LADY VIOLET	P1034	PORTSMOUTH	5.85	1.46	2007	POLAND
LAEBRAK	LK22	LERWICK	6.53	1.42	2004	CAMBORNE
LAIKA II	LK1017	LERWICK	7.28	1.41	2003	NORWAY
LAINEY	SH16	SCARBOROUGH	7.53	3.13	1979	ORKNEY
LAINY LASS	BA859	BALLANTRAE	6.95	3.19	2013	ANNALONG

UK Fishing Vessels 2015

Vessel Name	Code	Port Name	Loa	Ton Gt	Year	Construction Place
LAMORNA	SS28	ST IVES	11.93	13.28	1986	MEVAGISSEY
LANCER	PH48	PLYMOUTH	7.15	2.87	1981	PLYMOUTH
LANDY ELEANOR	GU130	GUERNSEY	6.12	1.24	2014	GBR
LANTIC BOW	SY889	STORNOWAY	4.40	0.74	1995	SOUTHBOURNE
LAPWING	PD972	PETERHEAD	24.35	144.00	1973	CAMPBELTOWN
LARA	M1149	MILFORD HAVEN	5.35	0.91	1995	SUFFOLK
LARA	OB18	OBAN	5.95	0.96	2006	NOT KNOWN
LARA B	CO577	CAERNARVON	5.60	1.47	1990	ARUNDEL WES SUSSEX
LARABELLE	SA7	SWANSEA	6.38	0.82	1995	CONNER DOWNS
LASS	CN714	CAMPBELTOWN	4.85	0.65	2003	Unk
LAST CHANCE	BS556	BEAUMARIS	5.33	0.76	2000	ENGLAND
LAST CHANCE	SM701	SHOREHAM	7.70	7.72	1984	HULL
LAST ORDERS	BS430	BEAUMARIS	5.00	0.73	1994	SUSSEX
LATIS	B1002	BELFAST	7.21	2.22	1981	GBR
LATNEY STAR	FE33	FOLKESTONE	7.40	3.67	1988	DEAL KENT
LAUNCH OUT	KY374	KIRKCALDY	17.20	40.00	1966	ST. MONANS
LAURA	N162	NEWRY	7.82	5.68	1986	KILKEEL
LAURA	SA374	SWANSEA	4.90	0.98	1989	NORFOLK
LAURA ANN	OB89	OBAN	16.42	50.00	1971	ANSTRUTHER
LAURA ANNE	IH68	IPSWICH	7.30	2.40	1988	POOLE DORSET
LAURA JAYNE	BH63	BLYTH	6.55	2.07	1978	PENRYN
LAURA JUNE II	CH102	CHESTER	7.96	3.61	1989	CORNWALL
LAURA K	LT974	LOWESTOFT	9.95	11.23	2007	CANVEY ISLAND
LAURA K	OB536	OBAN	7.15	1.82	1991	STONEHAVEN
LAURA MAY	M411	MILFORD HAVEN	5.36	0.70	1980	SHETLAND
LAURA THURLOW	MH96	MIDDLESBROUGH	9.30	3.80	1965	AMBLE
LAUREL	CY341	CASTLEBAY	16.58	60.25	1992	BUCKIE
LAUREN	PD19	PETERHEAD	6.11	1.80	1975	GARDENSTOWN
LAUREN	WH19	WEYMOUTH	6.00	1.31	1999	PRT
LAUREN ANN	KY8	KIRKCALDY	6.42	1.16	2007	GBR
LAUREN ANNE	CK304	COLCHESTER	13.33	26.61	1995	NORTH LINCS

UK Fishing Vessels 2015

Vessel Name	Code	Port Name	Loa	Ton Gt	Year	Construction Place
LAUREN G	SSS677	SOUTH SHIELDS	4.13	0.49	1990	WHITBY
LAUREN GIRL	CK68	COLCHESTER	7.89	4.67	1990	HAYLING ISLAND HANTS
LAUREN KARINE	CY836	CASTLEBAY	9.95	6.30	2005	CORNWALL
LAUREN KATE	FY836	FOWEY	9.95	6.24	2001	CORNWALL
LAUREN LOUISE	B883	BELFAST	7.86	4.67	1990	COUNTY DOWN
LAUREN LU	HL10	HARTLEPOOL	9.98	8.99	1999	SOUTH HUMBERSIDE
LAUREN ROSE	A6	ABERDEEN	6.02	1.27	2006	ANGUS
LAURIE JEAN	PZ453	PENZANCE	5.80	1.35	1973	GUNWALLOE HELSTON CORNWALL
LAURSCOTT	UL82	ULLAPOOL	8.59	1.77	1980	BRITAIN
LAURYN JACK	SD405	SUNDERLAND	6.26	1.26	2006	ORKNEY
LAUWERSZEE	MN182	MALDON	12.15	16.21	1976	HOLLAND
LAVINIA ROSE	FD547	FLEETWOOD	8.48	4.22	1970	FRA
LAWRET	BF880	BANFF	6.15	1.67	1999	CORNWALL
LAYLA MAY	PZ777	PENZANCE	4.43	0.67	1992	UK
LAZY DAYZ	M619	MILFORD HAVEN	5.05	1.38	2000	LANCASHIRE
LAZY SUNRISE	SM815	SHOREHAM	5.30	1.33	2009	SHOREHAM BY SEA
LE BELHARA	NN733	NEWHAVEN	9.83	10.42	2003	ESSEX
LE BONHEUR	PH600	PLYMOUTH	8.90	4.99	1976	ETEL
LE BULOTIER	J173	JERSEY	11.86	14.96	1991	Unk
LE MIRAGE	GU129	GUERNSEY	8.48	8.63	2006	CAMBOURNE & GUERNSEY
LE SOLEIL ROUGE	GU52	GUERNSEY	5.80	0.71	2007	FALMOUTH CORNWALL
LEA RIG	K8	KIRKWALL	5.56	1.53	1986	STROMNESS
LEA RIG	KY82	KIRKCALDY	7.06	4.42	1976	BURNTISLAND
LEAD US	SY144	STORNOWAY	16.79	43.00	1972	ST MONANCE
LEADER	PZ98	PENZANCE	5.49	1.28	1914	ST JUST
LEAH	YH2462	YARMOUTH	5.82	1.29	1999	NORFOLK
LEANA	N65	NEWRY	10.47	8.66	1987	ESSEX
LEANNE	PH89	PLYMOUTH	4.05	0.47	1989	PLYMOUTH
LEANNE	SM46	SHOREHAM	5.58	1.27	1989	UNKNOWN

UK Fishing Vessels 2015

Vessel Name	Code	Port Name	Loa	Ton Gt	Year	Construction Place
LEARIG 111	KY987	KIRKCALDY	8.08	5.63	1975	FRANCE
LEDA	PE1000	POOLE	5.12	0.58	1995	HAMPSHIRE
LEE	SM684	SHOREHAM	4.89	0.95	1975	NEWHAVEN
LEE-N	LT978	LOWESTOFT	4.88	0.65	1994	UNKNOWN
LEESON LADY	CS649	COWES	8.42	3.38	2001	ISLE OF WIGHT
LEEWARD	N956	NEWRY	5.60	1.12	1981	PLYMOUTH
LEIA B	M1172	MILFORD HAVEN	5.10	1.03	1994	DEVON
LENA	DE21	DUNDEE	6.40	3.15	1984	UNKNOWN
LENTEN ROSE	FY43	FOWEY	9.98	7.45	1959	FRASERBURGH
LEON	WY160	WHITBY	9.55	5.95	1987	WHITBY
LEONA JANE	LK783	LERWICK	8.00	3.19	1990	FALMOUTH
LEONIE JANE	IH105	IPSWICH	7.35	2.59	1991	FELIXSTOWE FERRY
LEONORA	M1185	MILFORD HAVEN	6.00	1.89	1995	DEVON
LEONORA	SC60	SCILLY	6.60	3.06	1982	PENRYN
LERINA	BM166	BRIXHAM	9.85	15.05	1997	ST MONANS
LESHAH	M1045	MILFORD HAVEN	6.45	2.18	2001	ENGLAND
LESLEY A	LK3452	LERWICK	6.85	1.55	1985	GBR
LESLEY ANN	PN7	PRESTON	6.48	2.24	1982	LANCASHIRE
LEVEN MOR	RO5	ROTHESAY	10.79	13.91	1977	GWEEK CORNWALL
LEVIATHAN	FH485	FALMOUTH	9.94	8.68	1979	FALMOUTH
LEWIS	TO11	TRURO	3.80	0.59	2003	NOT KNOWN
LEWIS ANDREW	LO20	LONDON	13.98	27.33	2008	EAST SUSSEX
LEX FERENDA	OB10	OBAN	9.94	11.72	1992	ENGLAND
LEXI MICHELLE	PE12	POOLE	6.95	0.98	2002	HANTS
LEXI ROSE	BF370	BANFF	5.99	1.14	2010	SCOTLAND
LIAM D	H141	HULL	6.18	1.63	1990	BRANSBURTON
LIAM JOHN II	BM11	BRIXHAM	6.36	1.38	1992	ARUNDEL WEST SUSSEX
LIANNE	LK149	LERWICK	8.10	3.80	1998	CORNWALL
LIBBY ALICE	SA568	SWANSEA	5.45	1.18	1989	GBR
LIBBY LOU	SM11	SHOREHAM	8.75	4.25	1984	GUERNSEY

UK Fishing Vessels 2015

Vessel Name	Code	Port Name	Loa	Ton Gt	Year	Construction Place
LIBERATOR	HH16	HARWICH	13.35	20.75	1986	NEWHAVEN
LIBERATOR	LO47	LONDON	13.84	23.35	2005	NEW HAVEN
LIBERTY	CK904	COLCHESTER	9.95	9.43	1985	NEWHAVEN
LIBERTY	FY431	FOWEY	8.10	5.13	1966	LOOE
LIBERTY	LK369	LERWICK	8.32	6.86	2000	BANFFSHIRE
LIBERTY	LN122	KINGS LYNN	8.55	3.07	1945	LEIGH ON SEA
LIBERTY	SD381	SUNDERLAND	9.98	14.91	1998	UNK
LIBRA	CT14	CASTLETOWN	6.55	3.79	2006	GBE
LIBRA STAR	PE5	POOLE	7.55	3.26	1985	PENRYN CORNWALL
LICHTIE LASS	AH2	ARBROATH	8.33	6.06	2008	CORNWALL
LIDDL'UN	WH700	WEYMOUTH	3.85	0.39	1975	WEYMOUTH
LIKELY LAD	WH324	WEYMOUTH	9.85	6.06	1989	HULL
LILACINA	BU37	BURNTISLAND	11.28	12.14	1980	CORNWALL
LILI MAE	BN439	BOSTON	9.97	11.53	2002	BARTON ON HUMBER
LILI MEI	FR7	FRASERBURGH	5.00	1.13	2002	SUFFOLK
LILIAN	LH596	LEITH	6.36	1.16	1986	WHITBY
LILLEY G	LO544	LONDON	9.89	10.98	1997	ABERYSTWYTH
LILLIAN R	GU45	GUERNSEY	5.62	1.49	1987	PLYMOUTH DEVON
LILLIE MAY	E43	EXETER	7.60	1.76	2006	GBR
LILLY	OB20	OBAN	5.10	0.70	1980	BALVICAR
LILY	OB457	OBAN	5.03	1.21	1974	PENZANCE CORNWALL
LILY	PD911	PETERHEAD	7.44	2.21	1992	STONEHAVEN
LILY B	BW14	BARROW	5.75	1.39	1988	ARUNDEL SUSSEX
LILY GRACE	CK191	COLCHESTER	9.75	5.97	1985	IPSWICH
LILY GRACE	FH444	FALMOUTH	11.40	29.06	1989	PADSTOW
LILY I	CY10	CASTLEBAY	8.43	4.78	1982	WICK
LILY LOLA	BM91	BRIXHAM	7.85	4.66	2010	BRIDGWATER
LILY MAE	INS52	INVERNESS	5.20	0.81	1990	UNKNOWN
LILY MAE	PE1221	POOLE	8.10	0.70	2012	VENTNOR
LILY MAY II	PW456	PADSTOW	6.90	1.62	2003	ISLE OF WIGHT

UK Fishing Vessels 2015

Vessel Name	Code	Port Name	Loa	Ton Gt	Year	Construction Place
LILY OAK V	BCK8	BUCKIE	9.96	15.16	1996	BARTON UPON HUMBER
LILY OF THE VALLEY	LH33	LEITH	9.54	4.73	1970	AMBLE
LILY ROSE	LA7	LLANELLI	5.40	1.10	2006	PEMBROKESHIRE
LILY V	BS482	BEAUMARIS	7.20	3.44	1985	CORNWALL
LILY V	WK46	WICK	10.30	10.36	1983	WICK SCOTLAND
LILYBEL	PE1111	POOLE	7.70	3.16	1980	SUSSEX
LILYS PRIDE	TO3	TRURO	6.55	1.90	2006	GBR
LINAN	N809	NEWRY	4.85	0.53	1986	ARUNDEL SUSSEX
LINDA	LR455	LANCASTER	5.65	1.03	2001	WEST SUSSEX
LINDA B	FY781	FOWEY	6.70	2.38	1986	UNKNOWN
LINDA LOUISE	LR38	LANCASTER	9.85	4.95	1989	LANCASTER
LINDY	R77	RAMSGATE	5.64	1.63	1989	MARGATE
LINDY LOU	LI93	LITTLEHAMPTON	6.00	1.28	1985	BOGNOR
LINGFIELD	J393	JERSEY	5.79	1.05	1984	GBR
LINKNESS	K1101	KIRKWALL	5.20	1.08	1967	ORKNEY
LIONEL THOMAS	NN750	NEWHAVEN	5.51	1.40	1990	BOGNOR
LISA	PZ395	PENZANCE	6.74	2.31	1960	APPLEDORE
LISA	RX385	RYE	4.85	1.04	1987	NEWHAVEN
LISA ANN	RX39	RYE	12.83	26.91	1989	NEWHAVEN
LISA CLARE	P265	PORTSMOUTH	9.95	4.10	1976	HOLLAND
LISA DIANE	YH9	YARMOUTH	5.85	1.52	2001	NORFOLK
LISA GEM	BS517	BEAUMARIS	4.86	0.67	2007	GBR
LISA JACQUELINE STEVENSON	PZ476	PENZANCE	24.20	112.00	1973	HOLLAND
LISA JAYNE	H67	HULL	9.70	9.43	1989	CORNWALL
LISA K	BM479	BRIXHAM	9.82	7.97	1973	FRANCE
LISA LEANNE	PH598	PLYMOUTH	9.60	10.56	1996	FALMOUTH
LISA MARIE	GU101	GUERNSEY	4.25	0.13	1985	GUERNSEY
LISA MARIE OF ARUN	LI114	LITTLEHAMPTON	9.87	5.61	1978	FALMOUTH & LITTLEHAMPTON
LISA MICHELLE	BW2	BARROW	8.95	3.38	1986	WALNEY ISLAND BARROW
LISANA	RX369	RYE	7.20	2.19	1991	HASTINGS

UK Fishing Vessels 2015

Vessel Name	Code	Port Name	Loa	Ton Gt	Year	Construction Place
LITTLE AMY	LI424	LITTLEHAMPTON	5.03	0.80	2002	GBR
LITTLE ANNE	FY765	FOWEY	4.88	1.09	1992	HAYLE CORNWALL
LITTLE AUK II	OB573	OBAN	5.14	0.90	1996	SUSSEX
LITTLE CHRISTINA	SS80	ST IVES	7.84	2.28	1989	ST. IVES
LITTLE DOT	P84	PORTSMOUTH	8.05	2.72	1989	UNKNOWN
LITTLE EMIEL	SE20	SALCOMBE	6.15	2.00	1980	UNK
LITTLE FISHER	R125	RAMSGATE	5.34	1.46	1962	RYE
LITTLE GEM	E456	EXETER	4.95	1.19	1986	PENRYN
LITTLE GEM	M1098	MILFORD HAVEN	6.25	1.11	1992	CORNWALL
LITTLE ISAAC	M622	MILFORD HAVEN	6.20	1.18	1996	ISLE OF WIGHT
LITTLE JEM	P989	PORTSMOUTH	7.90	4.67	2001	DEVON
LITTLE JOE	HL283	HARTLEPOOL	6.89	1.51	1990	Unk
LITTLE JOSH	PE1043	POOLE	6.25	0.84	1992	POOLE
LITTLE KAT	SA25	SWANSEA	8.82	3.06	2011	I.O.W
LITTLE LAUREN	FH22	FALMOUTH	4.60	0.73	2003	NORFOLK
LITTLE LAUREN	PZ14	PENZANCE	6.18	2.36	1982	CORNWALL
LITTLE LAUREN	WH606	WEYMOUTH	4.80	1.04	1990	CORNWALL
LITTLE LEER	BN434	BOSTON	9.98	10.31	2002	LINCOLNSHIRE
LITTLE LOUIS	PE550	POOLE	6.91	1.55	1995	PORTSMOUTH
LITTLE MAID	BM115	BRIXHAM	6.50	1.64	1988	CELLARDYKE
LITTLE MITE	BM526	BRIXHAM	5.65	0.83	2006	NEWTON ABBOT
LITTLE MO	FY7	FOWEY	4.75	0.52	2005	PENRYN
LITTLE OSCAR	PE11	POOLE	6.65	0.78	2000	DORSET
LITTLE PEARL	FY23	FOWEY	9.98	13.66	1997	HAYLE
LITTLE PEARL	PW60	PADSTOW	4.88	1.09	1980	PLYMOUTH
LITTLE PEARL	PZ8	PENZANCE	9.92	4.97	1954	PORT MELLON
LITTLE RED	R492	RAMSGATE	5.20	0.91	1973	GBR
LITTLE SHRUB	E80	EXETER	6.20	2.67	1987	TEIGNMOUTH
LITTLE SISTER	GU138	GUERNSEY	4.80	1.02	1996	PENRYN
LITTLE SISTER	M25	MILFORD HAVEN	9.32	4.84	1968	EXMOUTH

UK Fishing Vessels 2015

Vessel Name	Code	Port Name	Loa	Ton Gt	Year	Construction Place
LITTLE SISTER II	PE6	POOLE	9.80	9.51	2000	FALMOUTH
LITTLE STAR	P13	PORTSMOUTH	4.62	0.81	2008	PEMBROKESHIRE
LITTLE TERN	MH9	MIDDLESBROUGH	5.90	1.03	2004	CRAIL
LITTLE WONDER	CO81	CAERNARVON	6.91	3.22	1988	HOLYWELL CLWYD
LIVER BIRD	FY345	FOWEY	6.44	2.00	1980	FOWEY
LIVING WATERS	BF100	BANFF	5.62	0.83	2008	GBR
LIZANN	LL500	LIVERPOOL	4.95	1.27	2002	ENGLAND
LIZANN	SD41	SUNDERLAND	9.95	7.22	1988	RYE
LIZANNA	CY141	CASTLEBAY	11.86	16.59	1975	WICK
LIZY	FH693	FALMOUTH	9.97	5.92	2000	CORNWALL
LIZZIE B	BW263	BARROW	7.50	2.76	2006	ULVERSTON
LIZZIE M	LH10	LEITH	6.70	1.74	2010	PORTUGAL
LIZZY JANE	WH785	WEYMOUTH	5.31	1.31	2012	ENGLAND
LIZZY LOU	P612	PORTSMOUTH	4.50	0.75	1998	GBR
LLOYD TYLER	BM188	BRIXHAM	26.20	151.00	1970	BRESKENS HOLLAND
LOCH INCHARD II	UL44	ULLAPOOL	18.32	97.00	1985	BUCKIE
LOCH ROAG	K111	KIRKWALL	10.42	10.94	1970	MCAUGHEY WICK
LODE STAR	LH558	LEITH	8.83	6.86	2005	NOT KNOWN
LOLA K	PH516	PLYMOUTH	9.94	21.03	1996	SHEERNESS
LOLA KATE	YH1	YARMOUTH	6.50	1.59	2013	EDINGTHORPE
LONA M	LH112	LEITH	7.70	3.87	1977	HAYLE CORNWALL
LONESTAR	LH14	LEITH	6.96	3.35	2011	NORTHERN IRELAND
LONG SHOT	GY41	GRIMSBY	5.04	0.87	1988	SUSSEX
LORAN DAN	LI533	LITTLEHAMPTON	5.89	1.12	2000	WEST SUSSEX
LORD CHAD	LN123	KINGS LYNN	14.67	22.77	1981	HOLLAND
LORD SAM	LN86	KINGS LYNN	12.00	17.01	1981	KINGS LYNN
LORD SAM II	LN463	KINGS LYNN	13.71	25.79	2000	SINES
LOREN	ME3	MONTROSE	4.80	0.68	1981	JOHNSHAVEN
LORIS ELLIE	CY130	CASTLEBAY	7.95	2.52	1992	SHETLAND
LORRAINE	M210	MILFORD HAVEN	8.68	3.58	1990	ST CLEARS BOAT YARD
LORRAINE RUTH	PZ48	PENZANCE	4.80	0.71	1992	WESTON SUPER MARE

UK Fishing Vessels 2015

Vessel Name	Code	Port Name	Loa	Ton Gt	Year	Construction Place
LORRAINE RUTH	SA169	SWANSEA	8.28	4.04	2001	CORNWALL
LORRINE	WK108	WICK	8.84	6.95	1972	WICK
LOTTIE HOLLY	BS12	BEAUMARIS	26.92	187.00	2013	HOLLAND
LOU-ANNIE	IH36	IPSWICH	7.95	4.62	2007	CANBORNE
LOUANDRIC	UL24	ULLAPOOL	11.98	11.25	1973	WHITSTABLE
LOUELLA	PZ83	PENZANCE	4.45	0.59	1978	Unk
LOUIS B	J7	JERSEY	10.01	5.61	2003	ICELAND
LOUIS MARIE	J167	JERSEY	6.57	1.63	1996	UK
LOUISA	SY30	STORNOWAY	14.15	42.01	2009	FOWEY
LOUISA N	PZ101	PENZANCE	23.12	125.00	1990	POLAND/HOLLAND
LOUISE	RX378	RYE	9.54	8.07	1994	LYDD
LOUISE II	GU269	GUERNSEY	6.08	2.01	1997	GUERNSEY
LOUISE MAY	J229	JERSEY	5.80	1.24	1989	N/K
LOUP DE MER	J455	JERSEY	9.95	7.60	1997	GBR
LOUWE SENIOR	PW447	PADSTOW	36.60	432.00	2001	PONTEVERDA
LOWENA	SC2	SCILLY	6.90	1.22	2008	GBR
LOWENA - MOR	PZ47	PENZANCE	6.03	1.99	1986	PORTHLEVEN
LOWRI	CA125	CARDIGAN	4.98	0.70	1975	UK
LOYAL FRIEND	BA200	BALLANTRAE	7.70	3.30	1993	MACDUFF
LOYAL FRIEND	J79	JERSEY	7.39	2.63	1992	UK
LOYAL FRIEND	K1142	KIRKWALL	7.27	2.14	2000	MACDUFF
LOYAL FRIEND	M32	MILFORD HAVEN	8.59	2.24	2009	COLCHESTER
LOYAL FRIEND	WK676	WICK	11.70	18.71	1965	BANFF
LOYAL PARTNER	PZ30	PENZANCE	10.65	8.00	1982	HAYLE
LU-LU	GU51	GUERNSEY	3.56	0.37	2003	GUERNSEY
LUAIREAG	SY872	STORNOWAY	5.00	0.76	2006	NOT KNOWN
LUC	SN36	NORTH SHIELDS	17.80	69.00	1980	WALLSEND
LUCIA	HL1067	HARTLEPOOL	9.96	11.85	2000	CORNWALL
LUCIE FISHER	CA1	CARDIGAN	6.90	0.86	2005	ISLE OF WIGHT
LUCIE ROSE	SA386	SWANSEA	5.02	0.80	1985	GBR
LUCIUS	J279	JERSEY	5.00	0.84	1988	UK

UK Fishing Vessels 2015

Vessel Name	Code	Port Name	Loa	Ton Gt	Year	Construction Place
LUCKY	ME229	MONTROSE	4.90	0.80	2002	INVERBERVIE
LUCKY DIP	PO5	PORTLAND	3.85	0.50	1978	UK
LUCKY DOLPHIN	J116	JERSEY	4.40	0.77	2012	Unk
LUCKY II	ME18	MONTROSE	5.95	0.96	2000	GBR
LUCKY LAD	PE804	POOLE	7.30	3.10	1980	POOLE
LUCKY LADY	PE375	POOLE	8.75	5.21	1967	POOLE DORSET
LUCKY LOUISE	CY136	CASTLEBAY	5.75	1.38	1987	SUSSEX
LUCKY LUCY	RX442	RYE	7.95	7.54	2007	ROTTINGDEAN
LUCKY LUCY	SR48	STRANRAER	11.25	10.07	1989	POOLE
LUCKY LUKE	LN6	KINGS LYNN	13.71	25.79	2000	SINES
LUCKY ONE	K1149	KIRKWALL	5.22	0.83	2002	SUFFOLK
LUCKY SAM	GU3	GUERNSEY	5.58	1.47	1989	GUERNSEY
LUCKY SEVEN	E262	EXETER	10.29	8.68	1979	EXMOUTH
LUCKY STAR	N31	NEWRY	5.88	1.74	2001	FALMOUTH
LUCKY STAR	YH401	YARMOUTH	5.70	1.33	1994	SUSSEX
LUCKY THIRTEEN	LA19	LLANELLI	5.33	1.20	1987	SHETLAND
LUCY	SS4	ST IVES	6.82	2.17	2013	ENGLAND
LUCY	WY837	WHITBY	5.42	0.65	2009	UNKNOWN
LUCY ANN	WY821	WHITBY	5.85	0.91	1979	WHITBY
LUCY B	FY843	FOWEY	4.30	0.44	2003	NOT KNOWN
LUCY E	BRD657	BROADFORD	9.40	3.80	2002	GBR
LUCY J	RO50	ROTHESAY	9.15	11.18	2002	BANFFSHIRE
LUCY LOU	BF15	BANFF	5.70	1.76	1981	PLYMOUTH
LUCY M	E449	EXETER	5.10	0.94	1989	ARUNDEL ORKNEY
LUCY MARIANNA	FY239	FOWEY	9.14	4.25	1973	CHARLESTOWN
LUCY MARIE	BN80	BOSTON	13.30	27.70	1999	HULL
LUCY TOO	FY66	FOWEY	10.90	12.47	1989	POLRUAN
LULU	WK477	WICK	5.49	1.72	1977	UNKNOWN
LULWORTH FISHER	GU273	GUERNSEY	7.96	4.67	1965	WEYMOUTH
LUN	CO282	CAERNARVON	4.15	0.53	1974	ABERDARON

UK Fishing Vessels 2015

Vessel Name	Code	Port Name	Loa	Ton Gt	Year	Construction Place
LUNAN LASS	ME9	MONTROSE	6.94	1.28	2004	ISLE OF WIGHT
LUNAR BEAM	FY820	FOWEY	9.90	13.03	1998	CORNWALL
LUNAR BOW	PD265	PETERHEAD	69.30	2233.00	2008	NORWAY
LUNDY STAR	BD2	BIDEFORD	8.03	3.10	1985	ECCLES
LUSTRE	K1015	KIRKWALL	5.20	1.18	1996	ORKNEY
LUSTRE	LK315	LERWICK	9.98	8.31	1958	BANFF
LUSTY LISA	CA389	CARDIGAN	5.06	1.02	1982	ORKNEY
LUSTY LISA	J300	JERSEY	5.01	0.84	1988	Unk
LYCHETT LADY	PE21	POOLE	6.90	1.86	1999	POOLE
LYDON	M1050	MILFORD HAVEN	5.70	1.11	1988	ARUNDEL
LYMIRAC	FR16	FRASERBURGH	7.15	2.35	1978	ISLE OF WIGHT
LYN	CO121	CAERNARVON	5.00	0.65	1975	MORFA NEFYN
LYNAGUE	PL28	PEEL	6.90	0.02	2002	GBR
LYNANDER	LI182	LITTLEHAMPTON	9.16	7.17	1975	RYE
LYNDEN II	FR151	FRASERBURGH	26.23	168.00	1976	ABERDEEN
LYNN CATHERINE	M903	MILFORD HAVEN	9.97	4.83	1989	FALMOUTH
LYNN LOUISE	CN689	CAMPBELTOWN	5.62	1.16	1989	ARUNDEL
LYNN PRINCESS	LN175	KINGS LYNN	16.81	25.00	1989	HOLLAND
LYNNMARIE	N264	NEWRY	17.13	65.00	1973	BUCKIE
LYNSAY LOU	CN2	CAMPBELTOWN	4.95	0.70	2007	ISLAY
LYONESSE	FY555	FOWEY	7.14	2.20	1987	LOOE
LYONESSE	PZ81	PENZANCE	11.99	18.09	2008	CORNWALL
LYONESSE	SS713	ST IVES	5.95	1.21	2010	PORTUGAL
LYONESSE OF CAPE	PZ478	PENZANCE	4.39	0.60	1977	PORT ISAAC
M & J T	LN182	KINGS LYNN	11.34	6.58	1981	WALLSEND
M.J.T. 2	LI520	LITTLEHAMPTON	7.10	1.49	1997	CHESTERFIELD
MA FREEN	YH927	YARMOUTH	9.92	12.07	1985	GREAT YARMOUTH
MA VIE	PW228	PADSTOW	8.74	4.78	1977	MEVAGISSEY
MA-NICKS	AB229	ABERYSTWYTH	6.55	2.08	2006	PRT
MA-RONA	WK838	WICK	9.83	15.36	2004	COLCHESTER
MABEL	PE1123	POOLE	5.10	0.88	2001	GBR

UK Fishing Vessels 2015

Vessel Name	Code	Port Name	Loa	Ton Gt	Year	Construction Place
MAC II	INS104	INVERNESS	5.04	0.81	1988	Unk
MACE	KY984	KIRKCALDY	5.00	0.52	1978	FIFE
MACIE LOUIS	PE1155	POOLE	6.89	1.71	2003	CORNWALL
MAD CAT	NN782	NEWHAVEN	7.80	0.94	2009	ISLE OF WIGHT
MAD KAT	PE55	POOLE	5.80	1.10	2000	UNITED KINGDOM
MADADH CUAIN	UL594	ULLAPOOL	6.03	1.73	2013	NEWHAVEN
MADALIA	SN79	NORTH SHIELDS	14.99	41.16	1972	ARBROATH
MADASHELL	H41	HULL	5.58	1.49	1985	UNKNOWN
MADASHELL IV	H1073	HULL	7.99	2.75	2004	NORTHUMBERLAND
MADDY MARIE	PD320	PETERHEAD	9.36	8.74	1982	RYE
MADELEINE	FY926	FOWEY	5.90	1.12	2012	GBR
MADELEINE	SC187	SCILLY	4.86	1.13	1995	PLYMOUTH
MADELEINE ISABELLA	SH1	SCARBOROUGH	8.50	1.84	2000	NORTHUMBERLAND
MADKATLIZ	SY883	STORNOWAY	5.85	0.98	1990	SOUTHAMPTON
MADONNA	BK96	BERWICK ON TWEED	10.58	4.61	1969	ORKNEY
MAEZIE BELLE	CK956	COLCHESTER	8.10	2.31	2009	COLCHESTER
MAGAN D	AR1	AYR	38.06	263.00	1968	SPAIN
MAGDALENA	FH178	FALMOUTH	6.77	3.26	1989	MYLOR
MAGDALENE	CY70	CASTLEBAY	9.45	6.53	1976	CARDIFF
MAGGIE	LH537	LEITH	7.01	1.99	1999	UNK
MAGGIE	M492	MILFORD HAVEN	5.57	1.07	1986	PLYMOUTH
MAGGIE	SS35	ST IVES	4.70	0.97	1991	ST IVES
MAGGIE ANN	FR110	FRASERBURGH	26.60	111.00	1961	DORDRECHT
MAGGIE ANNE	CE804	COLERAINE	8.30	6.95	1997	MACDUFF
MAGGIE ANNE	WK823	WICK	9.67	7.52	2000	ABERDEENSHIRE
MAGGIE B	CN3	CAMPBELTOWN	10.10	14.31	1988	FALMOUTH
MAGGIE B	N511	NEWRY	9.95	14.60	2001	CORNWALL
MAGGIE G	M1060	MILFORD HAVEN	4.88	0.53	1981	CARDIGAN
MAGGIE J	K271	KIRKWALL	9.80	10.66	2006	ESSEX
MAGGIE JANE	K187	KIRKWALL	6.05	1.86	1906	WESTRAY
MAGGIE M MBE	SH170	SCARBOROUGH	26.54	284.00	1988	CAMPBELTOWN

UK Fishing Vessels 2015

Vessel Name	Code	Port Name	Loa	Ton Gt	Year	Construction Place
MAGGIE MAE	KY16	KIRKCALDY	6.74	0.97	1966	HAMPSHIRE
MAGGIE S	BN84	BOSTON	10.88	12.15	1989	HULL
MAGGIE-MARIE	DH60	DARTMOUTH	9.27	8.54	1976	MEVAGISSEY
MAGIC	SH296	SCARBOROUGH	9.99	6.15	1990	LOWESTOFT
MAGIE EVELYN	LO552	LONDON	5.50	0.79	1999	UNK
MAGLER-MOR	PZ26	PENZANCE	6.27	2.15	1970	GBR
MAGNET	LH248	LEITH	5.40	1.59	1989	UNKNOWN
MAGNET	M137	MILFORD HAVEN	5.87	2.76	1988	HAYLE
MAGNET	SD7	SUNDERLAND	9.89	5.16	1966	AMBLE NORTHUMBERLAND
MAGNUM	BM511	BRIXHAM	5.60	1.59	1992	PLYMOUTH
MAGNUM	DH20	DARTMOUTH	11.30	13.59	1979	PENRYN CORNWALL
MAGNUS	OB175	OBAN	6.92	3.96	1980	WICK
MAID MEL	SS673	ST IVES	5.65	1.45	1983	PENRYN CORNWALL
MAID OF BODINNICK	PW14	PADSTOW	6.25	1.43	1972	POLRUAN
MAID OF KENT	PH584	PLYMOUTH	4.98	0.70	2009	UK
MAIDEN BOWER	SC167	SCILLY	7.92	5.15	1984	PENRYN
MAILE	ME128	MONTROSE	4.50	0.74	1980	SUFFOLK
MAIMAI	FR432	FRASERBURGH	24.34	201.00	1988	ARDROSSAN
MAIREAD	OB274	OBAN	4.88	0.73	1976	ARUNDLE
MAIREAD M	OB164	OBAN	8.15	5.26	1980	CORNWALL
MAIRI	SY23	STORNOWAY	5.18	0.87	1980	UNK
MAIRI ANNA	UL573	ULLAPOOL	11.83	13.89	2007	COLCHESTER
MAIRI BHAN	SY474	STORNOWAY	5.50	0.87	1984	SOUTHAMPTON
MAIRI BHEAG	K991	KIRKWALL	13.20	16.91	1985	PLYMOUTH
MAIRI BHEAG	OB17	OBAN	5.61	1.52	1976	UNKNOWN
MAJESTIC	FY368	FOWEY	7.77	4.48	1977	CORNWALL
MAJESTIC	LK678	LERWICK	16.00	51.00	1977	APPLEDORE
MAJESTIC	UL26	ULLAPOOL	5.60	1.41	1989	DEVON
MAJESTIC III	BF234	BANFF	17.11	56.00	1973	MACDUFF
MAKO	FY400	FOWEY	7.98	2.76	1958	LOOE

UK Fishing Vessels 2015

Vessel Name	Code	Port Name	Loa	Ton Gt	Year	Construction Place
MALACCA	WH477	WEYMOUTH	8.20	2.32	1968	PORT HAMBLE
MALCOLM STUART	BH335	BLYTH	6.11	1.18	1990	FALMOUTH
MALIBU	WH311	WEYMOUTH	7.10	3.19	1974	SOUTHAMPTON
MALKERRY	BM147	BRIXHAM	13.72	44.70	1985	DUNSTAN ON TYNE
MALLAGAR	BD257	BIDEFORD	9.77	11.14	1995	BARNSTAPLE
MAMGEE	PH103	PLYMOUTH	6.00	1.33	2008	PORTUGAL
MAMOUNA	M1090	MILFORD HAVEN	4.72	0.56	1982	DEVON
MANANNAN	B4	BELFAST	5.93	1.05	1996	STONEHAVEN
MANATEE	PE1187	POOLE	5.05	1.07	2002	LANCASHIRE
MANDY KIM	YH29	YARMOUTH	5.68	0.96	1990	GREAT BRITAIN
MANG	SY69	STORNOWAY	7.50	4.22	2007	UNKNOWN
MANHAVEN LAD	SSS682	SOUTH SHIELDS	2.45	0.15	1996	GBR
MANTA RAY	E564	EXETER	4.40	0.61	1988	ICLANDER
MANUEL LAURA	FH725	FALMOUTH	36.00	338.00	2004	VIGO
MANX CAT	PL2	PEEL	7.95	6.76	2006	UNK
MANX MAID	DO18	DOUGLAS	9.15	4.90	2006	GBR
MANX PRIDE	CT140	CASTLETOWN	6.40	1.52	1990	UNITED KINGDOM
MANX RANGER	FY91	FOWEY	13.95	37.49	1991	CORNWALL
MANX RANGER	PL40	PEEL	9.96	12.59	2000	GBR
MANXMAN	DO22	DOUGLAS	5.97	2.97	2000	CORNWALL
MAPLE LEAF	WK122	WICK	7.93	7.31	1973	WICK
MAR	BE7	BARNSTAPLE	4.88	1.02	1997	PLYMOUTH
MAR BLANCO	FD85	FLEETWOOD	39.82	349.00	1989	SANTANDER
MAR CORAL	FD630	FLEETWOOD	39.10	499.00	2006	SPAIN
MAR DE BENS	TN40	TROON	46.85	468.00	1975	KOCHI
MAR DE CRETA	TN101	TROON	40.35	353.00	1957	VIGO
MAR-ROSE	GU121	GUERNSEY	8.32	5.72	1974	FRANCE
MARACESTINA	INS291	INVERNESS	23.94	240.00	1997	ASTURIAS
MARANATHA	B157	BELFAST	13.82	30.42	1988	DINGLE CO. KERRY
MARANATHA	SS149	ST IVES	5.94	1.74	1982	PENRYN

UK Fishing Vessels 2015

Vessel Name	Code	Port Name	Loa	Ton Gt	Year	Construction Place
MARANATHA	SY64	STORNOWAY	5.70	1.26	1988	HASTINGS
MARANDA MAY	LK3374	LERWICK	7.15	2.75	1988	GBR
MARAUDER	WH22	WEYMOUTH	9.22	1.99	2013	ISLE OF WIGHT
MARBELLA	H771	HULL	69.20	2882.00	1989	TOMREFJORD (NORWAY)
MARCAN SINE	CY211	CASTLEBAY	11.22	7.66	1974	ORKNEY
MARCUS J	LO580	LONDON	8.85	2.94	2007	ESSEX
MARDELL	SY816	STORNOWAY	4.90	0.71	1995	ARUNDEL
MARDESHAR	CS671	COWES	9.98	4.90	2007	ISLE OF WIGHT
MARE GRATIA	B932	BELFAST	43.51	315.00	2003	GBR
MAREA B	LK809	LERWICK	9.86	11.09	1997	BARTON UPON HUMBER
MAREA B II	WK868	WICK	9.96	9.50	2011	ABERDEENSHIRE
MAREEL	LK119	LERWICK	9.80	5.63	2004	HAFNARFJORDUR
MAREIXON	UL591	ULLAPOOL	29.30	223.00	1999	SPAIN
MARELANN	BF201	BANFF	16.48	52.00	1974	ANSTRUTHER
MARET	R159	RAMSGATE	12.16	15.05	1963	GERMANY
MARGARET	BA68	BALLANTRAE	5.50	0.97	2003	FIFE
MARGARET	SH232	SCARBOROUGH	9.53	4.93	1974	WHITBY
MARGARET	TH20	TEIGNMOUTH	5.48	1.17	1966	TEIGNMOUTH
MARGARET	UL541	ULLAPOOL	6.15	1.53	1998	DURNESS
MARGARET ANN	IH38	IPSWICH	6.10	2.12	1970	WOODBRIDGE
MARGARET ANN	PN1	PRESTON	5.60	1.02	1986	MANCHESTER
MARGARET ANN 11	B19	BELFAST	17.22	37.00	1968	DUNBAR SCOTLAND
MARGARET BERYL	LO526	LONDON	13.02	23.34	1992	HOLLAND
MARGARET ELIZABETH	WY812	WHITBY	6.30	1.05	1985	WHITBY
MARGARET ELLEN	WK104	WICK	6.25	2.71	1979	CORNWALL
MARGARET K	GU295	GUERNSEY	9.92	5.41	1975	GUERNSEY
MARGARET KERR II	BH218	BLYTH	9.99	11.00	1989	PENRYN CORNWALL
MARGARET MARIE	FR20	FRASERBURGH	5.02	0.76	1984	ABERDEEN
MARGARET ROSE	BF273	BANFF	7.36	2.79	1996	CORNWALL
MARGARET WILLIAM II	J274	JERSEY	5.80	1.06	1993	UK
MARGARETA II	OB69	OBAN	13.41	30.04	1982	MEVIGISSEY

UK Fishing Vessels 2015

Vessel Name	Code	Port Name	Loa	Ton Gt	Year	Construction Place
MARGARITA	TT26	TARBERT	13.38	31.58	1982	CO. DONEGALL
MARGRETA M	BRD7	BROADFORD	11.70	24.41	1989	FALMOUTH
MARGRIET	LT36	LOWESTOFT	40.72	441.00	2004	THE NETHERLANDS
MARI	MH92	MIDDLESBROUGH	7.38	3.58	1972	WHITBY
MARI DAWN	LK605	LERWICK	9.68	12.49	2007	GBR
MARI WYN	CO797	CAERNARVON	4.85	0.68	2000	GBR
MARIA	J437	JERSEY	5.50	0.82	1978	GBR
MARIA 2	FH669	FALMOUTH	7.13	1.47	1997	CORNWALL
MARIA LENA	N948	NEWRY	33.48	169.00	1983	NLD
MARIA Q	FH109	FALMOUTH	8.10	4.21	1981	FALMOUTH
MARIAN	TH8	TEIGNMOUTH	4.65	0.71	1978	TEIGNMOUTH
MARIANN	M94	MILFORD HAVEN	9.38	5.24	2002	GBR
MARIANNE	CO73	CAERNARVON	6.95	2.92	1984	CONWAY
MARIDA	DO37	DOUGLAS	15.36	39.45	1968	GBR
MARIE	LN158	KINGS LYNN	8.90	6.88	1992	KINGS LYNN
MARIE 'K'	SM45	SHOREHAM	6.02	1.32	1991	FALMOUTH
MARIE BHAN III	BRD621	BROADFORD	6.40	1.71	1984	CORNWALL
MARIE BHAN IV	BRD650	BROADFORD	8.18	6.28	1992	PENRYN CORNWALL
MARIE GALANTE	J486	JERSEY	11.90	17.72	1970	FRANCE
MARIE M	HL35	HARTLEPOOL	5.56	1.00	1988	ENGLAND
MARIE T	N93	NEWRY	9.99	6.24	1979	FISHGUARD
MARIE THERESE	CY183	CASTLEBAY	5.78	1.15	1990	INVERNESS
MARIGOLD	A52	ABERDEEN	15.78	34.00	1968	ANSTRUTHER FIFE
MARIGOLD	INS241	INVERNESS	28.30	450.00	1998	BROMBOROUGH
MARILYN CLARK III	SN3	NORTH SHIELDS	6.26	1.27	2000	YORKSHIRE
MARINA	B330	BELFAST	16.48	40.00	1964	MACDUFF
MARINA EMIEL	BM19	BRIXHAM	13.95	43.37	2012	NEWHAVEN
MARINA II	TO5	TRURO	7.27	4.86	1986	GBR
MARINER	SS224	ST IVES	5.09	0.69	1975	TRURO
MARINER III	DR170	DOVER	7.40	4.30	1989	ISLE OF WIGHT

UK Fishing Vessels 2015

Vessel Name	Code	Port Name	Loa	Ton Gt	Year	Construction Place
MARION	E15	EXETER	4.36	0.56	1964	LOOE
MARION	SY573	STORNOWAY	6.30	2.53	1997	UNKNOWN
MARIONA	B15	BELFAST	9.30	5.30	1990	RYE/ANNAN
MARISCO	B129	BELFAST	6.49	1.47	1998	FIFE
MARJORIE ANNE	MH294	MIDDLESBROUGH	6.99	2.00	1980	WHITBY
MARJORIE M	LR225	LANCASTER	5.70	1.24	1995	MORECAMBE
MARK & JAMES	PZ641	PENZANCE	5.49	1.59	1979	HAYLE
MARK ANTHONY	CO11	CAERNARVON	9.28	7.41	1973	MORCOMBE
MARKEV	KY204	KIRKCALDY	4.86	0.68	1982	CORNWALL
MARKIE	LI178	LITTLEHAMPTON	6.34	1.07	1987	BOGNOR
MARKIE	P62	PORTSMOUTH	6.58	1.47	1996	FALMOUTH
MARLENA	K529	KIRKWALL	8.84	10.63	1979	KIRKWALL
MARLENE	PW4	PADSTOW	4.46	0.64	1980	NEWQUAY
MARLI J	LO548	LONDON	9.89	10.54	1998	ABERYSTWYTH
MARLIN	TH1	TEIGNMOUTH	4.78	0.67	2000	PERTHSHIRE SCOTLAND
MARLIN G	SS683	ST IVES	6.14	0.68	1996	HAYLE
MARLU	J283	JERSEY	5.68	1.14	1987	SCOTLAND
MARLYN	LT603	LOWESTOFT	4.96	0.90	1985	ORKNEY
MARNIE	CK942	COLCHESTER	4.61	0.68	1994	LEA ON SEA
MARNIE ROSE	BS18	BEAUMARIS	5.89	1.55	2013	NORFOLK
MARNIK	ME15	MONTROSE	7.62	3.35	1976	PORTLEVEN
MARONA	BA792	BALLANTRAE	6.14	2.96	1977	GIRVAN
MARONA	CN89	CAMPBELTOWN	5.00	1.03	1980	ENGLAND
MARS	PE283	POOLE	9.34	7.08	1960	FRANCE
MARSALI	OB139	OBAN	9.15	4.19	1975	THURSO
MARSH MAID	J418	JERSEY	5.70	1.19	1997	ORKNEY
MARSYLV	OB7	OBAN	7.02	1.61	1990	GLASTECH GRAMPOUND CORNWALL
MARTA	E217	EXETER	4.00	0.49	1978	EXMOUTH
MARTHA M	CE522	COLERAINE	5.85	1.49	1999	CO. ANTRIM
MARTINA ROSE	N33	NEWRY	9.65	9.11	1980	TOTTON HANTS

UK Fishing Vessels 2015

Vessel Name	Code	Port Name	Loa	Ton Gt	Year	Construction Place
MARTINE	BM15	BRIXHAM	34.00	205.00	1973	NLD
MARTLET	SE158	SALCOMBE	6.00	2.46	1946	SALCOMBE
MARY	LR53	LANCASTER	5.74	1.18	1937	OVERTON
MARY - JESS	M22	MILFORD HAVEN	5.85	1.49	2000	FALMOUTH
MARY AMELIA	LO86	LONDON	13.93	27.25	2008	EAST SUSSEX
MARY ANN	FY913	FOWEY	4.64	0.57	1996	GBR
MARY ANN	K15	KIRKWALL	4.95	0.63	1995	ARUNDEL WEST SUSSEX
MARY ANN	WY779	WHITBY	9.87	4.21	1997	PENRYN
MARY ANN	YH213	YARMOUTH	6.21	2.40	1972	POTTER HEIGHAM
MARY ANNE	BH196	BLYTH	7.00	3.06	1978	UNKNOWN
MARY ANNE	BM482	BRIXHAM	11.98	18.07	1997	ABERDEEN
MARY ANNE	CN712	CAMPBELTOWN	8.05	2.95	1988	CORNWALL
MARY ANNE II	H1101	HULL	7.45	1.59	2001	GBR
MARY D	YH299	YARMOUTH	8.51	3.33	1989	STIFFKEY
MARY EILEEN	FY811	FOWEY	4.80	1.14	1986	HAYLE
MARY ELIZABETH	N3	NEWRY	9.10	7.01	1987	NEWRY
MARY ELLEN	B945	BELFAST	14.95	60.84	2004	EYEMOUTH
MARY J	GU135	GUERNSEY	8.30	6.62	2013	GUERNSEY
MARY J	WH4	WEYMOUTH	6.00	1.21	2010	PORTUGAL
MARY JAMES	RY8	RAMSEY	9.98	12.79	1988	HULL
MARY JANE	LN5	KINGS LYNN	5.20	1.10	1970	SALTHOUSE
MARY JAYNE	N1016	NEWRY	7.96	4.67	1980	Unk
MARY JEAN	K978	KIRKWALL	6.58	4.13	1992	SHAPINSAY
MARY K	SH107	SCARBOROUGH	7.95	6.86	1983	WORCESTER
MARY LOUISE	CY231	CASTLEBAY	6.54	1.53	1980	PENRYN CORNWALL
MARY MANSON	OB19	OBAN	17.80	40.00	1970	DUNBAR
MARY MARIA	N974	NEWRY	12.59	15.55	2004	BORTON HILL
MARY MO	SS46	ST IVES	5.46	1.24	2011	GBR
MARY OAKLEY	MH162	MIDDLESBROUGH	6.70	1.63	1961	THORNABY
MARY ROSE	PZ477	PENZANCE	5.60	1.54	1987	NEWLYN
MARY-KAY	CY433	CASTLEBAY	9.70	5.77	1990	RYE

UK Fishing Vessels 2015

Vessel Name	Code	Port Name	Loa	Ton Gt	Year	Construction Place
MARYEARED	TT57	TARBERT	17.07	75.00	1979	FRASERBURGH
MASADA	WH515	WEYMOUTH	7.20	1.33	1989	SOUTHAMPTON
MASCARAID	CO820	CAERNARVON	11.99	12.69	1980	POOLE
MASTER B	J121	JERSEY	4.40	0.59	1980	UK
MATAURI BAY	J45	JERSEY	7.38	3.06	1990	UK
MATT DEE	SY862	STORNOWAY	6.10	1.52	2005	GBR
MATTANJA	TN36	TROON	32.50	217.00	1973	WEST GRAFTDIJK HOLLAND
MATTY JAY	LO541	LONDON	13.91	22.77	1997	DYFED
MAUDIE	CK127	COLCHESTER	6.19	1.11	1990	TOLLESBURY ESSEX
MAUREEN FRANCES	BRD423	BROADFORD	9.90	7.66	1976	HAMBLE
MAUREEN PATRICIA	CT76	CASTLETOWN	13.97	27.91	1970	GBR
MAVERICK	CK79	COLCHESTER	9.98	14.88	1999	POLRUAN
MAVERICK	E565	EXETER	7.95	4.09	2013	PLYMOUTH
MAVERICK	H1069	HULL	6.83	1.40	1984	BARTON UPON HUMBER
MAVERICK	HH984	HARWICH	9.34	5.57	1974	RYE
MAVERICK	PH589	PLYMOUTH	9.45	4.57	1995	CANEWDON
MAVERICK	PL165	PEEL	9.21	6.04	2005	SOUTHAMPTON
MAVERICK	R486	RAMSGATE	9.80	7.32	2002	CORNWALL
MAVERICK II	J94	JERSEY	10.73	9.62	2012	Unk
MAXINE	ML129	METHIL	9.95	12.55	2001	ENGLAND
MAXINE CHARLOTTE	SS759	ST IVES	5.20	1.19	2006	LANCASHIRE
MAXINES PRIDE	FY38	FOWEY	11.89	26.26	1984	POLRUAN NR FOWEY
MAY	CK355	COLCHESTER	8.16	2.13	1982	WEST MERSEA
MAY C	SY213	STORNOWAY	5.79	1.45	1989	YAPTON
MAY LILY	FR607	FRASERBURGH	6.40	1.42	1978	FALMOUTH
MAY QUEEN	SE138	SALCOMBE	4.02	0.42	1900	SALCOMBE
MAYBE	SY891	STORNOWAY	5.31	0.78	2002	UK
MAYFAIR	GU362	GUERNSEY	7.68	4.03	1978	BERWICH
MAYFLOWER	FD535	FLEETWOOD	6.10	0.96	1996	ISLE OF WIGHT
MAYFLOWER	WK20	WICK	5.95	1.51	1902	STROMA SCOTLAND

UK Fishing Vessels 2015

Vessel Name	Code	Port Name	Loa	Ton Gt	Year	Construction Place
MAYFLOWER A	WY237	WHITBY	9.94	5.79	1964	WHITBY
MAYFLOWER OF PORTAVOGIE	B44	BELFAST	19.86	59.00	1957	BUCKIE
MAYFLY	DH8	DARTMOUTH	7.27	2.23	2004	PLYMOUTH
MAYFLY	LI111	LITTLEHAMPTON	11.98	19.41	1985	NEWHAVEN
MAYHEM	BS539	BEAUMARIS	5.90	1.22	2007	PORTUGAL
MAYHEM	NN770	NEWHAVEN	5.20	0.78	1986	LLANELLI
MAYHEM 2	SE33	SALCOMBE	7.95	3.26	2010	COLCHESTER ESSEX
MEDINA MIST	N286	NEWRY	9.84	3.25	1989	NORFOLK/COWES
MEDWAY IV	BN109	BOSTON	9.60	8.51	1999	BOSTON
MEER	FY2	FOWEY	9.75	6.44	2007	SOUTHAMPTON
MEG	CO25	CAERNARVON	6.90	1.73	2004	ISLE OF WIGHT
MEGAN	B1	BELFAST	5.69	1.61	1991	UNKNOWN
MEGAN DENISE	LI539	LITTLEHAMPTON	4.50	0.70	2002	SIDESHAM
MEGANJANE	SH2	SCARBOROUGH	6.74	1.63	2012	UK
MEGELLEN	ME12	MONTROSE	6.93	1.16	1999	VENTNOR
MEGWYN	SS14	ST IVES	5.50	1.29	2003	BELGIUM
MEHEFIN	M96	MILFORD HAVEN	8.90	3.51	1992	NEWPORT PEMBROKESHIRE
MELANIE DAWN	PE1038	POOLE	8.75	10.34	2000	UK
MELANIE LOUISE	RX46	RYE	9.90	13.71	1989	SUNDERLAND
MELANIE S	CE542	COLERAINE	9.20	3.60	1975	MALAHIDE
MELESSA	CO366	CAERNARVON	9.75	7.50	1976	KEYHAVEN
MELINKA	B40	BELFAST	5.60	1.66	1980	UNKNOWN
MELISSA CLARE	BS2	BEAUMARIS	10.75	12.27	1989	SUNDERLAND
MELISSA E	F57	FAVERSHAM	9.15	3.85	1975	WHITSTABLE KENT
MELISSA LOUISE	LK347	LERWICK	7.10	2.72	2001	GBR
MELITA	LN125	KINGS LYNN	9.91	7.59	1966	KINGS LYNN
MENACE	R487	RAMSGATE	9.20	1.76	2007	ISLE OF WIGHT
MERBREEZE	PZ179	PENZANCE	4.66	0.57	1970	LAMORNA
MERCURIUS	M277	MILFORD HAVEN	27.20	99.00	1963	HOLLAND
MERCURY	PE541	POOLE	6.41	0.80	1976	POOLE

UK Fishing Vessels 2015

Vessel Name	Code	Port Name	Loa	Ton Gt	Year	Construction Place
MERDINA II	K20	KIRKWALL	10.55	5.13	2004	ESSEX
MERIDIAN	NN757	NEWHAVEN	9.83	8.58	2007	COLCHESTER
MERLIN	BN39	BOSTON	11.98	14.81	2007	HUMBER
MERLIN	BS255	BEAUMARIS	7.00	4.80	1982	ISLE OF WIGHT
MERLIN	J38	JERSEY	6.80	1.86	2009	PORTUGAL
MERLIN	LH580	LEITH	6.40	1.47	2009	KILKEEL CO.DOWN
MERLIN	LK780	LERWICK	9.99	12.42	1997	PLYMOUTH
MERLIN	M1133	MILFORD HAVEN	9.81	5.33	1990	SAUNDERSFOOT
MERLIN	OB963	OBAN	8.00	3.41	2001	GBR
MERLIN	PH1017	PLYMOUTH	11.50	9.03	2013	CORNWALL
MERLIN 11	K69	KIRKWALL	11.34	11.61	1969	NESS SLIPWAY STROMNESS
MERMAID	AD4	ARDROSSAN	4.80	0.63	2003	ARUNDEL
MERMAID	BS226	BEAUMARIS	6.30	2.16	1989	PETERHEAD
MERMAID	FY909	FOWEY	3.94	0.46	1991	Unk
MESMERIST	NN755	NEWHAVEN	8.50	7.20	2007	ESSEX
METAN	PH322	PLYMOUTH	8.29	5.42	1980	CAMELFORD CORNWALL
METEOR	YH206	YARMOUTH	6.40	1.49	1996	HAISBRO
MHAIRI KIRSTEEN	WK306	WICK	5.20	1.38	1980	UK
MI AMOR	FD1	FLEETWOOD	9.38	10.32	1976	LOOE
MI JENNY	IH47	IPSWICH	7.35	5.39	1987	FELIXSTOWE FERRY
MI TIME	P193	PORTSMOUTH	5.65	1.16	2012	PORTUGAL
MIA B	E520	EXETER	9.88	6.18	2005	EXMOUTH
MIA BLUE	LT231	LOWESTOFT	9.60	8.13	2004	GBR
MIA JANE W	FR443	FRASERBURGH	24.40	199.00	1989	FRANCE
MIA LOU	M628	MILFORD HAVEN	4.90	1.29	2000	BLACKPOOL
MIABELLA	BD310	BIDEFORD	4.38	0.47	1976	GBR
MIANN	PD52	PETERHEAD	6.48	1.21	1988	LIVERPOOL
MICHAEL J	CT21	CASTLETOWN	6.04	1.56	1956	GBR
MICHAEL J	K390	KIRKWALL	10.84	13.33	1957	GIRVAN
MICHANNDA	KY222	KIRKCALDY	7.01	0.79	1982	WHITEHAVEN CUMBRIA

UK Fishing Vessels 2015

Vessel Name	Code	Port Name	Loa	Ton Gt	Year	Construction Place
MICHELLE	BRD117	BROADFORD	10.70	5.05	1982	WEYMOUTH DORSET
MICHELLE ANNE I	CN365	CAMPBELTOWN	5.80	1.30	1993	STONEHAVEN
MICHELLE NA MARA	N1042	NEWRY	9.95	9.53	2013	UK
MICHELLE WISEMAN	UL181	ULLAPOOL	11.48	8.60	1979	GUERNSEY
MIDGE	SS694	ST IVES	5.55	1.38	1985	PLYMOUTH
MIDNIGHT SUN	RX374	RYE	6.70	1.99	2009	SHOREHAM BY SEA WEST SUSSEX
MIDNIGHT SUN	TH24	TEIGNMOUTH	11.99	27.67	1996	PENRYN
MIGRANT	CK962	COLCHESTER	5.52	1.69	1965	FELIXTOWE
MIKAL	PE1098	POOLE	5.20	0.49	2002	PORTSMOUTH
MILEY ADELLE	SN10	NORTH SHIELDS	10.00	13.36	1972	FRANCE
MILI	PE8	POOLE	4.37	0.53	1990	GBR
MILL STAR	B728	BELFAST	5.01	0.70	1991	COMBER N IRELAND
MILLBURN	FR83	FRASERBURGH	21.76	143.00	1975	BUCKIE
MILLENNIA	PZ54	PENZANCE	9.98	8.96	1999	BARTON UPON HUMBER
MILLENNIUM	K108	KIRKWALL	8.88	3.92	1998	FALMOUTH
MILLIE	SE18	SALCOMBE	4.83	0.64	1984	KINGSBRIDGE
MILLIE G	FH21	FALMOUTH	9.80	5.99	2002	MACDUFF
MILLIE G	R502	RAMSGATE	9.98	8.25	1991	WHITBURN SUNDERLAND
MILLY II	FH746	FALMOUTH	5.86	1.97	1986	CORNWALL
MINCH HUNTER	N236	NEWRY	16.70	46.00	1975	D-OLONNE FRANCE
MINERVA	FR147	FRASERBURGH	24.80	311.00	2000	MACDUFF
MINERVA	K53	KIRKWALL	6.80	4.17	1980	SHETLAND
MINGA	LI548	LITTLEHAMPTON	5.50	1.43	1979	BOGNOR REGIS
MINNEHAHA	SE6	SALCOMBE	4.77	0.55	1990	ALDRIDGE WEST MIDLANDS
MINSTREL	FH744	FALMOUTH	4.64	1.09	2007	CORNWALL
MINUIT	J2	JERSEY	6.60	2.29	1982	UK
MIRAGE II	H1075	HULL	11.15	10.16	1990	WEYMOUTH
MIRANDA	DH11	DARTMOUTH	4.75	0.77	1982	PORTLEMOUTH
MIRANDA	P224	PORTSMOUTH	37.75	373.00	1987	NETHERLANDS

UK Fishing Vessels 2015

Vessel Name	Code	Port Name	Loa	Ton Gt	Year	Construction Place
MIRANDA FAYE	PD92	PETERHEAD	7.93	3.61	1980	UK
MISCHIEF	SE344	SALCOMBE	4.60	0.54	2006	DEVON
MISCHIEF	WO41	WORKINGTON	6.30	1.91	1988	WORKINGTON
MISS CONNIE	GU85	GUERNSEY	7.00	2.76	1992	LA HURE MARE
MISS DARCIE K	N114	NEWRY	6.25	1.43	2008	FALMOUTH CORNWALL
MISS GRACE II	CK70	COLCHESTER	7.07	1.56	2006	ENGLAND
MISS MOLLY	DE133	DUNDEE	5.59	1.25	1990	GBR
MISS PATTIE	GU58	GUERNSEY	9.75	8.28	2014	Unk
MISTLETOE	SY13	STORNOWAY	4.93	1.13	1980	GBR
MISTRAL	P1016	PORTSMOUTH	6.65	1.66	1985	CHANNEL ISLANDS
MISTRAL	PE266	POOLE	6.32	2.42	1981	UNK
MISTRESS	DR174	DOVER	4.56	0.63	1991	GBR
MISTRESS III	M146	MILFORD HAVEN	9.90	8.41	1988	CORNWALL
MISTRESS OF SOUTHWOLD	LT2	LOWESTOFT	9.63	10.61	2010	COWES - I.O.W
MISTY	GU143	GUERNSEY	3.62	0.46	2004	GUERNSEY
MISTY	R3	RAMSGATE	9.50	4.45	1979	WESTON SUPER MARE
MISTY BLUE	H1070	HULL	7.78	2.32	1994	SOUTHAMPTON
MISTY BLUE	PW30	PADSTOW	6.00	1.46	2008	GBR
MISTY DAWN	P247	PORTSMOUTH	6.58	2.19	1976	SHOREHAM
MISTY ISLE	K75	KIRKWALL	8.23	5.67	1972	KIRKWALL
MISTY LADY	OB4	OBAN	8.50	4.20	2010	EDINBURGH
MISTY MORN	CY458	CASTLEBAY	8.09	4.54	1993	MEVAGISSEY CORNWALL
MISTY MORN	GU35	GUERNSEY	6.40	1.78	1988	ST SAMPSONS
MISTY NIGHT	PE59	POOLE	3.91	0.25	1983	NEW MILTON HANTS
MIXON LADY	LI201	LITTLEHAMPTON	8.40	7.49	1983	SELSEY
MIZPAH	CY145	CASTLEBAY	5.78	1.54	2004	DEVON
MIZPAH	HL1	HARTLEPOOL	9.95	20.02	2001	GBR
MIZPAH	LK497	LERWICK	8.45	3.99	1991	QUENDALE SHETLAND
MIZPAH	MH64	MIDDLESBROUGH	4.42	0.44	1989	SANDSEND
MIZPAH	N455	NEWRY	6.49	1.85	1979	WEYMOUTH
MIZPAH	PE32	POOLE	9.77	11.26	1990	FALMOUTH

UK Fishing Vessels 2015

Vessel Name	Code	Port Name	Loa	Ton Gt	Year	Construction Place
MIZPAH 11	SM221	SHOREHAM	7.01	3.91	1976	ISLE OF WIGHT
MIZPAH III	PE981	POOLE	9.20	5.04	1982	POOLE
MIZPAH LK	LK173	LERWICK	26.88	254.00	1988	CAMPBELTOWN ARGYLL
MO CHAILINI	CE600	COLERAINE	9.15	3.84	2008	CO.DONEGAL
MO MHAIRI	TT87	TARBERT	10.00	6.73	1975	ORKNEY
MOA	NN702	NEWHAVEN	5.40	0.80	1996	SWANSEA
MOANER	CA187	CARDIGAN	4.50	0.46	1980	UNK
MOBY DICK	PH326	PLYMOUTH	9.24	10.40	1976	GUILVENEC FRANCE
MOIAN	BA820	BALLANTRAE	7.68	3.58	1988	BOGNOR REGIS
MOIRA F	TH82	TEIGNMOUTH	4.14	0.36	1991	DAWLISH
MOJO	WH737	WEYMOUTH	9.95	2.91	2004	CORNWALL
MOL	GU82	GUERNSEY	3.63	0.46	2013	Unk
MOLLIE ANN	GU226	GUERNSEY	7.35	4.45	1989	CORNWALL
MOLLIE DAWN	SS6	ST IVES	5.80	0.80	2004	GBE
MOLLY	BA854	BALLANTRAE	6.55	1.49	2009	MACDUFF
MOLLY	KY1030	KIRKCALDY	6.67	1.73	2007	UK
MOLLY	WK858	WICK	5.70	1.06	1992	GBR
MOLLY C	KY2	KIRKCALDY	6.15	1.48	1985	GBR
MOLLY JAYNE	WH3	WEYMOUTH	8.06	5.03	2001	WADEBRIDGE
MOLLY MAI	FY890	FOWEY	4.80	0.59	2000	GBR
MOLLY OG	CY91	CASTLEBAY	9.15	3.78	2008	ROSS-SHIRE
MOLLY T	TO2	TRURO	7.80	1.84	2007	ESSEX
MONA LISA	RX258	RYE	6.00	2.59	1975	NEWHAVEN
MONARCH	BF212	BANFF	5.86	1.30	2009	GBS
MONKS BAY	CS70	COWES	6.90	0.37	2008	ISLE OF WIGHT
MONTANA	LH5	LEITH	8.00	2.79	1987	RAMSGATE
MONTE MAZANTEU	FD521	FLEETWOOD	27.30	200.00	1989	NAVIE ASTILLERN ARMON S A
MOO MOO	SM806	SHOREHAM	5.50	1.43	1995	GBR
MOOGIE	FY898	FOWEY	6.09	2.20	2008	CORNWALL
MOON SHINE	GU121	GUERNSEY	6.54	1.53	2004	PEMBROKESHIRE

UK Fishing Vessels 2015

Vessel Name	Code	Port Name	Loa	Ton Gt	Year	Construction Place
MOON STAR	RX444	RYE	6.60	3.23	2008	WEST SUSSEX
MOONFLEET	DH62	DARTMOUTH	5.60	0.91	1986	CORNWALL
MOONLIGHTER II	CK51	COLCHESTER	9.50	4.76	1978	RYE
MOONRAKER	NN483	NEWHAVEN	4.90	0.65	1992	EASTBOURNE
MOONRAKER	RX10	RYE	6.44	1.93	2006	EAST SUSSEX
MOONRAKER	SA410	SWANSEA	5.90	1.04	2010	WADEBRIDGE CORNWALL
MOONSHINE	B1001	BELFAST	6.12	2.14	2001	GBR
MOONSHINE	J74	JERSEY	5.35	0.97	1983	UK
MOONSHINE	RX118	RYE	6.28	2.94	1967	NEWHAVEN
MOONSHINE	WH332	WEYMOUTH	5.63	1.46	1979	WEYMOUTH
MORA	GU142	GUERNSEY	5.60	1.51	2014	GBR
MORAG	AH92	ARBROATH	4.80	0.79	1980	ABERDEEN
MORAY ENDEAVOUR	BCK17	BUCKIE	21.20	189.00	1997	MACDUFF
MORAY PEARL	BF17	BANFF	8.11	2.59	1980	PENRYN
MORDROS	FY523	FOWEY	9.23	9.34	1978	LOOE
MOREL MARGH	FH12	FALMOUTH	10.93	12.73	1989	SUNDERLAND
MOREMMA	PD135	PETERHEAD	22.95	172.00	1988	BUCKIE
MOREN-DEK	N627	NEWRY	9.50	9.98	1980	SOUTHAMPTON
MORENA	CY457	CASTLEBAY	7.04	4.08	1990	GRIMSAY NORTH UIST
MORFRAN III	CO815	CAERNARVON	6.93	1.28	2007	ISLE OF WIGHT
MORGELYN	FY872	FOWEY	6.00	1.46	1980	MEVAGISSEY
MORLO	CO324	CAERNARVON	4.35	0.76	1982	KINGSBRIDGE DEVON
MORNING DAWN	N252	NEWRY	16.95	46.00	1970	ARBROATH
MORNING DAWN	PD359	PETERHEAD	44.98	565.00	1987	STELLENDAM
MORNING STAR	P8	PORTSMOUTH	13.47	25.69	1984	BIRKENHEAD & FLEETWOOD
MORNING STAR	PZ9	PENZANCE	7.67	4.20	1989	CORNWALL
MORNING STAR	SN87	NORTH SHIELDS	9.75	17.56	1989	RETFORD NOTTS.
MORNINGTON BAY	LT182	LOWESTOFT	8.36	1.60	1988	SOUTHBEN FLEET
MORVRAN	FH745	FALMOUTH	5.85	0.91	2007	SUFFOLK
MOSS ROSE	DR110	DOVER	8.20	5.54	1980	WALMER

UK Fishing Vessels 2015

Vessel Name	Code	Port Name	Loa	Ton Gt	Year	Construction Place
MOSS ROSE	LR90	LANCASTER	7.02	2.02	1922	MORECAMBE
MOWGLI	FD520	FLEETWOOD	5.00	0.67	1986	PRESTON
MOWZER	BM236	BRIXHAM	6.90	1.52	2007	ISLE OF WIGHT
MOXIE	PE25	POOLE	7.95	1.41	2009	SOMERSET
MOYALLON	SH24	SCARBOROUGH	11.92	23.55	1985	GIRVAN AYRSHIRE
MOYRA JANE	BRD675	BROADFORD	7.22	1.92	1985	ISLE OF WIGHT
MOYUNA	N938	NEWRY	15.34	43.00	1973	PORTAVOGIE
MUDDY WATERS	SU927	SOUTHAMPTON	6.91	1.00	2002	BEDHAMPTON
MULLET	P1014	PORTSMOUTH	4.50	0.50	2006	Unk
MUNCHKIN MADNESS	GU122	GUERNSEY	6.47	2.38	2002	PEMBROKESHIRE
MURRAY V	K28	KIRKWALL	11.78	12.93	1997	FALMOUTH
MY AMBER	CY303	CASTLEBAY	10.30	9.08	1990	CORNWALL
MY DANIELLE	PH338	PLYMOUTH	5.30	0.75	1988	PLYMOUTH
MY GIRLS	PH572	PLYMOUTH	7.75	2.49	1992	TURNCHAPEL
MY GIRLS II	YH293	YARMOUTH	5.74	1.06	1992	ARUNDEL
MY GIRLS J L L II	BRD645	BROADFORD	9.95	6.30	1999	ANGLESEY
MY GIRLS J.L.L	CY824	CASTLEBAY	11.20	6.62	2003	ICELAND
MY JANE	SH32	SCARBOROUGH	9.98	16.46	1999	ABERYSTWYTH
MY JEM	J159	JERSEY	9.95	5.79	1998	FALMOUTH
MY LADS	WA223	WHITEHAVEN	9.80	8.66	1975	ISLE OF WIGHT
MY LADY	E28	EXETER	5.60	1.40	2002	GBR
MY LASS	PZ291	PENZANCE	9.10	5.31	1977	RYE
MY OWN	LI339	LITTLEHAMPTON	5.49	1.15	1983	BOGNOR REGIS
MY QUEST	LK2	LERWICK	9.95	8.08	2006	SOUTH HUMBERSIDE
MY SARA	RX419	RYE	9.95	11.84	2002	HASTINGS SUSSEX
MY SIOBHAN	OB564	OBAN	9.46	8.80	1981	WORCESTER
MY TARA	OB73	OBAN	10.30	9.08	1990	HAYLE
MY WAY	CK926	COLCHESTER	9.92	10.59	1998	LINCOLNSHIRE
MY WAY	CS451	COWES	12.02	7.84	1980	BEMBRIDGE
MY YACHT	J228	JERSEY	4.47	0.63	1994	UK

UK Fishing Vessels 2015

Vessel Name	Code	Port Name	Loa	Ton Gt	Year	Construction Place
MYGHAL	FH750	FALMOUTH	8.47	8.40	2008	CORNWALL
MYRA G	BA230	BALLANTRAE	9.95	9.57	1990	ANNAN
MYROSS MIST	SS16	ST IVES	9.90	8.23	1989	RYE
MYSTERY	GU61	GUERNSEY	6.31	2.31	1939	GUERNSEY
MYSTERY	GY480	GRIMSBY	8.90	4.02	1938	LEIGH-ON-SEA
MYSTICAL ROSE	CY121	CASTLEBAY	6.25	2.34	1980	AYR
MYSTICAL ROSE II	B24	BELFAST	15.85	41.00	1981	APPLEDORE
MYSTIQUE II	FY869	FOWEY	9.40	6.05	2005	GBR
MYTILUS	B449	BELFAST	27.00	158.25	1999	BRUINISSE
MYTILUS	FY27	FOWEY	6.70	1.45	2007	PORTUGAL
NA'TANT	LI73	LITTLEHAMPTON	7.26	3.01	1981	HIGHCLIFFE
NAN	FD79	FLEETWOOD	9.60	7.17	1992	FLEETWOOD
NANCY ELLEN	CT58	CASTLETOWN	9.50	5.47	2003	FALMOUTH
NANCY ELLEN	DH44	DARTMOUTH	6.40	1.48	1982	SOUTHAMPTON
NANCY GLEN	TT100	TARBERT	12.98	26.41	1991	EYEMOUTH
NAOMI G	PZ778	PENZANCE	4.48	0.56	1992	THE LIZARD CORNWALL
NAOMI M	WK30	WICK	9.30	5.44	1976	WEST MERSEA
NARWHAL	CO204	CAERNARVON	7.43	2.04	1971	SCARBOROUGH
NATALIE	FY602	FOWEY	11.35	18.97	1990	MORVAL LOOE
NATALIE	LI199	LITTLEHAMPTON	6.25	0.92	2006	WEST SUSSEX
NATALIE B	A107	ABERDEEN	26.36	124.00	1967	GRONIGAN HOLLAND
NATALIE D	B173	BELFAST	6.81	2.96	1989	GLEN SHIPYARD
NATALIE H	CO816	CAERNARVON	8.50	2.83	2006	I.O.W
NATALIE KRISTEN II	BH306	BLYTH	9.98	9.15	2008	SUSSEX
NATALIE ROSE	BW27	BARROW	9.49	7.24	1986	PORTAVOGIE
NATALIE ROSE II	OB40	OBAN	10.97	13.64	1983	WORCESTER
NATASHA A	PD780	PETERHEAD	6.50	2.52	1972	NORWAY
NATHALIE	TN16	TROON	18.35	65.00	1971	ST MONANCE
NATIVE	CK12	COLCHESTER	9.14	5.66	1978	HULL
NATTY	M589	MILFORD HAVEN	3.96	0.30	2008	UK

UK Fishing Vessels 2015

Vessel Name	Code	Port Name	Loa	Ton Gt	Year	Construction Place
NAURU	BCK635	BUCKIE	14.95	53.98	1974	BERWICK ON TWEED
NAVADA	PD1026	PETERHEAD	6.75	2.68	1974	GBR
NAVICULA	OB526	OBAN	6.00	1.45	2001	GBR
NAZANNA	WY780	WHITBY	7.93	4.78	1998	FALMOUTH
NAZARENE	PZ336	PENZANCE	8.36	5.23	2001	CORNWALL
NAZARENE	SC21	SCILLY	4.75	1.06	1989	HAYLE
NECORA	BS36	BEAUMARIS	6.85	1.21	2009	UK
NEELTJE	H426	HULL	28.80	329.00	2000	DEMARK
NEFERTARI	OB978	OBAN	5.05	0.75	2000	UNITED KINGDOM
NEMESIS	BRD115	BROADFORD	11.98	10.28	1988	PENRYN CORNWALL
NEMO	BD288	BIDEFORD	12.83	13.33	2004	CORK
NEMO	SE8	SALCOMBE	4.80	0.78	1991	OYSTER BOATS
NEMO	SN219	NORTH SHIELDS	4.30	0.58	1987	NOT KNOWN
NEPTUNE	BD69	BIDEFORD	6.40	1.92	1970	APPLEDORE
NEPTUNE	K36	KIRKWALL	5.24	0.79	2000	SUFFOLK
NEPTUNE	SD201	SUNDERLAND	9.95	13.51	1991	SUNDERLAND
NEPTUNES BRIDE	FY304	FOWEY	4.81	1.00	1976	DOWNDERRY
NEPTUNES PRIDE II	FY767	FOWEY	7.09	2.19	1993	PLYMOUTH
NER E NOUGH	PE237	POOLE	5.98	2.13	1980	CORNWALL
NEREUS	INS172	INVERNESS	19.00	183.00	2012	PORTUGAL
NEREUS	ML6	METHIL	9.30	6.04	1980	GBR
NESTAN 3	M17	MILFORD HAVEN	5.30	1.68	2001	MILFORD HAVEN
NET GAIN	PE556	POOLE	6.00	1.10	1990	BEDHAMPTON HANTS
NETTA	UL85	ULLAPOOL	6.84	1.24	1995	ISLE OF WIGHT
NETTY	PE390	POOLE	5.60	0.90	1992	PLYMOUTH
NETTY'S WAY	GU28	GUERNSEY	6.31	0.95	1998	LES HERBIERS
NEV NEV	BS119	BEAUMARIS	4.64	0.71	2002	ORKNEY
NEVER AGAIN	RX371	RYE	6.80	1.23	1991	RYE
NEVER CAN TELL A	WY341	WHITBY	9.99	8.31	1982	WHITBY

UK Fishing Vessels 2015

Vessel Name	Code	Port Name	Loa	Ton Gt	Year	Construction Place
NEVER DESPAIR	GU132	GUERNSEY	7.45	3.08	1998	DORSET
NEW AQUARIUS	NN92	NEWHAVEN	9.37	4.88	1971	EXMOUTH
NEW DAWN	CN303	CAMPBELTOWN	14.00	24.65	1989	BEVERLEY
NEW DAWN	FR470	FRASERBURGH	14.95	52.63	2004	MACDUFF
NEW DAWN	FY16	FOWEY	6.95	1.64	2013	PORTUGAL
NEW DAWN	GU11	GUERNSEY	9.93	5.32	1998	CORNWALL
NEW DAWN	PL1	PEEL	13.75	31.60	2005	GBR
NEW DAWN	R203	RAMSGATE	6.05	2.85	1980	SEATON DEVON
NEW DAWN	SY884	STORNOWAY	6.60	2.01	1989	LOCHGILPHEAD
NEW DAWN	WH57	WEYMOUTH	4.93	0.88	1967	WEYMOUTH
NEW HARMONY OF HELFORD	FH60	FALMOUTH	9.60	13.04	1995	CORNWALL
NEW SEEKER	E12	EXETER	11.95	25.93	2012	Unk
NEW VENTURE	B914	BELFAST	13.70	39.63	2000	KILKEEL
NEW VENTURE	CL12	CARLISLE	8.80	7.14	1999	BARRY
NEW VENTURE	DR173	DOVER	6.77	1.19	1997	IRELAND
NEW VENTURE	FH5	FALMOUTH	12.38	21.06	1985	CORNWALL
NEW VENTURE	FR39	FRASERBURGH	8.40	5.55	2010	GBR
NEW VENTURE	K112	KIRKWALL	15.93	37.00	1982	APPLEDORE
NEW VENTURE	N304	NEWRY	17.99	84.00	1979	SOUTHAMPTON
NEW VENTURE	WO5	WORKINGTON	9.88	10.02	2011	ENGLAND
NEWBROOK	DH149	DARTMOUTH	14.31	20.25	1960	APPLEDORE
NEWLEK-MOR	FH229	FALMOUTH	4.87	1.09	2000	GBR
NEXT DRIFT	DH410	DARTMOUTH	6.65	1.75	2011	PORTUGAL
NEXT WEEK	LH518	LEITH	8.45	5.88	1996	BORTH YNYSLAS
NIA-G	M27	MILFORD HAVEN	7.93	5.89	1981	FALMOUTH
NIAROO	N998	NEWRY	9.30	4.55	1980	UNKNOWN
NIC NAT	H1077	HULL	5.42	0.73	1974	HORNSEA
NICHOLA JAYNE	MH1	MIDDLESBROUGH	6.40	1.51	2004	NORFOLK
NICHOLAS C	LI90	LITTLEHAMPTON	9.93	6.60	1968	EXMOUTH
NICKS	SE142	SALCOMBE	3.85	0.44	1986	KINGSBRIDGE
NICKY NOO	PH993	PLYMOUTH	3.95	0.65	1998	UK

UK Fishing Vessels 2015

Vessel Name	Code	Port Name	Loa	Ton Gt	Year	Construction Place
NICKY V	DH1	DARTMOUTH	9.80	7.09	1983	CAMELFORD
NICOLA A J	RX82	RYE	5.90	1.91	1981	GBR
NICOLA ANNE	CK305	COLCHESTER	14.30	41.88	1988	FRANCE
NICOLA D	AH26	ARBROATH	4.80	0.91	1986	GLENROTHES
NICOLA D	PH217	PLYMOUTH	5.80	1.68	1982	PLYMOUTH
NICOLA DAWN	LT539	LOWESTOFT	9.97	13.16	1978	KENT
NICOLA FAITH	BS58	BEAUMARIS	10.69	10.89	1987	HULL
NICOLA JANE	OB1043	OBAN	11.32	20.22	1987	FALMOUTH
NICOLA JAYNE	BM491	BRIXHAM	5.00	0.71	1997	BEDHAMPTON
NICOLA L	WY37	WHITBY	13.60	35.65	1984	TEES MARINE
NICOLA MAY	PZ660	PENZANCE	14.98	26.65	1969	FRANCE
NICOLA-JOANNE	N5	NEWRY	10.80	13.34	1982	SUNDERLAND
NICOLAIRE J	SA43	SWANSEA	5.00	1.14	1988	ALDRIDGE
NICOLE	OB900	OBAN	4.97	1.07	1982	PLYMOUTH
NICOLE B	RX390	RYE	9.81	9.47	1997	CORNWALL
NIGHEAN DONN	TT237	TARBERT	4.30	0.43	1984	ORKNEY
NIGHT OWL	KY454	KIRKCALDY	7.70	3.89	1992	CORNWALL
NIGHTHAWK	WO115	WORKINGTON	5.18	1.08	1959	GBR
NIGHTRIDER OF KEYHAVEN	SU388	SOUTHAMPTON	9.75	8.97	1977	KEYHAVEN
NIK NAK	PZ611	PENZANCE	5.62	1.02	1977	PLYMOUTH
NIKI LOU	FH17	FALMOUTH	6.00	1.23	2012	LEYLAND PRESTON
NIKKI LOU	AB52	ABERYSTWYTH	9.45	5.65	1974	CORNWALL
NIKKI LOUISE	SS126	ST IVES	6.25	2.54	1989	HAYLE CORNWALL
NIL DESPERANDUM	DH390	DARTMOUTH	9.02	5.24	1981	WORCESTER
NIL DESPERANDUM	MR3	MANCHESTER	9.75	7.08	1998	BANFFSHIRE
NIMBLE	BF569	BANFF	5.86	1.05	1991	STONEHAVEN
NIMBLE	WH478	WEYMOUTH	7.14	1.25	1961	HAMBLE SOUTHAMPTON
NIMROD	B926	BELFAST	16.28	64.00	1976	ARBROATH
NIMROD	BH227	BLYTH	16.50	95.00	1989	ARBROATH
NIMROD	MH6	MIDDLESBROUGH	6.72	1.11	2006	CLEVELAND

UK Fishing Vessels 2015

Vessel Name	Code	Port Name	Loa	Ton Gt	Year	Construction Place
NIMROD II	MH2	MIDDLESBROUGH	6.65	1.67	2007	PORTUGAL
NINA	E7	EXETER	5.50	1.06	2008	GBR
NINA MAY	E538	EXETER	4.80	0.56	2000	GBR
NIORD	ME10	MONTROSE	6.50	1.54	2005	FIFE
NIPPER	BM44	BRIXHAM	5.92	1.67	1986	PENRYN CORNWALL
NIPPY	CY449	CASTLEBAY	3.70	0.43	1991	NORWAY
NO 8 WILLING HANDS	INS157	INVERNESS	6.07	1.49	1975	HILTON FEARN
NO MORE	SU6	SOUTHAMPTON	9.95	13.29	1989	LONDON
NOAH GIL	SE26	SALCOMBE	6.40	1.54	1990	CORNWALL
NOAH-C	GU65	GUERNSEY	6.57	0.53	2007	PENICHE PORTUGAL
NOMAD	NN485	NEWHAVEN	6.10	0.98	1993	ISLE OF WIGHT
NOMAD	OB474	OBAN	5.80	1.15	1989	VALENTIA MARINE EIRE
NONAKIE	BK83	BERWICK ON TWEED	11.35	6.33	2005	UK
NOORDZEE	TN30	TROON	31.10	249.00	1980	NETHERLANDS
NORAH-T	SS53	ST IVES	5.64	1.48	1987	ST IVES CORNWALL
NORANN	BRD70	BROADFORD	7.46	3.26	1981	SUSSEX
NORDIC BRIDE	LK703	LERWICK	7.35	4.07	1983	SCARFSKERRY
NORDIC WAY	CY340	CASTLEBAY	15.52	59.00	1992	STROMNESS
NORDSTJERNEN	GY1477	GRIMSBY	15.60	32.00	1976	DENMARK
NORFOLK GIRL	LT399	LOWESTOFT	6.40	1.52	2006	NORFOLK
NORLAN	BF362	BANFF	24.80	309.00	1999	MACDUFF
NORLAND WIND	KY992	KIRKCALDY	7.49	1.50	1999	VENTNOR
NORLYN	BCK3	BUCKIE	8.26	7.54	1996	CORNWALL
NORMA ANN	OB497	OBAN	7.12	2.91	1991	FALMOUTH
NORMA MARY	H110	HULL	73.40	2342.00	1989	FAROE ISLANDS
NORNESS	A860	ABERDEEN	5.96	1.11	1992	KINEFF
NORONYA	K733	KIRKWALL	18.46	138.00	2008	WHITBY
NORSE COURAGE	WK28	WICK	6.40	2.13	2010	CORNWALL
NORSEMAN	K972	KIRKWALL	5.90	1.03	1990	STONEHAVEN
NORTH EASTERN	SN45	NORTH SHIELDS	11.51	8.03	1983	AMBLE

UK Fishing Vessels 2015

Vessel Name	Code	Port Name	Loa	Ton Gt	Year	Construction Place
NORTHEASTERN	FR85	FRASERBURGH	7.09	2.50	1988	MONTROSE
NORTHERN CLIPPER	DH119	DARTMOUTH	13.04	27.45	1971	GRANVILLE FRANCE
NORTHERN DAWN	N10	NEWRY	20.50	86.00	1969	FRANCE
NORTHERN ISLE	CE121	COLERAINE	7.10	4.57	1970	LISBURN N IRELAND
NORTHERN ISLE	WY28	WHITBY	8.07	3.43	1991	FALMOUTH
NORTHERN LIGHT	AR861	AYR	6.00	1.70	1992	ISLE OF WHITHORN
NORTHERN LIGHTS	UL138	ULLAPOOL	6.59	1.16	1980	PENRYN CORNWALL
NORTHERN LIGHTS	YH320	YARMOUTH	9.50	8.12	1978	FALMOUTH CORNWALL
NORTHERN LIGHTS II	PO17	PORTLAND	8.00	5.76	1989	UNKNOWN
NORTHERN PRIDE	BK64	BERWICK ON TWEED	10.37	4.60	1977	AMBLE
NORTHERN PRIDE	YH115	YARMOUTH	6.25	1.71	1983	AMBLE HUMBERSIDE
NORTHERN QUEST	N777	NEWRY	19.27	89.00	1980	FRANCE
NORTHERN STAR	SC16	SCILLY	4.45	0.67	1978	PENZANCE
NORTHERN STAR	SY11	STORNOWAY	16.46	39.00	1968	ST MONANS
NORTHERN STAR	WK828	WICK	7.15	1.89	1984	GBR
NORTHERN STAR II	FY583	FOWEY	7.80	3.62	1982	POLRUAN CORNWALL ENGLAND
NORTHERN VENTURE	N77	NEWRY	19.90	110.00	1982	CO.CORK
NORTHERN VIKING	N74	NEWRY	20.40	112.00	1983	FRANCE
NORTHWESTERN	GU76	GUERNSEY	8.64	2.66	2006	WADEBRIDGE
NORTHWOOD	SC25	SCILLY	7.47	2.27	1990	HAYLE
NORWASTERN	LK29	LERWICK	11.70	17.76	2012	KYLE OF LOCHALSH
NOVA SPERO	PZ187	PENZANCE	20.43	110.00	1973	ARBROATH
NOVA STAR	OB395	OBAN	6.00	1.89	1993	CORNWALL
NOVANTAE	SH270	SCARBOROUGH	13.90	37.58	1990	SUNDERLAND
NYELLA	R109	RAMSGATE	7.01	2.75	1972	MANSTON KENT
NYUGGEL	LK3440	LERWICK	6.96	2.67	1955	GBR
O GENITA	FD529	FLEETWOOD	33.30	315.00	1977	SPAIN
O.C.A.	GU126	GUERNSEY	8.40	3.96	2006	PENRYN & GUERNSEY
OBI I	WH755	WEYMOUTH	4.94	0.72	1990	GBR
OBSESSION	K99	KIRKWALL	11.00	11.48	1986	PENRYN

UK Fishing Vessels 2015

Vessel Name	Code	Port Name	Loa	Ton Gt	Year	Construction Place
OBSESSION	PE1188	POOLE	7.90	2.44	2008	GBR
OBSESSION H	K553	KIRKWALL	5.60	0.98	1990	ORKNEY BOAT BUILDERS
OCEAN BOUNTY	PD182	PETERHEAD	24.26	266.00	1998	MACDUFF
OCEAN BREEZE	PZ775	PENZANCE	5.62	1.48	1991	POLRUAN
OCEAN BRIDE	WK8	WICK	6.05	1.43	1985	GBR
OCEAN CHALLENGE	BF85	BANFF	21.30	202.00	2000	MACDUFF
OCEAN CHALLENGE	FR771	FRASERBURGH	9.65	6.09	2010	FALMOUTH CORNWALL
OCEAN CREST	BF854	BANFF	6.42	1.45	2002	ABERDEENSHIRE
OCEAN CREST	LH87	LEITH	8.14	3.89	1977	SCARBOROUGH
OCEAN DANCER	J72	JERSEY	5.78	1.11	1999	UK
OCEAN DAWN	A200	ABERDEEN	4.78	0.63	1998	MACDUFF
OCEAN DAWN	BH7	BLYTH	5.57	0.76	1985	Unk
OCEAN DAWN	H347	HULL	26.50	224.00	1987	ST MONANS FIFE
OCEAN DIVINE	B1005	BELFAST	11.35	11.71	1982	PENRYN CORNWALL
OCEAN HARVEST	FY12	FOWEY	11.37	14.66	1985	PENRYN
OCEAN HARVEST	PD198	PETERHEAD	28.35	349.00	2008	DNK
OCEAN HARVESTER	N273	NEWRY	22.78	151.00	1976	SWEDEN
OCEAN HERALD	CN322	CAMPBELTOWN	14.94	28.95	1970	EYEMOUTH
OCEAN HUNTER	SY503	STORNOWAY	17.22	66.00	1969	ST MONANCE FIFE
OCEAN MAID	BA55	BALLANTRAE	19.62	60.00	1973	ST. MONANCE
OCEAN MAID	CY84	CASTLEBAY	10.99	14.83	1974	ORKNEY
OCEAN PEARL	WY81	WHITBY	5.85	1.33	1988	RUSWARP NR WHITBY
OCEAN PIONEER	FR928	FRASERBURGH	19.00	161.00	2000	SPAIN
OCEAN PRIDE	FH24	FALMOUTH	18.75	131.00	1987	BUCKIE
OCEAN QUEEN	FY26	FOWEY	8.27	6.15	1969	LOOE
OCEAN QUEST	BF77	BANFF	61.50	1632.00	2002	ESP
OCEAN QUEST	DO33	DOUGLAS	5.80	1.65	1989	UNITED KINGDOM
OCEAN QUEST	FR375	FRASERBURGH	21.28	138.00	1982	CAMPBELTOWN
OCEAN REAPER IV	FR273	FRASERBURGH	21.30	189.00	1999	MACDUFF
OCEAN REWARD IV	BCK83	BUCKIE	21.22	180.00	1997	MACDUFF
OCEAN SPIRIT	BM493	BRIXHAM	13.70	29.69	1999	CORNWALL

UK Fishing Vessels 2015

Vessel Name	Code	Port Name	Loa	Ton Gt	Year	Construction Place
OCEAN SPIRIT	N1013	NEWRY	9.93	9.36	1989	HULL
OCEAN SPIRIT	SY2	STORNOWAY	13.10	31.20	1979	PORTAUOGIE
OCEAN SPRAY	CN65	CAMPBELTOWN	7.32	2.94	1988	FALMOUTH
OCEAN SPRAY	CY113	CASTLEBAY	6.20	1.29	1991	FALMOUTH
OCEAN SPRAY	SH94	SCARBOROUGH	14.11	40.34	1990	POLRUAN
OCEAN STAR	OB48	OBAN	6.83	0.56	2009	HAVANT
OCEAN SURF	FR9	FRASERBURGH	5.70	1.00	1970	GBR
OCEAN TRUST	FR152	FRASERBURGH	21.31	164.00	1985	MACDUFF
OCEAN TRUST	PD787	PETERHEAD	18.04	121.00	1982	MACDUFF
OCEAN VENTURE	B282	BELFAST	19.46	74.00	1971	GRAMPIAN
OCEAN VENTURE	FR77	FRASERBURGH	61.50	1632.00	2003	VIZCAYA
OCEAN VENTURE II	PD340	PETERHEAD	30.50	370.00	1992	ST MONANS FIFE
OCEAN WAY	BF878	BANFF	18.23	134.00	1987	MACDUFF
OCEAN WAY	FR349	FRASERBURGH	17.07	80.00	1974	BUCKIE
OCEAN WAY	LK207	LERWICK	24.30	268.00	1996	BUCKIE
OCEANA	BF840	BANFF	9.95	18.78	2000	PETERHEAD
OCEANA	INS1	INVERNESS	8.53	5.20	1984	FALMOUTH
OCEANS GIFT	NN2	NEWHAVEN	5.30	1.30	2011	SHOREHAM
OCEANUS	N924	NEWRY	18.51	106.00	1983	DINGLE
OCTOBER MORNING	BE9	BARNSTAPLE	8.07	3.99	2000	Unk
ODD TIMES	IH219	IPSWICH	8.70	4.53	1963	IPSWICH
ODESSA	GU99	GUERNSEY	6.54	1.53	2003	NEYLAND PEMBROKESHIRE
ODETTE	K710	KIRKWALL	9.00	5.23	1987	BIRKENHEAD
ODILIA	GU388	GUERNSEY	6.70	1.78	1990	GUERNSEY
ODIN	CN92	CAMPBELTOWN	5.51	1.20	1989	SOUTHAMPTON
ODIN	GU80	GUERNSEY	8.14	5.87	1976	CORNWALL
ODIN	LA572	LLANELLI	5.10	0.70	1997	UNKNOWN
ODIN	M12	MILFORD HAVEN	4.59	0.80	2009	Unk
ODYSSEY	SH44	SCARBOROUGH	7.80	3.86	2013	KENT
OHIO	FY123	FOWEY	5.60	1.11	1985	PLYMOUTH

UK Fishing Vessels 2015

Vessel Name	Code	Port Name	Loa	Ton Gt	Year	Construction Place
OKAVANGO	OB951	OBAN	7.01	1.99	1976	FARLINGTON
OLED	LI537	LITTLEHAMPTON	5.02	0.64	1975	BOGNOR REGIS
OLIVE BRANCH	BA9	BALLANTRAE	18.59	71.00	1971	SANDHAVEN FRASERBURGH
OLIVE C	PH5	PLYMOUTH	14.70	33.24	1970	FRANCE
OLIVER HENRY	RX427	RYE	8.30	5.23	2005	FALMOUTH
OLIVIA J	GU203	GUERNSEY	8.62	8.08	1985	JERSEY
OLIVIA JEAN	TN35	TROON	33.86	242.00	1980	GIESSENDAM HOLLAND
OLIVIA N	P993	PORTSMOUTH	7.00	1.06	2002	GBR
OLIVIA ROSE	LK806	LERWICK	8.40	4.79	2001	WHITBY
OLIVIA ROSE	WY806	WHITBY	9.73	8.18	2013	WHITBY
OLLY	WO15	WORKINGTON	5.49	1.45	1974	HARRINGTON
OLWEN GEORGE	NN743	NEWHAVEN	5.10	0.81	2002	CORNWALL
OLWEN MAY	NN241	NEWHAVEN	5.30	1.30	1985	EASTBOURNE
OLY-RAY	F52	FAVERSHAM	13.95	18.76	2002	Unk
ON WARD	PH74	PLYMOUTH	5.64	1.92	1971	CORNWALL
ONDAS VERDES	RX412	RYE	4.90	0.77	2002	GBR
ONTARIO	LA4	LLANELLI	5.00	0.86	2009	LANCASHIRE
ONWARD	HH55	HARWICH	7.40	3.31	2000	SUFFOLK
ONWARD	K52	KIRKWALL	4.52	0.55	2011	ORKNEY
ONWARD	LK3398	LERWICK	8.96	4.66	1981	BEAUMARIS
ONWARD	LN47	KINGS LYNN	9.20	4.13	1982	WEST MERSEA
ONWARD	M954	MILFORD HAVEN	6.37	1.36	1996	MACDUFF
ONWARD	MT100	MARYPORT	18.07	108.00	1981	FRASERBURGH
ONWARD	PD349	PETERHEAD	9.06	5.66	2011	IRELAND
ONWARD	PE482	POOLE	6.00	3.09	1989	FALMOUTH
ONWARD	PZ768	PENZANCE	4.73	1.05	1989	HAYLE
ONWARD	SY799	STORNOWAY	11.83	15.61	1987	WICK
ONWARD	UL1	ULLAPOOL	11.62	16.74	1988	HAVANT
ONWARD STAR	SH165	SCARBOROUGH	16.54	43.00	1966	FRASERBURGH
OOR LASS	AH1	ARBROATH	6.93	1.19	2002	ISLE OF WIGHT

UK Fishing Vessels 2015

Vessel Name	Code	Port Name	Loa	Ton Gt	Year	Construction Place
OOR SAUND	KY1026	KIRKCALDY	6.52	1.30	2004	GBR
OPHELIA	B41	BELFAST	9.64	10.73	1971	FRANCE
OPPORTUNE	LK209	LERWICK	23.60	176.04	1984	SMOGEN
OPPORTUNE	UL29	ULLAPOOL	6.55	1.83	1980	HOYLAKE
OPPORTUNE	WK171	WICK	25.90	204.05	1979	CAMPBELTOWN
OPPORTUNITY	FE6	FOLKESTONE	8.20	4.49	1992	PORTLAND
OPPORTUNUS IV	PD96	PETERHEAD	19.95	153.10	2007	DENMARK
OPPOSITION	BRD190	BROADFORD	8.10	4.16	1973	GBR
OPTIMIST	LO70	LONDON	9.90	12.40	1989	HEYBRIDGE
OPTIMISTIC	BF891	BANFF	5.25	1.01	1995	Unk
OPTIMISTIC	SH50	SCARBOROUGH	9.60	5.70	2013	UNUITED KINGDOM
ORCA	A971	ABERDEEN	9.80	9.70	2012	UK
ORCA	BW255	BARROW	4.87	1.00	1999	PRESTON
ORCA	CT52	CASTLETOWN	9.56	4.40	1999	FALMOUTH
ORCA	GU73	GUERNSEY	6.50	2.77	1995	GUERNSEY
ORCA	LH521	LEITH	6.77	1.29	1997	UNKNOWN
ORCA	M26	MILFORD HAVEN	9.83	10.98	2004	COLCHESTER
ORCA	PZ3	PENZANCE	4.88	0.62	1999	SUSSEX
ORCA	SE71	SALCOMBE	4.95	0.81	2004	SPAIN
ORCA	SS707	ST IVES	6.90	0.96	2002	ISLE OF WIGHT
ORCADES II	PW364	PADSTOW	12.19	5.04	2002	NEWHAVEN
ORCADIA	WK115	WICK	3.81	0.70	1983	WICK
ORCADIS	FR22	FRASERBURGH	6.08	2.25	1994	STONEHAVEN
ORCAT	SH11	SCARBOROUGH	8.27	3.22	2000	VENTNOR
ORIANNE	AH268	ARBROATH	9.90	5.57	2001	ICELAND
ORIENT	PW458	PADSTOW	8.40	5.75	1988	ROCHESTER
ORION	BA813	BALLANTRAE	7.26	2.56	1991	STONEHAVEN
ORION	BF432	BANFF	19.90	195.00	2000	ABERDEENSHIRE
ORION	FD10	FLEETWOOD	6.60	2.80	1980	FALMOUTH
ORION	FR2	FRASERBURGH	6.21	1.37	2006	NOT KNOWN

UK Fishing Vessels 2015

Vessel Name	Code	Port Name	Loa	Ton Gt	Year	Construction Place
ORION	K40	KIRKWALL	9.45	5.86	1983	POOLE
ORION	LK67	LERWICK	6.70	3.24	1987	ORKNEY
ORION	LT15	LOWESTOFT	9.98	14.28	1989	LOWESTOFT
ORION	OB151	OBAN	9.90	7.53	1991	BARTON ON HUMBER
ORION	PD158	PETERHEAD	6.49	3.38	1981	PENZANCE
ORION	SS273	ST IVES	8.02	3.88	1978	HAYLE
ORION	SY22	STORNOWAY	5.65	0.91	1991	GBR
ORION II	WK21	WICK	5.51	1.10	1986	WICK
ORKNEY DOLPHIN	LT1022	LOWESTOFT	5.75	1.32	1992	GBR
ORKNEY STAR	CY193	CASTLEBAY	5.69	1.20	1990	SUSSEX
ORTAC	BD99	BIDEFORD	7.38	3.13	1974	APPLEDORE NORTH DEVON
ORTANCA	J70	JERSEY	4.97	0.81	1992	UK
ORTHELES	LT220	LOWESTOFT	7.48	3.00	1961	LEIGH-ON-SEA
OSIRIS	PE1125	POOLE	5.50	1.23	2001	GBR
OSPREY	AH35	ARBROATH	8.32	5.72	2008	CORNWALL
OSPREY	BK516	BERWICK ON TWEED	8.80	3.85	1997	UNKNOWN
OSPREY	CO37	CAERNARVON	9.93	6.87	1983	HAYLE CORNWALL
OSPREY	FH774	FALMOUTH	4.67	1.06	2004	ENGLAND
OSPREY	INS35	INVERNESS	6.15	1.73	2000	NORWICH
OSPREY	K839	KIRKWALL	8.69	5.42	1989	BURRAY ORKNEY
OSPREY	KY445	KIRKCALDY	6.50	3.23	1991	ANSTRUTHER FIFE
OSPREY	LK158	LERWICK	7.28	2.89	1983	BURRA ISLE SHETLAND
OSPREY	M216	MILFORD HAVEN	7.69	2.37	2001	ST. DAVIDS
OSPREY	MN39	MALDON	4.85	0.89	1983	REDGRAVE SUFFOLK
OSPREY	N902	NEWRY	11.59	25.62	1989	PENRYN
OSPREY	RO22	ROTHESAY	9.95	7.65	1961	PETERHEAD
OSPREY	SS17	ST IVES	5.02	0.68	1994	DORSET
OSPREY	SU71	SOUTHAMPTON	6.80	1.64	1986	PORTSMOUTH
OSPREY	SY300	STORNOWAY	7.80	4.40	2007	SOMERSET
OSPREY	WK14	WICK	13.84	31.57	1965	UNKNOWN

UK Fishing Vessels 2015

Vessel Name	Code	Port Name	Loa	Ton Gt	Year	Construction Place
OSPREY A	CO530	CAERNARVON	6.20	1.33	2001	GBR
OSPREY II	PE332	POOLE	5.19	0.55	1999	DORSET
OSPREY JA	LK321	LERWICK	9.99	7.93	1957	FRASERBURGH
OSPREY.	PZ127	PENZANCE	9.85	3.73	1987	CORNWALL
OSSIE I	LI525	LITTLEHAMPTON	5.30	0.56	2000	SUSSEX
OTAKI	FR53	FRASERBURGH	4.93	0.80	1985	WEST SUSSEX
OTRANTO II	AB107	ABERYSTWYTH	7.01	2.26	1972	RYDE ISLE OF WIGHT
OTTER	BE6	BARNSTAPLE	4.40	0.55	1990	Unk
OTTER	E25	EXETER	3.79	0.61	1988	BUDLEIGH SALTERTON
OTTER	OB523	OBAN	6.52	2.14	1992	POOLE DORSET
OTTER III	SM803	SHOREHAM	5.31	1.29	2004	CHORLEY
OUR ANNA	PZ657	PENZANCE	40.20	465.00	1992	STELLENDAM
OUR BELLE ANN	PW100	PADSTOW	11.73	13.28	1985	WADEBRIDGE
OUR BESS	IH314	IPSWICH	8.00	9.53	1999	FALMOUTH
OUR BESS	RX432	RYE	7.90	5.64	2006	GBR
OUR BETTY	SM807	SHOREHAM	7.95	6.18	2005	SUSSEX
OUR BOYS	LT972	LOWESTOFT	4.60	0.73	1980	UNK
OUR BRIA LEA	AB11	ABERYSTWYTH	4.82	0.61	2004	UK
OUR CARA	B957	BELFAST	5.10	0.86	2001	N. IRELAND
OUR CAROLINE	LT163	LOWESTOFT	9.48	7.42	1974	FRANCE
OUR CAROLL II	CK924	COLCHESTER	9.15	4.20	1985	RYE
OUR CARRIE	ML384	METHIL	9.82	8.54	1978	PORTSMOUTH
OUR CATHERINE	BRD77	BROADFORD	9.99	8.93	1989	HEREFORD
OUR CATHLENE	RX435	RYE	6.50	2.26	1964	DUNGENESS
OUR CHRISTINE	SE44	SALCOMBE	6.68	1.70	1992	CORNWALL
OUR DORIS	J626	JERSEY	6.25	1.33	1995	FRA
OUR ENDEAVOUR	CK96	COLCHESTER	9.38	8.92	1981	SOUTHAMPTON
OUR ENDEAVOUR	E161	EXETER	9.95	14.45	1988	DORSET
OUR GIRLS	FY37	FOWEY	5.73	1.56	1980	WOLVERHAMPTON
OUR GRACE	N464	NEWRY	9.96	11.85	2001	PENRYN
OUR GRACE	TH3	TEIGNMOUTH	5.60	1.15	1995	GBR

UK Fishing Vessels 2015

Vessel Name	Code	Port Name	Loa	Ton Gt	Year	Construction Place
OUR HAZEL	UL543	ULLAPOOL	19.97	157.00	1994	NAVIA
OUR HERITAGE	FR237	FRASERBURGH	16.89	53.00	1976	NOBLES FRASEBURGH
OUR HOLLY	RX55	RYE	7.26	3.44	2011	SUSSEX
OUR JACK	GU88	GUERNSEY	3.60	0.47	1994	GUERNSEY
OUR JAMES	MT66	MARYPORT	13.57	24.92	1965	ST. MONANS
OUR JENNY	BD4	BIDEFORD	11.75	12.97	2011	HOLYHEAD ANGLESEY
OUR JESSY	PW18	PADSTOW	5.84	1.08	1987	BRANDESBURTON
OUR JOE	WY805	WHITBY	4.95	1.26	2000	CAMBORNE
OUR JOSIE GRACE	BD287	BIDEFORD	14.95	50.72	2002	NEWHAVEN
OUR JULIA	SH310	SCARBOROUGH	14.19	23.12	1965	DENMARK
OUR KATE	DR165	DOVER	8.70	4.98	1991	RYE SUSSEX
OUR KATIE	PZ260	PENZANCE	6.98	2.43	1962	PORTHLEVEN
OUR KATY	CF24	CARDIFF	5.60	1.45	1978	DUNBARTONSHIRE
OUR LADS	BK36	BERWICK ON TWEED	7.82	2.01	1985	CORNWALL
OUR LADS	RY12	RAMSEY	7.76	4.74	1993	GBR
OUR LADS III	SS699	ST IVES	5.94	1.46	2001	CARMBORNE
OUR LADY	BM189	BRIXHAM	9.85	4.65	1981	LEIGH ESSEX
OUR LADY	CF6	CARDIFF	9.75	8.43	1957	WHITSTABLE
OUR LASS III	WY261	WHITBY	25.94	261.00	2012	UK
OUR LASSIE	LN177	KINGS LYNN	12.02	16.87	1955	FRASERBURGH
OUR LISA	GU13	GUERNSEY	4.75	1.16	1989	GUERNSEY
OUR LIZ	FY47	FOWEY	8.68	5.17	1983	LOOE CORNWALL
OUR LOUISE	SA316	SWANSEA	9.75	10.80	1992	SWANSEA
OUR MARIA	OB150	OBAN	10.00	14.81	1987	PENRYN CORNWALL
OUR MAXINE	FY35	FOWEY	4.54	0.67	1992	MARAZION
OUR MELISSA	SD403	SUNDERLAND	14.75	16.89	1979	DENMARK
OUR MIRANDA	BM27	BRIXHAM	25.28	155.00	1982	KATWIJK NETHERLANDS
OUR NINA	SM423	SHOREHAM	5.50	1.41	2000	GBR
OUR OLIVIA BELLE	BD277	BIDEFORD	14.95	73.35	2005	FIFE
OUR PAMMY	DH135	DARTMOUTH	8.48	6.14	1974	MYLOR BRIDGE FALMOUTH

UK Fishing Vessels 2015

Vessel Name	Code	Port Name	Loa	Ton Gt	Year	Construction Place
OUR PORTLAND FISHER	GU417	GUERNSEY	8.54	8.58	1987	CORNWALL
OUR PRIDE	PD77	PETERHEAD	18.25	104.00	1984	MACDUFF
OUR RITA	SM72	SHOREHAM	5.00	0.58	1977	NEWHAVEN
OUR ROSEANNE	PH5547	PLYMOUTH	9.99	10.34	1997	LINCOLNSHIRE
OUR RUBY	RX447	RYE	4.90	0.68	2009	GBR
OUR SAMMY	PE526	POOLE	8.16	5.42	1990	POOLE
OUR SARAH JANE	CT141	CASTLETOWN	13.98	30.39	1999	NEWHAVEN
OUR SARAH JANE	NN710	NEWHAVEN	9.83	10.15	2006	ESSEX
OUR SARAH JAYNE	BM116	BRIXHAM	14.02	28.24	1973	APPLEDORE
OUR SHARON	SH7	SCARBOROUGH	9.60	6.35	2009	CANVEY ISLAND
OUR SIAN GRACE	RX90	RYE	9.00	4.15	1998	HASTINGS
OUR VALERIE ANN	FD515	FLEETWOOD	6.20	2.03	1997	ISLE OF WIGHT
OUR VENTURE	K355	KIRKWALL	12.75	33.27	1982	TROON
OUR WENDY	BM342	BRIXHAM	5.64	1.08	2008	PORTUGAL
OUR WINNIE	PW242	PADSTOW	3.96	0.36	1965	FOWEY
OUR ZOE	PW28	PADSTOW	7.40	3.76	1992	RYE
OUT OF THE BLUE	GU30	GUERNSEY	9.90	10.63	1983	CARDIFF
OUT OF THE BLUE	GU30	GUERNSEY	9.77	7.05	2014	GBR
OUT RIGGER	LN453	KINGS LYNN	8.66	3.23	1982	UNKNOWN
OUTCAST	E544	EXETER	7.60	1.85	2003	ISLE OF WHITE
OUTCAST 2	E56	EXETER	8.40	3.03	2003	ISLE OF WIGHT
OUTLAW	CE160	COLERAINE	7.32	3.70	1977	ISLE OF WIGHT
OUTRAGE	J238	JERSEY	4.38	0.65	1964	UK
OUTSETTER	SE46	SALCOMBE	6.45	3.41	1984	PENRYN CORNWALL
OUTSIDER	OB983	OBAN	7.90	2.27	2004	VENTNOR
OYSTER CATCHER	FR12	FRASERBURGH	6.38	1.44	2007	NOT KNOWN
OZ 5	R491	RAMSGATE	4.65	0.74	2000	GBR
P G K	RX405	RYE	8.50	6.75	1984	NEWHAVEN
P.W.S	DH92	DARTMOUTH	4.40	0.61	1991	KINGSBRIDGE
PACEMAKER	GY165	GRIMSBY	16.45	49.00	1970	BUCKIE

UK Fishing Vessels 2015

Vessel Name	Code	Port Name	Loa	Ton Gt	Year	Construction Place
PAGE THREE	M732	MILFORD HAVEN	9.75	5.45	1978	EXMOUTH
PAIR I	BD249	BIDEFORD	5.35	0.86	1990	SOUTHAMPTON
PAL O MINE	BF9	BANFF	5.79	1.54	1992	UNK
PALATINE	FY149	FOWEY	9.95	10.64	1985	CORNWALL
PALINDRA	FE58	FOLKESTONE	9.17	4.98	1987	ROCHESTER
PALORES	PW75	PADSTOW	7.93	7.33	1980	PADSTAW
PAM	WH442	WEYMOUTH	4.80	0.74	1998	DORSET
PAMELA JANE	FY888	FOWEY	6.90	1.20	2008	GBR
PAMELA MARY	LN471	KINGS LYNN	12.18	14.96	2002	BARTON UPON HUMBER
PAMELA S	WY38	WHITBY	16.76	41.00	1969	FRASEBURGH
PAN ARCTIC	CO359	CAERNARVON	4.80	0.69	1986	ORKNEY
PANDION	GY356	GRIMSBY	9.15	5.76	1987	HULL
PANDORA	WK62	WICK	6.00	1.26	2004	KINNEFF
PANIA	FY918	FOWEY	6.20	1.80	2003	CORNWALL
PAPAS BOYS	N1024	NEWRY	7.00	2.34	1980	UK
PARAVEL	FY369	FOWEY	10.88	16.48	1979	LOOE
PATHFINDER	AB199	ABERYSTWYTH	8.50	5.61	1987	FALMOUTH
PATHFINDER	AH717	ARBROATH	7.39	1.81	2004	HAMPSHIRE
PATHFINDER	LK431	LERWICK	8.08	2.86	1977	FALMOUTH
PATHFINDER	OB181	OBAN	18.16	42.00	1964	GIRVAN
PATHFINDER II	SH209	SCARBOROUGH	9.90	4.59	1980	GBR
PATHWAY	PD165	PETERHEAD	66.60	2194.00	2003	FLEKKFJORD
PATRICE	PZ125	PENZANCE	8.00	4.11	1988	PORTHLEVEN
PATRICE 11	FH55	FALMOUTH	7.78	3.16	1988	FALMOUTH
PATRICIA ANNE	FH734	FALMOUTH	5.82	1.83	1984	FALMOUTH
PATRICIA B	BN438	BOSTON	13.94	21.53	2003	SOUTH HUMBERSIDE
PATRICIA CHRISTINE	WY53	WHITBY	7.38	2.11	1984	SANDSEND WHITBY
PATRICIA JANE	SA66	SWANSEA	8.33	4.84	1995	WEST SUSSEX
PATRICIA MARTA	OB113	OBAN	32.99	291.00	1995	SPAIN
PATRICIA O'MELIA	BH98	BLYTH	6.10	2.43	1980	CORNWALL
PATRIOT	WY127	WHITBY	6.42	1.35	2006	NORTH YORKSHIRE

UK Fishing Vessels 2015

Vessel Name	Code	Port Name	Loa	Ton Gt	Year	Construction Place
PATSY ANNE	WA5	WHITEHAVEN	11.58	11.86	1969	STROMNESS
PATSY B	FR925	FRASERBURGH	11.41	9.61	1984	NEWHAVEN
PATSY DEE	OB34	OBAN	5.70	0.68	1983	FALMOUTH
PATSY J	CE68	COLERAINE	9.80	5.74	1990	PEMBROKE DOCK
PAUL ARRAN	PZ140	PENZANCE	5.90	1.98	1978	WITHAM
PAUL PATRICK	H1103	HULL	9.98	9.70	2001	BARTON UPON HUMBER
PAULA	PE436	POOLE	5.50	0.45	1962	POOLE
PAULA B	OB933	OBAN	7.40	5.18	1999	VENTNOR
PAULA LEE II	RX310	RYE	5.80	2.49	1991	RYE
PAULA ROSE	FH300	FALMOUTH	7.19	2.15	1980	HULL
PAULA'S FOLLY II	NN740	NEWHAVEN	5.36	1.93	2005	LANCASHIRE
PAULINE B	GU108	GUERNSEY	6.50	3.16	1991	GUERNSEY
PAULINE CLAIRE	NN311	NEWHAVEN	5.30	1.30	2011	WEST SUSSEX
PAULINE J	CO245	CAERNARVON	9.98	11.58	1987	PLYMOUTH
PAVALINE G	GU144	GUERNSEY	4.28	0.60	1994	GUERNSEY
PEACE AND PLENTY III	BM24	BRIXHAM	11.73	27.47	1983	SWANSEA
PEACEFUL WATERS	DO162	DOUGLAS	6.80	2.31	2011	GBR
PEADAR MARIE	GU199	GUERNSEY	18.35	89.18	1992	DEN HELDER
PEARL	SY869	STORNOWAY	4.88	0.67	1986	NOT KNOWN
PEARL III	WY232	WHITBY	6.77	1.74	1970	WHITBY
PEBBLE	CO796	CAERNARVON	4.90	0.52	2000	HORNSEA
PEBBLES	WK17	WICK	5.54	0.98	1990	GBR
PECTEN	DH402	DARTMOUTH	3.20	0.29	1989	ISSY LES MOULINEAUX
PEDDEN	PZ67	PENZANCE	4.80	0.71	1980	UK
PEDRYN	CO83	CAERNARVON	6.90	0.85	2003	ISLE OF WIGHT
PEGASUS	BH3	BLYTH	8.10	2.73	2010	ENGLAND
PEGASUS	GK1	GREENOCK	5.91	2.21	1972	PORT HEIGHAM
PEGASUS	GU5072	GUERNSEY	5.49	1.38	1977	GUERNSEY
PEGASUS	KY442	KIRKCALDY	9.98	15.49	1990	SUNDERLAND
PEGASUS	OB216	OBAN	11.75	10.49	1989	GBR

UK Fishing Vessels 2015

Vessel Name	Code	Port Name	Loa	Ton Gt	Year	Construction Place
PEGASUS	P958	PORTSMOUTH	6.85	2.09	1982	ISLE OF WIGHT
PEGASUS	PE998	POOLE	5.49	1.51	1984	UNKNOWN
PEGASUS	PZ729	PENZANCE	6.42	2.79	1981	ST JUST
PEGASUS A	LK520	LERWICK	7.10	4.09	1988	ORKNEY
PEGGY II	LR212	LANCASTER	6.23	1.19	1995	MIDDLETON
PELICAN	E531	EXETER	5.70	1.01	1975	PLYMOUTH
PELICAN	PL14	PEEL	7.00	0.01	1976	GBR
PELICAN	SC76	SCILLY	4.46	0.54	1989	UNKNOWN
PEN DINAS	AB77	ABERYSTWYTH	11.98	13.72	2007	CORNWALL
PEN GLAS	SE34	SALCOMBE	18.40	62.00	1960	CAMARET
PEN KERNOW	PZ84	PENZANCE	4.54	0.59	1973	MARAZION
PENDOWER	PZ118	PENZANCE	5.59	1.56	1992	BOATLINERS NEWLYN
PENNY LYNN	PZ747	PENZANCE	5.61	1.49	1982	SENNEN COVE
PENOLVA	BCK479	BUCKIE	9.14	6.71	1978	PORTHLEVEN
PENVER	PZ631	PENZANCE	4.63	0.96	1978	SENNEN
PEPSI	LI559	LITTLEHAMPTON	5.35	1.23	2003	WEST SUSSEX
PERCY-VERE	PE96	POOLE	8.60	7.26	1969	EXMOUTH
PERFECT STORM	LH44	LEITH	7.87	3.26	2005	JOHN WEBB
PERSERVERENCE II	AB213	ABERYSTWYTH	6.31	1.04	1982	GBR
PERSEUS	M105	MILFORD HAVEN	4.90	0.68	1997	GBR
PERSEVERANCE	CN17	CAMPBELTOWN	9.98	6.18	1975	RYE
PERSEVERANCE	J649	JERSEY	6.27	1.52	1999	GBR
PERSEVERANCE	K247	KIRKWALL	5.90	1.08	1987	KIRKWALL ORKNEY
PERSEVERANCE II	H11	HULL	14.00	30.42	2013	GRIMSBY
PERSEVERE	PL144	PEEL	9.95	8.22	1992	UNK
PESCADOR	M2	MILFORD HAVEN	6.75	1.93	2011	PORTUGAL
PESCOSO	SM419	SHOREHAM	4.88	0.96	1980	BOGNOR
PETER JOHN II	FH690	FALMOUTH	8.02	3.29	1999	CORNWALL
PETER M	CA31	CARDIGAN	6.90	2.69	1988	POOLE
PETER M	PL25	PEEL	14.90	44.67	1970	UNITED KINGDOM

UK Fishing Vessels 2015

Vessel Name	Code	Port Name	Loa	Ton Gt	Year	Construction Place
PETER MICHAEL	J109	JERSEY	9.77	6.29	2008	UK
PETER PAN	SS138	ST IVES	5.68	1.97	1985	PLYMOUTH
PETER PAUL	FE74	FOLKESTONE	9.90	7.64	1989	WALMER DEAL KENT
PETER PAUL 11	SM694	SHOREHAM	9.40	4.18	1981	RYE
PETIT BATEAU	E82	EXETER	4.90	0.65	1980	ENGLAND
PETIT FLEUR	GU344	GUERNSEY	5.50	1.68	1983	SARK
PETIT MICHELLE	GU87	GUERNSEY	4.89	1.01	1986	UK/GUERNSEY
PETIT MOUSSE II	J399	JERSEY	7.40	2.19	1999	FRANCE
PETITE FOLIE	PH1	PLYMOUTH	9.10	9.39	1974	PAMPAL
PETITE MEL	FH730	FALMOUTH	9.33	5.13	2000	CORNWALL
PETREL	BS24	BEAUMARIS	4.86	0.80	1987	GBR
PETREL	FY881	FOWEY	6.25	1.82	2007	CORNWALL
PHANTOM	P300	PORTSMOUTH	10.55	5.23	1972	POOLE
PHEOBE	WY825	WHITBY	4.88	0.65	1989	NOT KNOWN
PHILOMENA	TN37	TROON	30.57	176.00	1970	VISSER HOLLAND
PHOEBE	BD3	BIDEFORD	6.20	1.27	1980	STANLEY
PHOEBE ALICE	PO14	PORTLAND	6.10	0.55	2004	PORTSMOUTH
PHOENIX	BS90	BEAUMARIS	5.80	1.90	1992	CONNAHS QUAY WALES
PHOENIX	FR941	FRASERBURGH	26.50	237.00	1988	FIFE
PHOENIX	FY804	FOWEY	9.98	4.91	1974	POLRUAN CORNWALL
PHOENIX	K27	KIRKWALL	9.35	8.60	1988	MONTROSE
PHOENIX	NN3	NEWHAVEN	5.79	1.05	1995	SUSSEX
PHOENIX	RX59	RYE	6.80	0.91	1995	ISLE OF WIGHT
PHOENIX	SY35	STORNOWAY	9.97	5.03	1990	CORNWALL
PHOENIX	UL100	ULLAPOOL	8.55	6.50	1994	CLWYD
PHOSPHORESCENT	WH1	WEYMOUTH	7.93	3.01	1996	WADEBRIDGE CORNWALL
PHRA - NANG	SS66	ST IVES	8.25	3.40	1990	HAYLE
PHYLLIS JOHN	P77	PORTSMOUTH	9.58	9.00	2001	COWES
PICALO	BS52	BEAUMARIS	6.20	0.13	1997	VENTNOR
PICASO II	J650	JERSEY	7.50	1.51	1996	GBR
PICKLES	BS3	BEAUMARIS	4.70	0.63	1970	ENGLAND

UK Fishing Vessels 2015

Vessel Name	Code	Port Name	Loa	Ton Gt	Year	Construction Place
PIEDRAS	FD528	FLEETWOOD	35.50	295.00	1976	VIGO
PIERETTE	J25	JERSEY	4.90	0.79	1988	UK
PIEWACKET	B93	BELFAST	6.18	2.13	1993	SCARFSKERRY
PIGLET	CK919	COLCHESTER	5.00	1.03	1996	UNKNOWN
PILOT	PE822	POOLE	5.60	1.47	1987	PLYMOUTH
PILOT STAR	B85	BELFAST	16.32	40.00	1964	MACDUFF
PILOT STAR	BF335	BANFF	6.00	1.21	2007	SCOTLAND
PILOT US	B145	BELFAST	17.77	52.00	1969	FRASERBURGH
PIMPERNEL II	GU97	GUERNSEY	4.80	1.09	1996	ST AUSTELL
PIONEER	AB67	ABERYSTWYTH	9.20	6.25	2000	GBR
PIONEER	BRD44	BROADFORD	9.99	9.59	1990	FORT WILLIAM
PIONEER	E447	EXETER	9.23	3.54	1975	MEECHING QUARRY NEWHAVEN
PIONEER	NN200	NEWHAVEN	7.94	3.28	1988	WARMER DOVER
PIONEER	OB11	OBAN	11.90	11.44	1990	HAYLE CORNWALL
PIONEER	PD152	PETERHEAD	9.06	3.52	1977	MACDUFF
PIONEER	SC41	SCILLY	8.02	4.95	1963	EXMOUTH
PISCATIO	BF826	BANFF	6.18	1.43	2000	MORAY
PISCES	BF8	BANFF	5.70	1.18	1996	ORKNEY
PISCES	BH11	BLYTH	6.10	1.18	2003	ANSTROTHER
PISCES	DH74	DARTMOUTH	4.87	1.03	1968	GBR
PISCES	FD512	FLEETWOOD	9.96	14.61	2004	BIRKENHEAD
PISCES	HL12	HARTLEPOOL	8.60	1.19	2013	ASHINTON
PISCES	ME16	MONTROSE	9.90	4.16	2010	ISLE OF WIGHT
PISCES	NN15	NEWHAVEN	5.03	0.79	1989	HORNDEAN HANTS
PISCES	PE331	POOLE	8.75	2.82	1934	UNK
PISCES	TH2	TEIGNMOUTH	8.38	4.44	1969	FRANCE
PISCES 11	PW105	PADSTOW	4.90	0.71	1984	ARUNDEL SUSSEX
PISMO	AD1	ARDROSSAN	9.95	6.89	2004	AYR
PITULLIE	FR961	FRASERBURGH	4.95	0.75	2002	GBR
PLANET	LK79	LERWICK	11.98	19.08	1952	FRASERBURGH

UK Fishing Vessels 2015

Vessel Name	Code	Port Name	Loa	Ton Gt	Year	Construction Place
PLEIADES	BF155	BANFF	17.50	122.00	2008	WHITBY
PLOVER	DR169	DOVER	6.32	0.89	1996	ISLE OF WIGHT
POACHER	LA51	LLANELLI	4.52	0.73	2000	Unk
POCO LOCO	YH537	YARMOUTH	4.27	0.71	1989	UNK
POL PRY II	PZ770	PENZANCE	4.84	0.74	1989	YAPTON W. SUSSEX
POLARIS	SY886	STORNOWAY	4.95	0.97	2000	ORKNRY
POLARIS II	SH295	SCARBOROUGH	7.60	4.63	2012	SOMERSET
POLARLYS	TT71	TARBERT	5.00	1.04	1997	KENT
POO	LH24	LEITH	3.67	0.26	1980	GBR
POO II	LH3	LEITH	4.76	0.65	1997	CYGNUS MARINE
POPEYE	H1	HULL	6.10	1.71	1994	EAST YORKSHIRE
POPPY	HL14	HARTLEPOOL	5.92	1.89	2010	CORNWALL
POPPY	SM246	SHOREHAM	5.49	1.22	1984	BOGNOR REGIS
POPSO	SA389	SWANSEA	4.84	1.05	1993	NORFOLK
PORT OF AYR	FD527	FLEETWOOD	31.12	254.00	1974	BILBAO
PORTH ENYS	PZ7	PENZANCE	5.60	1.08	1976	GBR
PORTIA OF POOLE	INS111	INVERNESS	9.13	5.30	1999	PENRYN
PORTLAND FISHER	PO7	PORTLAND	5.80	0.94	2009	ENGLAND
PORTLAND ISLE	WH296	WEYMOUTH	12.00	18.87	1990	FALMOUTH
PORTLAND PREFECT	WH34	WEYMOUTH	7.68	1.70	1990	ENGLAND
PORTPATRICK LADY	SR89	STRANRAER	6.95	1.53	2005	GBR
PORTUNUS	LN91	KINGS LYNN	17.65	46.00	1983	ZOUTKAMPT
POSEIDON	NN359	NEWHAVEN	6.61	1.74	1979	NEWHAVEN
POST HASTE	BW136	BARROW	6.22	1.20	1997	ISLE OF WIGHT
POT LUCK	CS679	COWES	4.20	0.43	1999	ORKNEY
PRAWN CRACKER	BN28	BOSTON	6.42	1.69	1999	HOLLAND
PRAWN STAR	FD530	FLEETWOOD	6.20	1.10	2009	ISLE OF WIGHT
PRECIOUS	BD292	BIDEFORD	4.50	0.61	1997	CORNWALL
PREDATOR	DH6	DARTMOUTH	7.00	1.74	2007	GBR
PREDATOR	DO14	DOUGLAS	6.92	1.83	2003	AQUEDA
PREDATOR	GU63	GUERNSEY	6.44	1.46	2002	PEMBROKESHIRE WALES

UK Fishing Vessels 2015

Vessel Name	Code	Port Name	Loa	Ton Gt	Year	Construction Place
PREDATOR	GY4	GRIMSBY	8.60	3.86	2011	NORTHUMBERLAND
PREDATOR	LI556	LITTLEHAMPTON	8.87	6.09	2004	COLCHESTER
PREDATOR	PH6	PLYMOUTH	6.06	1.13	2011	PORTUGAL
PREDATOR	R471	RAMSGATE	9.99	6.73	1999	DEAL
PREDATOR	YH2490	YARMOUTH	6.40	1.61	2006	NORFOLK
PREDITOR	LA619	LLANELLI	5.06	0.92	2006	GBR
PREVAIL	BF319	BANFF	6.70	3.18	2000	PENRYN
PREVAIL	GU26	GUERNSEY	6.50	1.75	1975	GUERNSEY
PREVAIL	LK117	LERWICK	22.46	147.00	1981	MACDUFF SCOTLAND
PREVAIL	P9	PORTSMOUTH	12.73	19.58	1972	EXETER
PREVAIL	PE227	POOLE	5.30	0.74	1990	GBR
PRIDE AND JOY	WY218	WHITBY	10.90	14.91	1989	WHITBY
PRIDE N JOY	TT276	TARBERT	9.95	4.25	2007	ISLE OF WIGHT
PRIDE OF CORNWALL	SS87	ST IVES	9.90	7.47	2005	HAYLE
PRIDE OF PERELLE	BS57	BEAUMARIS	6.97	1.30	1999	ISLE OF WIGHT
PRIDE OF WALES	GK291	GREENOCK	12.59	31.24	1982	EAST LOTHIAN
PRIME TIME	M593	MILFORD HAVEN	4.99	1.20	2002	LEYLAND LANCASHIRE
PRIMITIVE	BK112	BERWICK ON TWEED	6.49	2.04	1956	ORKNEY
PRIMROSE	CN18	CAMPBELTOWN	6.25	1.79	1995	ALASKA 600
PRIMROSE	CY233	CASTLEBAY	16.25	37.00	1968	ARBROATH
PRIMROSE	SD2	SUNDERLAND	5.50	0.95	2005	UNK
PRINCESS	NN130	NEWHAVEN	9.98	13.14	1988	NEWHAVEN
PRINCESS FREYA	B87	BELFAST	5.82	1.34	1995	ISLE OF WIGHT
PRINCESS KEELY	FE386	FOLKESTONE	7.95	7.09	2012	NEWHAVEN
PRINCESS KLEO	M615	MILFORD HAVEN	8.89	3.50	1992	HUNTINGDON CAMBS
PRINCESS ROYAL	BS63	BEAUMARIS	4.88	0.87	1989	NEWHAVEN
PRISCILLA ANN	GU67	GUERNSEY	4.30	0.67	2008	VALE GUERNSEY
PRISCILLA JEAN	N50	NEWRY	8.20	3.62	2010	KILKEEL CO.DOWN
PRO NAV	J604	JERSEY	5.80	1.21	1994	UK
PROCEED	SY659	STORNOWAY	5.60	2.79	1995	ISLE OF LEWIS

UK Fishing Vessels 2015

Vessel Name	Code	Port Name	Loa	Ton Gt	Year	Construction Place
PROFIT	H1135	HULL	7.52	2.00	1987	GBR
PROGRESS	FE69	FOLKESTONE	9.95	11.35	1989	SANDWICH
PROGRESS	J444	JERSEY	11.80	23.10	1989	GBR
PROGRESS	LH229	LEITH	10.15	8.61	1981	WORCESTER
PROGRESS	SN77	NORTH SHIELDS	13.54	26.45	1989	GRIMSBY
PROLIFIC	LK986	LERWICK	19.00	166.00	2008	WHITBY
PROMISE	UL59	ULLAPOOL	6.70	1.49	1991	CORNWALL
PROMISED LAND	BK103	BERWICK ON TWEED	9.17	3.79	1976	CORNWALL
PROPER JOB	SS738	ST IVES	6.93	1.19	2004	I.O.W
PROPER JOB II	BS458	BEAUMARIS	7.00	1.51	1999	PORTSMOUTH
PROPHET	FH722	FALMOUTH	6.85	2.49	2000	FALMOUTH
PROPITIOUS	TH181	TEIGNMOUTH	9.99	13.93	2000	ABERDEEN
PROSPECT	GU166	GUERNSEY	8.10	5.14	1981	PENRYN
PROSPECTOR	J189	JERSEY	16.95	48.73	1974	SCOTLAND
PROSPECTOR	WH264	WEYMOUTH	9.89	7.61	1974	RYE
PROSPERITY	H483	HULL	9.00	2.79	1978	WHITBY
PROSPERITY	M642	MILFORD HAVEN	17.73	38.00	1966	HULL
PROSPERITY	P238	PORTSMOUTH	8.57	4.35	1979	BOTLEY
PROSPERITY	PD987	PETERHEAD	9.69	5.69	2001	MACDUFF
PROSPERITY	WY60	WHITBY	7.30	2.48	1990	SANDHAVEN
PROTERA	OB1045	OBAN	10.00	11.07	1999	NORTH LINCS
PROVIDENCE	FY887	FOWEY	5.85	1.25	2007	NOT KNOWN
PROVIDENCE	H144	HULL	11.83	7.41	2005	COLCHESTER
PROVIDENCE II	BH438	BLYTH	9.90	8.80	1995	AMBLE
PROVIDENCE IV	B923	BELFAST	18.09	65.00	1975	ARBROATH
PROVIDER	AH71	ARBROATH	16.83	60.00	1972	ARBROATH
PROVIDER	BH57	BLYTH	10.87	15.82	1989	WHITBY
PROVIDER	CE517	COLERAINE	9.98	12.95	2000	GBR
PROVIDER	E87	EXETER	9.95	8.16	1990	SHEPPEY
PROVIDER	H2	HULL	5.03	0.69	1992	Unk

UK Fishing Vessels 2015

Vessel Name	Code	Port Name	Loa	Ton Gt	Year	Construction Place
PROVIDER	KY19	KIRKCALDY	11.43	40.13	1990	PEMBROKE DOCK
PROVIDER	M643	MILFORD HAVEN	11.10	15.08	1990	FALMOUTH
PROVIDER	N434	NEWRY	9.96	15.87	1998	ENGLAND
PROVIDER	PE47	POOLE	6.11	0.59	1998	DORSET
PROVIDER	PL184	PEEL	9.66	5.88	2001	CORNWALL
PROVIDER	RX72	RYE	7.08	2.30	1984	RYE DORSET
PROVIDER	SM37	SHOREHAM	5.30	1.30	2010	WEST SUSSEX
PROVIDER	SY801	STORNOWAY	8.75	5.58	1982	GBR
PROVIDER II	BM422	BRIXHAM	14.00	36.03	2001	LEVEN
PROVIDING STAR	FD366	FLEETWOOD	13.11	26.75	1982	BIRKENHEAD
PROWESS	CY720	CASTLEBAY	60.20	1332.00	1988	NORWAY
PRUE ESTHER II	CY550	CASTLEBAY	11.60	15.54	1987	WADEBRIDGE CORNWALL
PRUSAK.K	WY245	WHITBY	7.30	3.03	2002	FALMOUTH
PTARMIGAN	BRD175	BROADFORD	7.10	2.32	1979	ISLE OF WIGHT
PUFFIN	FY278	FOWEY	7.37	6.02	1989	FLAMOUTH/PORTMELLON
PURBECK 11	SU461	SOUTHAMPTON	11.03	14.23	1981	APPLEDORE
PURBECK ISLE	DH104	DARTMOUTH	11.64	6.76	1960	APPLEDORE
PURSUIT	KY338	KIRKCALDY	5.00	0.62	2006	NOT KNOWN
Q-VARL	RY1	RAMSEY	18.25	85.00	1988	PAULL
Q18	GU316	GUERNSEY	5.00	0.30	1980	ISLE OF WIGHT
QUAKER	AB7	ABERYSTWYTH	11.90	22.74	1980	FRANCE
QUANTAS	KY996	KIRKCALDY	9.95	11.98	1999	SCOTLAND
QUANTUS	PD379	PETERHEAD	65.48	2084.00	2008	NORWAY
QUANTUS	SY830	STORNOWAY	8.15	3.96	1992	CORNWALL
QUARTER BELL	WH425	WEYMOUTH	11.00	13.94	1986	RYE SUSSEX
QUEEN OF HEARTS	LK95	LERWICK	9.86	4.86	1980	WEYMOUTH
QUEENIE	SY888	STORNOWAY	5.07	1.21	1987	DELL QUAY
QUEENSBERRY	BA156	BALLANTRAE	15.90	35.00	1971	ARBROATH
QUELINE	K1138	KIRKWALL	11.90	20.01	1983	GUERNSEY
QUENON	GU125	GUERNSEY	5.03	1.07	1984	PLYMOUTH

UK Fishing Vessels 2015

Vessel Name	Code	Port Name	Loa	Ton Gt	Year	Construction Place
QUEQUEG	J22	JERSEY	6.42	1.55	2006	FRANCE
QUEST	BS500	BEAUMARIS	9.80	9.24	1988	PLYMOUTH
QUEST	FR17	FRASERBURGH	5.86	1.30	2010	BANFF
QUEST	K924	KIRKWALL	7.02	3.65	1967	ORKNEY
QUEST	OB87	OBAN	11.10	10.74	1976	FALMOUTH
QUEST	UL52	ULLAPOOL	11.15	14.94	1985	WICK
QUEST	WY143	WHITBY	9.95	14.01	1991	ALLERSTON SCARBOROUGH
QUEST 1V	ME70	MONTROSE	6.82	1.88	1964	ST MONANCE
QUEST II	K26	KIRKWALL	7.20	5.31	1989	SHAPINSAY ORKNEY
QUICKSILVER	CE88	COLERAINE	9.83	12.09	2002	COLCHESTER
QUIET WATERS	OB330	OBAN	6.05	1.51	2006	NOT KNOWN
QUO VADIS	BCK40	BUCKIE	42.36	499.00	1996	STELLENDAM
QUO VADIS	BK1	BERWICK ON TWEED	8.25	6.73	1997	CORNWALL
QUO VADIS	LA22	LLANELLI	5.10	0.81	1982	UNKNOWN
QUO VADIS	PE1219	POOLE	3.79	0.34	1990	DEVON
R KYD K	P910	PORTSMOUTH	5.12	0.69	1991	GOSPORT
R. LAURA	HH163	HARWICH	8.88	6.09	1980	WOODBRIDGE
R.E.M.	GU174	GUERNSEY	5.80	1.36	1980	ISLE OF WIGHT
R.E.M.	J174	JERSEY	5.73	1.14	2011	GBR
RABBIE B	KY446	KIRKCALDY	9.98	7.97	1988	SOUTH SHIELDS
RACHAEL	PZ756	PENZANCE	6.95	2.97	2013	GBR
RACHAEL LINDA	LT336	LOWESTOFT	6.40	2.91	1979	ALDEBURGH
RACHAEL MARIE	CY855	CASTLEBAY	8.85	6.48	2004	SALTERTON
RACHAEL S	GY305	GRIMSBY	20.10	83.00	1974	DENMARK
RACHEAL B	PE980	POOLE	6.40	0.89	2003	GBR
RACHEL	A974	ABERDEEN	4.77	0.67	2004	SCOTLAND
RACHEL & PAUL	PZ612	PENZANCE	5.60	1.46	1980	NEWLYN
RACHEL ANNE	CE19	COLERAINE	5.78	1.12	1989	ARUNDEL SUSSEX
RACHEL ANNE	PO16	PORTLAND	9.14	7.55	1972	NEWHAVEN
RACHEL CLAIRE	WA224	WHITEHAVEN	9.65	8.04	1991	SCARFSKERRY

UK Fishing Vessels 2015

Vessel Name	Code	Port Name	Loa	Ton Gt	Year	Construction Place
RACHEL DAN II	GU24	GUERNSEY	5.58	1.43	1992	GUERNSEY
RACHEL MAY	LH23	LEITH	7.55	3.06	1998	ROUSDEN
RACHEL STAR	TN45	TROON	9.96	5.43	1980	SCOTLAND
RADIANCE	FR1	FRASERBURGH	9.95	14.62	1999	EYEMOUTH
RADIANCE	INS240	INVERNESS	19.68	89.00	1980	NORWAY
RADIANCE	LK101	LERWICK	12.01	21.89	1968	GIRVAN
RADIANCE	LT3	LOWESTOFT	14.00	36.69	2011	ISLE OF WHITHORN
RADIANT MORN	FR141	FRASERBURGH	16.85	52.00	1974	FRASERBURGH
RADIANT STAR	LK71	LERWICK	23.07	219.84	2007	GBR
RADIANT STAR	PE2	POOLE	7.45	4.51	1995	POOLE
RADIANT STAR	WA73	WHITEHAVEN	12.80	29.17	1980	WHITBY
RADJEL	FY270	FOWEY	6.55	2.60	1988	MEVAGISSEY
RAE OF HOPE	PO29	PORTLAND	6.80	1.51	2009	ISLE OF WIGHT
RAFIKI	OB227	OBAN	5.25	1.53	1986	AYR
RAINBOW	N714	NEWRY	7.00	1.60	1998	CORNWALL
RAINBOW	WH370	WEYMOUTH	5.65	3.27	1979	LULWORTH
RAINBOW CHASER	LO66	LONDON	8.08	3.25	1990	CANVEY
RAINBOW CHASER	R4	RAMSGATE	7.30	1.97	1978	UNK
RALPH CLEGG	SU529	SOUTHAMPTON	8.07	3.71	1985	CORNWALL
RAMBLIN ROSE	WK13	WICK	8.10	3.17	2001	CANTERBURY
RAMBLING ROSE	N108	NEWRY	18.59	91.00	1981	GIRVAN
RAMBLING ROSE	OB780	OBAN	16.81	48.00	1979	ARBROATH
RAMBLING ROSE	WK839	WICK	5.89	1.13	1980	PENRYN
RAMPANT	WH148	WEYMOUTH	5.55	1.75	1984	WEYMOUTH
RAMSEY JAK	RY161	RAMSEY	9.98	8.11	2012	UNITED KINGDOM
RAN	WY803	WHITBY	7.10	2.91	2000	YORKSHIRE
RANA	FY31	FOWEY	3.95	0.35	1981	NORWAY
RANGER	SR82	STRANRAER	9.92	7.69	2000	UNKNOWN
RANGER	UL551	ULLAPOOL	4.85	0.64	2000	Unk
RANGER A	SY37	STORNOWAY	16.60	42.00	1966	GIRVAN
RAONAID	SY118	STORNOWAY	9.60	14.13	1985	KILKEEL

UK Fishing Vessels 2015

Vessel Name	Code	Port Name	Loa	Ton Gt	Year	Construction Place
RAPID RETURN	M77	MILFORD HAVEN	10.06	9.44	1988	COLCHESTER/POOLE
RAPIDO	PE1141	POOLE	5.05	1.15	1999	Unk
RARA AVIS	WK664	WICK	7.65	3.19	1992	WICK
RAVEN	SS748	ST IVES	4.77	1.07	2007	CORNWALL
RAZORBILL	R94	RAMSGATE	8.50	5.99	1989	GUERNSEY
RAZORBILL	SS268	ST IVES	5.60	1.51	1979	HAYLE CORNWALL
REAP	YH214	YARMOUTH	6.91	3.25	1976	BRIGHLINGSEA
REAPER	M123	MILFORD HAVEN	9.75	12.16	1987	BARNSTAPLE
REBECCA	CO92	CAERNARVON	9.97	11.47	1991	PENRYN CORNWALL
REBECCA	FH665	FALMOUTH	9.95	15.59	2011	NEWHAVEN EAST SUSSEX
REBECCA	FR143	FRASERBURGH	21.22	191.00	2008	GBS
REBECCA	GU19	GUERNSEY	6.37	2.29	2000	EYEMOUTH
REBECCA	KY982	KIRKCALDY	9.79	10.05	1998	ST MONANS
REBECCA	LH11	LEITH	21.53	155.00	1987	BUCKIE
REBECCA ANN	BF250	BANFF	6.30	1.57	1997	MACDUFF
REBECCA ANNE	PZ800	PENZANCE	5.58	1.48	1991	PENZANCE
REBECCA D	FR21	FRASERBURGH	6.30	1.07	1990	GBR
REBECCA GRACE	SS681	ST IVES	5.65	1.57	1995	GBR
REBECCA J	CA83	CARDIGAN	9.98	11.74	2001	GBR
REBECCA JAYNE A	SSS49	SOUTH SHIELDS	7.90	2.42	2006	ISLE OF WIGHT
REBECCA JAYNE II	M1102	MILFORD HAVEN	5.35	0.77	2001	GBR
REBECCA JENEEN	OB38	OBAN	16.69	105.00	2008	HULL
REBECCA LOUISE	CK15	COLCHESTER	7.90	2.14	1989	GBR
REBECCA M	BS60	BEAUMARIS	7.24	2.23	1985	UNITED KINGDOM
REBECCA M	LK125	LERWICK	9.44	5.38	1982	PETERHEAD
REBECCA MARIE	FR222	FRASERBURGH	7.20	2.78	2012	CORNWALL
REBECCA R	CN383	CAMPBELTOWN	9.95	13.70	1992	RYE
REBECCA TOO	FH740	FALMOUTH	5.75	1.87	1980	CORNWALL
REBECCAN	CK134	COLCHESTER	13.20	29.37	1994	NEWHAVEN
REBEKAH	B769	BELFAST	5.20	0.92	1990	UNKNOWN
REBEKAH ERIN	SY345	STORNOWAY	5.96	1.94	2006	GBR

UK Fishing Vessels 2015

Vessel Name	Code	Port Name	Loa	Ton Gt	Year	Construction Place
REBEKAH JAYNE	OB235	OBAN	17.20	76.00	1978	FRASERBURGH
REBEL	LA606	LLANELLI	4.32	0.44	1990	KINGSBRIDGE
REBEL	LK3447	LERWICK	4.92	0.84	1974	GBR
REBENA BELLE	N313	NEWRY	14.02	27.94	1963	GIRVAN
RED	LO586	LONDON	5.30	0.83	1990	SHOEBURYNESS
RED DAWN	B685	BELFAST	8.65	7.21	1974	FALMOUTH
RED DRAGON	GU351	GUERNSEY	9.95	5.23	1996	PORT ISAAC
RED DWARF	DH12	DARTMOUTH	7.75	1.70	1997	WEST MERSEA
RED HACKLE	BF913	BANFF	6.45	2.81	1984	SAWTRY
RED MIST	J85	JERSEY	4.88	0.83	1994	UK
RED RIB	OB393	OBAN	6.18	0.65	1985	CHESHIRE
RED ROSE	PO11	PORTLAND	8.08	5.43	1982	YARMOUTH
RED VIXEN	FY111	FOWEY	10.42	9.16	1986	LOOE CORNWALL
REDEEMED	SY172	STORNOWAY	5.85	1.74	1987	CORNWALL
REDEMPTION	M1117	MILFORD HAVEN	4.60	0.57	1986	CHANNEL ISLANDS
REEL EASY	DH87	DARTMOUTH	4.80	0.97	2006	GBR
REGAL STAR	PL200	PEEL	9.90	16.48	1991	Unk
REIVER	E50	EXETER	10.00	11.97	1988	ISLE OF SHEPPY
REIVER II	AH63	ARBROATH	8.84	7.10	1983	WORCESTER
REJOICE	BH220	BLYTH	11.99	32.80	1989	SUNDERLAND
REJOICE	DH88	DARTMOUTH	6.22	2.65	1989	TYNEMOUTH
RELENTLESS	IH327	IPSWICH	9.90	12.90	2009	ENGLAND
RELENTLESS	R470	RAMSGATE	9.99	11.95	1992	CANVEY ISLAND
RELENTLESS	SM811	SHOREHAM	5.60	0.99	1980	GBR
RELENTLESS II	FE3	FOLKESTONE	10.13	9.71	2007	ESSEX
RELIANCE	BF80	BANFF	18.11	126.00	1988	MACDUFF
RELIANCE	CY189	CASTLEBAY	7.15	1.82	1991	STONEHAVEN
RELIANCE	E247	EXETER	9.45	5.32	1948	EXMOUTH
RELIANCE 111	LO33	LONDON	14.00	28.59	1986	GRAVESEND
RELIANCE II	BF800	BANFF	19.00	166.00	2009	GBR
RELIANT	CY799	CASTLEBAY	8.74	6.29	2000	CORNWALL

UK Fishing Vessels 2015

Vessel Name	Code	Port Name	Loa	Ton Gt	Year	Construction Place
RELIEF	LK968	LERWICK	6.70	2.62	1994	CORNWALL
RELIENCE	NN745	NEWHAVEN	5.55	1.25	1994	GBR
REMEMBRANCE	FR6	FRASERBURGH	9.99	12.28	2011	MACDUFF
REMUS	NN73	NEWHAVEN	9.78	7.46	1968	BIDEFORD
REMY D	PZ124	PENZANCE	5.12	1.18	1995	PENZANCE
RENE	E519	EXETER	5.96	2.06	2005	PENRYN
RENE B	IH2	IPSWICH	6.40	1.86	1968	IPSWICH
RENOWN	FR246	FRASERBURGH	24.41	201.00	1987	ARDROSSAN
RENOWN	LO88	LONDON	12.68	14.28	1991	NEWHAVEN
RENOWN	SD379	SUNDERLAND	9.80	3.08	1972	WHITBY
RENOWN IV	LO50	LONDON	11.98	11.40	1989	QUEENSBOROUGH I. OF SHEPPEY
RENOWN J W	LK52	LERWICK	16.14	57.00	1989	HULL
REPLENISH	BF28	BANFF	26.50	299.00	1998	MACDUFF
RESEARCH W	LK62	LERWICK	70.70	2430.00	2003	FLEKKEFJORD
RESILIENT	LK195	LERWICK	24.26	266.00	1997	MACDUFF
RESILIENT III	FR327	FRASERBURGH	26.21	154.00	1973	ABERDEEN
RESOLUTE	BF50	BANFF	64.00	1759.00	2003	OLENSVAG
RESOLUTE	FR795	FRASERBURGH	8.26	6.35	2000	ST COMBS
RESOLUTE	FY119	FOWEY	9.95	13.29	2004	CAMBORNE
RESOLUTE	LK395	LERWICK	9.96	7.00	1996	FALMOUTH
RESOLUTION	SC173	SCILLY	7.95	3.28	2000	KENT
RESOLUTION	WY78	WHITBY	23.99	158.00	1981	BUCKIE
RESPLENDENT	B42	BELFAST	8.00	2.89	1981	CORNWALL
RESTLESS WAVE	B617	BELFAST	10.65	8.39	1978	IRL
RESTLESS WAVE	BH51	BLYTH	9.76	8.97	1971	EYEMOUTH
RESTLESS WAVE	LK466	LERWICK	7.92	5.16	1977	SHETLAND
RESTLESS WAVE	N976	NEWRY	9.20	5.51	1980	HULL
RESTLESS WAVE II	CY468	CASTLEBAY	9.81	10.88	1991	TARBERT
RESULT	SM80	SHOREHAM	4.88	0.98	1979	BOGNOR REGIS
RESURGAM	PZ1001	PENZANCE	26.22	134.00	1969	HOLLAND

UK Fishing Vessels 2015

Vessel Name	Code	Port Name	Loa	Ton Gt	Year	Construction Place
REUBEN WILLIAM	IH212	IPSWICH	7.00	2.74	2006	SUFFOLK
REUL-A-CHUAIN	CY807	CASTLEBAY	7.23	3.35	2002	GBR
REUL-A-CHUAIN	OB915	OBAN	18.00	47.00	1959	DENMARK
REVELRY	K100	KIRKWALL	11.39	15.80	2013	CORNWALL
REVENGE	K591	KIRKWALL	12.20	26.06	1976	FRANCE
REVENGE	LO2	LONDON	13.08	18.45	1989	BRIGHTLINGSEA ESSEX
REVENGE	WA39	WHITEHAVEN	9.45	5.65	1976	BIGRIGG
REWARD	BH6	BLYTH	6.57	1.78	2007	CORNWALL
REWARD	CN12	CAMPBELTOWN	6.11	1.04	1990	ISLAND PLASTICS
REWARD	FR26	FRASERBURGH	9.99	12.71	1970	SHETLAND
RHEA	WK7	WICK	6.76	3.30	1964	STROMNESS
RHIANNON	LH598	LEITH	7.42	2.30	1980	CORNWALL
RHIANNON	NN105	NEWHAVEN	6.85	2.11	1985	NEWHAVEN
RHIANNON	PZ76	PENZANCE	6.21	1.80	2007	GBR
RHIANNON	TT159	TARBERT	6.40	2.07	1982	CONWAY WALES
RHIANNON JANE	SS173	ST IVES	5.88	2.01	1980	NEWQUAY
RHODA	SY864	STORNOWAY	4.98	1.00	2005	GBR
RHODA MARY	FH8	FALMOUTH	8.38	3.55	1980	FALMOUTH
RHODANNA	B14	BELFAST	20.20	82.00	1970	BUCKIE
RHONA ANN	CA7	CARDIGAN	6.15	1.44	1982	WEYMOUTH
RIAINNE	N100	NEWRY	6.80	2.83	1994	ISLE OF WIGHT
RIAN JOHN	N20	NEWRY	9.73	12.73	2009	GBR
RIBBLE RANGER	PN23	PRESTON	5.65	1.17	2000	GBR
RIBBLE REAPER	PN22	PRESTON	5.65	1.17	1998	GBR
RIBHINN BEAG	OB489	OBAN	8.15	3.48	1989	NORWICH
RIBHINN DONN II	B140	BELFAST	19.30	57.00	1973	GIRVAN
RICHARD ANN OF PLYMOUTH	PH5562	PLYMOUTH	9.95	5.09	1979	BAGILLT
RICHARD HEAD	NN12	NEWHAVEN	5.05	0.71	1970	GBR
RICHARD WILLIAM	YH3	YARMOUTH	9.95	5.24	2011	ISLE OF WIGHT
RIPCURL	LI503	LITTLEHAMPTON	5.78	1.01	1995	ARUNDEL

UK Fishing Vessels 2015

Vessel Name	Code	Port Name	Loa	Ton Gt	Year	Construction Place
RIPPLE	SS19	ST IVES	13.35	18.18	1896	ST IVES
RIPTIDE	H10	HULL	12.49	16.45	1990	PORT ISAAC
RIPTIDE OF ST HELIER	J145	JERSEY	12.83	12.27	1990	UK
RISING DAWN	BM556	BRIXHAM	10.00	9.92	2000	ARROCHER
RISING DAWN	RX8	RYE	9.80	11.69	2005	GBR
RISKY	J152	JERSEY	5.00	0.69	2013	UK
RITA JOYCE	WH448	WEYMOUTH	5.48	1.85	1980	WEYMOUTH
RIVAL II	SY274	STORNOWAY	14.64	29.78	1974	AMBLE NORTHUMBERLAND
RIVER ISLAND	B183	BELFAST	9.99	8.03	1988	BIRKENHEAD
RIVER RASCAL	E559	EXETER	5.80	1.23	2013	CYGNUS MARINE BOATS
RO-MI-CHRIS	PZ638	PENZANCE	4.88	0.82	1979	HAYLE
ROAMS	PW46	PADSTOW	4.84	1.03	1998	GBR
ROB ROY	DH21	DARTMOUTH	4.27	0.53	1982	KINGSBRIDGE
ROB ROY	KY32	KIRKCALDY	7.20	3.66	1962	LOOE CORNWALL
ROBBYN	WY839	WHITBY	5.06	1.30	1995	GBR
ROBERT LOUISE	P902	PORTSMOUTH	9.80	11.52	1998	FALMOUTH
ROBERTA	LH287	LEITH	8.07	2.79	1978	POOLE DORSET
ROBERTA HELEN	P344	PORTSMOUTH	5.90	1.42	1983	FAFLMOUTH
ROBINA INGLIS	LH179	LEITH	9.15	7.25	1923	NEWHAVEN
ROCK	WK677	WICK	4.83	0.68	1996	ABERDEEN
ROCK DODGER II	B179	BELFAST	5.54	1.33	1992	PLYMOUTH
ROCK HOPPER	SS769	ST IVES	6.20	1.39	2013	CHICHESTER
ROCK HOPPER	TH135	TEIGNMOUTH	4.88	0.92	1988	TEIGNMOUTH
ROCK N ROLLER	WH10	WEYMOUTH	6.70	1.94	1991	FALMOUTH
ROCKHOPPER	SC4	SCILLY	4.73	0.62	1981	PENRYN
ROCKHOPPER	WH715	WEYMOUTH	4.96	1.09	1983	CHICKERELL
ROCKHOPPER OF PERCUEL	LH138	LEITH	9.90	9.35	1975	FALMOUTH
ROCKLEY	LT1028	LOWESTOFT	7.60	1.03	2007	ISLE OF WIGHT
ROCKY	IH319	IPSWICH	7.37	1.97	1973	SHOREHAM
ROCKY	J404	JERSEY	4.90	1.07	1988	GBR

UK Fishing Vessels 2015

Vessel Name	Code	Port Name	Loa	Ton Gt	Year	Construction Place
ROCKY BOTTOM	M639	MILFORD HAVEN	5.00	1.31	1992	NORFOLK
ROCMOR	INS10	INVERNESS	5.80	1.46	2012	NORFOLK
ROEBUCK	RX174	RYE	5.50	1.75	1971	NEWHAVEN
ROIS MHAIRI	OB45	OBAN	18.90	125.00	2005	WHITBY
ROISIN DUBH	B150	BELFAST	5.88	0.98	1973	PORTAFERRY
ROMA IV	BA279	BALLANTRAE	7.01	4.38	1972	NEWHAVEN
ROMULUS	LI120	LITTLEHAMPTON	9.75	7.02	1964	EXMOUTH
RONA	CN778	CAMPBELTOWN	9.98	8.40	1997	MACDUFF
RONA	CY2	CASTLEBAY	6.45	2.04	1968	GBR
RONA II	SR79	STRANRAER	5.85	0.98	1996	MONTOSE
RONAN ORLA	CO10	CAERNARVON	9.98	9.14	1988	PENRYN
RORY JAMES	YH2473	YARMOUTH	6.09	1.31	2001	NORTH WALSHAM
ROS BUIDHE	CN332	CAMPBELTOWN	5.70	0.77	1982	FALMOUTH
ROSE	E445	EXETER	4.17	0.42	2008	GBR
ROSE	FH4	FALMOUTH	4.77	1.05	1992	ST AUSTELL
ROSE DAWN	LT278	LOWESTOFT	6.00	1.52	1996	Unk
ROSE III	DE6	DUNDEE	5.78	1.66	1999	CRAIL
ROSE OF MOUSEHOLE	PZ816	PENZANCE	5.60	1.47	1990	GBR
ROSE OF SHARON	LH202	LEITH	5.49	1.12	1981	CORNWALL
ROSEANNE	R488	RAMSGATE	8.00	1.82	1985	BECCLES
ROSEBANK	B17	BELFAST	8.84	9.18	1981	STROMNESS
ROSEBLOOM	INS353	INVERNESS	23.95	240.00	2003	SCOTLAND
ROSEBUD	PZ1209	PENZANCE	4.86	1.03	2003	CAMBORNE
ROSEBUD	SS30	ST IVES	4.72	0.50	1980	HAYLE
ROSEMARY ANN	B279	BELFAST	13.72	26.15	1965	GIRVAN
ROSEMOUNT	PD313	PETERHEAD	26.00	176.00	1983	CAMPBELTOWN
ROSEN	FH3	FALMOUTH	6.17	2.39	2006	GBR
ROSIE	SM176	SHOREHAM	4.30	0.76	1960	NEWHAVEN
ROSIE	TH276	TEIGNMOUTH	5.75	1.39	1991	SUSSEX
ROSIE B	CY57	CASTLEBAY	6.56	1.94	2002	CAMBORNE

UK Fishing Vessels 2015

Vessel Name	Code	Port Name	Loa	Ton Gt	Year	Construction Place
ROSIE MAE	NN756	NEWHAVEN	7.98	7.13	2007	SUSSEX
ROSIE-ANNE	RX394	RYE	8.17	4.90	1972	HAMPSHIRE
ROSLYN-M	OB939	OBAN	7.15	2.58	1992	UIG ISLE OF SKYE
ROSMARA	INS6	INVERNESS	4.57	0.64	2006	SEAKING BOATS
ROSS	WY793	WHITBY	8.43	2.64	1988	WHITBY
ROSSNESS FALCON	KY1004	KIRKCALDY	6.61	3.24	1991	KINGHORN FIFE
ROTTEN SHAMBLE	ME69	MONTROSE	7.93	3.57	2007	HAMPSHIRE
ROUGET	WH233	WEYMOUTH	5.57	1.49	1989	PUTTON LANE CHICKERELL
ROUSSE RAIDER	GU366	GUERNSEY	8.04	5.34	1981	ISLE OF WIGHT
ROWENA	FE75	FOLKESTONE	10.64	11.68	1989	RYE
ROY WILLIAM	BS56	BEAUMARIS	5.15	0.74	1986	RHOSNEIGN
ROYAL CHARLOTTE	FE50	FOLKESTONE	11.24	10.63	1976	MEDWAY
ROYAL ESCAPE	WH768	WEYMOUTH	11.95	14.39	1974	ENGLAND
ROYAL REBEL	SM3	SHOREHAM	9.99	10.07	2010	CAMBORNE CORNWALL
ROYAL SOVEREIGN	DH148	DARTMOUTH	17.03	53.00	1984	APPLEDORE
ROYAL SOVEREIGN	KY75	KIRKCALDY	6.15	0.94	1996	ABERDEEN
ROYAL SOVEREIGN	SN356	NORTH SHIELDS	9.99	4.13	2000	GBR
ROYS BOYS	RX150	RYE	9.90	9.29	2000	SUSSEX
RUBEN LUKE	FH704	FALMOUTH	6.08	1.35	2002	CORNWALL
RUBY	F177	FAVERSHAM	4.60	0.65	1990	KENT
RUBY	FY81	FOWEY	4.51	0.66	2000	UNKNOWN
RUBY	M7	MILFORD HAVEN	6.75	0.84	2002	MILFORD HAVEN
RUBY	RX2	RYE	5.18	0.90	2006	SHETLAND
RUBY MAE	PZ343	PENZANCE	4.88	0.52	1964	NORWAY
RUBY MAY	BRD8	BROADFORD	7.50	1.18	2002	NORTHUMBERLAND
RUBY ROE	BS534	BEAUMARIS	7.70	2.46	2008	KENT
RUBY SUSAN	FR3	FRASERBURGH	6.75	0.77	2000	ENGLAND
RUBY TUESDAY	BM554	BRIXHAM	6.99	1.47	2008	ESSEX
RUM RUNNER	WH709	WEYMOUTH	7.62	2.58	1999	WEYMOUTH
RUSSA TAIGN	K193	KIRKWALL	27.41	354.00	1997	MACDUFF

UK Fishing Vessels 2015

Vessel Name	Code	Port Name	Loa	Ton Gt	Year	Construction Place
RUTH IMELDA	BN64	BOSTON	11.28	15.04	1989	HULL
RUTH R	PD30	PETERHEAD	8.00	4.51	1978	PENRYN
RYAN AMY	INS32	INVERNESS	5.55	1.74	2008	GBR
RYAN BOY	RX17	RYE	6.40	1.30	2011	UK
RYANWOOD	FR307	FRASERBURGH	23.47	230.00	1988	BUCKIE
RYDS	E144	EXETER	4.65	0.62	1990	SWEDEN
RYE BABY	SU421	SOUTHAMPTON	6.20	1.06	1990	ISLE OF WIGHT
S'AALIN MADRAN	CT139	CASTLETOWN	9.84	7.25	1980	GBR
SABAI-DEE	GU161	GUERNSEY	3.50	0.38	2013	GBR
SABRE	E5	EXETER	6.44	1.84	1995	CORNWALL
SABRE II	BRD628	BROADFORD	9.45	4.02	1971	NEWHAVEN
SABU	GU102	GUERNSEY	3.57	0.46	1995	ST SAMPSONS
SACRE BLEU	J494	JERSEY	5.78	1.19	1994	GBR
SADIE	CE37	COLERAINE	8.49	3.29	1965	REPUBLIC OF IRELAND
SADIE JOAN	LK987	LERWICK	9.99	7.06	1961	FRASERBURGH
SAFIA ROSE	LA13	LLANELLI	8.50	2.86	2008	ISLE OF WHITE
SAGITTARIUS	B313	BELFAST	20.21	146.00	1985	MACDUFF
SAGITTARIUS	HL15	HARTLEPOOL	9.80	15.36	2000	GBR
SAIL AWAY	LA37	LLANELLI	5.28	1.25	1999	GBR
SAIL FREE	TT244	TARBERT	6.30	2.31	1994	PENRYN
SAILFISH II	M20	MILFORD HAVEN	4.90	0.91	1994	DEVON
SAINT JUDE	J607	JERSEY	5.78	1.11	1986	UK
SAINT PETER	LH22	LEITH	7.80	2.80	1993	BERWICKSHIRE
SAINT PIERRE	BM547	BRIXHAM	9.98	7.14	1988	FRANCE
SAIR ANNE	NN227	NEWHAVEN	4.40	0.58	1968	NEWHAVEN
SAJENN	NN444	NEWHAVEN	13.99	38.44	1995	NEWHAVEN
SALACIA	GU54	GUERNSEY	6.42	3.00	1993	PENRYN CORNWALL
SALAMANDA	PZ677	PENZANCE	6.86	2.54	1985	LITTLEHAMPTON
SALCOMBE LASS	SE74	SALCOMBE	11.00	6.54	1966	SALCOMBE
SALLIANN	BD179	BIDEFORD	9.99	7.40	1977	NEWHAVEN

UK Fishing Vessels 2015

Vessel Name	Code	Port Name	Loa	Ton Gt	Year	Construction Place
SALLY	R53	RAMSGATE	4.92	0.82	2000	NEWHAVEN
SALLY ANN	CA67	CARDIGAN	6.40	1.56	1978	FALMOUTH
SALLY ANN III	SM6	SHOREHAM	6.70	1.51	2007	ISLE OF WIGHT
SALLY ROSE OF NAVAX	PZ1191	PENZANCE	7.34	1.50	2000	WHITSTABLE
SALOME	M391	MILFORD HAVEN	5.09	1.81	1986	GBR
SALTEE II	J275	JERSEY	4.94	0.83	1986	UK
SALTIRE	CY741	CASTLEBAY	4.90	0.76	2003	GBR
SALTIRE	LH42	LEITH	9.72	4.93	1998	PENRYN
SALTIRE	ME234	MONTROSE	6.98	1.55	2003	VENTNOR
SALTIRE	SY892	STORNOWAY	6.74	1.63	1998	ABERDEEN
SALTPETER	DH58	DARTMOUTH	3.10	0.29	1985	KINGSBRIDGE
SALTY 1	E468	EXETER	4.44	0.70	2001	GBR
SALUTE	NN786	NEWHAVEN	6.28	1.46	1989	UK
SALVA MEA	R2	RAMSGATE	7.38	2.13	1982	ISLE OF WIGHT
SAM LEWETTE II	MT123	MARYPORT	12.20	27.87	1990	NEWHAVEN
SAM-TORI	SU916	SOUTHAMPTON	8.32	5.85	1998	FALMOUTH
SAMALLEN	P40	PORTSMOUTH	9.26	8.52	1975	FALMOUTH
SAMANTHA	MH111	MIDDLESBROUGH	6.40	2.36	1988	DEVON
SAMANTHA ANN	P252	PORTSMOUTH	7.35	2.09	1987	POOLE
SAMANTHA JANE	K94	KIRKWALL	12.60	19.62	2006	ESSEX
SAMANTHA JAYNE	GU181	GUERNSEY	6.40	1.90	1985	PENRYN
SAMANTHA KAY	M47	MILFORD HAVEN	9.98	7.00	1989	PEMBROKE DOCK
SAMANTO	LR226	LANCASTER	5.70	1.24	1995	MORECAMBE
SAMAR	WK71	WICK	6.40	1.04	2001	CRAIL
SAMARA	YH27	YARMOUTH	5.85	1.39	2005	NORTHWALSHAM
SAMBE	E515	EXETER	7.97	4.40	2003	PENRYN
SAME DIFFERENCE	N8	NEWRY	6.93	2.39	1985	UNITED KINGDOM
SAMIE 2	E8	EXETER	6.95	1.62	1988	YAPTON SUSSEX
SAMMY B	TH86	TEIGNMOUTH	6.00	1.28	2008	PORTUGAL
SAMMY I	LA575	LLANELLI	4.56	0.64	1998	NORTH YORKSHIRE
SAMMY JAYNE	FY817	FOWEY	4.76	0.62	1998	GBR

UK Fishing Vessels 2015

Vessel Name	Code	Port Name	Loa	Ton Gt	Year	Construction Place
SAMPHIRE	BS467	BEAUMARIS	5.10	0.73	2001	GBR
SAMPHIRE	PH350	PLYMOUTH	7.20	4.00	1980	PLYMOUTH
SAMUEL JAMES	FY885	FOWEY	6.00	1.30	2007	PRT
SAMUEL JAY	CS144	COWES	7.20	1.64	1977	PLYMOUTH REBUILD SELSEY
SAMYORK	LR205	LANCASTER	9.10	6.86	1991	SUNDERLAND POINT
SAMYRA	A950	ABERDEEN	5.46	0.74	2002	ABERDEEN
SAN MIGUEL	N818	NEWRY	9.40	6.56	1992	KILKEEL
SANAMEDIO	FD525	FLEETWOOD	36.00	317.00	1994	SPAIN
SANCTA MARIA	N29	NEWRY	20.37	106.00	1979	FRANCE
SAND JULIE	P311	PORTSMOUTH	10.51	9.24	1972	UNKNOWN
SANDELLA	LI79	LITTLEHAMPTON	7.32	1.45	1988	FORD SUSSEX
SANDERLING	AB4	ABERYSTWYTH	11.43	10.13	1979	ORKNEY ISLANDS
SANDHOPPER	P370	PORTSMOUTH	6.97	1.24	1981	ISLE OF WIGHT
SANDIE ANN	SU370	SOUTHAMPTON	6.64	3.42	1967	AXMOUTH
SANDPIPER	BRD668	BROADFORD	4.94	0.66	1982	YORKSHIRE
SANDPIPER	OB657	OBAN	7.65	2.16	2004	ISLE OF WIGHT
SANDPIPER	SH309	SCARBOROUGH	5.30	0.89	2008	GBR
SANDPIPER	SS41	ST IVES	4.95	1.06	1980	GBR
SANDRA H	FR1017	FRASERBURGH	7.10	2.30	2010	BANFF
SANDRA J	GU301	GUERNSEY	8.15	4.96	2000	GUERNSEY
SANDRA JAMES	BH447	BLYTH	8.55	3.43	1978	WHITBY
SANDUKY	J54	JERSEY	8.20	2.85	2004	UK
SANDY BELLE	P14	PORTSMOUTH	8.00	7.19	1980	PORTSMOUTH
SANELA	KY459	KIRKCALDY	11.85	24.20	1989	HAYLING ISLAND
SANGSARA	BRD200	BROADFORD	8.08	6.86	1978	CORNWALL
SANRENE	GY152	GRIMSBY	17.82	51.00	1969	DENMARK
SANS PEUR	WK158	WICK	6.94	1.05	1976	ORKNEY
SANS PEUR II	WK19	WICK	7.47	2.58	1981	UNKNOWN
SANTA FE	AB23	ABERYSTWYTH	7.52	4.81	1982	EASTBOURNE

UK Fishing Vessels 2015

Vessel Name	Code	Port Name	Loa	Ton Gt	Year	Construction Place
SANTA MARIA IIII	CY38	CASTLEBAY	11.22	20.40	1979	WHITBY
SANTOY	TH115	TEIGNMOUTH	4.88	0.65	1992	ORKNEY
SAPPHIRE	CS665	COWES	6.93	1.19	2000	ISLE OF WIGHT
SAPPHIRE	CY4	CASTLEBAY	11.58	7.72	2004	HAYLE
SAPPHIRE	DR161	DOVER	7.50	4.70	1991	RYE
SAPPHIRE	FH748	FALMOUTH	6.68	2.92	2003	POL
SAPPHIRE	K43	KIRKWALL	7.44	4.95	1979	KIRKWALL
SAPPHIRE	LK108	LERWICK	7.32	5.88	1985	AITH SHETLAND
SAPPHIRE	M24	MILFORD HAVEN	9.92	7.79	1998	HAYLING ISLAND
SAPPHIRE	PZ66	PENZANCE	25.05	91.00	1958	HOLLAND
SAPPHIRE	SY841	STORNOWAY	5.20	0.97	2002	GBR
SAPPHIRE II	PZ115	PENZANCE	26.50	180.00	1981	HOLLAND
SAPPHIRE STONE	B221	BELFAST	20.58	103.00	1968	SANDHAVEN
SARA J	K983	KIRKWALL	7.93	7.33	1994	PENRYN
SARA JANE	K326	KIRKWALL	7.53	3.51	1977	LYMINGTON
SARA JANE	PE891	POOLE	6.45	0.06	1982	POOLE
SARA LENA	BM30	BRIXHAM	18.21	82.00	1990	HOLLAND
SARA MAY	LH406	LEITH	5.49	1.27	1989	ISLE OF WIGHT
SARA NAOMI	YH333	YARMOUTH	5.78	1.10	2007	GBR
SARADA	GU140	GUERNSEY	6.71	3.32	1970	GUERNSEY
SARAFINA	PW23	PADSTOW	7.15	2.17	1990	TORPOINT
SARAH	K22	KIRKWALL	6.93	3.48	1984	STROMNESS
SARAH	UL565	ULLAPOOL	6.70	0.73	1988	Unk
SARAH - M	PZ22	PENZANCE	5.91	2.36	1980	NEWLYN
SARAH ANN	J280	JERSEY	5.00	0.84	1992	UK
SARAH B	PE1090	POOLE	5.76	0.90	1998	UNK
SARAH BETH	PZ1	PENZANCE	8.76	6.20	2006	GUERNSEY
SARAH BUNN	BW122	BARROW	8.50	6.03	1978	BARROW IN FURNESS
SARAH C	SE121	SALCOMBE	8.13	3.45	1977	PORT MELLON
SARAH H	CO377	CAERNARVON	17.58	46.00	1939	DENMARK

UK Fishing Vessels 2015

Vessel Name	Code	Port Name	Loa	Ton Gt	Year	Construction Place
SARAH HELEN	SN92	NORTH SHIELDS	9.70	5.89	1992	ANGLESEY
SARAH J	OB922	OBAN	6.90	1.63	1998	HAVANT
SARAH JANE	DH39	DARTMOUTH	9.70	8.74	1991	NEWHAVEN
SARAH JANE	FD64	FLEETWOOD	9.53	6.04	1981	HULL
SARAH JANE	SM692	SHOREHAM	5.52	1.49	1985	UNK
SARAH JANE	TO10	TRURO	4.93	0.60	1989	ST. AGNES
SARAH JANE T	PZ155	PENZANCE	4.60	0.61	1996	CORNWALL
SARAH JAYNE	BM249	BRIXHAM	14.94	32.89	1979	TRURO
SARAH LEANNE	SH255	SCARBOROUGH	5.15	0.87	1987	BRANDSBURTON DRIFFIELD
SARAH LEE	LA581	LLANELLI	5.33	1.14	1993	GBS
SARAH LENA	CT18	CASTLETOWN	13.44	34.84	1998	EAST SUSSEX
SARAH LENA	NN712	NEWHAVEN	13.64	28.85	2007	EAST SUSSEX
SARAH LOU	GU180	GUERNSEY	7.00	1.76	1992	FALMOUTH
SARAH LOUISA	R48	RAMSGATE	8.50	6.51	1989	RAMSGATE
SARAH LOUISE	BH526	BLYTH	9.95	12.71	1987	SHAPINSAY
SARAH LOUISE	BM41	BRIXHAM	23.99	164.00	1991	HOLLAND
SARAH LOUISE	CO74	CAERNARVON	9.90	10.26	1986	WALES
SARAH LOUISE	LI575	LITTLEHAMPTON	6.23	1.09	2012	GBR
SARAH LOUISE	MT115	MARYPORT	9.95	11.37	2004	NORTH LINCOLNSHIRE
SARAH LOUISE	WH256	WEYMOUTH	9.49	7.56	1998	GUERNSEY
SARAH LOUISE	WK669	WICK	6.28	2.28	1992	SCARFSKERRY CAITHNESS
SARAH LYNN	HL122	HARTLEPOOL	6.57	2.03	1994	LITTLE NESTON
SARAH LYNN II	HL2	HARTLEPOOL	7.52	1.21	2000	GBR
SARAH LYNN R	HL17	HARTLEPOOL	7.92	4.21	2008	FIFIE
SARAH MO	DR168	DOVER	7.92	2.04	1996	CANTERBURY
SARAH RAY	R490	RAMSGATE	9.95	9.54	2009	ROTTINGDEAN BRIGHTON
SARAH STEVE	PZ1218	PENZANCE	8.01	3.75	2005	GBR
SARAH-P	GU399	GUERNSEY	14.32	38.86	1989	SOUTHAMPTON
SARAHS SPIRIT	LL506	LIVERPOOL	5.83	0.90	2012	WARRIOR BOATS
SARDIA LOUISE	WY335	WHITBY	10.85	16.02	1982	WHITBY

UK Fishing Vessels 2015

Vessel Name	Code	Port Name	Loa	Ton Gt	Year	Construction Place
SARDIUS	N934	NEWRY	16.77	89.00	1988	HULL
SARDONYX II	BF206	BANFF	18.38	119.00	1993	PAULL HULL
SARDONYX II	WK350	WICK	11.45	18.04	1989	HULL
SARNIA -ANN	BRD646	BROADFORD	5.75	1.16	2004	TOTNES
SARO II	BS39	BEAUMARIS	6.84	1.90	1952	FIFE SCOTLAND
SASHA EMIEL	BM181	BRIXHAM	23.97	150.00	1998	NETHERLANDS
SATURNUS	KY43	KIRKCALDY	24.00	156.00	1990	NETHERLANDS
SAUCY SUE	J112	JERSEY	6.98	1.84	2009	FRANCE
SAXON	MN60	MALDON	6.30	1.26	1987	GOSPORT
SAXON LADY	WY102	WHITBY	9.48	5.79	1984	WHITBY
SAYLAVEE	P5	PORTSMOUTH	6.40	2.11	1990	NORFOLK
SCALLY	J156	JERSEY	3.58	0.35	2010	UK
SCALLY	PE1151	POOLE	4.70	0.28	2001	BJORKELANGEN
SCALPAY ISLE	SY818	STORNOWAY	6.48	1.60	1979	WORCESTER
SCARLET CORD	R7	RAMSGATE	10.39	10.49	2013	PETERHEAD
SCARLET PRIVATEER	CS632	COWES	6.90	1.00	1997	ISLE OF WIGHT
SCARLET THREAD	PD57	PETERHEAD	8.07	2.65	1988	FALMOUTH
SCARLETT LOU	BS1	BEAUMARIS	13.58	47.29	1988	HARTLEPOOL
SCATH DU	FH85	FALMOUTH	6.80	2.68	1982	FALMOUTH
SCATHMAS	PH356	PLYMOUTH	4.35	0.76	1976	PORTWRINKLE
SCEPTRE	LK443	LERWICK	6.98	2.81	2011	KILKEEL CO. DOWN
SCHIEHALLION	LH591	LEITH	6.40	2.41	1987	PENRYN
SCOOBY 2	BD19	BIDEFORD	4.75	0.45	1998	BIDEFORD
SCOOBY DOO	UL588	ULLAPOOL	5.89	1.09	2004	YAPTON WEST SUSSEX
SCOOBY-DOO	BH5	BLYTH	6.23	1.79	1991	GBR
SCORPIO	PZ707	PENZANCE	7.75	2.25	1996	PENRYN
SCORPION	LH183	LEITH	9.26	8.24	1980	WORCESTER
SCORPION LASS	BM102	BRIXHAM	6.05	1.66	1980	CHELMSFORD ESSEX
SCOTIA	BCK1	BUCKIE	6.18	1.57	2011	PETERHEAD
SCOTIA	WA37	WHITEHAVEN	11.25	20.06	1955	BANFF

UK Fishing Vessels 2015

Vessel Name	Code	Port Name	Loa	Ton Gt	Year	Construction Place
SCOTIA	WK48	WICK	7.90	5.46	1974	ORKNEY
SCOTIA STAR	TT267	TARBERT	11.87	18.16	2003	GBR
SCOTSMAN	N46	NEWRY	6.21	1.56	1980	WARRENPOINT
SCOTT K	B73	BELFAST	6.20	1.49	2010	FALMOUTH CORNWALL
SCOTTIES PRIDE	LK68	LERWICK	8.64	8.56	1984	BURRA ISLE
SCRAAYL	CT8	CASTLETOWN	8.05	5.29	1980	FOWEY
SCRATCHER	PD777	PETERHEAD	5.83	1.66	1991	STONEHAVEN
SEA BIRD	FH10	FALMOUTH	5.90	1.18	1998	UK
SEA BISCUIT	BA287	BALLANTRAE	4.88	0.59	1962	ISLE OF WHITHORN WIGTOWNSHIRE
SEA BREEZE	BS204	BEAUMARIS	7.20	3.64	1988	APPLEDORE
SEA BREEZE	CY272	CASTLEBAY	6.79	4.19	2001	GBR
SEA BREEZE	GU60	GUERNSEY	4.98	0.83	2013	Unk
SEA BREEZE	HL7	HARTLEPOOL	9.96	15.14	1991	POLRUAN CORNWALL
SEA BREEZE	LH81	LEITH	8.30	6.18	1995	FALMOUTH
SEA BREEZE	SR4	STRANRAER	5.65	1.19	1990	ORKNEY
SEA BREEZE	SS32	ST IVES	9.00	5.83	2006	NOT KNOWN
SEA CAT	H1134	HULL	6.45	1.73	2002	GBR
SEA CINDERS	SN370	NORTH SHIELDS	5.06	0.93	1979	NR DORCHESTER
SEA CREST	SU349	SOUTHAMPTON	11.15	10.59	1981	SOUTHAMPTON
SEA DART	SY192	STORNOWAY	7.01	2.95	1988	BEDHAMPTON
SEA DART II	TT270	TARBERT	7.47	2.21	2005	HAVANT
SEA DIAMOND	J613	JERSEY	5.63	1.01	1990	GBR
SEA DOG	BN2	BOSTON	13.92	22.94	2008	GBR
SEA ELF	B308	BELFAST	6.10	1.56	1978	ST JOHNS POINT
SEA FEVER	BM3	BRIXHAM	9.07	5.05	2007	CORNWALL
SEA FOAM	FH11	FALMOUTH	7.38	2.50	1955	PORTHLEVEN
SEA FOAM II	FH33	FALMOUTH	7.47	1.99	2010	HAYLE CORNWALL
SEA FOX	HH661	HARWICH	9.96	10.42	2002	ESSEX
SEA FOX	PZ62	PENZANCE	5.87	1.84	1991	FLAMOUTH
SEA GEM	SM690	SHOREHAM	5.08	1.07	1992	YAPTON ARUNDEL SUSSEX

UK Fishing Vessels 2015

Vessel Name	Code	Port Name	Loa	Ton Gt	Year	Construction Place
SEA GIPSY	BS216	BEAUMARIS	5.95	1.62	1980	UNKNOWN
SEA GLORY	CK930	COLCHESTER	6.82	0.73	1998	GBR
SEA GOBLIN	PZ1199	PENZANCE	4.85	0.71	2002	CAMBORNE
SEA GOOSE	LR204	LANCASTER	5.10	0.64	1982	OVERTON LANCS
SEA GULL	LK901	LERWICK	6.20	1.30	1989	MALAHIDE CO.DUBLIN
SEA HARVEST	WY115	WHITBY	9.85	4.48	1957	WHITBY
SEA HARVESTER	N822	NEWRY	19.97	73.00	1968	BUCKIE
SEA HAWK	WA257	WHITEHAVEN	4.97	0.66	1989	GBR
SEA HOUND II	P944	PORTSMOUTH	8.25	4.13	1995	EMSWORTH
SEA HUNTER	GU25	GUERNSEY	8.10	3.26	1996	DEVON & HOLLAND
SEA HUNTER	J15	JERSEY	5.96	0.99	2004	UK
SEA HUNTER	PZ410	PENZANCE	5.20	0.99	1981	LONDON
SEA HUNTER II	HH512	HARWICH	9.50	4.55	1980	ENGLAND
SEA IMP TOO	J50	JERSEY	4.83	0.69	1989	UK
SEA JAY	NN96	NEWHAVEN	4.97	0.80	1985	ENGLAND
SEA JEWEL	FE265	FOLKESTONE	7.91	3.93	1986	RYE SUSSEX
SEA KING	BS40	BEAUMARIS	5.30	1.30	2010	GBR
SEA KING	J194	JERSEY	5.28	1.03	1992	UK
SEA LADY	TN20	TROON	32.80	239.00	1985	HOLLAND
SEA LASS	FH610	FALMOUTH	5.85	0.94	2003	BECCLES SUFFOLK
SEA LASS	K11	KIRKWALL	6.42	1.03	2003	SUFFOLK
SEA LION	PZ882	PENZANCE	5.09	1.29	1992	PENZANCE
SEA MAIDEN	PZ1052	PENZANCE	7.99	3.57	2011	HAYLE CORNWALL
SEA MAIDEN II	SS744	ST IVES	6.80	1.12	2007	PORTUGAL
SEA MARINER	INS1023	INVERNESS	4.90	0.69	1996	UNKNOWN
SEA MASTER	BS540	BEAUMARIS	5.79	1.76	1985	UNKNOWN
SEA MOON	LO345	LONDON	9.40	6.61	1982	RYE
SEA MOURNE	B92	BELFAST	13.70	39.63	2005	KILKEEL
SEA NYMPH	CN70	CAMPBELTOWN	9.90	9.71	1987	CORNWALL
SEA OTTER	BM222	BRIXHAM	14.97	40.33	1984	NEYLAND DYFED

UK Fishing Vessels 2015

Vessel Name	Code	Port Name	Loa	Ton Gt	Year	Construction Place
SEA OTTER	RX31	RYE	7.09	1.99	1994	GBR
SEA OTTER	SY524	STORNOWAY	5.65	1.35	1993	ARUNDEL
SEA PIRATE	SM470	SHOREHAM	5.54	1.49	1982	BOGNOR REGIS
SEA QUEEN	MH308	MIDDLESBROUGH	8.20	5.43	1985	WHITBY
SEA QUEST	CO7	CAERNARVON	8.40	7.17	1982	CORNWALL
SEA QUEST	SM259	SHOREHAM	6.93	1.42	1974	PENRYN
SEA RANGER	BRD632	BROADFORD	9.87	10.97	1998	ISLE OF SKYE
SEA ROVER	LN464	KINGS LYNN	9.40	5.87	2001	GBR
SEA SCAMP	GU75	GUERNSEY	5.58	3.23	1979	ENGLAND
SEA SEEKER	E68	EXETER	11.15	17.06	1985	BRISTOL
SEA SHANTY	LA59	LLANELLI	5.05	0.83	1990	NEW MILL CRUGUBAR LLANWRDA
SEA SHELL	BF23	BANFF	6.92	1.42	1988	WHITEHILLS
SEA SOLDIER	DH179	DARTMOUTH	5.90	1.27	1982	EXETER
SEA SPIRIT	PZ317	PENZANCE	6.50	0.65	2005	ST IVES
SEA SPRAY	A929	ABERDEEN	7.71	1.85	1989	IRELAND
SEA SPRAY	CN15	CAMPBELTOWN	5.74	0.99	1989	FORD SUSSEX
SEA SPRAY	FY8	FOWEY	4.90	1.25	1980	ENGLAND
SEA SPRAY	INS386	INVERNESS	4.85	0.84	1985	UK
SEA SPRAY	LH12	LEITH	5.72	0.97	2002	WEST SUSSEX
SEA SPRAY	LI162	LITTLEHAMPTON	6.23	1.09	2013	ENGLAND
SEA SPRAY	LT61	LOWESTOFT	9.93	12.58	1988	LODDON
SEA SPRAY	PD1054	PETERHEAD	6.75	3.78	1984	GBR
SEA SPRAY	TT93	TARBERT	9.98	7.73	1999	BARTON UPON HUNBER
SEA SPRAY	UL5	ULLAPOOL	5.93	1.06	1998	ABERDEENSHIRE
SEA SPRAY II	N15	NEWRY	9.43	4.41	1978	BANGOR
SEA STAR	LK273	LERWICK	7.14	1.89	1992	SHETLAND
SEA STAR	PW346	PADSTOW	5.60	0.80	1981	FALMOUTH
SEA STRIKER	PE1212	POOLE	4.70	0.62	2000	GBR
SEA SWALLOW	LN20	KINGS LYNN	17.60	35.00	1967	GERMANY

UK Fishing Vessels 2015

Vessel Name	Code	Port Name	Loa	Ton Gt	Year	Construction Place
SEA TONIC	J84	JERSEY	4.50	0.74	1994	UK
SEA TREK	GU210	GUERNSEY	6.60	2.57	1994	CREDITON
SEA TURKEY	PE443	POOLE	5.30	1.02	1984	LITTLEHAMPTON
SEA URCHIN	FH119	FALMOUTH	4.76	1.00	1988	PENRYN
SEA VENTURE	CN779	CAMPBELTOWN	10.34	14.24	1996	NOT KNOWN
SEA VENTURE	UL4	ULLAPOOL	7.80	2.98	1972	SCARBOROUGH
SEA VENTURE	YH34	YARMOUTH	8.80	9.29	1989	GREAT YARMOUTH
SEA WITCH	PD85	PETERHEAD	9.00	5.76	2001	GBR
SEABASS	J419	JERSEY	5.79	1.05	1993	GBR
SEABIRD	WH481	WEYMOUTH	7.22	2.96	1992	LYMINGTON
SEABREEZE	DR179	DOVER	5.39	0.97	1975	GBR
SEABREEZE	SY137	STORNOWAY	8.85	6.14	1982	BANGOR CO DOWN
SEAFISHER	CH202	CHESTER	8.21	4.88	1978	CORNWALL
SEAFORTH	J58	JERSEY	7.96	2.64	2010	FRANCE
SEAGLORY TT	ST2	STOCKTON	8.85	5.56	2007	UK
SEAGULL	BA111	BALLANTRAE	4.79	0.84	1963	FRASERBURGH
SEAGULL	BF74	BANFF	27.41	349.00	1995	MACDUFF
SEAGULL	LN22	KINGS LYNN	17.20	38.00	1968	EMDEN
SEAHAWK	CL1	CARLISLE	7.19	3.72	1983	SILLOTH
SEAHAWK	M1096	MILFORD HAVEN	6.00	1.66	2000	LANCASHIRE
SEAJAY	KY54	KIRKCALDY	6.10	1.74	2009	GBR
SEAJAY V	WK341	WICK	7.92	5.74	1978	WEST BAY
SEAKAY	LI545	LITTLEHAMPTON	5.57	1.51	1986	BOGNOR REGIS
SEALG BRIGH	WH2	WEYMOUTH	6.93	1.28	2008	GBR
SEALGAIR	BF303	BANFF	9.77	9.19	1996	MACDUFF
SEALGAIR MARA	SY132	STORNOWAY	11.89	8.77	1984	PENRYN CORNWALL
SEAMOUSE	GU72	GUERNSEY	4.05	0.29	1988	LLANELLI DYFED
SEAPIE	NT28	NEWPORT	9.88	8.50	1991	GBR
SEAQUEST	NN760	NEWHAVEN	4.80	0.82	1987	SHETLAND
SEAQUEST	YH16	YARMOUTH	9.26	8.28	1969	SUSSEX
SEARCHER	BF205	BANFF	23.71	227.00	1988	ST.MONANCE

UK Fishing Vessels 2015

Vessel Name	Code	Port Name	Loa	Ton Gt	Year	Construction Place
SEARCHER	CO28	CAERNARVON	7.01	3.48	1990	NOT KNOWN
SEARIDER	GU89	GUERNSEY	7.12	3.34	1996	VALE GUERNSEY
SEASCAPE	KY38	KIRKCALDY	5.35	0.74	1960	GBR
SEASHELL	J284	JERSEY	5.49	1.04	1980	UK
SEASPRAY	LK3463	LERWICK	5.90	1.03	1980	NORTH HUMBERSIDE
SEASPRAY II	KY11	KIRKCALDY	10.97	8.60	1981	WORCESTER
SEASTAR	GU429	GUERNSEY	5.13	1.08	1968	GUERNSEY
SEATRACTOR	LO578	LONDON	5.15	0.74	1989	GBR
SEAVIEW	CO110	CAERNARVON	8.12	2.41	2003	NORTHUMBERLAND
SEAWOLF	FR1026	FRASERBURGH	6.10	1.48	2002	GBR
SEAWOLF	SE346	SALCOMBE	3.84	0.36	2006	NORWAY
SECOND DEGREE	DS2	DUMFRIES	12.00	23.98	1989	KIRKGUNZEON
SECRET STAR	PH2	PLYMOUTH	7.18	3.82	1996	BECCLES
SEDNA	LK655	LERWICK	8.10	3.83	1983	PENRYN
SEEKER	P253	PORTSMOUTH	6.09	1.68	1970	EMSWORTH
SEIONT A	BM114	BRIXHAM	16.99	38.00	1968	HOLLAND
SELACHOS	BD297	BIDEFORD	5.95	2.06	1998	ENGLAND
SELINA MAY	LK897	LERWICK	7.10	2.84	1990	WORKINGTON
SELKIE	SY840	STORNOWAY	6.00	1.03	1999	MONTROSE
SELSEY PEARL	LI215	LITTLEHAMPTON	11.69	8.16	1974	POOLE
SEMIRA	MH1014	MIDDLESBROUGH	7.40	3.31	1991	HUMMERSEA LOFTUS
SEMPER FIDELIS	NN94	NEWHAVEN	8.12	4.39	1989	FALMOUTH
SEMPER VICTORIA	TT282	TARBERT	17.20	44.00	1967	HOLLAND
SEMPER VIGILO	SY248	STORNOWAY	5.58	1.26	1978	GRIMSAY NORTH UIST
SENLAC JACK	RX1066	RYE	9.83	16.30	2005	COLCHESTER
SENNA	LA602	LLANELLI	9.86	7.11	1984	WADEBRIDGE
SEONAG	CY797	CASTLEBAY	5.17	0.81	2001	GBR
SEREN	SA314	SWANSEA	8.25	5.19	2008	CORNWALL
SEREN-Y-MOR	CN114	CAMPBELTOWN	9.58	3.46	1988	HAYLE CORNWALL

UK Fishing Vessels 2015

Vessel Name	Code	Port Name	Loa	Ton Gt	Year	Construction Place
SERENE	BF453	BANFF	6.15	1.25	2008	CORNWALL
SERENE	BRD75	BROADFORD	11.80	17.47	2006	SCOTLAND
SERENE	LK297	LERWICK	71.66	2943.00	2008	NORWAY
SERENE	PZ642	PENZANCE	5.88	1.84	1979	PENRYN
SERENE	R12	RAMSGATE	9.75	8.84	2012	ABERDEENSHIRE
SERENE	SY6	STORNOWAY	7.25	1.66	1990	GBR
SERENE	UL562	ULLAPOOL	8.55	6.19	1977	MACDUFF
SERENE	WK9	WICK	7.65	6.17	1984	ORKNEY
SERENE DAWN	LT7	LOWESTOFT	11.60	21.79	1982	KILBIRNIE
SERENE DAWN	PW156	PADSTOW	11.86	27.57	1989	PENRYN
SERENE II	CY436	CASTLEBAY	6.77	2.34	1994	ESSEX
SERENITY	BF24	BANFF	20.85	158.00	1991	MACDUFF
SERENITY	BH10	BLYTH	8.46	4.15	2007	ASHINGTON
SERIATIM	NN7	NEWHAVEN	6.20	1.09	1986	DEVON
SERINAH	GH116	GRANGEMOUTH	9.99	16.22	2000	BERWICKSHIRE
SERPICO	PL156	PEEL	11.29	14.50	1979	FLAMOUTH
SEVEN SISTERS	BN445	BOSTON	13.86	21.89	2007	ENGLAND
SEVEN SISTERS	CY202	CASTLEBAY	7.62	4.17	1977	GRIMSAY
SGIAN	OB350	OBAN	9.45	6.29	1983	GBR
SGIATHAN	OB1040	OBAN	3.99	0.41	2006	MALLAIG
SHADWELL	LA5	LLANELLI	5.04	1.05	1998	U.K.
SHAKIRA	FY14	FOWEY	4.23	0.64	2011	PEMBROKESHIRE
SHALAIR	K38	KIRKWALL	8.20	2.92	2001	ORKNEY
SHALANNA	BF843	BANFF	18.42	97.00	1988	SANDHAVEN
SHALIMAR	BCK598	BUCKIE	22.86	168.00	1985	BUCKIE
SHALIMAR	K49	KIRKWALL	11.95	19.51	1979	POLRUAN CORNWALL
SHALIMAR	KY989	KIRKCALDY	12.19	13.92	1970	ORKNEY
SHALIMAR	LK176	LERWICK	7.86	5.28	1975	BURRA ISLE SHETLAND
SHALIMAR II	PD303	PETERHEAD	26.55	246.00	1988	ST MONANS
SHALIMAR L.M	LK803	LERWICK	7.00	3.50	1988	BURNTISLAND

UK Fishing Vessels 2015

Vessel Name	Code	Port Name	Loa	Ton Gt	Year	Construction Place
SHALLOW WATERS	J323	JERSEY	7.31	2.51	1996	UK
SHALOM	PD194	PETERHEAD	6.43	2.25	1938	GARDENSTOWN
SHAMAN	WH777	WEYMOUTH	8.20	3.96	1999	FALMOUTH CORNWALL
SHAMARA II	AH721	ARBROATH	5.95	1.03	2008	HAVANT HAMPSHIRE
SHAMARIAH	FR245	FRASERBURGH	22.07	140.24	1989	SANDHAVEN
SHAMARNIC	A177	ABERDEEN	7.20	2.99	2000	MACDUFF
SHAMROCK	BF173	BANFF	6.40	1.27	1982	PORTSMOUTH
SHAMROCK	CY837	CASTLEBAY	5.91	1.70	2001	CAMBORNE
SHAMROCK	E524	EXETER	7.60	1.64	2008	ISLE OF WIGHT
SHAMROCK	LH604	LEITH	5.90	1.22	2008	UK
SHAMROCK	PD154	PETERHEAD	6.20	1.29	1958	Unk
SHAMROCK	SM609	SHOREHAM	4.94	1.29	1989	BOGNOR REGIS
SHAMROCK	TO46	TRURO	5.95	1.48	2001	GBR
SHANGRI-LA	CN394	CAMPBELTOWN	16.49	42.00	1967	ANSTRUTHER
SHANIA	PE1124	POOLE	7.35	3.29	2001	Unk
SHANKRILA	R271	RAMSGATE	5.30	1.05	1974	FOLKSTONE
SHANMAR	PW6	PADSTOW	5.02	0.93	1995	ISLE OF WIGHT
SHANNON	LH541	LEITH	5.62	0.96	1999	GBR
SHANNON	LI547	LITTLEHAMPTON	5.30	1.09	2004	UK
SHANNON	OB562	OBAN	6.60	3.27	1996	LUING
SHANNON	SH268	SCARBOROUGH	9.97	6.18	1999	PENRYN
SHANNON	SS45	ST IVES	9.15	3.09	1998	PENRYN
SHANNON BHAN	N9	NEWRY	8.25	5.43	1997	CORNWALL
SHANNON C	SR96	STRANRAER	5.70	0.77	2000	SUSSEX
SHANNON LOUISE	BW269	BARROW	6.14	1.19	1992	ISLE OF WIGHT
SHANRINE	B6	BELFAST	9.99	8.77	1988	UNK
SHARANDAN	J620	JERSEY	5.32	1.03	1995	UK
SHARATAN	SY828	STORNOWAY	9.15	5.17	2000	CORNWALL
SHARICMAR	PW104	PADSTOW	7.68	5.87	1988	PENRYN
SHARKIE TOO	J569	JERSEY	10.39	8.76	1978	UK
SHARKY	J165	JERSEY	5.60	1.20	1998	UK

UK Fishing Vessels 2015

Vessel Name	Code	Port Name	Loa	Ton Gt	Year	Construction Place
SHARNIC	J389	JERSEY	5.40	0.78	1994	Unk
SHARON ANN	N17	NEWRY	12.90	26.53	1992	POLRUAN CORNWALL
SHARON ANNE	CA2	CARDIGAN	5.00	0.91	2000	ORKNEY
SHARON II	BN444	BOSTON	6.99	1.53	1990	GBR
SHARON ROSE	SY190	STORNOWAY	16.92	75.00	1979	BUCKIE
SHARONA	K23	KIRKWALL	9.14	7.82	1985	SCARFSKERRY CAITHNESS
SHARONA	ME47	MONTROSE	14.96	35.57	1976	MACDUFF
SHARONELLE	BF18	BANFF	6.79	1.95	1989	CORNWALL
SHARYN LOUISE	LK250	LERWICK	18.80	111.00	1987	MACDUFF
SHAULORA	BF794	BANFF	17.64	87.00	1974	KNOTTINGLEY
SHAUN M	CE537	COLERAINE	6.73	1.66	1999	PENRYN
SHAUNA	CE66	COLERAINE	5.72	1.28	1987	SUSSEX
SHAUNAD	LA272	LLANELLI	3.81	0.45	1978	CARDIGAN
SHAUNETTE	K157	KIRKWALL	13.40	29.10	1991	STROMNESS
SHAUNKELLY	FR18	FRASERBURGH	5.70	1.02	2009	GBR
SHE-D-LEA	WO51	WORKINGTON	6.63	4.31	1984	WORKINGTON
SHEARMA	A869	ABERDEEN	5.92	1.11	1997	KINCARDINESHIRE
SHEARWATER	BA790	BALLANTRAE	9.98	5.78	1992	KIRKOSWALD
SHEARWATER	CA273	CARDIGAN	8.30	4.22	1946	GREAT BRITAIN
SHEARWATER	CT3	CASTLETOWN	6.53	2.83	1977	GBR
SHEARWATER	FY182	FOWEY	7.30	2.98	2006	NOT KNOWN
SHEARWATER	J482	JERSEY	5.90	1.17	1996	UK
SHEARWATER	OB272	OBAN	7.17	0.70	1987	PORTSMOUTH
SHEARWATER	SA2	SWANSEA	6.90	1.64	2005	UK
SHEARWATER II	KY110	KIRKCALDY	7.20	5.45	1989	ENGLAND
SHEARWATER II	SU206	SOUTHAMPTON	10.64	8.94	1974	EXMOUTH
SHEIGRA	M46	MILFORD HAVEN	8.90	7.17	2009	Unk
SHEIGRA	SY7	STORNOWAY	17.04	43.00	1971	GBR
SHEIGRA	WK70	WICK	8.20	3.64	2003	GBR
SHEILA C	K1170	KIRKWALL	6.82	1.69	1981	GBR

UK Fishing Vessels 2015

Vessel Name	Code	Port Name	Loa	Ton Gt	Year	Construction Place
SHEILA II	SY135	STORNOWAY	6.40	3.71	1985	TEIGNMOUTH
SHEILA JOYCE	LN456	KINGS LYNN	6.70	2.99	1985	BLAKENEY
SHEILA L	H129	HULL	5.56	1.64	1989	UNKNOWN
SHELANG	H1109	HULL	6.93	1.19	2002	ISLE OF WIGHT
SHELLEY MARIE	PH429	PLYMOUTH	11.62	39.15	1988	HAYLING ISLAND
SHELLEY MARIE	PZ77	PENZANCE	5.92	1.85	1993	FALMOUTH
SHELLFISHER	A946	ABERDEEN	4.77	0.58	2000	GBS
SHELLY	ME246	MONTROSE	5.88	1.07	1990	STONEHAVEN
SHELLY	WA258	WHITEHAVEN	7.20	3.17	1977	GBR
SHELTIE TWO	M1016	MILFORD HAVEN	5.02	1.08	1987	UNK
SHEMARA	SN168	NORTH SHIELDS	11.43	12.65	1982	HULL
SHEMARA II	LK27	LERWICK	6.99	3.67	2008	GLASGOW
SHEMARAH	B640	BELFAST	9.90	10.92	2001	LINCOLNSHIRE
SHEMARAH II	LH65	LEITH	26.30	301.00	1995	CAMPBELTOWN
SHEONA	SD396	SUNDERLAND	7.10	1.62	1990	PLYMOUTH
SHEPERTON	SA335	SWANSEA	8.00	3.33	1997	CORNWALL
SHERI LOUISE	PE1119	POOLE	5.70	1.08	1995	POOLE
SHERPA	P107	PORTSMOUTH	5.79	1.61	1968	ISLE OF WIGHT
SHETLAND SUN	YH394	YARMOUTH	6.94	1.93	1992	SEA PALLING
SHIKARI	SS716	ST IVES	5.68	1.49	1980	GBR
SHINING LIGHT	B996	BELFAST	6.55	1.92	1990	PORTAVOGIE
SHINY 1	PH3	PLYMOUTH	4.46	0.27	2006	SOUTH AFRICA
SHIP SHAPE	K140	KIRKWALL	10.50	4.96	1990	SOUTH RONALDSAY ORKNEY
SHIPMATES	YH529	YARMOUTH	4.63	0.62	1980	UNKNOWN
SHIRALEE	BM35	BRIXHAM	9.82	11.39	1979	GRANVILLE FRANCE
SHIRALEE	J211	JERSEY	6.58	2.89	1977	UK
SHIRALEE	PH585	PLYMOUTH	8.20	3.07	1963	FRANCE
SHIRLEY	GU32	GUERNSEY	5.87	1.05	2007	PENRYN
SHIRLEY ANN II	P142	PORTSMOUTH	6.10	1.40	2006	HAVANT
SHIRLEY BETTY	DH50	DARTMOUTH	9.81	9.35	1973	POLRUAN

UK Fishing Vessels 2015

Vessel Name	Code	Port Name	Loa	Ton Gt	Year	Construction Place
SHIRLEY II	KY130	KIRKCALDY	6.71	1.92	1957	ST MONANS FIFE
SHOAL WATER	CK7	COLCHESTER	5.00	0.74	2000	SUFFOLK
SHONA	OB90	OBAN	9.00	4.46	1968	STROMNESS
SHONALEE	WH11	WEYMOUTH	5.60	1.52	1978	PAIGNTON
SHOOTING STAR	AD6	ARDROSSAN	5.54	1.13	2007	KILKEEL
SHOOTING STAR	SU135	SOUTHAMPTON	8.12	6.22	1991	FALMOUTH
SHUNA	BRD202	BROADFORD	7.01	4.27	1973	KYLESKU
SHYLOCK	J388	JERSEY	5.72	1.31	1986	GBR
SIARACH III	SY85	STORNOWAY	19.45	70.00	1986	HAMBURG
SIDEWINDER	BS5	BEAUMARIS	8.56	1.58	2002	AYRSHIRE
SIENNA	R6	RAMSGATE	10.90	12.08	2011	PETERHEAD
SIGMA	LK206	LERWICK	7.62	4.98	1988	BRITAIN
SILENT HUNTER	P4	PORTSMOUTH	6.83	1.23	2013	WEST SUSSEX
SILENUS	PZ771	PENZANCE	6.50	2.89	1989	FALMOUTH
SILIS	BRD680	BROADFORD	7.90	2.52	1995	SUSSEX
SILVER BAY	B967	BELFAST	5.66	1.21	1995	ORKNEY
SILVER BREEZE	N931	NEWRY	8.22	2.63	2000	GBR
SILVER CARRS	BH337	BLYTH	4.46	0.36	1980	ENGLAND
SILVER CAT	BRD17	BROADFORD	6.99	1.22	1998	CHEETAH MARINE
SILVER CHORD	SY101	STORNOWAY	16.42	78.00	1973	BUCKIE
SILVER CLOUD II	WK80	WICK	16.55	42.00	1972	ARBROATH
SILVER COQUET	SN8	NORTH SHIELDS	9.74	3.28	1960	AMBLE
SILVER CREST II	LH19	LEITH	15.71	40.30	1969	ANSTRUTHER
SILVER DARLINGS	B30	BELFAST	6.93	3.20	1980	ISLE OF WIGHT
SILVER DAWN	N295	NEWRY	7.80	2.89	1977	ANNALONG
SILVER DAWN	OB333	OBAN	17.61	51.00	1970	GIRVAN AYRSHIRE
SILVER DAWN	PZ1196	PENZANCE	17.93	118.00	2001	FALMOUTH
SILVER DEE	B310	BELFAST	18.54	63.00	1971	FRASERBURGH
SILVER DOLLAR	M30	MILFORD HAVEN	5.79	0.83	1982	UK
SILVER E	BRD32	BROADFORD	8.70	1.55	2010	COLCHESTER

UK Fishing Vessels 2015

Vessel Name	Code	Port Name	Loa	Ton Gt	Year	Construction Place
SILVER EEL	PE250	POOLE	9.46	3.24	1990	POOLE DORSET
SILVER FERN	B889	BELFAST	13.09	20.76	1973	FRASERBURGH
SILVER FERN	FR416	FRASERBURGH	17.99	97.00	1982	BUCKIE
SILVER FERN	OB84	OBAN	16.27	47.00	1971	ARBROATH
SILVER FISH	BRD670	BROADFORD	9.88	14.22	1996	FISHBOURNE
SILVER FJORD	UL50	ULLAPOOL	8.72	5.22	1971	BALTASOUND
SILVER FOAM	PE723	POOLE	5.97	1.72	1976	DORSET
SILVER HARVEST	IH311	IPSWICH	6.25	2.85	1996	SUFFOLK
SILVER HARVESTER	B713	BELFAST	22.12	164.00	1989	DINGLE
SILVER J	BRD28	BROADFORD	9.98	4.24	2006	ISLE OF WIGHT
SILVER JUBILEE	WY268	WHITBY	9.75	5.26	1977	WHITBY
SILVER LANCE	FH506	FALMOUTH	5.55	1.55	1980	CADGWITH
SILVER LINE	H488	HULL	9.91	4.27	1979	SCARBOROUGH
SILVER LINE W	WY68	WHITBY	9.99	11.98	1988	WHITBY
SILVER LINING	K462	KIRKWALL	8.54	6.98	1975	ORKNEY ISLES
SILVER LINING III	TT37	TARBERT	16.61	39.00	1973	ST MONANCE
SILVER QUEEN	FH324	FALMOUTH	7.46	2.60	2009	CORNWALL
SILVER QUEST	AR190	AYR	16.92	56.00	1971	FRASERBURGH
SILVER QUEST	BH225	BLYTH	7.69	1.49	1990	AMBLE NORTHUMBERLAND
SILVER RAY	OB295	OBAN	9.10	3.57	1979	ORMESBY
SILVER ROSE	DS12	DUMFRIES	5.60	0.85	2001	GBR
SILVER SEA	BH19	BLYTH	5.85	1.30	2008	CYGNUS MARINE
SILVER SEA	BRD5	BROADFORD	7.30	3.43	1989	BANFF
SILVER SPIRIT	WH719	WEYMOUTH	8.30	5.61	1995	THETFORD
SILVER SPOON TWO	LI494	LITTLEHAMPTON	5.52	0.80	1991	BOGNOR REGIS
SILVER SPRAY	LI220	LITTLEHAMPTON	5.51	0.84	1975	BOGNOR
SILVER SPRAY	OB140	OBAN	12.10	22.71	1972	FRASERBURGH
SILVER SPRAY	SY559	STORNOWAY	4.40	0.56	1991	TAMWORTH
SILVER SPRAY	YH5	YARMOUTH	6.80	2.68	1991	YAPTON ARUNDEL SUSSEX

UK Fishing Vessels 2015

Vessel Name	Code	Port Name	Loa	Ton Gt	Year	Construction Place
SILVER SPRAY 111	TT77	TARBERT	11.73	24.93	1986	STROMNESS
SILVER STAR	FR821	FRASERBURGH	18.21	128.00	1990	NORWAY
SILVER STAR	LK341	LERWICK	6.37	1.57	1955	BURRA ISLE
SILVER STAR	LN2	KINGS LYNN	9.30	2.72	1997	ALNWICK
SILVER STAR	OB86	OBAN	9.42	6.46	1979	FALMOUTH
SILVER STEELE	BRD663	BROADFORD	9.83	12.09	2002	COLCHESTER
SILVER STRAND	N28	NEWRY	9.15	8.89	1987	TAMWORTH STAFFORDSHIRE
SILVER STREAM	PH411	PLYMOUTH	14.55	36.17	1966	FRANCE
SILVER T	BRD21	BROADFORD	7.30	2.48	1999	ISLE OF WIGHT
SILVER VIKING	PL19	PEEL	14.60	34.77	1973	GBR
SILVER WAKE	AB15	ABERYSTWYTH	9.98	3.66	1968	ABERYSTWYTH
SILVER WAVE	BF372	BANFF	18.18	76.00	1974	KNOTTINGLEY
SILVER WAVE	BRD84	BROADFORD	10.04	10.17	1986	STROMNESS
SILVERFISH	DH90	DARTMOUTH	7.90	1.93	2011	ISLE OF WIGHT
SILVERLINE	B475	BELFAST	9.30	3.17	1981	YARMOUTH
SILVERMINE	BRD671	BROADFORD	9.84	8.67	2004	ISLE OF SKYE
SILVERSAL	SM795	SHOREHAM	4.80	0.97	2000	GBR
SILVERWOOD	H132	HULL	9.99	8.40	1989	HULL
SILVERY SEA	FY570	FOWEY	9.60	9.51	1980	LOOE
SIMON ISAAC	RX43	RYE	9.30	5.47	1989	RYE
SIMPLY RED	PE9	POOLE	6.60	0.85	2005	DORSET
SINCERE V	AH3	ARBROATH	11.20	20.05	1989	HULL
SINCERITY	SY70	STORNOWAY	18.62	69.79	1971	ARBROATH
SINCERITY II	MT188	MARYPORT	13.39	24.33	1962	PETERHEAD
SINCERITY S	SD1	SUNDERLAND	13.95	23.68	1960	FRASERBURGH
SINE BHAN	ME27	MONTROSE	10.00	9.57	1984	HAYLE
SINE BHAN I	CY441	CASTLEBAY	4.98	0.79	1977	ORKNEY
SIOBHAN III	CE307	COLERAINE	11.95	22.95	1997	CO DONEGAL
SIOLTA	CY243	CASTLEBAY	6.82	2.10	1980	GRIMSAY

UK Fishing Vessels 2015

Vessel Name	Code	Port Name	Loa	Ton Gt	Year	Construction Place
SIR JACK	SS723	ST IVES	4.80	0.77	2002	PORTUGAL
SIRENE	CS434	COWES	9.75	10.61	1980	BEMBRIDGE
SIRENE	FY120	FOWEY	6.50	3.11	1987	DOWNDERRY CORNWALL
SIRIUS	K1136	KIRKWALL	7.83	4.03	1970	ORKNEY
SIRIUS	LR33	LANCASTER	5.55	1.08	1923	OVERTON
SIRIUS RP	LK76	LERWICK	7.23	2.75	1998	MACDUFF
SISTER MC B	BM107	BRIXHAM	6.70	2.87	1982	NEWPORT GWENT
SISTERS	K414	KIRKWALL	8.03	3.83	1980	ORKNEY
SITH	CY9	CASTLEBAY	4.49	0.59	2005	CORNWALL
SIWRENGALE	H77	HULL	14.95	46.23	2003	WHITBY
SKATE	CT1	CASTLETOWN	6.13	0.20	1969	GBR
SKERRY BELLE	DH63	DARTMOUTH	11.52	10.50	1974	EXMOUTH
SKINDEEPER	WH12	WEYMOUTH	11.00	8.44	2007	ISLE OF WIGHT
SKINT	PT90	PORT TALBOT	9.30	4.80	1979	HULL
SKUA	BF863	BANFF	6.30	1.76	2003	UNK
SKUA	BRD672	BROADFORD	6.37	1.45	1994	MACDUFF
SKUA	CO9	CAERNARVON	5.69	1.31	1980	BANGOR
SKUA	SD272	SUNDERLAND	9.90	9.56	1991	LOWESTOFT
SKUA	UL341	ULLAPOOL	5.51	0.82	1960	HULL
SKUA	WH685	WEYMOUTH	3.76	0.47	1990	PORTLAND
SKUA	WK148	WICK	6.40	1.46	1989	UNK
SKUA II	A17	ABERDEEN	8.27	6.61	2002	FALMOUTH
SKYE	J490	JERSEY	5.80	1.07	2001	UK
SKYTENDER	LH7	LEITH	9.99	4.24	1990	CORNWALL
SLIPPERY DICK	BM20	BRIXHAM	8.23	3.44	1988	RAMSGATE
SMIFFYS	INS238	INVERNESS	5.01	0.84	1992	SUSSEX
SMILING MORN	LK891	LERWICK	6.46	3.12	1978	CORNWALL
SNAPPER	PE229	POOLE	6.50	2.63	1979	POOLE
SNOW GOOSE	M23	MILFORD HAVEN	7.18	1.27	1992	EAST COAST
SNOWMAN	CS41	COWES	7.51	5.33	1975	GOSPORT

183

UK Fishing Vessels 2015

Vessel Name	Code	Port Name	Loa	Ton Gt	Year	Construction Place
SNOWY OWL	SD76	SUNDERLAND	6.54	1.88	1994	PAIGNTON
SOAY II	SY678	STORNOWAY	5.92	1.69	2011	Unk
SOIXANTE NEUF	J69	JERSEY	8.88	4.59	1988	Unk
SOLA FIDE	RN1	RUNCORN	43.97	527.00	1989	HOLLAND
SOLAN	SN9	NORTH SHIELDS	13.42	34.64	1980	CORNWALL
SOLAR STAR	YH481	YARMOUTH	9.98	10.23	1980	GREAT YARMOUTH
SOLARIS	KY36	KIRKCALDY	6.50	3.23	1990	ANSTRUTHER
SOLAS	B3	BELFAST	9.50	7.05	1978	GISBURN - CLITHEROE - LANCS'
SOLE FISH	NN470	NEWHAVEN	4.50	1.24	1990	HAVANT HAMPSHIRE
SOLE TRADER	BL1	BRISTOL	5.70	1.15	1983	FALMOUTH
SOLE VENTURE	WH704	WEYMOUTH	8.00	2.02	1988	HAYLING ISLAND
SOLENT STAR	P6	PORTSMOUTH	9.20	11.33	1991	NEWHAVEN
SOLI DEO GLORIA	PH63	PLYMOUTH	44.98	546.00	1987	NETHERLANDS
SOLITAIRE	FH443	FALMOUTH	6.49	3.18	1976	FALMOUTH
SOLITAIRE	SD409	SUNDERLAND	7.85	2.02	1986	CYGNUS
SOLO	E549	EXETER	6.10	2.03	1980	BRITAIN
SOLO	LH40	LEITH	6.30	1.71	1987	PORTSMOUTH
SOLO	UL560	ULLAPOOL	7.34	1.45	1979	ISLE OF WIGHT
SOLO II	KY1013	KIRKCALDY	5.67	1.08	1992	ARUNDEL SUSSEX
SOLO VENTURE	M241	MILFORD HAVEN	6.20	2.77	1991	CORNWALL
SOLSTICE	BF56	BANFF	23.92	212.00	2000	NAVIA
SOLSTICE	CN199	CAMPBELTOWN	9.90	10.72	2000	GBR
SOLUIS	SY571	STORNOWAY	4.90	0.86	1995	UNKNOWN
SOLWAY PROSPECTOR	MT49	MARYPORT	13.41	24.12	1989	HULL
SOLWAY PROVIDER	CL26	CARLISLE	13.34	16.85	1995	BEVERLEY
SOMEDAY SOON	E461	EXETER	5.25	0.51	1980	UNKNOWN
SOMERSET MORN	FR920	FRASERBURGH	9.20	5.90	1989	RYE
SON DE MER	CY120	CASTLEBAY	6.63	3.42	1988	GRIMSAY NORTH UIST
SON-A-MOR	FH494	FALMOUTH	6.16	2.38	1979	HAYLE
SONAS	OB70	OBAN	9.96	9.85	1999	MUIR-OF-ORD

UK Fishing Vessels 2015

Vessel Name	Code	Port Name	Loa	Ton Gt	Year	Construction Place
SONDRA	LK365	LERWICK	13.48	41.09	1989	LERWICK
SONIA ST CLAIR	GU253	GUERNSEY	5.59	1.52	1982	PLYMOUTH
SONSIE	OB3	OBAN	6.13	1.50	2009	Unk
SOPH-ASH	CN519	CAMPBELTOWN	9.95	5.29	1983	CORNWALL
SOPH-ASH-JAY	LH60	LEITH	11.21	10.68	2007	ICELAND
SOPHIE	R16	RAMSGATE	9.90	4.98	2010	ISLE OF WIGHT
SOPHIE 1	PO8	PORTLAND	6.65	1.31	2006	ESSEX
SOPHIE B	LN481	KINGS LYNN	4.84	0.65	1995	YAPTON WEST SUSEX
SOPHIE DAWN	LT22	LOWESTOFT	9.98	10.60	1989	LOWESTOFT
SOPHIE JANE	BD36	BIDEFORD	5.62	1.03	1989	GBR
SOPHIE JAYNE	LO106	LONDON	13.95	24.97	1992	E SUSSEX
SOPHIE LEIGH	HL9	HARTLEPOOL	9.90	5.43	1985	TARBERT
SOPHIE LOUISE	WY168	WHITBY	22.36	180.00	1988	ST.MONANS
SOPHIE ROSE	PE1199	POOLE	5.93	0.51	2000	Unk
SORRENTO	GY189	GRIMSBY	21.77	74.00	1974	DENMARK
SOUTH RIVER	PE523	POOLE	7.55	2.49	1991	POOLE
SOUTHERN BELLE	SU7	SOUTHAMPTON	9.95	11.56	2005	NOT KNOWN
SOUTHERN CROSS	LT1033	LOWESTOFT	7.95	0.85	2009	COLCHESTER
SOUTHERN GIRL	KY41	KIRKCALDY	7.62	6.21	1972	SOUTHAMPTON
SOUTHERN HEAD	NN99	NEWHAVEN	9.80	6.65	1973	EXMOUTH
SOUTHERN STAR	FH71	FALMOUTH	7.32	2.04	1959	PORTHLEVEN
SOUTHERN STAR	FY125	FOWEY	9.73	10.47	1990	PENRYN CORNWALL
SOUTHERN STAR	N904	NEWRY	4.72	0.70	1997	CO ANTRIM
SOUTHERN STAR	P31	PORTSMOUTH	9.93	11.15	1989	EMSWORTH NR. PORTSMOUTH
SOUTHERN VENTURE	GU182	GUERNSEY	6.00	0.97	1994	PORTSMOUTH
SOUTHWEST ISLE	SU301	SOUTHAMPTON	8.76	6.53	1974	FRANCE
SOUWEST LADY	SE21	SALCOMBE	11.02	11.32	1961	EXMOUTH
SOUWESTER	PZ5	PENZANCE	5.48	1.40	1990	GBR
SOVEREIGN	BN19	BOSTON	10.90	16.83	1989	HULL
SOVEREIGN	FH25	FALMOUTH	8.02	7.29	1983	LOOE

UK Fishing Vessels 2015

Vessel Name	Code	Port Name	Loa	Ton Gt	Year	Construction Place
SOVEREIGN	LN266	KINGS LYNN	10.95	8.05	1970	SOUTH SHIELDS
SOVEREIGN	SY28	STORNOWAY	7.90	3.07	1976	GBR
SOWENNA	SC181	SCILLY	7.85	4.86	2009	BRIDGWATER
SOWENNA III	SC3	SCILLY	7.95	5.41	2007	CORNWALL
SPANISH EYES III	E509	EXETER	9.99	9.89	2001	BARTON UPON HUMBER
SPARKLING LINE	PW3	PADSTOW	17.30	119.00	1989	MACDUFF
SPARKLING SEA	N183	NEWRY	23.21	195.00	1988	GORINCHEM HOLLAND
SPARKLING STAR	CY137	CASTLEBAY	6.40	1.71	1988	DUBLIN
SPARKLING STAR III	BD247	BIDEFORD	14.95	52.95	2004	WHITBY
SPARKLING STAR IV	BCK29	BUCKIE	17.60	130.00	2001	ST PETERSBURG
SPARKLING WATERS	FR894	FRASERBURGH	14.95	47.00	2003	METHIL
SPAVEN MOR	CT77	CASTLETOWN	17.85	55.87	1965	GBR
SPAVEN MOR II	CT142	CASTLETOWN	6.58	1.57	2003	UNK
SPECTRUM	FR667	FRASERBURGH	6.14	1.36	2009	SCOTLAND
SPEEDBIRD	B944	BELFAST	7.17	1.88	1990	GILLIE
SPEEDWELL	B2	BELFAST	7.30	5.95	1989	CORNWALL
SPEEDWELL	LH133	LEITH	7.01	2.40	1972	GARDENSTOWN BANFFSHIRE
SPEEDWELL	LN477	KINGS LYNN	9.47	15.05	2007	COLCHESTER
SPEEDWELL	SY412	STORNOWAY	5.48	1.59	1985	CORNWALL
SPEEDWELL II	N411	NEWRY	9.11	4.09	2006	GBR
SPEEDWELL OF GLENARIFFE	CN318	CAMPBELTOWN	8.20	4.76	1995	CORNWALL
SPES BONA V	BA107	BALLANTRAE	14.95	51.56	2004	ISLE OF BUTE
SPES MARIS	N193	NEWRY	13.87	32.85	1973	FIFE
SPICA	FH713	FALMOUTH	34.60	320.00	2002	PONTEVEDRA
SPINDRIFT	N57	NEWRY	9.12	6.97	2004	PENRYN
SPINDRIFT	PD1	PETERHEAD	7.01	1.87	1989	PENRYN
SPINDRIFT	PW485	PADSTOW	5.64	1.15	1991	SUSSEX
SPINDRIFT	R485	RAMSGATE	6.90	1.78	2006	CORNWALL
SPINDRIFT	SY128	STORNOWAY	10.62	10.18	1985	SHAPINSAY ORKNEY
SPINDRIFT	WK302	WICK	5.92	1.48	1989	CORNWALL

UK Fishing Vessels 2015

Vessel Name	Code	Port Name	Loa	Ton Gt	Year	Construction Place
SPINDRIFT III	BRD693	BROADFORD	9.95	4.12	2007	ISLE OF WIGHT
SPIRIT	WH14	WEYMOUTH	8.02	2.88	2010	ENGLAND
SPIRIT OF NAVAN	NN779	NEWHAVEN	8.00	2.76	2003	NEWHAVEN
SPIRIT OF PORTLAND	PO21	PORTLAND	6.45	1.53	1983	ENGLAND
SPIRIT OF THE WHITE WOLF	CS361	COWES	6.20	1.09	1998	VENTNOR
SPIRITED LADY III	SU516	SOUTHAMPTON	12.95	23.61	2013	NEWHAVEN
SPITFIRE	CA169	CARDIGAN	7.15	2.82	1975	CAERNARFON
SPITFIRE	LH107	LEITH	11.27	14.31	1974	DUNBAR
SPITFIRE	PZ16	PENZANCE	5.65	1.01	1999	ARUNDELWEST SUSSEX
SPLENDOUR	PH307	PLYMOUTH	7.50	3.03	1988	FALMOUTH
SPORTSMAN KNIGHT	P16	PORTSMOUTH	10.76	10.41	1985	WOOLSTON
SPRAY	CN691	CAMPBELTOWN	9.08	3.87	1974	EIRE
SPRAY	WK811	WICK	4.76	0.95	2003	PLYMOUTN
SPRAY I	CY40	CASTLEBAY	11.75	11.66	1989	LYMINGTON
SPRIGHTLY	LK3395	LERWICK	8.94	4.89	1998	SCALLOWAY
SPRIGS OF HEATHER	PZ218	PENZANCE	5.58	1.50	1975	MULLION COVE
SPRING TIDE	B124	BELFAST	5.85	1.54	1993	UNK
SPRING TIDE	LT1018	LOWESTOFT	7.00	3.64	2000	ALDEBURGH
SPRING TIDE	NN785	NEWHAVEN	6.45	1.72	2012	NORFOLK
SPRING TIDE	SM183	SHOREHAM	5.55	1.38	1980	BOGNOR REGIS
SPRINGER	M109	MILFORD HAVEN	4.00	0.48	1984	NORWAY
SPRINGTIDE	LK714	LERWICK	11.70	18.01	1960	FRASERBURGH
SPRITE	OB565	OBAN	5.64	0.80	1995	UNK
SPURN LIGHT	H22	HULL	6.02	1.50	1986	BRANDESBURTON
SQUIDSIN	PW493	PADSTOW	4.76	0.72	1980	ORKNEY
ST ADRIAN	KY360	KIRKCALDY	12.94	24.89	1970	GRAVESEND
ST ALOYSIUS	CY359	CASTLEBAY	6.40	2.67	1987	MALAHIDE DUBLIN
ST ANDREW	OB67	OBAN	8.50	6.24	1949	BANFF
ST APOLLO	BA359	BALLANTRAE	18.21	51.00	1979	HULL
ST BRENDAN	N105	NEWRY	10.45	12.99	1990	PORTAFERRY

UK Fishing Vessels 2015

Vessel Name	Code	Port Name	Loa	Ton Gt	Year	Construction Place
ST CLAIR	SY606	STORNOWAY	6.40	2.96	1994	CORNWALL
ST ELVAN	PZ64	PENZANCE	5.87	1.92	1994	PENRYN
ST GEORGES	PZ1053	PENZANCE	34.78	237.00	1973	HOLLAND
ST GWENFAEN	CO171	CAERNARVON	5.70	0.86	2000	Unk
ST KILDA	BF142	BANFF	5.68	0.85	1992	ANGUS
ST KILDA	LK991	LERWICK	5.80	1.16	2002	SHETLAND
ST NICHOLAS II	CO484	CAERNARVON	6.10	1.29	1994	CORNWALL
ST RUAN	FH243	FALMOUTH	9.85	9.27	1976	FALMOUTH
ST. NINIAN	LH868	LEITH	7.75	3.47	1923	EYEMOUTH
ST.GWENFAEN	BS171	BEAUMARIS	4.40	0.54	1980	GBR
STACEY ANNE	BM16	BRIXHAM	5.59	1.50	1994	PLYMOUTH
STACEY E	SN332	NORTH SHIELDS	9.90	3.54	1992	NOT KNOWN
STACEY JAYNE	LH18	LEITH	6.40	1.01	1988	WORKINGTON
STACY MARIA	MH1022	MIDDLESBROUGH	5.61	0.90	1997	WAYCROSS
STALKA VIKING	N111	NEWRY	8.32	3.95	2001	CUMBRIA
STAN	DH22	DARTMOUTH	4.70	0.82	1999	DEVON
STAND SURE	BK552	BERWICK ON TWEED	9.83	16.30	2000	GBR
STAR	GU145	GUERNSEY	5.20	0.75	1986	HAMPSHIRE
STAR	LK850	LERWICK	6.53	1.96	1970	SHETLAND
STAR	YH26	YARMOUTH	6.58	3.04	1979	POTTER HEIGHAM
STAR 'O' BUCHAN	FR116	FRASERBURGH	9.89	7.01	1989	BRANCASTER
STAR DIVINE	BH230	BLYTH	11.58	19.24	1982	EYEMOUTH BERWICKSHIRE
STAR INA	B128	BELFAST	7.10	3.93	1972	ISLE OF WIGHT
STAR O' STAXIGOE	WK6	WICK	4.70	1.17	1991	BRITANNIA YARD PENRYN
STAR OF ANNAN	OB50	OBAN	18.29	80.00	1982	APPLEDORE
STAR OF HENNOCK	E499	EXETER	7.97	4.86	2000	EXMOUTH
STAR OF HOPE	LK277	LERWICK	6.55	3.32	1985	LERWICK
STAR OF JURA	OB278	OBAN	19.00	125.00	2006	WHITBY
STAR OF PEACE	BH77	BLYTH	9.81	4.34	1973	AMBLE
STAR OF THE NORTH	SC14	SCILLY	8.49	4.18	1974	GUERNSEY

UK Fishing Vessels 2015

Vessel Name	Code	Port Name	Loa	Ton Gt	Year	Construction Place
STAR ORION	ME231	MONTROSE	5.94	1.83	1972	NORWAY
STARBANK	H8	HULL	6.59	1.15	1980	GBR
STARDUST	CN56	CAMPBELTOWN	9.82	2.05	1980	PLYMOUTH
STARDUST	CY174	CASTLEBAY	6.71	2.44	1963	ST. MONANS FIFE
STARDUST	LH871	LEITH	8.30	5.61	1970	JERSEY
STARDUST	N227	NEWRY	19.92	88.00	1974	ARBROATH
STARFISH	LN449	KINGS LYNN	9.90	7.88	1996	BARTON ON HUMBER
STARFISH	PE567	POOLE	10.40	5.90	1974	LYTCHETT BAY BOATYARD POOLE
STARGAZER	J499	JERSEY	9.74	6.90	1978	UK
STARGAZER	WH686	WEYMOUTH	3.75	0.32	1985	UNKNOWN
STARLIGHT	FH414	FALMOUTH	7.62	3.84	1977	GWEEK
STARLIGHT	PD786	PETERHEAD	24.82	270.00	1995	BUCKIE
STARLIGHT	RX934	RYE	9.20	11.04	2000	GBR
STARLIGHT SPLENDOUR	B224	BELFAST	19.81	76.00	1975	BANGOR
STARLITE	PD150	PETERHEAD	7.92	3.37	1974	RYE
STARWARD	N737	NEWRY	19.27	88.00	1980	GLEHEN
STATELY	PD1025	PETERHEAD	9.30	7.13	1989	PORTLAND
STEADFAST	INS16	INVERNESS	5.85	1.20	2011	BANFF
STEADFAST	K388	KIRKWALL	6.60	2.21	2001	GOSPORT
STEEL PRINCESS	LI176	LITTLEHAMPTON	9.99	8.17	1981	BRISTOL
STEEL VENTURE	CO452	CAERNARVON	9.03	5.60	1996	KINGS LYNN
STEELE	BRD23	BROADFORD	6.00	0.91	1985	CORNWALL
STEFANIE - M	N265	NEWRY	49.28	631.00	1987	FLEKKEEFJORD NORWAY
STELIMAR	CY163	CASTLEBAY	12.78	25.56	1988	BUCKIE
STELISSA	PZ498	PENZANCE	20.60	140.00	1991	FRANCE
STELLA AMY	PE71	POOLE	5.60	0.91	1983	FALMOUTH
STELLA ANN	WH29	WEYMOUTH	5.10	1.24	1969	WEYMOUTH
STELLA MARIA	FE269	FOLKESTONE	7.31	3.17	1994	BROADSTAIRS
STELLA MARIS	CY250	CASTLEBAY	17.80	81.00	1980	FRASERBURGH
STELLA MARIS	DR167	DOVER	9.98	12.10	1981	PENRYN

UK Fishing Vessels 2015

Vessel Name	Code	Port Name	Loa	Ton Gt	Year	Construction Place
STELLA MARIS	HL705	HARTLEPOOL	9.96	11.85	1999	PENRYN
STELLA MARIS	TT183	TARBERT	11.20	13.17	1988	HAYLING ISLAND
STELLA MARIS OF NEWQUAY	PH97	PLYMOUTH	14.99	40.73	1968	FRASERBURGH
STELLANOVA	PD1024	PETERHEAD	4.60	0.70	2000	LANCASHIRE
STEPHANIE	M177	MILFORD HAVEN	23.98	97.00	2003	GBR
STEPHANIE	WK45	WICK	5.60	0.99	1979	GBR
STEPHANIE R	CS64	COWES	9.90	3.73	2010	VENTNOR ISLE OF WIGHT
STEPHEN JOHN	FR30	FRASERBURGH	4.85	0.64	1983	SUSSEX
STEPHEN WILLIAM	M1034	MILFORD HAVEN	5.36	0.94	1976	BURY ST EDMUNDS
STEREN - MOR	SC73	SCILLY	7.10	1.99	1985	NR SALTASH
STERENNYK	FH728	FALMOUTH	9.20	6.84	2005	POLRUAN-BY-FOWEY
STERGAN	PZ428	PENZANCE	8.00	4.19	1974	PORTHLEVEN
STERINA	BH47	BLYTH	9.00	3.96	1971	DUNBAR
STILL GAME	FR29	FRASERBURGH	9.82	12.77	2013	NORTHERN IRELAND
STILL OSTREA	B98	BELFAST	28.50	92.00	1987	HOLLAND
STILL WATERS	FH52	FALMOUTH	9.87	12.16	1990	BEVERLY HUMBERSIDE
STILL WATERS	SS209	ST IVES	6.25	1.98	1975	PORTSMOUTH
STJERNEN	WA31	WHITEHAVEN	11.54	18.82	1959	GIRVAN
STORM CHILD	BD6	BIDEFORD	7.00	2.06	2006	CORNWALL
STORM CHILD	FY3	FOWEY	7.17	4.38	1989	LOOE
STORM CHILD	M83	MILFORD HAVEN	9.98	5.02	2012	ISLE OF WIGHT
STORM PETREL	FH683	FALMOUTH	5.25	0.95	2007	CORMWALL
STORM PETREL	PZ594	PENZANCE	4.47	0.69	2010	CORNWALL
STORMALONG	CS119	COWES	7.92	1.82	1986	POOLE
STORMBRINGER	J445	JERSEY	5.04	0.86	1998	UK
STORMDRIFT	GU147	GUERNSEY	6.25	1.17	1986	PORTSMOUTH
STORMY C	GY451	GRIMSBY	17.06	41.00	1960	DENMARK
STORMY C	WY818	WHITBY	9.96	15.91	2003	BARTON UPON HUMBER
STORMY DAWN	E9	EXETER	6.01	3.10	1968	AXMOUTH
STRATHBEG	FR583	FRASERBURGH	4.90	0.87	1992	UNK

UK Fishing Vessels 2015

Vessel Name	Code	Port Name	Loa	Ton Gt	Year	Construction Place
STRATHDONAN	WK818	WICK	7.44	4.67	1999	CAITHNESS
STRATHMORE	B788	BELFAST	23.09	202.00	1984	SANDHAVEN
STRENUOUS	SY205	STORNOWAY	7.14	4.61	1988	SCARFSKERRY CAITHNESS
STRIKE	PW443	PADSTOW	5.10	0.84	1997	DEVON
STRIKER	E163	EXETER	5.10	0.95	1989	UNKNOWN
STROMA	INS146	INVERNESS	7.73	3.14	1997	GBR
STROMA ISLE	ME216	MONTROSE	12.20	15.67	1974	STROMNESS
STRONSAY LAD	K1124	KIRKWALL	11.27	21.72	1988	SUNDERLAND
STRONSAY MAID	K1113	KIRKWALL	9.80	12.26	1998	WIGTOWN
STROWA II	K981	KIRKWALL	8.17	6.56	1992	STROMNESS
STUMARK II	HH986	HARWICH	9.81	4.78	1986	RYE SUSSEX
STUMPY	M44	MILFORD HAVEN	4.85	0.68	1996	ARUNDEL SUSSEX
STUPID	M627	MILFORD HAVEN	4.50	0.59	1999	LLANELLI
STURDY	AB129	ABERYSTWYTH	8.00	2.34	1979	PORTLEVEN CORNWALL
SUCCESS III	WY212	WHITBY	20.90	174.00	1990	BANFF
SUD AYRE	LK41	LERWICK	7.60	4.04	1983	SCALLOWAY
SUE	PE167	POOLE	6.00	1.04	2000	GBR
SUE ELLEN	BM211	BRIXHAM	11.93	23.10	1985	TRURO CORNWALL
SUFFOLK CHIEFTAIN	LT372	LOWESTOFT	38.25	400.00	1968	APPLEDORE NORTH DEVON
SUKAT II	GY3	GRIMSBY	8.90	3.01	2009	ISLE OF WIGHT
SULA	FH1	FALMOUTH	6.10	1.48	1951	TRURO
SULA	SA17	SWANSEA	4.87	0.67	1985	ARUNDEL
SULA BASSANA	PH25	PLYMOUTH	8.20	1.69	1990	TORPOINT
SULAIRE	CN49	CAMPBELTOWN	4.87	1.15	1989	UNK
SUMMER DAWN	PD97	PETERHEAD	26.00	188.00	1973	FLEKKEFIELD
SUMMER ROSE	H358	HULL	9.39	3.53	1976	WHITBY
SUMMERTIME BLUES	SC5	SCILLY	6.80	2.57	2007	GBR
SUN CHASER	CO813	CAERNARVON	6.00	1.21	2007	GBR
SUNBEAM	E94	EXETER	6.50	3.38	1972	AXMOUTH
SUNBEAM	FR487	FRASERBURGH	56.17	1349.00	1999	SPAIN

UK Fishing Vessels 2015

Vessel Name	Code	Port Name	Loa	Ton Gt	Year	Construction Place
SUNBEAM	ME240	MONTROSE	5.03	0.58	1998	STONEHAVEN
SUNBEAM	TT251	TARBERT	12.16	20.25	1959	ST MONANCE
SUNBEAM	WK47	WICK	7.02	3.87	1974	ISLE OF WIGHT
SUNDANCE	WH452	WEYMOUTH	9.07	3.31	1980	WEYMOUTH
SUNDOWNER	FH222	FALMOUTH	9.30	3.96	1977	CAMBOURNE
SUNLIGHT RAY	BF101	BANFF	15.75	95.00	2002	Unk
SUNNY JIM	SY1	STORNOWAY	9.88	9.35	1979	PENRYN
SUNNY MORN	LN475	KINGS LYNN	13.98	22.26	2005	KINGS LYNN
SUNRISE	FR359	FRASERBURGH	26.00	201.00	1984	CAMPELTOWN
SUNRISE	H1136	HULL	6.16	1.16	1988	NORWAY
SUNRISE	K350	KIRKWALL	9.33	6.97	1977	RYE
SUNRISE	NN766	NEWHAVEN	5.30	1.08	1993	HAVANT
SUNRISE	PZ53	PENZANCE	4.39	0.62	1972	PENBERTH
SUNRISE	SH302	SCARBOROUGH	7.82	2.49	2006	KENT
SUNSEEKER	CN33	CAMPBELTOWN	8.00	5.44	1977	LOOE
SUNSEEKER II	SE29	SALCOMBE	6.93	3.27	1981	LOOE CORNWALL
SUNSHINE	E284	EXETER	5.63	1.04	1964	SEATON
SUNSHINE	FH699	FALMOUTH	3.66	0.38	2001	GBR
SUNSHINE	FY826	FOWEY	6.40	2.75	1999	FALMOUTH
SUNSHINE II	YH432	YARMOUTH	5.00	0.71	2003	CAISTER-ON-SEA
SUNSTRIKER	J115	JERSEY	13.26	22.41	1972	NORWAY
SUNTAN	R489	RAMSGATE	7.60	2.23	1985	DEVON
SUPERB 11	FY509	FOWEY	8.53	7.92	1978	MEVAGISSEY
SUPERB-US	DH99	DARTMOUTH	13.57	22.96	1964	CREMYLL PLYMOUTH
SUPERBITCH 2	M19	MILFORD HAVEN	4.85	1.10	2012	LANCASHIRE
SUPERSTAR	WH586	WEYMOUTH	8.65	2.63	1968	SOUTHAMPTON
SUPESAM	CK169	COLCHESTER	5.59	1.82	1989	CLACTON-ON-SEA
SUPREME	LH109	LEITH	19.81	103.00	1975	EYEMOUTH
SUPREME	N180	NEWRY	16.16	46.00	1969	SANDHAVEN SCOTLAND
SUPREME	UL210	ULLAPOOL	8.31	6.13	1993	FALMOUTH
SUPREME II	BK50	BERWICK ON TWEED	10.00	5.37	1979	SEAHOUSES

UK Fishing Vessels 2015

Vessel Name	Code	Port Name	Loa	Ton Gt	Year	Construction Place
SURF DANCER	YH365	YARMOUTH	5.73	1.12	1992	BRITTAIN
SURLY MERMAID	J71	JERSEY	7.05	1.41	2011	Unk
SURMOUNT	LK400	LERWICK	7.60	3.95	1982	STROMNESS ORKNEY
SURMOUNT	PD368	PETERHEAD	24.29	243.00	1995	NAVIA
SURPRISE	FY759	FOWEY	6.72	2.15	1992	GORRAN HAVEN. CORNWALL
SURPRISE	GU451	GUERNSEY	5.03	1.40	1986	SARK
SURSUM CORDA	R10	RAMSGATE	8.96	3.57	2011	COLCHESTER
SUS	K566	KIRKWALL	4.84	0.57	1973	GBR
SUSA UNO	FH707	FALMOUTH	32.10	287.00	2003	PONTE VEDRA
SUSAN	BRD398	BROADFORD	8.25	4.10	1986	HAYLING ISLAND
SUSAN AMANDA	SM262	SHOREHAM	5.52	1.31	1986	LITTLEHAMPTON
SUSAN BIRD	FR357	FRASERBURGH	24.80	88.00	1964	HOLLAND
SUSAN ELIZABETH	BM46	BRIXHAM	5.92	1.68	2008	CORNWALL
SUSAN II	J316	JERSEY	5.57	1.56	1985	UK
SUSAN K	PD146	PETERHEAD	4.70	0.55	2002	ABERDEENSHIRE
SUSAN L	BS10	BEAUMARIS	9.60	2.97	1980	NOT KNOWN
SUSIE D	P10	PORTSMOUTH	6.90	1.27	2002	VENTNOR
SUSIE H	BM8	BRIXHAM	9.21	6.67	1989	FELIXSTOWE
SUSIE J	LA2	LLANELLI	6.55	1.75	1992	FALMOUTH
SUSIE MO II	BS506	BEAUMARIS	6.00	1.79	1974	I.O.W.
SUSIE TOO	J130	JERSEY	4.93	0.81	1988	UK
SUSTAIN	BCK62	BUCKIE	16.76	65.82	1971	BUCKIE
SUSTAIN	PD378	PETERHEAD	27.96	219.00	1986	IHLOW
SUVERA	HL1054	HARTLEPOOL	9.80	11.35	1992	MIDDLESBROUGH
SUZANNE II	BH14	BLYTH	5.18	0.82	1995	GBR
SUZI	LI562	LITTLEHAMPTON	5.58	0.82	2006	GBR
SUZIE	PZ454	PENZANCE	4.85	0.94	1974	ST LEVAN
SUZIE P	PH9	PLYMOUTH	7.53	6.60	2012	SUSSEX
SWALLOW	FY59	FOWEY	11.65	11.36	1989	RYE
SWALLOW	LK61	LERWICK	7.56	2.63	1968	LERWICK

UK Fishing Vessels 2015

Vessel Name	Code	Port Name	Loa	Ton Gt	Year	Construction Place
SWAN	M291	MILFORD HAVEN	3.85	0.42	1977	NORWAY
SWAN DANCER	HL46	HARTLEPOOL	9.75	7.70	1977	PENRYN CORNWALL
SWEET AS	SS13	ST IVES	5.95	2.05	2005	Unk
SWEET PROMISE	BK7	BERWICK ON TWEED	8.24	4.39	2000	GBR
SWEET WATER OF NEWLYN	PZ685	PENZANCE	9.90	15.86	1982	PENRYN
SWELL	BRD296	BROADFORD	7.10	1.37	1992	WATERNISH ISLE OF SKY
SWIFT	H145	HULL	9.99	6.15	1990	SULTON ON THE BROADS
SWIFT	LK17	LERWICK	6.28	1.11	1963	SHETLAND
SWIFT SURE	B480	BELFAST	9.95	6.30	2001	HOLYHEAD
SWIFT SURE	OB825	OBAN	9.80	6.54	1999	WEST LOOE
SWN-Y-MOR	SA384	SWANSEA	4.20	0.58	2006	GBR
SWORDFISH	WH15	WEYMOUTH	8.90	6.20	1992	PENRYN
SYDO	BM12	BRIXHAM	13.75	28.01	1954	NORWAY
SYLMARIAN	BRD40	BROADFORD	5.97	1.10	1991	STONEHAVEN
SYLVIA	HH11	HARWICH	10.97	8.39	1938	BRUNDALL NORFOLK
SYLVIA BOWERS	DS8	DUMFRIES	36.75	413.00	1988	BELGIUM
SYLVIA K	GU331	GUERNSEY	7.71	2.63	1980	WEYMOUTH DORSET
SYLVIA MAY	YH2485	YARMOUTH	6.40	1.56	2004	NORFOLK
SYLVIA ROSE	SH79	SCARBOROUGH	8.66	3.39	1975	WHITBY
SYLVIA T	BM112	BRIXHAM	23.98	119.62	2011	HOLLAND
SYLVIES DAWN	J17	JERSEY	3.74	0.42	1980	UK
SYLVIES GRACE	J11	JERSEY	7.57	2.59	2004	WALES
SYLVIES JOY	J53	JERSEY	8.72	4.25	2012	Unk
SYRINEN	WA2	WHITEHAVEN	11.60	18.91	1959	GIRVAN
T J ROCKHOPPER	J127	JERSEY	5.80	1.08	1989	UK
TAHUME	UL666	ULLAPOOL	35.28	315.00	1957	PETERHEAD
TAITS	FR227	FRASERBURGH	70.60	1965.00	2000	NORWAY
TALENE	SH240	SCARBOROUGH	8.49	4.15	1979	SCARBOROUGH
TALISKER	BW7	BARROW	9.80	15.38	1989	LLANELLI
TALISMAN	SD280	SUNDERLAND	9.33	4.77	1965	POLRUAN CORNWALL

UK Fishing Vessels 2015

Vessel Name	Code	Port Name	Loa	Ton Gt	Year	Construction Place
TALISMAN II	BK176	BERWICK ON TWEED	8.55	3.18	1978	EYEMOUTH
TALLY-HO	BS242	BEAUMARIS	4.40	0.51	1990	HOLYHEAD
TALON	CA6	CARDIGAN	8.71	6.15	1981	PORT ISAAC CORNWALL
TAMAHINE	FY892	FOWEY	4.75	0.65	1990	GBR
TAMARA	FY332	FOWEY	8.45	4.55	1965	LOOE
TAMARA	PZ564	PENZANCE	4.54	0.62	1977	PENZANCE
TAMARA	SA80	SWANSEA	6.50	1.50	1988	TEIGNMOUTH
TAMARALYN	DE35	DUNDEE	11.58	25.49	1981	FOWEY
TAMESIS	PH34	PLYMOUTH	9.49	5.55	2009	BRIDGEWATER SOMERSET
TAMMIE NORRIE	WK806	WICK	5.60	0.47	1980	PLYMOUTH
TAMSIN T	PZ315	PENZANCE	5.51	1.39	1989	NEWLYN
TANAMERA	GU20	GUERNSEY	6.54	1.43	1988	ISLE OF WIGHT
TANEGAN	FY778	FOWEY	6.43	2.91	1996	DOWNDERRY
TANGA ROA	LH602	LEITH	8.12	5.96	2013	UK
TANMAR II	YH2472	YARMOUTH	7.03	1.49	2001	HAMPSHIRE
TANNIE CHRISTINA	BS98	BEAUMARIS	26.45	62.00	1905	HOLLAND
TANYA	BE31	BARNSTAPLE	5.07	0.46	1962	FREMINGTON
TARA	PZ209	PENZANCE	4.96	1.23	1972	ST LEVEN NR PENZANCE
TARA LOUISE	UL121	ULLAPOOL	9.36	10.29	1983	MALLAIG
TARA ROSE	PZ94	PENZANCE	4.39	0.58	2010	GBR
TARKA	CN345	CAMPBELTOWN	4.95	0.91	1988	ANSTRUTHER
TARKA	TT101	TARBERT	11.90	19.10	1996	WADEBRIDGE
TARPON	P1	PORTSMOUTH	7.50	1.49	2002	GBR
TAURUS	UL77	ULLAPOOL	5.86	1.30	2010	GAMRIE BANFF
TAY-LEE	BA821	BALLANTRAE	9.93	13.46	1999	MANCHESTER
TAYMOR ONE	OB1030	OBAN	9.96	5.39	2005	HOLYHEAD
TE-BHEAG	BRD256	BROADFORD	6.40	1.71	1980	PENRYN CORNWALL
TEA LEAF TWO	BS503	BEAUMARIS	8.23	2.22	1970	CORNWALL
TEAL	M264	MILFORD HAVEN	4.88	0.53	1978	PEMBROKE

UK Fishing Vessels 2015

Vessel Name	Code	Port Name	Loa	Ton Gt	Year	Construction Place
TEAL	PE658	POOLE	3.77	0.43	1970	SWANAGE
TEDDERA	WA72	WHITEHAVEN	9.45	12.67	1992	BECKERMET
TEDDIE BOY	FE25	FOLKESTONE	5.90	1.10	1983	WALLINGFORD
TEEGAN LOUISE	CS5	COWES	6.10	2.32	1991	COWES
TEGAN	WK837	WICK	4.85	0.58	1980	GBR
TEGEN MOR	SS88	ST IVES	10.84	9.72	1985	HAYLE
TELA	FH484	FALMOUTH	7.62	4.98	1975	RYE
TELESIS	N345	NEWRY	11.89	23.43	1988	HAYLING ISLAND
TELLSTAR	AA38	ALLOA	7.02	2.13	1977	ISLE OF WIGHT
TELMAR	WH69	WEYMOUTH	8.17	2.77	1975	GBR
TELSTAR	K141	KIRKWALL	9.69	12.57	1974	WICK
TELSTAR II	J77	JERSEY	4.50	0.74	1991	Unk
TEMERAIRE	N850	NEWRY	16.41	90.00	1990	THE SLIPWAY ARBROATH
TENACIOUS	DH95	DARTMOUTH	14.97	31.72	1975	CREMYLL SHIPYARD PLYMOUTH
TENDER TO	SU952	SOUTHAMPTON	4.60	0.56	2000	SIDLESHAM WEST SUSSEX
TENDER TO HEATSEEKER	DH79	DARTMOUTH	3.50	0.24	1982	FRANCE
TERN	A879	ABERDEEN	9.82	8.01	1961	BUCKIE
TERN	BA187	BALLANTRAE	7.50	2.95	1981	Unk
TERN	LH53	LEITH	9.11	7.43	1966	SCOTLAND
TERN	PD76	PETERHEAD	5.85	1.94	1985	CORNWALL
TERRY DAVID	SE15	SALCOMBE	6.30	1.32	1990	CYGNUS MARINE LTD
TERRY WILLIAM	LT199	LOWESTOFT	10.56	7.50	1989	LOWESTOFT
TESS	DH85	DARTMOUTH	4.98	0.90	1993	ARUNDEL SUSSEX
THANKFUL	BM488	BRIXHAM	7.62	3.54	1974	ISLE OF WIGHT
THATS IT	WH251	WEYMOUTH	4.59	0.75	1980	PORTLAND
THE GAMBLER	J28	JERSEY	6.50	1.75	1966	JERSEY
THE LITTLE OLD LADY	SM115	SHOREHAM	4.90	0.71	1947	WHITBY
THE SHILLING	J164	JERSEY	5.05	0.88	1998	Unk
THE VITAL SPARK	M217	MILFORD HAVEN	8.51	5.64	1953	ANSTRUTHER SCOTLAND
THE WAY	B268	BELFAST	16.50	36.00	1965	MCDUFF BORFFSHIRE

UK Fishing Vessels 2015

Vessel Name	Code	Port Name	Loa	Ton Gt	Year	Construction Place
THELMA	K11	KIRKWALL	4.88	0.94	1966	WESTRAY
THEODORON	BH165	BLYTH	6.99	1.84	1980	WHITBY
THERESA	PE16	POOLE	9.14	4.29	1975	NEYLAND
THESEUS II	J365	JERSEY	11.53	7.63	2002	IRELAND
THETIS	AB204	ABERYSTWYTH	4.00	0.25	2001	GBR
THISTLE	PH7	PLYMOUTH	6.90	1.92	1980	PENRYN CORNWALL
THOMAS ANDREW	PW214	PADSTOW	9.83	12.56	2004	UK
THOMAS H	BK280	BERWICK ON TWEED	7.90	3.72	1981	PORT ISAAC
THOMAS HENRY	BA218	BALLANTRAE	7.00	2.85	1974	NEWHAVEN
THOMAS IAN	BK548	BERWICK ON TWEED	9.95	9.98	2013	SUSSEX
THOMAS V	GU49	GUERNSEY	3.75	0.47	2010	CASTEL GUERNSEY
THREE BOYS	FH339	FALMOUTH	5.46	1.56	1976	PORTLOE
THREE BOYS	K905	KIRKWALL	10.47	7.48	1966	ORKNEY
THREE BOYS	PZ718	PENZANCE	5.04	1.01	1978	COWES ISLE OF WIGHT
THREE BROTHERS	CA93	CARDIGAN	6.40	1.98	1980	FALMOUTH
THREE BROTHERS	CN203	CAMPBELTOWN	9.15	6.29	1966	ST MONANS
THREE BROTHERS	IH51	IPSWICH	7.35	2.13	1988	COLYTON DEVON
THREE BROTHERS	OB431	OBAN	9.75	10.94	1990	WEST BAY
THREE BUOYS	OB60	OBAN	6.53	1.65	2011	ENGLAND
THREE GIRLS	CN722	CAMPBELTOWN	6.36	1.56	1986	ORKNEY
THREE J'S	CH49	CHESTER	7.47	5.63	1990	PARKGATE SOUTH WIRRAL
THREE J'S	GU46	GUERNSEY	6.84	3.87	1993	GUERNSEY
THREE J'S	PW371	PADSTOW	8.41	4.00	1981	PORTHLEVEN
THREE JAYS	E507	EXETER	7.60	3.66	2001	GBR
THREE JAYS	FY1	FOWEY	4.78	0.87	2004	PENRYN
THREE JAYS	SS84	ST IVES	11.05	9.81	1989	HAYLE
THREE LASSES	BS303	BEAUMARIS	4.93	0.80	1987	SUSSEX
THREE NIECES II	LA608	LLANELLI	5.00	1.10	2004	HAMPSHIRE
THREE SISTERS	BRD584	BROADFORD	9.91	8.61	1978	PENRYN
THREE SISTERS	CA64	CARDIGAN	9.90	4.91	1989	FALMOUTH

UK Fishing Vessels 2015

Vessel Name	Code	Port Name	Loa	Ton Gt	Year	Construction Place
THREE SISTERS	CL7	CARLISLE	7.01	3.12	1976	SILLOTH
THREE SISTERS	GU396	GUERNSEY	6.57	2.86	1990	CORNWALL
THREE SISTERS	N147	NEWRY	9.70	3.50	1998	CORNWALL
THREE SISTERS	RX410	RYE	8.01	3.33	2001	RYE
THREE SISTERS	SY808	STORNOWAY	4.92	0.71	1998	NOT KNOWN
THREE SISTERS R	BH86	BLYTH	9.55	3.67	1986	AMBLE
THREE WISHES	PW7	PADSTOW	11.05	7.83	1972	MEVAGISSEY
TIA LILY	RX445	RYE	6.65	3.48	2008	GBR
TIA MARIA	LI570	LITTLEHAMPTON	9.35	5.19	1982	RYE
TIA-G	E23	EXETER	6.10	1.39	2008	PORTUGAL
TICINO	F44	FAVERSHAM	13.80	24.31	1971	WHITSTABLE
TICKETY BOO	NN780	NEWHAVEN	7.09	1.59	2006	FRANCE
TICKETY TWO	J342	JERSEY	5.78	0.99	1997	UK
TIDOS	FH731	FALMOUTH	5.55	1.44	1972	GBR
TIGER	SS21	ST IVES	5.60	1.43	1974	PLYMOUTH
TIGHT LINES II	SM802	SHOREHAM	7.09	2.06	2001	SUSSEX
TIGRIS	BA856	BALLANTRAE	4.85	0.67	1978	GBR
TILLERMAN	SS76	ST IVES	5.85	1.87	1988	HAYLE
TILLIE BLOSSOM	CK961	COLCHESTER	6.48	1.38	2007	SHETLAND
TILLY II	BK11	BERWICK ON TWEED	5.70	0.98	1985	NOT KNOWN
TIME 'N' TIDE	J21	JERSEY	8.85	6.12	1997	UK
TIME AND TIDE	PE1159	POOLE	8.22	4.90	2012	POOLE
TIME BANDIT	J107	JERSEY	7.71	3.73	1977	UK
TIMMYHAM	FY884	FOWEY	4.01	0.46	2005	SWEDEN
TIN CAN	BRD688	BROADFORD	6.35	1.47	1990	GBR
TINA	CY72	CASTLEBAY	4.30	0.38	1986	ORKNEY
TINA	SD47	SUNDERLAND	11.25	14.02	1973	DENMARK
TINA J	B8	BELFAST	5.60	0.93	2000	PLYMOUTH
TINA LOUISE	KY17	KIRKCALDY	5.82	1.64	2001	UK
TIRRICK	FR52	FRASERBURGH	4.90	0.74	1990	GBR

UK Fishing Vessels 2015

Vessel Name	Code	Port Name	Loa	Ton Gt	Year	Construction Place
TIZ	INS7	INVERNESS	5.64	1.26	1998	SUSSEX
TIZZARDLEE ON	PW16	PADSTOW	9.30	5.33	2008	FALMOUTH
TJEERD JACOBA	BS186	BEAUMARIS	25.30	133.00	1968	ZAANDAM
TOBRACH N	TN2	TROON	23.07	146.51	1999	HULL
TOBY II	BD155	BIDEFORD	4.82	0.66	1982	UNK
TOBY ROC	NN404	NEWHAVEN	11.45	12.00	1981	EXMOUTH
TOBY TOO	J669	JERSEY	3.90	0.38	2002	UK
TOL BAR	SS40	ST IVES	5.76	1.60	2005	NEWQUAY
TOM BOFFIN	LH35	LEITH	7.56	3.75	2005	WORKINGTON
TOMALI	OB1024	OBAN	5.80	1.62	1996	SHETLAND
TOMENNA	NN324	NEWHAVEN	5.86	0.57	1988	NEWHAVEN
TOMKAT	YH273	YARMOUTH	6.80	1.80	1990	CAISTER ON SEA
TOMKAT OF SELSEY	P1010	PORTSMOUTH	9.88	8.21	2005	HAYLING ISLAND
TOMKIT	YH116	YARMOUTH	4.66	0.64	1972	STALHAM
TOMMY	PE7	POOLE	8.05	2.28	1992	POOLE
TON LAS	RO83	ROTHESAY	9.33	4.76	1974	MEVAGISSEY
TOOBOYS	GU92	GUERNSEY	5.65	1.25	1992	ARUNDEL
TOP CAT	LA210	LLANELLI	6.13	1.20	1995	ISLE OF WIGHT
TOP DOG	PH5580	PLYMOUTH	4.00	0.51	1990	PLYMOUTH
TOPAZ	M58	MILFORD HAVEN	9.17	5.00	1979	WORCESTER
TOPCAT II	ME5	MONTROSE	9.98	4.26	2005	VENTNOR
TORRI BEE	SS144	ST IVES	5.84	2.41	1991	FALMOUTH
TORRI GWYNT	FY11	FOWEY	4.80	1.15	1990	FISHGUARD
TOUCAN	BRD12	BROADFORD	7.10	2.67	1983	FALMOUTH
TRACE SEA	E20	EXETER	9.88	7.17	1995	SUSSEX
TRACEY CLARE	SS67	ST IVES	9.94	6.80	1980	POLRUAN
TRACEY ELAINE	BN5	BOSTON	13.90	29.08	2007	LINCS
TRACEY ELIZABETH	PO12	PORTLAND	4.70	0.72	2000	PORTLAND
TRACEY LYNN	E81	EXETER	7.57	4.85	1989	CHARD SOMERSET

UK Fishing Vessels 2015

Vessel Name	Code	Port Name	Loa	Ton Gt	Year	Construction Place
TRACY CLARE	BRD619	BROADFORD	9.91	7.70	1978	ST LEVAN
TRACY K	SY27	STORNOWAY	9.30	7.89	1973	LOOE CORNWALL
TRACY LOUISE	CO5	CAERNARVON	7.30	3.44	1988	SEATON DELAVAL NEWCASTLE
TRADE WINDS	LT230	LOWESTOFT	6.49	2.41	1953	LOWESTOFT
TRADE WINDS	R14	RAMSGATE	9.30	4.64	1987	RAMSGATE
TRADEWINDS 2	YH2478	YARMOUTH	5.74	1.03	2003	NORFOLK
TRADITION	BN447	BOSTON	6.14	1.20	2008	Unk
TRADITION	H232	HULL	13.60	26.38	1973	SOUTH SHIELDS
TRANQUILITY	LK63	LERWICK	26.64	222.00	1986	ST MONANS
TRANQUILITY	PD35	PETERHEAD	23.99	218.00	2000	FIFE
TRANQUILLITY	BF7	BANFF	20.60	169.00	1988	MACDUFF
TRANQUILLITY	LH528	LEITH	8.00	5.27	1990	SOUTHAMPTON
TRANSCEND	BF61	BANFF	19.92	168.00	2000	NAVIA
TREASURE	BF300	BANFF	6.02	1.00	1984	GARDENSTOWN
TREASURE	LK257	LERWICK	9.90	12.23	1999	CAITHNESS
TREBLA	CL2	CARLISLE	9.15	6.77	1989	SILLOTH CUMBRIA
TREEN	PZ23	PENZANCE	4.86	0.69	2000	CAMBORNE
TREGLOWN	FH49	FALMOUTH	7.87	2.31	1987	HAYLE CORNWALL
TRELAWNEY OF CORNWALL	OB409	OBAN	10.66	13.75	1985	HAYLE
TRENEGLOS	FH395	FALMOUTH	8.05	3.31	1977	FALMOUTH
TRENOW GIRL	PZ1228	PENZANCE	4.50	0.62	2005	HELSTON
TRERYN CASTLE	CY27	CASTLEBAY	8.72	5.06	1978	POLRUAN BY FOWEY
TREVALLY	FH2	FALMOUTH	7.95	4.52	2007	HAMPSHIRE
TREVESSA 1V	PZ193	PENZANCE	26.15	135.00	1969	HOLLAND
TREVOSE	PW64	PADSTOW	12.44	18.23	1986	GALMPTON DEVON
TRI CAT	H600	HULL	6.90	1.75	2001	ISLE OF WIGHT
TRI STAR II	H1066	HULL	5.53	1.64	1971	UNK
TRIBUTE	B123	BELFAST	16.66	47.00	1965	BUCKIE
TRICIA B	BN429	BOSTON	9.96	8.05	2000	HUMBERSIDE

UK Fishing Vessels 2015

Vessel Name	Code	Port Name	Loa	Ton Gt	Year	Construction Place
TRINA A	FD514	FLEETWOOD	5.03	0.60	2005	ENGLAND
TRISH	PE582	POOLE	6.00	0.93	2004	BEDHAMPTON
TRISHA JAMES	N1015	NEWRY	6.40	1.89	2009	KILKEEL CO. DOWN
TRISTY	PZ70	PENZANCE	5.85	1.87	1989	GBR
TRITON	J19	JERSEY	5.84	0.91	2004	UK
TRITON	LH145	LEITH	11.04	9.09	1975	WHITBY
TROJAN	MN103	MALDON	8.75	6.95	1983	WORCESTER
TROSTAN	CE320	COLERAINE	6.35	1.74	1991	CUSHENDALL N.IRELAND
TRUE BLUE	LI9	LITTLEHAMPTON	7.38	3.17	1989	SELSEY
TRUE GRIT	DH387	DARTMOUTH	9.20	5.07	1999	PENRYN
TRUE LIGHT	CE533	COLERAINE	7.91	2.17	2000	UK
TRUE TO THE CORE	HH62	HARWICH	10.50	7.00	1988	OULTON BROAD
TRUE TOKEN	N298	NEWRY	18.15	46.00	1965	GIRVAN
TRUE VINE	BH21	BLYTH	6.97	3.97	2005	MACDUFF
TRUE VINE	KY7	KIRKCALDY	15.24	35.00	1974	ST MONANS
TRUE VINE II	UL545	ULLAPOOL	9.94	7.81	1999	SCOTLAND
TRUI VAN HINTE	FD283	FLEETWOOD	40.25	474.00	1989	STELLENDAM
TRUST	AR871	AYR	16.83	58.00	1974	EYEMOUTH
TRUST	BK8	BERWICK ON TWEED	9.95	7.41	2000	ISLE OF LEWIS
TRUST	CY7	CASTLEBAY	8.54	5.68	1978	GARDENSTOWN
TRUST	FY108	FOWEY	7.40	2.37	1982	STOKE IN TEIGHN HEAD
TRUST	UL590	ULLAPOOL	9.15	7.31	1981	GARDENSTOWN
TRUSTFUL	SN12	NORTH SHIELDS	11.43	20.81	1969	FRASERBURGH
TRY AGAIN	WH587	WEYMOUTH	4.02	0.51	1990	ABBOTSBURY ENGLAND
TRYPHENA	SS233	ST IVES	5.63	1.44	1978	ROCK WADEBRIDGE CORNWALL
TUB	BW169	BARROW	5.65	1.19	1990	YAPTON
TUDOR ROSE	SS258	ST IVES	5.53	1.24	1988	GBR
TULNA	GU91	GUERNSEY	6.54	1.53	2008	MILFORD HAVEN
TULNA TOO	GU91	GUERNSEY	6.54	0.86	2013	Unk
TUNNAG	OB544	OBAN	5.18	0.85	1990	FISHBOURNE I O W

UK Fishing Vessels 2015

Vessel Name	Code	Port Name	Loa	Ton Gt	Year	Construction Place
TUPPENCE	PZ826	PENZANCE	5.54	1.40	1990	PLYMOUTH
TURKS HEAD	SC180	SCILLY	4.75	0.67	2009	GBS
TUSKA FIVE	CA5	CARDIGAN	9.98	6.78	1989	POOLE
TUSSAN	LK165	LERWICK	9.14	7.89	1970	STROMNESS
TWA GORDONS	M41	MILFORD HAVEN	9.75	8.44	1980	PENRYN
TWENTY THREE	BS191	BEAUMARIS	6.99	1.47	1988	FALMOUTH
TWILIGHT	BH12	BLYTH	9.87	10.66	2013	PLYMOUTH
TWILIGHT	NN1	NEWHAVEN	6.23	1.09	2012	WEST SUSSEX
TWILIGHT	PW43	PADSTOW	5.71	0.87	2004	SUFFOLK
TWILIGHT	PZ499	PENZANCE	8.02	4.24	1969	SOUTHAMPTON
TWILIGHT III	PZ137	PENZANCE	29.10	141.00	1969	HOLLAND
TWILIGHT STAR	BK116	BERWICK ON TWEED	10.67	8.14	1959	SEAHOUSES
TWIN SISTERS	LI110	LITTLEHAMPTON	9.41	5.22	1999	CORNWALL
TWINS II	GU192	GUERNSEY	7.53	3.24	1996	HAVANT
TWO BOYS	CN707	CAMPBELTOWN	9.95	8.82	1979	MEVAGISSEY
TWO BOYS	PD178	PETERHEAD	6.95	3.28	2012	COUNTY DOWN
TWO BOYS	PE587	POOLE	7.62	1.49	1975	POOLE
TWO BOYS	PZ828	PENZANCE	7.90	2.18	2009	ISLE OF WIGHT
TWO BOYS	SE3	SALCOMBE	5.85	1.84	2001	PENRYN
TWO BOYS	SR83	STRANRAER	9.71	11.67	1991	SUNDERLAND
TWO BROTHERS	BA110	BALLANTRAE	9.84	15.57	2000	CUMBRIA
TWO BROTHERS	BK452	BERWICK ON TWEED	6.95	2.48	2011	CORNWALL
TWO BROTHERS	BM516	BRIXHAM	9.99	7.46	1979	HAMBLE
TWO BROTHERS	LN1	KINGS LYNN	9.83	13.49	2008	GBR
TWO BROTHERS	N588	NEWRY	10.70	13.27	1989	PENRYN
TWO BROTHERS	RX433	RYE	9.60	4.40	2005	EAST SUSSEX
TWO BROTHERS II	SM241	SHOREHAM	11.49	16.02	1987	NEWHAVEN
TWO GIRLS	PL8	PEEL	13.88	27.43	1991	UNK
TWO MARKS	LN458	KINGS LYNN	13.98	22.98	1999	HOLLAND
TWO SISTERS	RY35	RAMSEY	8.17	5.88	1996	GBR
TWO SISTERS	SM198	SHOREHAM	5.52	1.14	1978	BOGNOR REGIS

UK Fishing Vessels 2015

Vessel Name	Code	Port Name	Loa	Ton Gt	Year	Construction Place
TWO SISTERS	UL142	ULLAPOOL	9.05	4.62	1983	LIVERPOOL
TWO SUNS	LO13	LONDON	10.64	7.76	1985	BARLING ESSEX
TYPHOON	FY850	FOWEY	9.95	5.87	2004	PENRYN
UBEROUS	FR50	FRASERBURGH	18.60	163.00	2005	MACDUFF
UBIQUE	KY28	KIRKCALDY	16.67	41.00	1974	ST MONANS FIFE
UDRA	FD526	FLEETWOOD	35.00	355.00	1988	SPAIN
UIST ISLE	CY98	CASTLEBAY	7.15	1.82	1990	STONEHAVEN
ULTIMATE	GY60	GRIMSBY	6.34	1.77	1988	NORFOLK
UNCLE LEN	PH5595	PLYMOUTH	9.00	2.64	1982	WEYMOUTH
UNDER 7	BS11	BEAUMARIS	6.95	2.07	2012	HOLYHEAD
UNITY	BK86	BERWICK ON TWEED	10.75	9.53	1986	SEAHOUSES
UNITY	BM96	BRIXHAM	5.70	1.03	1980	ORKNEY
UNITY	FR165	FRASERBURGH	38.10	850.00	2005	NORWAY
UNITY	LL120	LIVERPOOL	7.32	3.73	1977	PLYMOUTH
UNITY.	LL57	LIVERPOOL	9.89	10.93	1988	WEST KIRBY
UPHILL STRUGGLE	CO803	CAERNARVON	11.90	10.26	2002	BRYNSIENCYN
UPTIDE 4	R97	RAMSGATE	5.90	0.89	2004	WEST SUSSEX
URCHIN	OB127	OBAN	11.98	11.38	1990	CARDIFF
US TWO	PE455	POOLE	5.49	0.75	2006	GBR
USANER	ME228	MONTROSE	4.86	0.65	1992	UK
UTILISE	LK3	LERWICK	8.30	5.63	1990	HAMNAVOE
UTSKER	LK332	LERWICK	7.95	3.99	1996	HAFRUAFJORDUR
UTSKER	WH1236	WEYMOUTH	6.60	2.32	1990	HAFNAFJODUR
VAGABOND	M98	MILFORD HAVEN	5.35	0.86	2001	SHETLAND
VAGABOND	UL23	ULLAPOOL	4.85	0.76	1990	TEIGNMOUTH
VAGABOND II	DO180	DOUGLAS	9.83	5.74	2011	PLYMOUTH
VAGRANT	LK141	LERWICK	7.22	2.82	1973	SHETLAND
VAL B	MH1044	MIDDLESBROUGH	6.40	1.72	2011	NORFOLK
VAL G	B767	BELFAST	17.01	63.00	1967	AKERBOON BERGUM - HOLLAND

UK Fishing Vessels 2015

Vessel Name	Code	Port Name	Loa	Ton Gt	Year	Construction Place
VALAHOPE	KY12	KIRKCALDY	5.77	1.02	2008	GBR
VALAURA	BA256	BALLANTRAE	13.40	32.39	1987	GIRVAN
VALDAR	LK15	LERWICK	9.15	5.88	2005	PENRYN
VALDEZ	N63	NEWRY	9.95	5.23	1982	FISHGUARD
VALENTE	BS8	BEAUMARIS	43.19	388.00	2002	GDANSK
VALENTIA	LK21	LERWICK	9.20	5.74	2012	COUNTY KERRY IRELAND
VALENTINE	FE20	FOLKESTONE	9.90	11.82	1999	CORNWALL
VALERIE	LI127	LITTLEHAMPTON	5.85	1.48	1947	SOUTHWOLD
VALERIE ANN	IH322	IPSWICH	7.99	2.26	2006	GBR
VALERIE ANN	RX142	RYE	6.80	1.85	2013	SUSSEX
VALERIE E	SA12	SWANSEA	5.20	1.01	2011	WALES
VALETTA	PO2	PORTLAND	4.84	0.73	2000	GBR
VALHALLA	AD2	ARDROSSAN	6.77	3.37	1985	RYE
VALHALLA	BA234	BALLANTRAE	6.79	1.79	1988	MALAHIDE DUBLIN
VALHALLA	BH9	BLYTH	10.70	16.39	1989	STROMNESS ORKNEY
VALHALLA	BRD659	BROADFORD	9.95	7.37	2002	HOLYHEAD
VALHALLA	FR268	FRASERBURGH	25.60	201.00	1999	NAVIA
VALHALLA	LK687	LERWICK	18.15	85.00	1985	ST. MONANCE
VALHALLA	N845	NEWRY	6.50	3.10	1984	HAYLE
VALHALLA II	WK84	WICK	8.90	4.25	1984	UNK
VALHALLA V	AH5	ARBROATH	6.79	1.35	2007	FAREHAM
VALHALLA VI	AH6	ARBROATH	6.20	1.13	1996	ISLE OF WIGHT
VALIANT	OB77	OBAN	8.15	4.03	1997	PENRYN
VALIANT	SY197	STORNOWAY	5.80	1.45	1988	SOUTHAMPTON
VALIRON	WH856	WEYMOUTH	8.13	6.99	1992	CORNWALL
VALKYRIE	CK4	COLCHESTER	9.30	6.40	1978	GBR
VALKYRIE	NN70	NEWHAVEN	7.85	3.38	1983	RYE
VALKYRIE	TH417	TEIGNMOUTH	5.62	1.65	1998	PLYMOUTH
VALKYRIE II	CK5	COLCHESTER	9.99	9.95	1989	HULL
VALODEST	BA852	BALLANTRAE	6.89	1.07	2009	CO.ANTRIM

UK Fishing Vessels 2015

Vessel Name	Code	Port Name	Loa	Ton Gt	Year	Construction Place
VALONIA	BF263	BANFF	7.19	2.01	1989	STONEHAVEN SCOTLAND
VALONIA	PL63	PEEL	16.86	53.43	1975	GBR
VAN DIJCK	BM362	BRIXHAM	33.53	203.00	1974	ZEEBRUGGE BELGIUM
VANQUISH	B74	BELFAST	24.80	246.00	2003	UK
VAR LISA	WK120	WICK	8.66	5.51	1978	BURRAY ORKNEY
VARUNA	BRD684	BROADFORD	8.30	5.07	2005	GBR
VECTIS ENTERPRISE	CO18	CAERNARVON	10.64	8.91	1982	RYE SUSSEX
VENTNOR BAY	CS672	COWES	7.95	2.24	2006	GBR
VENTNOR PRIDE II	CS644	COWES	9.00	3.96	1999	I.O.W.
VENTURA	P975	PORTSMOUTH	6.90	3.38	1997	FALMOUTH
VENTURE	AB5	ABERYSTWYTH	7.40	2.91	1980	POOLE
VENTURE	AH36	ARBROATH	9.77	3.94	2012	GBR
VENTURE	BH179	BLYTH	9.88	8.71	1959	FRASERBURGH
VENTURE	BS4	BEAUMARIS	3.67	0.26	1963	UNK
VENTURE	CH45	CHESTER	8.37	4.56	1984	LIVERPOOL
VENTURE	CK925	COLCHESTER	9.97	17.25	1998	CEREDIGION
VENTURE	LK641	LERWICK	24.70	227.00	1991	ST MONANCE
VENTURE	OB459	OBAN	7.50	3.57	1981	MACDUFF
VENTURE	PZ166	PENZANCE	5.49	1.34	1946	PORTHLEVEN
VENTURE	TT56	TARBERT	5.94	2.05	2001	CORNWALL
VENTURE	WK498	WICK	6.95	2.65	1973	TARBERT
VENTURE 11	OB28	OBAN	8.16	8.00	1980	HAYLING ISLAND
VENTURE AGAIN	PL39	PEEL	15.39	38.19	1966	GBR
VENTURE AGAIN II	KY239	KIRKCALDY	13.65	27.50	1998	EYEMOUTH
VENTURE II	BF326	BANFF	28.00	468.00	2001	MACDUFF
VENTURE JH	LK712	LERWICK	6.27	1.38	1989	DEVON
VENTURER	HL1063	HARTLEPOOL	8.05	2.31	1986	NEWCASTLE-UPON-TYNE
VENTUROUS	LK75	LERWICK	26.19	244.00	1989	HESSLE
VENUS	CY42	CASTLEBAY	7.32	3.74	1977	WICK SCOTLAND
VENUS	FY58	FOWEY	9.95	7.43	1992	CORNWALL

UK Fishing Vessels 2015

Vessel Name	Code	Port Name	Loa	Ton Gt	Year	Construction Place
VENUS	KY22	KIRKCALDY	4.98	0.69	2008	FIFE
VENUS II	BS6	BEAUMARIS	5.70	0.82	1989	UNKNOWN
VENUS II	K574	KIRKWALL	11.25	12.10	1979	CORNWALL
VENUS II	KY34	KIRKCALDY	8.05	4.83	1987	FALMOUTH
VERA	LK345	LERWICK	5.95	1.25	1993	UNKNOWN
VERA D	DH16	DARTMOUTH	4.85	0.62	1981	ARUNDEL SUSSEX
VERANIA II	LK298	LERWICK	8.20	2.58	1996	CAITHNESS
VERANN	B54	BELFAST	18.52	59.00	1977	GBR
VERONA	FY803	FOWEY	5.42	1.42	1997	UNKNOWN
VERONICA ANN	PW99	PADSTOW	11.60	24.66	1993	FEARN SCOTLAND
VERSATILE	P598	PORTSMOUTH	7.68	5.15	1974	RYE SUSSEX
VERTROUWEN	DS11	DUMFRIES	26.24	144.50	1968	WEST-GRAFTDIJK HOLLAND
VERVINE	BA842	BALLANTRAE	16.90	47.00	1970	GBR
VESPER II	FY606	FOWEY	6.45	2.52	1988	MEVAGISSEY
VESTA	FY529	FOWEY	7.10	3.24	1979	CHARLESTOWN
VI-KING	LH679	LEITH	5.63	1.46	1995	GBR
VICHANA	PD5	PETERHEAD	9.81	10.41	1988	RYE
VICKY ANNA	SC32	SCILLY	9.78	6.67	1991	FALMOUTH CORNWALL
VICKY ELLEN	BN86	BOSTON	13.38	25.96	1992	THORNE NR DONCASTER
VICKY LEIGH	LL273	LIVERPOOL	12.95	23.12	1992	HANSWEED
VICTAM	BS450	BEAUMARIS	5.80	1.29	1989	ARUNDEL
VICTORIA	CK923	COLCHESTER	9.90	7.06	1997	CORNWALL
VICTORIA	E556	EXETER	6.05	1.18	1993	CORNWALL
VICTORIA	YH71	YARMOUTH	5.58	1.04	1985	DRIFFIELD YORKSHIRE
VICTORIA ANNE	FH706	FALMOUTH	5.90	1.25	2002	CAMBORNE
VICTORIA LEIGH	N70	NEWRY	7.30	2.90	2008	Unk
VICTORY	FR5	FRASERBURGH	5.94	1.28	2007	GBR
VICTORY II	LK356	LERWICK	8.38	5.31	1950	BANFF
VICTORY OF HELFORD	SC11	SCILLY	10.73	7.36	1975	LOOE
VIDDY	PW473	PADSTOW	4.91	0.33	1991	GBR

UK Fishing Vessels 2015

Vessel Name	Code	Port Name	Loa	Ton Gt	Year	Construction Place
VIGILANT	BF190	BANFF	18.60	163.00	2004	MACDUFF
VIGILANT	KY71	KIRKCALDY	9.21	5.81	2001	CORNWALL
VIGILANT	PD65	PETERHEAD	6.22	1.37	1996	MACDUFF
VIGILANT B	SY136	STORNOWAY	6.06	2.13	1987	PLYMOUTH
VIGILANTE	PE753	POOLE	9.25	7.87	1978	BOTLEY
VII LOONS	FR69	FRASERBURGH	4.87	0.55	1992	ARRUNDEL
VIKING	GU120	GUERNSEY	7.00	2.10	2003	FRANCE
VIKING	PZ88	PENZANCE	9.62	4.30	1995	LOCHIN
VIKING	UL231	ULLAPOOL	6.57	1.43	1984	ACHILTIBUIE
VIKING III	UL572	ULLAPOOL	7.95	6.54	2006	INVERFORDON
VIKING MONARCH	K58	KIRKWALL	40.00	611.00	1998	TROON
VIKING PRINCESS	FE137	FOLKESTONE	9.86	11.67	1995	LINCOLN
VIKING WARRIOR	BS188	BEAUMARIS	14.97	28.57	1969	DENMARK
VIKINGBORG	OB285	OBAN	16.62	44.00	1975	BUCKIE
VILLAGE BELLE	LH54	LEITH	9.55	6.66	1971	DUNBAR - EAST LOTHIAN
VILLAGE BELLE IV	B377	BELFAST	18.10	47.00	1970	GIRVAN
VILLAGE MAID	BRD13	BROADFORD	7.90	1.89	1987	INVERNESS
VILLAGE MAID	TT25	TARBERT	8.84	4.24	1966	UK
VINE	K9	KIRKWALL	3.66	0.47	1971	WESTRAY ORKNEY
VIOLET EILEEN	H80	HULL	9.95	4.25	2007	ISLE OF WIGHT
VIOLET EVA	CS659	COWES	6.30	0.61	2004	GBR
VIOLET MAY	NN752	NEWHAVEN	5.27	0.94	2005	EASTBOURNE
VIOLET MAY	SC80	SCILLY	5.80	0.81	1997	CORNWALL
VIORA	LK177	LERWICK	8.30	6.89	1993	FALMOUTH
VIPA	PZ481	PENZANCE	6.25	2.91	1992	ZENNOR CORNWALL
VIRGO	ST7	STOCKTON	11.33	16.39	1984	POLRUAN
VIRLEY NATIVE	CK935	COLCHESTER	7.91	2.54	1981	FALMOUTH
VIRTUE	PD1021	PETERHEAD	5.91	1.24	2005	CLACKMANNANSHIRE
VIRTUOUS	FR253	FRASERBURGH	23.30	210.00	2010	WHITBY
VISION III	BF191	BANFF	23.00	227.00	2013	UK

UK Fishing Vessels 2015

Vessel Name	Code	Port Name	Loa	Ton Gt	Year	Construction Place
VITAL SPARK II	WK456	WICK	5.67	1.53	1975	PLYMOUTH
VITALITE	BW247	BARROW	7.00	2.41	1994	BARROW-IN-FURNESS
VIVERRINA	P970	PORTSMOUTH	9.75	6.06	1999	HAVANT
VMOS	BS25	BEAUMARIS	5.20	1.15	1989	UNK
VOE	OB504	OBAN	6.34	1.37	1990	SHETLAND
VOYAGER	LI522	LITTLEHAMPTON	9.58	7.87	1999	EAST COWES
VOYAGER	N905	NEWRY	75.40	3145.00	2010	DNK
WAHOO	E52	EXETER	5.80	1.37	2009	EXMOUTH
WAHOO	P981	PORTSMOUTH	9.90	4.03	1999	NORFOLK
WAHOO	WH744	WEYMOUTH	7.24	2.69	1990	SUSSEX
WAIKIKI	WH511	WEYMOUTH	6.90	1.83	1985	FAIREY MARINE
WAKEFUL	PD294	PETERHEAD	11.32	12.14	1974	CARDIFF
WAKIL II	BW147	BARROW	9.88	7.69	1973	BARROW
WALRUS	UL25	ULLAPOOL	10.86	10.88	1989	WHITBY
WALTER GEORGE	RX414	RYE	9.80	6.54	2002	RYE
WANDERER	J396	JERSEY	3.60	0.48	1973	FRANCE
WANDERER	K169	KIRKWALL	8.70	7.36	1982	UNK
WANDERER	WK106	WICK	5.55	1.50	1978	PLYMOUTH
WANDERER II	SY378	STORNOWAY	16.76	37.00	1972	GIRVAN
WANNY LOU	LR459	LANCASTER	6.98	2.07	1968	LANCASTER
WANORTU	K980	KIRKWALL	5.00	0.75	1998	SUSSEX
WANSBECK	BH68	BLYTH	9.99	12.17	2009	PETERHEAD
WARREN B	SM214	SHOREHAM	4.96	1.25	1986	BOGNOR REGIS
WARREN EDWARDS	M15	MILFORD HAVEN	9.90	3.90	2013	ISLE OF WIGHT
WASH PILGRIM	BN1	BOSTON	12.99	19.24	1992	BARTON ON HUMBER ENGLAND
WASH PRINCESS	LN161	KINGS LYNN	13.10	19.95	1992	KINGS LYNN
WATER-RAIL	ME235	MONTROSE	4.80	0.77	2007	GBR
WATERLILY	N51	NEWRY	10.76	15.59	1972	STROMNESS
WAVE CREST	HL198	HARTLEPOOL	9.14	4.74	1980	WHITBY
WAVE DANCER	M1134	MILFORD HAVEN	5.09	1.17	2004	LIVERPOOL

UK Fishing Vessels 2015

Vessel Name	Code	Port Name	Loa	Ton Gt	Year	Construction Place
WAVE ON	GU218	GUERNSEY	6.38	1.41	1993	YAPTON
WAVE RIDER	J479	JERSEY	5.05	0.76	1995	GBR
WAVECREST	SY3	STORNOWAY	16.34	41.00	1968	SANDHAVEN
WAVEDANCER	SS12	ST IVES	4.85	0.55	1997	CORNWALL
WAY TU GO	GU59	GUERNSEY	5.60	1.11	1991	ARUNDEL WEST SUSSEX
WAYFARER	SH9	SCARBOROUGH	11.54	8.39	1982	SOUTHAMPTON
WAYPOINT 1	R9	RAMSGATE	6.50	1.74	1997	UK
WAYWARD LAD	RX6	RYE	9.98	12.95	1982	RYE
WE LIKE IT	WO1	WORKINGTON	9.76	9.07	1976	KEYHAVEN
WE-RE HERE	PZ3	PENZANCE	3.17	0.28	1980	PENZANCE
WE'LL TRY	RO25	ROTHESAY	9.68	10.59	1995	FALMOUTH
WEE BESS	LH16	LEITH	5.50	1.05	1986	SCOTLAND
WEE BOAT	B20	BELFAST	5.20	1.02	1991	COUNTY DURHAM
WEEMARA	TT242	TARBERT	4.95	0.90	1988	TAMWORTH STAFFORDSHIRE
WELCOME HOME	BRD3	BROADFORD	8.01	3.96	1979	CORNWALL
WELCOME HOME	N347	NEWRY	7.86	6.62	1979	ANNALONG CO DOWN
WELSH MAID	CO332	CAERNARVON	9.75	6.60	1938	COWES
WENDON	CO257	CAERNARVON	3.75	0.36	1989	UNKNOWN
WENDY G	WY321	WHITBY	7.07	1.63	1997	ANSTRUTHER
WENDY II	WO130	WORKINGTON	5.92	1.97	1977	WORKINGTON
WENDY J	LI578	LITTLEHAMPTON	10.00	5.03	1978	UNITED KINGDOM
WENDY JANE	SM91	SHOREHAM	6.50	0.88	1984	UNKNOWN
WENDY LIAM	TT35	TARBERT	9.80	9.97	1986	MELTON
WENDY PATRICIA	BH22	BLYTH	9.85	12.09	2007	SCOTLAND
WENDY SUE	LH4	LEITH	7.38	3.03	1981	MARYPORT
WENNAJO	FY20	FOWEY	5.60	1.51	2003	UK
WEST COASTER	WK864	WICK	4.91	0.70	1973	NOT KNOWN
WEST WIND	SE371	SALCOMBE	4.40	0.52	1996	KINGSBRIDGE
WEST WINDS	WK10	WICK	4.90	0.84	1978	TAMSBRIG AYR
WESTERLY WARRIOR	INS24	INVERNESS	9.99	10.56	1984	PENRYN

UK Fishing Vessels 2015

Vessel Name	Code	Port Name	Loa	Ton Gt	Year	Construction Place
WESTERN CHIEF	SY842	STORNOWAY	5.30	0.66	2002	UNITED KINGDOM
WESTERN FISHER	GU260	GUERNSEY	7.95	3.46	1983	PLYMOUTH & GUERNSEY
WESTERN LADY Y	LI8	LITTLEHAMPTON	8.08	5.73	1979	GUERNSEY
WESTERN LASS	GU136	GUERNSEY	9.68	6.65	1988	GUERNSEY
WESTERN PROMISE	SM304	SHOREHAM	9.30	6.49	1971	FRANCE
WESTERN VENTURE	LK122	LERWICK	11.15	20.88	1991	WICK CAITHNESS
WESTHAVEN	OB51	OBAN	7.13	2.50	1982	SCOTLAND
WESTHAVEN III	KY5	KIRKCALDY	11.28	13.46	1978	FALMOUTH
WESTON BAY	OB129	OBAN	12.20	21.28	1985	PENRYN
WESTRAL WARRIOR	CA385	CARDIGAN	7.10	1.82	1995	GBR
WESTS	BF25	BANFF	5.94	1.19	2006	SCOTLAND
WESTWARD ISLE	SM575	SHOREHAM	9.14	7.84	1980	RYE
WEXFORDIAN 3	LK1011	LERWICK	8.45	3.79	1988	SAETON DEVON
WHINIVER	SY8	STORNOWAY	8.02	5.83	1975	ORKNEY
WHISKY GALORE	CT5	CASTLETOWN	9.98	11.53	1991	PENRYN
WHITBY CREST	WY318	WHITBY	9.91	8.63	1980	WHITBY
WHITBY LASS	WY789	WHITBY	6.85	1.71	1975	WHITBY
WHITE HEATHER	PE1	POOLE	6.97	0.84	2002	POOLE
WHITE HEATHER	PZ272	PENZANCE	5.61	1.59	1973	HELSTON CORNWALL
WHITE HEATHER	SS33	ST IVES	12.40	26.40	1988	PENRYN
WHITE HEATHER	TT273	TARBERT	9.83	5.94	2006	ESSEX
WHITE HEATHER IV	B26	BELFAST	14.94	36.08	1968	EYEMOUTH
WHITE HEATHER VI	LH1	LEITH	20.82	86.00	1981	CAMPBELTOWN
WHITE LADY	BS530	BEAUMARIS	5.70	1.04	1982	SOUTHBOURNE NR EMSWORTH
WHITE LADY	J3	JERSEY	7.97	6.06	2007	GBR
WHITE MARLIN II	TO64	TRURO	6.95	0.92	2006	ISLE OF WIGHT
WHITE OSPREY	GU58	GUERNSEY	8.45	3.31	2007	FALMOUTH CORNWALL
WHITE ROSE	OB299	OBAN	10.87	10.04	1987	HULL
WHITE ROSE OF FISHGUARD	CA42	CARDIGAN	7.20	2.22	1979	CORNWALL
WHITE SURF	B12	BELFAST	7.25	0.87	2006	ISLAND PLASTICS

UK Fishing Vessels 2015

Vessel Name	Code	Port Name	Loa	Ton Gt	Year	Construction Place
WHITE WATERS	J100	JERSEY	9.75	9.54	1993	UK
WHITELINK	CY208	CASTLEBAY	9.45	4.33	1974	CARDIFF
WHO CARES	SH10	SCARBOROUGH	9.31	4.71	1990	BERWICK ON TWEED
WICKED HEN	DO16	DOUGLAS	8.00	2.07	1986	UNITED KINGDOM
WICKED WENDY	IE3	IRVINE	9.75	3.92	1988	CORNWALL
WILD CAT	WY833	WHITBY	9.64	6.00	2008	GBR
WILD CHORUS	GY1476	GRIMSBY	4.58	0.15	2007	LINCS
WILD ROSE	OB401	OBAN	9.50	11.07	1981	SHAPINSAY
WILD ROVER	HL707	HARTLEPOOL	7.78	4.06	1970	WHITBY
WILD SPIRIT	BS53	BEAUMARIS	5.18	0.86	1990	ORKNEY BOATS/WEST SUSSEX
WILD WAVE	GU42	GUERNSEY	5.98	2.93	1972	PAIMPOL
WILD WEST	NN10	NEWHAVEN	5.30	1.65	2005	WEST SUSSEX
WILD WILLY	GU66	GUERNSEY	4.05	0.32	1970	HAMPSHIRE
WILHELMINA	LT60	LOWESTOFT	40.00	428.00	1991	STELLENDAM HOLLAND
WILLIAM ALEXANDER	B48	BELFAST	9.70	5.24	1973	GBR
WILLIAM AND MOLLY	HL321	HARTLEPOOL	6.50	2.87	1987	PENRYN
WILLIAM ARNOLD	LR173	LANCASTER	5.92	1.70	1977	OVERTON
WILLIAM CONNOR	BA857	BALLANTRAE	9.95	4.25	2008	ISLE OF WIGHT
WILLIAM GEORGE	GU266	GUERNSEY	7.90	5.01	1977	ENGLAND
WILLIAM HARVEY	PZ75	PENZANCE	12.64	20.71	1958	FRANCE
WILLIAM HENRY	FY929	FOWEY	5.80	0.73	1998	UK
WILLIAM HENRY	NN711	NEWHAVEN	9.83	10.15	2006	ESSEX
WILLIAM HENRY II	DH5	DARTMOUTH	22.50	185.00	1989	DEN HELDER (HOLLAND)
WILLIAM JOHN	N60	NEWRY	9.98	9.98	1975	ANNALONG
WILLIAM JOHN	PD298	PETERHEAD	9.98	12.84	1988	HULL
WILLIAM MARY	NN729	NEWHAVEN	13.95	30.09	2003	NEWHAVEN SUSSEX
WILLIAM SAMPSON STEVENSON	PZ191	PENZANCE	28.24	142.00	1969	HOLLAND
WILLIAM STANLEY	CO814	CAERNARVON	6.00	1.16	2007	GWYNEDD
WILLIAM STEVENSON	PZ195	PENZANCE	25.99	104.00	1967	NETHERLANDS

UK Fishing Vessels 2015

Vessel Name	Code	Port Name	Loa	Ton Gt	Year	Construction Place
WILLIAM T	FE368	FOLKESTONE	9.66	4.79	1999	CORNWALL
WILLIAM WALTER	LO582	LONDON	8.15	2.29	2008	ISLE OF WIGHT
WILLING BOYS	YH533	YARMOUTH	6.48	1.78	1947	SOUTH COAST
WILLING LAD	N102	NEWRY	18.75	115.35	2009	SCOTLAND
WILLSBRY	IH1	IPSWICH	9.91	6.00	1998	BARTON-UPON-HUMBER
WILLY BOY	IH263	IPSWICH	6.71	3.00	1969	FELIXSTOWE FERRY
WILMA JOHN	K45	KIRKWALL	6.40	2.62	1967	BURRAY ORKNEY
WILZY LOU	LA441	LLANELLI	5.00	0.59	1980	GBR
WIN	NN500	NEWHAVEN	5.37	1.29	1973	SUFFOLK
WINAWAY	KY279	KIRKCALDY	11.40	20.99	1988	HAVANT
WINDERMERE	LK423	LERWICK	7.47	3.99	1979	ORKNEY
WINDWARD	LK185	LERWICK	6.98	1.25	1984	ISLE OF WIGHT
WINDY ISLE	SY5	STORNOWAY	9.75	8.13	1991	LOOE
WINIFRED	FY919	FOWEY	5.37	0.88	2013	UNKNOWN
WINKLE	SS247	ST IVES	4.42	0.57	1978	WADEBRIDGE
WINNER	K1127	KIRKWALL	8.29	7.55	1979	WICK
WINNIE	SA368	SWANSEA	9.40	5.27	2002	GBR
WINNIE THE POOH	PW393	PADSTOW	7.99	2.28	2005	NORTHUMBERLAND
WINSOME	N611	NEWRY	15.18	31.00	1966	ST MONANS
WIRON 1	PH110	PLYMOUTH	51.44	1059.00	1995	SPAIN
WIRON 2	PH220	PLYMOUTH	51.44	1068.00	1996	SPAIN
WIRON 5	PH1100	PLYMOUTH	50.63	1230.00	2002	SPAIN
WIRON 6	PH2200	PLYMOUTH	50.63	1230.00	2002	SPAIN
WISHERMAN	GU34	GUERNSEY	6.20	1.08	2002	AUGUSTOW
WIZARD	P66	PORTSMOUTH	6.85	1.17	1982	ISLE OF WIGHT
WONKY	SA357	SWANSEA	9.95	9.72	2000	KIDWALLY
WONOVER	BA840	BALLANTRAE	5.20	0.72	1967	SCARBOROUGH
WORTHY LASS	PZ97	PENZANCE	6.15	1.59	1982	DEVON
WRIGGLER	M328	MILFORD HAVEN	3.79	0.43	1979	NORWAY
WYVILLESS	SH26	SCARBOROUGH	9.60	5.85	2013	NORTHUMBERLAND

UK Fishing Vessels 2015

Vessel Name	Code	Port Name	Loa	Ton Gt	Year	Construction Place
XERCES	LO3	LONDON	6.90	1.31	1997	ISLE OF WIGHT
XMAS ROSE	BH197	BLYTH	9.51	3.54	1963	AMBLE
Y NOT	PE1094	POOLE	6.95	3.72	1999	YEOVIL
Y PRIS	LT63	LOWESTOFT	4.94	1.00	1999	LANCASHIRE
YANUCA	J32	JERSEY	5.80	0.89	2007	GBR
YDON	CK1	COLCHESTER	9.20	7.13	1979	HULL
YELLOWHAMMER	MT107	MARYPORT	9.61	8.67	2000	GBR
YN DREAN	CT133	CASTLETOWN	6.53	3.12	1978	PENRYN
YOUNG LAUREN	YH1044	YARMOUTH	5.75	1.04	1992	YAPTON SUSSEX
YUNG DHAL	WK190	WICK	6.10	1.67	1993	NORWAY
YVONNE ANNE	HH118	HARWICH	9.93	15.70	1988	RAMSGATE
YVONNE TEST	CF307	CARDIFF	13.00	31.32	1997	CARDIFF
ZAC B	PE107	POOLE	6.20	0.72	1992	POOLE
ZARA	SS270	ST IVES	6.20	2.30	1985	ST IVES
ZARANATHAX	WH707	WEYMOUTH	9.95	11.85	1999	FALMOUTH
ZARVAN	PW122	PADSTOW	8.10	6.56	1988	PENRYN
ZEALANDER	P101	PORTSMOUTH	3.38	0.26	1912	GOSPORT
ZEBEC	J209	JERSEY	7.78	2.41	1980	UK
ZENITH	B470	BELFAST	21.42	116.00	1972	BUCKIE
ZENITH	BA806	BALLANTRAE	5.97	1.22	1985	UNK
ZENITH	BF106	BANFF	24.85	192.00	1986	BUCKIE
ZENITH	BH133	BLYTH	14.64	49.30	1983	SEAHOUSES
ZENITH	SY874	STORNOWAY	7.68	2.41	1989	RYE
ZENITH	UL222	ULLAPOOL	16.80	41.00	1964	FRASERBURGH
ZEPHYR	FR444	FRASERBURGH	11.15	16.80	1982	SANDHAVEN
ZEPHYR	LK394	LERWICK	72.80	2060.00	1996	NORWAY
ZEPHYR	N203	NEWRY	14.98	31.85	1974	ST MONANS
ZEPHYR	SC50	SCILLY	5.84	2.26	1984	ENGLAND
ZEPHYR	SY807	STORNOWAY	8.45	3.72	1987	POULDEN BERWICKSHIRE
ZEUS	LI135	LITTLEHAMPTON	11.85	8.89	1991	NEWPORT - I.O.W.

UK Fishing Vessels 2015

Vessel Name	Code	Port Name	Loa	Ton Gt	Year	Construction Place
ZEUS FABER	J82	JERSEY	7.01	1.60	2008	UK
ZIGGY	DH180	DARTMOUTH	3.85	0.68	1982	KINGSBRIDGE
ZILLIW	BS426	BEAUMARIS	6.35	2.59	1992	AMLWCH
ZOE ANN	N708	NEWRY	9.80	7.91	1992	FALMOUTH
ZOEY	GU179	GUERNSEY	8.01	3.01	1980	EYEMOUTH
ZOLEE	CN53	CAMPBELTOWN	11.80	9.52	2007	ESSEX
ZOLOTOY	SD406	SUNDERLAND	9.98	4.26	2009	ISLE OF WIGHT
ZONA	TO4	TRURO	4.30	0.45	1994	UNK
ZOOM	DH15	DARTMOUTH	5.70	0.94	1983	CHICHESTER
ZORA JAY	CN51	CAMPBELTOWN	9.85	4.04	1974	WEYMOUTH
ZULU	KY21	KIRKCALDY	7.73	2.65	2004	NORTHUMBERLAND
ZULU	LT171	LOWESTOFT	8.00	2.75	1979	CORNWALL

FISHING VESSELS CODE/NAME INDEX

CODE	NAME	CODE	NAME	CODE	NAME
A1	GOOD DESIGN	AB67	PIONEER	B12	WHITE SURF
A10	KELLIN STAR	AB7	QUAKER	B123	TRIBUTE
A107	NATALIE B	AB71	GRATITUDE	B124	SPRING TIDE
A13	JACQUELINE	AB77	PEN DINAS	B126	INCENTIVE II
A15	JACKIE B	AB8	BAARAGUTT II	B127	GOLDEN REAPER
A17	SKUA II	AD1	PISMO	B128	STAR INA
A177	SHAMARNIC	AD2	VALHALLA	B129	MARISCO
A200	OCEAN DAWN	AD4	MERMAID	B14	RHODANNA
A272	AVIT	AD5	KARA LOUISE	B140	RIBHINN DONN II
A3	IRENE K	AD6	SHOOTING STAR	B144	ALLIANCE
A344	BARRY JEAN	AD7	DILEAS	B145	PILOT US
A40	GRAMPIAN ADMIRAL	AH1	OOR LASS	B15	MARIONA
A440	JEANNIE	AH136	ENDURANCE	B150	ROISIN DUBH
A441	BOY GORDON V	AH153	FORTUNA II	B152	ILENE
A5	DAG DAN	AH180	HARRIET J	B157	MARANATHA
A52	MARIGOLD	AH2	LICHTIE LASS	B163	KINDLY LIGHT
A53	CRAWPEEL	AH20	LADY ANNE	B17	ROSEBANK
A6	LAUREN ROSE	AH24	ASPIRE	B173	NATALIE D
A73	AURORA	AH26	NICOLA D	B179	ROCK DODGER II
A8	KIT KAT	AH268	ORIANNE	B182	EX MARE GRATIA
A857	CLAIRE L	AH28	IRIS	B183	RIVER ISLAND
A860	NORNESS	AH3	SINCERE V	B185	ASTERIA
A865	HARVESTER	AH35	OSPREY	B19	MARGARET ANN 11
A869	SHEARMA	AH36	VENTURE	B198	EVENTIDE
A879	TERN	AH39	GOOD FRIEND	B2	SPEEDWELL
A913	DALWHINNIE	AH4	BONNIE LASS II	B20	WEE BOAT
A929	SEA SPRAY	AH45	KIROAN	B200	FREEDOM
A94	HALCYON	AH5	VALHALLA V	B209	ADELE II
A946	SHELLFISHER	AH59	BONNIE LASS	B210	HANDA ISLE
A950	SAMYRA	AH6	VALHALLA VI	B22	ELLEN
A955	JOHNY II	AH63	REIVER II	B221	SAPPHIRE STONE
A971	ORCA	AH67	FAITHFUL	B224	STARLIGHT SPLENDOUR
A974	RACHEL	AH708	HARMONY	B230	DAWNLIGHT
AA38	TELLSTAR	AH709	GEMINI	B235	GOLDEN JUBILEE
AB1	HARMONY	AH71	PROVIDER	B236	GIRL MARY
AB104	BOY SCOTT	AH711	GLORIA VICTUS	B238	GIRL JILL II
AB107	OTRANTO II	AH714	GRETAS GIRL	B24	MYSTICAL ROSE II
AB11	OUR BRIA LEA	AH717	PATHFINDER	B249	HOOVER IT
AB125	DONNA J	AH721	SHAMARA II	B26	WHITE HEATHER IV
AB128	AERON BELLE	AH728	LADY CLAIRE	B260	ALISA
AB129	STURDY	AH92	MORAG	B268	THE WAY
AB14	CELTIC SPIRIT	AH95	DAY DAWN	B27	JAY
AB15	SILVER WAKE	AR1	MAGAN D	B279	ROSEMARY ANN
AB170	ABBA-CAT	AR190	SILVER QUEST	B28	ABIGAIL III
AB199	PATHFINDER	AR325	ESPEMAR DOS	B282	OCEAN VENTURE
AB2	CARASUE	AR861	NORTHERN LIGHT	B291	AMANDA J
AB201	AQUA	AR865	CABO ORTEGAL	B3	SOLAS
AB204	THETIS	AR871	TRUST	B30	SILVER DARLINGS
AB206	ANGELA MARY	AR89	AQUILA ROI	B308	SEA ELF
AB210	CLAIRE	AR94	AYR QUEEN	B310	SILVER DEE
AB213	PERSERVERENCE II	B1	MEGAN	B313	SAGITTARIUS
AB22	JESSICA IONE	B10	GIRL ANN III	B317	KAREN
AB229	MA-NICKS	B1001	MOONSHINE	B330	MARINA
AB23	SANTA FE	B1002	LATIS	B336	AURELIA
AB29	D.H.S.	B1003	BLACK TOM	B338	BOLD VENTURE
AB3	BARBOSSA	B1005	OCEAN DIVINE	B340	ENDURANCE
AB30	AMBUSH	B1012	GUIDING LIGHT	B350	BENAIAH IV
AB33	DOVEY BELLE	B104	ISLAND VENTURE	B351	ABBACY ANNIE
AB4	SANDERLING	B11	GENESIS	B358	BAHR NAGASH
AB5	VENTURE	B113	ALICE	B377	VILLAGE BELLE IV
AB52	NIKKI LOU	B116	GOOD HOPE	B4	MANANNAN

FISHING VESSELS CODE/NAME INDEX

CODE	NAME	CODE	NAME	CODE	NAME
BCK40	QUO VADIS	BE6	OTTER	BF370	LEXI ROSE
BCK479	PENOLVA	BE7	MAR	BF372	SILVER WAVE
BCK50	COURAGE II	BE9	OCTOBER MORNING	BF4	GIRL JULIE
BCK595	DEESIDE	BF1	ENTERPRISE II	BF405	EMMA JANE
BCK598	SHALIMAR	BF10	ELLIE TESSA	BF41	INTEGRITY W
BCK608	INTREPID	BF100	LIVING WATERS	BF410	FLOURISH
BCK612	CASTLEBAY	BF101	SUNLIGHT RAY	BF42	JEWEL
BCK617	KINGFISHER	BF103	GRATITUDE	BF420	INTEGRITY
BCK619	CULANE	BF106	ZENITH	BF432	ORION
BCK62	SUSTAIN	BF109	CELESTIAL DAWN	BF440	BERYL
BCK624	LADY ANN III	BF11	CONNOR BOY	BF453	SERENE
BCK625	KELLY	BF110	EXCEL	BF47	JACINTH III
BCK626	INSCHALLA	BF111	COASTAL QUEEN	BF5	GUIDING STAR
BCK630	BEADNAL	BF12	ELLORAH	BF50	RESOLUTE
BCK635	NAURU	BF142	ST KILDA	BF500	HALCYON II
BCK70	HELENUS	BF15	LUCY LOU	BF505	GENESIS
BCK8	LILY OAK V	BF151	DAYSTAR	BF515	ENDEAVOUR IV
BCK81	KESTREL	BF155	PLEIADES	BF55	HOPEFUL
BCK83	OCEAN REWARD IV	BF16	CAMANNA	BF555	KALISTO
BCK9	CARONA	BF17	MORAY PEARL	BF56	SOLSTICE
BD1	GUIDING LIGHT III	BF173	SHAMROCK	BF569	NIMBLE
BD11	CEOL NA MARA B	BF177	HARVEST REAPER II	BF6	HALCYON
BD155	TOBY II	BF18	SHARONELLE	BF600	CONFIDENCE
BD169	J O	BF182	ATLAS	BF61	TRANSCEND
BD179	SALLIANN	BF19	AMETHYST	BF64	JUST REWARD
BD18	GEMINI	BF190	VIGILANT	BF7	TRANQUILLITY
BD19	SCOOBY 2	BF191	VISION III	BF70	KROSSFJORD
BD2	LUNDY STAR	BF2	HELENA	BF73	JENNA MAREE
BD217	BOYS PRIDE	BF201	MARELANN	BF74	SEAGULL
BD22	ANN LOUISE	BF205	SEARCHER	BF77	OCEAN QUEST
BD228	ARGONAUT	BF206	SARDONYX II	BF777	EMMALEY
BD247	SPARKLING STAR III	BF21	EXPLORER	BF79	BOUNTIFUL
BD249	PAIR I	BF212	MONARCH	BF794	SHAULORA
BD257	MALLAGAR	BF223	ACHIEVE	BF8	PISCES
BD267	LADY OF LUNDY	BF23	SEA SHELL	BF80	RELIANCE
BD277	OUR OLIVIA BELLE	BF234	MAJESTIC III	BF800	RELIANCE II
BD279	CERI-LEE	BF24	SERENITY	BF803	CARINA
BD287	OUR JOSIE GRACE	BF240	FRUITFUL VINE	BF826	PISCATIO
BD288	NEMO	BF25	WESTS	BF83	AUDACIOUS
BD292	PRECIOUS	BF250	REBECCA ANN	BF840	OCEANA
BD297	SELACHOS	BF263	VALONIA	BF843	SHALANNA
BD3	PHOEBE	BF268	DISCOVERY	BF849	IONA
BD310	MIABELLA	BF27	ANTARIES	BF85	OCEAN CHALLENGE
BD33	HANNAH MARIE	BF272	JACINTH W	BF854	OCEAN CREST
BD36	SOPHIE JANE	BF273	MARGARET ROSE	BF863	SKUA
BD4	OUR JENNY	BF28	REPLENISH	BF878	OCEAN WAY
BD5	K C H	BF285	DAY DAWN	BF880	LAWRET
BD6	STORM CHILD	BF296	CHARISMA	BF89	AQUARIUS
BD69	NEPTUNE	BF3	JASPER II	BF891	OPTIMISTIC
BD7	KEVLOU	BF300	TREASURE	BF9	PAL O MINE
BD76	BOY LEE	BF303	SEALGAIR	BF91	GOLDEN CHANCE
BD78	COMPASS ROSE II	BF319	PREVAIL	BF913	RED HACKLE
BD8	FRANCIS ANNE	BF324	CHANCE	BH1	ENDURANCE II
BD87	CHALE BAY	BF326	VENTURE II	BH10	SERENITY
BD88	GREEN EYE	BF335	PILOT STAR	BH108	EMMA JANE N
BD9	ANNA	BF340	FLOURISH N	BH11	PISCES
BD99	ORTAC	BF36	KAIROS	BH111	GLAD TIDINGS
BE1	JAN B	BF362	NORLAN	BH115	GOLDEN LILY
BE13	CARLA JANE	BF365	KESTREL	BH12	TWILIGHT
BE29	K-SANDS	BF366	KINWAIN	BH120	HOMELAND
BE31	TANYA	BF37	BRACODEN	BH121	FREYA

FISHING VESSELS CODE/NAME INDEX

CODE	NAME	CODE	NAME	CODE	NAME
BH133	ZENITH	BH7	OCEAN DAWN	BM12	SYDO
BH138	JINGLING GEORDIE	BH77	STAR OF PEACE	BM126	BEARS WATCHING
BH14	SUZANNE II	BH85	FAIR HARVEST	BM127	HARVESTER
BH15	JOANNE	BH86	THREE SISTERS R	BM128	HOLLY ANNE
BH155	BORDER QUEEN	BH9	VALHALLA	BM14	GRACE
BH156	GREEN PASTURES	BH92	FIDELITY	BM140	GEESKE
BH165	THEODORON	BH95	CRYSTAL SEA	BM147	MALKERRY
BH174	HARTLEY	BH98	PATRICIA O'MELIA	BM15	MARTINE
BH179	VENTURE	BK1	QUO VADIS	BM16	STACEY ANNE
BH18	EMULATE A	BK10	GLAD TIDINGS VII	BM166	LERINA
BH182	HAUXLEY HAVEN	BK103	PROMISED LAND	BM172	KERRIE MARIE
BH188	BOLD VENTURE II	BK108	FORTUNE II	BM176	EBONNIE
BH19	SILVER SEA	BK11	TILLY II	BM177	LA CREOLE
BH196	MARY ANNE	BK111	GIRL JACKIE	BM18	GUYONA
BH197	XMAS ROSE	BK112	PRIMITIVE	BM181	SASHA EMIEL
BH2	ADVENTURE	BK116	TWILIGHT STAR	BM188	LLOYD TYLER
BH20	DAYDA B	BK155	JACQUELINE	BM189	OUR LADY
BH21	TRUE VINE		STEPHENSON	BM19	MARINA EMIEL
BH212	CONSTANT FRIEND	BK172	GOOD FELLOWSHIP	BM192	ELOISE
BH218	MARGARET KERR II	BK176	TALISMAN II	BM2	HANNAH D
BH22	WENDY PATRICIA	BK224	HARVEST HOME	BM20	SLIPPERY DICK
BH220	REJOICE	BK226	GLAD TIDINGS II	BM208	JACOMINA
BH225	SILVER QUEST	BK241	ENDEAVOUR	BM211	SUE ELLEN
BH227	NIMROD	BK27	HELEN	BM218	HARINGVLIET
BH229	EMBRACE	BK279	GLAD TIDINGS III	BM222	SEA OTTER
BH230	STAR DIVINE	BK280	THOMAS H	BM224	AMBER J
BH24	HARVEST DAWN	BK312	GUIDE ME	BM225	JORDAN A
BH243	INCENTIVE	BK36	OUR LADS	BM23	CARHELMAR
BH26	DAYDA II	BK411	BALTIC	BM236	MOWZER
BH27	CHARISMA	BK452	TWO BROTHERS	BM24	PEACE AND PLENTY III
BH3	PEGASUS	BK50	SUPREME II	BM249	SARAH JAYNE
BH306	NATALIE KRISTEN II	BK516	OSPREY	BM254	BLUE GATE
BH314	BRITANNIA II	BK522	AMATHUS	BM258	HELEN CLAIRE
BH335	MALCOLM STUART	BK524	KINDLY LIGHT D	BM26	ISABEL MARY
BH337	SILVER CARRS	BK533	FULMAR 2	BM265	JOANNA C
BH36	ENDEAVOUR	BK535	ISAAC EDWARD	BM27	OUR MIRANDA
BH37	FRANCES ANN D	BK536	FREEDOM	BM271	ANGELENA
BH4	LADY FRANCES	BK548	THOMAS IAN	BM276	BELINDA BEE
BH438	PROVIDENCE II	BK552	STAND SURE	BM28	EMILY ROSE
BH44	BORDER LASSIE	BK64	NORTHERN PRIDE	BM3	SEA FEVER
BH441	CLAIRE MADISON	BK69	JENNA H	BM30	SARA LENA
BH447	SANDRA JAMES	BK7	SWEET PROMISE	BM342	OUR WENDY
BH45	BOLD ENDEAVOUR	BK8	TRUST	BM35	SHIRALEE
BH450	BOLD VENTURE	BK83	NONAKIE	BM361	BARENTSZEE
BH453	BONAVENTURE	BK86	UNITY	BM362	VAN DIJCK
BH456	AQUARIUS II	BK96	MADONNA	BM367	BON ACCORD
BH462	ELIZABETH JADE	BL1	SOLE TRADER	BM397	HELEN B
BH467	ELLIE JOY	BL57	BARBARA L	BM4	GOLDFISH
BH47	STERINA	BM1	EMULATE	BM40	BOY PHILLIP
BH471	HELEN	BM10	EMILIA JAYNE	BM41	SARAH LOUISE
BH476	CRYSTAL RIVER A	BM100	LADY T EMIEL	BM42	KAYLEIGH ANN
BH477	CHRISTOPHER	BM102	SCORPION LASS	BM422	PROVIDER II
BH479	BROTHERS	BM107	SISTER MC B	BM44	NIPPER
BH5	SCOOBY-DOO	BM11	LIAM JOHN II	BM454	KELLY MARENA II
BH51	RESTLESS WAVE	BM110	LADY LOU	BM46	SUSAN ELIZABETH
BH526	SARAH LOUISE	BM111	CATHARINA	BM478	DANIELLE
BH56	FREEDOM II	BM112	SYLVIA T	BM479	LISA K
BH57	PROVIDER	BM113	GRETEL K	BM482	MARY ANNE
BH6	REWARD	BM114	SEIONT A	BM484	CONSTANT FRIEND
BH63	LAURA JAYNE	BM115	LITTLE MAID	BM487	KATY JANE
BH68	WANSBECK	BM116	OUR SARAH JAYNE	BM488	THANKFUL

FISHING VESSELS CODE/NAME INDEX

CODE	NAME	CODE	NAME	CODE	NAME
BM491	NICOLA JAYNE	BRD120	JAMIAIN II	BRD676	GLADLY ANNE II
BM493	OCEAN SPIRIT	BRD123	DUNAN STAR II	BRD678	LADY LYNNE
BM499	ATLANTIS II	BRD13	VILLAGE MAID	BRD679	FRAM OF SHIELDAIG
BM5	DEE J	BRD149	EILIDH	BRD680	SILIS
BM51	HARM JOHANNES	BRD15	JEANNIE	BRD682	GIRL SARAH
BM511	MAGNUM	BRD16	GIRL MARGARET	BRD684	VARUNA
BM516	TWO BROTHERS	BRD17	SILVER CAT	BRD685	JOSEPH COOK II
BM517	KASEY MARIE	BRD175	PTARMIGAN	BRD686	CRABSTER
BM522	JOHN B	BRD18	ALEX C	BRD687	FAMILYS PRIDE II
BM526	LITTLE MITE	BRD180	CATRIONA	BRD688	TIN CAN
BM529	BOLD VENTURE	BRD185	AMITY	BRD693	SPINDRIFT III
BM547	SAINT PIERRE	BRD19	IRIS II	BRD694	BOY CORRIN
BM55	ANGEL EMIEL	BRD190	OPPOSITION	BRD695	CADENZA
BM554	RUBY TUESDAY	BRD2	CHRISTINE	BRD7	MARGRETA M
BM556	RISING DAWN	BRD200	SANGSARA	BRD70	NORANN
BM557	BLUE THUNDER	BRD202	SHUNA	BRD73	GREEN ISLE III
BM558	BLUE TINNY	BRD21	SILVER T	BRD74	ENCHANTED
BM6	ALAN C	BRD212	AMPS	BRD75	SERENE
BM63	LADY L	BRD23	STEELE	BRD77	OUR CATHERINE
BM65	ELSIE B	BRD250	ASTERIA	BRD8	RUBY MAY
BM7	LADY MAUREEN	BRD256	TE-BHEAG	BRD83	GREEN ISLE
BM77	JACOBA	BRD259	CLAIRE JAYNE II	BRD84	SILVER WAVE
BM78	CALYPSO	BRD273	INSHALLAH	BRD9	BOLTON GIRL
BM79	ADELA	BRD279	JACQUELINE	BRD90	HELEN BRUCE
BM8	SUSIE H	BRD28	SILVER J	BRD97	JULIA ANN
BM9	LADY JEAN	BRD296	SWELL	BS1	SCARLETT LOU
BM91	LILY LOLA	BRD3	WELCOME HOME	BS10	SUSAN L
BM96	UNITY	BRD32	SILVER E	BS100	GOLDEN STRAND III
BN1	WASH PILGRIM	BRD323	EVELYN	BS11	UNDER 7
BN109	MEDWAY IV	BRD362	GRACE ANN	BS115	GWEN PAUL M
BN19	SOVEREIGN	BRD38	BOY RYAN	BS119	NEV NEV
BN190	KATHRYN JAMES	BRD398	SUSAN	BS12	LOTTIE HOLLY
BN2	SEA DOG	BRD40	SYLMARIAN	BS125	CAITLIN
BN23	JAIME LOUISE	BRD423	MAUREEN FRANCES	BS14	LADY K
BN24	ABIGAIL	BRD438	LADY JADE	BS15	AURORA
BN28	PRAWN CRACKER	BRD44	PIONEER	BS16	CALAMARI
BN39	MERLIN	BRD5	SILVER SEA	BS17	JAN LE CLAIR
BN428	ITSIE BITSIE	BRD518	EILANE	BS171	ST.GWENFAEN
BN429	TRICIA B	BRD584	THREE SISTERS	BS18	MARNIE ROSE
BN430	CALLY SERANNE	BRD619	TRACY CLARE	BS186	TJEERD JACOBA
BN434	LITTLE LEER	BRD621	MARIE BHAN III	BS188	VIKING WARRIOR
BN435	FIVE JS	BRD628	SABRE II	BS191	TWENTY THREE
BN438	PATRICIA B	BRD629	CORAL SEA	BS2	MELISSA CLARE
BN439	LILI MAE	BRD632	SEA RANGER	BS204	SEA BREEZE
BN444	SHARON II	BRD639	DANNY J	BS216	SEA GIPSY
BN445	SEVEN SISTERS	BRD645	MY GIRLS J L L II	BS218	KAYLEIGH C
BN447	TRADITION	BRD646	SARNIA -ANN	BS219	ANITA
BN5	TRACEY ELAINE	BRD650	MARIE BHAN IV	BS226	MERMAID
BN64	RUTH IMELDA	BRD652	DARIEN	BS234	LADY JEN
BN67	INTREPID	BRD657	LUCY E	BS235	JEAN M
BN77	ANGELENA	BRD658	ISA	BS24	PETREL
BN78	JAANA B	BRD659	VALHALLA	BS242	TALLY-HO
BN80	LUCY MARIE	BRD663	SILVER STEELE	BS25	VMOS
BN84	MAGGIE S	BRD664	IONA	BS255	MERLIN
BN86	VICKY ELLEN	BRD668	SANDPIPER	BS3	PICKLES
BR116	GALWAD Y MOR	BRD669	DEALAN-DE	BS303	THREE LASSES
BRD1	FRAM III	BRD670	SILVER FISH	BS33	CLOUDY
BRD109	GOLDEN RULE	BRD671	SILVERMINE	BS36	NECORA
BRD115	NEMESIS	BRD672	SKUA	BS39	SARO II
BRD117	MICHELLE	BRD674	JOSA	BS4	VENTURE
BRD12	TOUCAN	BRD675	MOYRA JANE	BS40	SEA KING

FISHING VESSELS CODE/NAME INDEX

CODE	NAME	CODE	NAME	CODE	NAME
BS418	BARBRA ANN	BW255	ORCA	CE500	GIRL NICOLA
BS425	CKS	BW256	CATATONIA	CE509	GREEN ISLE V
BS426	ZILLIW	BW260	BOY SAM	CE510	BOY MATTHEW
BS427	J B	BW262	AMY KATE	CE515	FIVE BROTHERS
BS430	LAST ORDERS	BW263	LIZZIE B	CE517	PROVIDER
BS446	C SHARP	BW269	SHANNON LOUISE	CE52	CARELLIN
BS448	CORVINA	BW27	NATALIE ROSE	CE521	FOUR BOYS
BS450	VICTAM	BW7	TALISKER	CE522	MARTHA M
BS456	GYPSY	CA1	LUCIE FISHER	CE525	EMERALD ISLE II
BS457	CERI	CA103	AFONDALE	CE526	BLUE MARLIN
BS458	PROPER JOB II	CA125	LOWRI	CE531	LADY JADE
BS467	SAMPHIRE	CA169	SPITFIRE	CE533	TRUE LIGHT
BS474	CAT FISH	CA182	AWEL-Y-MOR	CE537	SHAUN M
BS475	CIMWCH 2	CA187	MOANER	CE538	BOY SEAN II
BS482	LILY V	CA192	GWALCH Y MOR III	CE539	CIARA NAOIMH
BS485	EMILY JAYNE	CA2	SHARON ANNE	CE542	MELANIE S
BS494	KEIRAN TREFOR	CA273	SHEARWATER	CE545	FULMAR OF COLERAINE
BS5	SIDEWINDER	CA306	AQUARIUS	CE546	COMPASS ROSE
BS500	QUEST	CA31	PETER M	CE56	LADY CLARE
BS501	BILLY B	CA32	GLAS-Y-DORLAN I	CE6	BLACK PEARL II
BS503	TEA LEAF TWO	CA33	CHANNEL FISHER	CE600	MO CHAILINI
BS505	DARK HARVESTER	CA369	HOWNI	CE66	SHAUNA
BS506	SUSIE MO II	CA372	CLARICE	CE68	PATSY J
BS515	EMILY MAY	CA373	BARBARA JONES	CE694	INTREPID
BS517	LISA GEM	CA375	KATHLEEN MAY	CE695	KERIOLET
BS519	ENDEAVOUR	CA385	WESTRAL WARRIOR	CE707	ALASKA
BS52	PICALO	CA386	LADY JAYNE	CE79	IMELDA M
BS526	AMY M	CA387	CHRISTINE ANN	CE804	MAGGIE ANNE
BS53	WILD SPIRIT	CA389	LUSTY LISA	CE88	QUICKSILVER
BS530	WHITE LADY	CA42	WHITE ROSE OF	CF1	AGAINST ALL ODDS
BS534	RUBY ROE		FISHGUARD	CF167	KYRENIA
BS539	MAYHEM	CA44	CALIOPE	CF24	OUR KATY
BS540	SEA MASTER	CA5	TUSKA FIVE	CF307	YVONNE TEST
BS541	CALYPSO	CA57	JOANNA	CF319	BLUE BOY
BS556	LAST CHANCE	CA6	TALON	CF6	OUR LADY
BS56	ROY WILLIAM	CA63	ANERITA	CF7	ELKIE B
BS57	PRIDE OF PERELLE	CA64	THREE SISTERS	CH102	LAURA JUNE II
BS58	NICOLA FAITH	CA67	SALLY ANN	CH202	SEAFISHER
BS6	VENUS II	CA7	RHONA ANN	CH257	DARK STAR
BS60	REBECCA M	CA83	REBECCA J	CH45	VENTURE
BS63	PRINCESS ROYAL	CA84	DONNA	CH49	THREE J'S
BS66	EMMA MARIE	CA9	D.J.P.	CH537	EMMA
BS7	GOOD ONE	CA93	THREE BROTHERS	CH66	KATHLEEN
BS79	BILLEN	CE10	GLEN ISLE	CK1	YDON
BS8	VALENTE	CE12	BOY PAUL	CK109	BOY MICHAEL
BS9	ALICE	CE121	NORTHERN ISLE	CK110	ELISE
BS90	PHOENIX	CE133	EMMY LOU	CK12	NATIVE
BS98	TANNIE CHRISTINA	CE135	CRYSTAL TIDE	CK127	MAUDIE
BU37	LILACINA	CE160	OUTLAW	CK134	REBECCAN
BW1	BALLAST	CE19	RACHEL ANNE	CK14	JON BOY
BW10	KELLIN STAR	CE208	GREEN BRAE	CK15	REBECCA LOUISE
BW106	ANNE MARIE	CE226	CAROL	CK157	JESSICA M
BW12	LADY JULIA	CE235	IRISH ROVER	CK168	CHRISTINA CARA
BW122	SARAH BUNN	CE239	FIONA	CK169	SUPESAM
BW136	POST HASTE	CE277	HOMEWARD BOUND	CK191	LILY GRACE
BW14	LILY B	CE279	INCENTIVE	CK20	FOX
BW147	WAKIL II	CE3	CAROLI-JEN	CK23	BASS VILLIAN
BW169	TUB	CE307	SIOBHAN III	CK230	KARLEE
BW2	LISA MICHELLE	CE311	ISLAND FISHER	CK3	HOT SHOT
BW23	ELAINALEE	CE320	TROSTAN	CK304	LAUREN ANNE
BW247	VITALITE	CE37	SADIE	CK305	NICOLA ANNE

FISHING VESSELS CODE/NAME INDEX

CODE	NAME	CODE	NAME	CODE	NAME
CK351	JAMES GARY	CN200	HARVESTER	CN9	EQUINOX
CK355	MAY	CN203	THREE BROTHERS	CN92	ODIN
CK38	KAREN	CN207	ALLIANCE	CN96	CLANSMAN
CK4	VALKYRIE	CN21	AOIFE OG	CO1	JEAN KELLY
CK5	VALKYRIE II	CN213	ANA - MOSKEEN	CO10	RONAN ORLA
CK51	MOONLIGHTER II	CN25	DIONNE	CO106	GOOD PROSPECT
CK6	ASTERIX	CN258	ATLAS	CO11	MARK ANTHONY
CK68	LAUREN GIRL	CN3	MAGGIE B	CO110	SEAVIEW
CK7	SHOAL WATER	CN303	NEW DAWN	CO118	AMSER
CK70	MISS GRACE II	CN318	SPEEDWELL OF	CO121	LYN
CK78	CHERYL SARAH		GLENARIFFE	CO137	CARIAD
CK79	MAVERICK	CN322	OCEAN HERALD	CO170	HEATHER JUNE
CK8	CAITLIN BEE	CN323	FIADH OR	CO171	ST GWENFAEN
CK896	BOY STEVEN 11	CN324	DAWN QUEST	CO18	VECTIS ENTERPRISE
CK898	EXCEL	CN33	SUNSEEKER	CO186	EWYN
CK9	DRIFTER	CN332	ROS BUIDHE	CO204	NARWHAL
CK904	LIBERTY	CN345	TARKA	CO217	KRILL 3
CK91	FISHER LASSIE	CN35	AMY HARRIS IV	CO22	CELTIC LADY
CK919	PIGLET	CN357	CLIFFORD NOEL	CO245	PAULINE J
CK922	CATHY ANNE	CN365	MICHELLE ANNE I	CO25	MEG
CK923	VICTORIA	CN367	ESCAPE	CO257	WENDON
CK924	OUR CAROLL II	CN373	HAZEL ANN	CO267	GERTRUDE
CK925	VENTURE	CN383	REBECCA R	CO28	SEARCHER
CK926	MY WAY	CN394	SHANGRI-LA	CO281	JIM
CK930	SEA GLORY	CN397	JUST MINE	CO282	LUN
CK934	ALVIC	CN4	KATIE CLAIRE	CO30	COLLEEN
CK935	VIRLEY NATIVE	CN40	IAIN OG	CO316	IVY ROSS
CK941	JACK	CN43	CRIMSON ARROW	CO324	MORLO
CK942	MARNIE	CN444	GLEANER	CO328	JORY
CK945	BOY LEW	CN49	SULAIRE	CO332	WELSH MAID
CK946	JESS	CN5	DEFIANCE IV	CO34	BOY JASON
CK948	BASSET	CN50	JULIE	CO359	PAN ARCTIC
CK956	MAEZIE BELLE	CN51	ZORA JAY	CO365	CELTIC STAR
CK958	HONIE BEAU	CN519	SOPH-ASH	CO366	MELESSA
CK96	OUR ENDEAVOUR	CN53	ZOLEE	CO37	OSPREY
CK961	TILLIE BLOSSOM	CN56	STARDUST	CO377	SARAH H
CK962	MIGRANT	CN57	JACAMAR	CO394	DWYFOR
CK97	ENDEAVOUR	CN65	OCEAN SPRAY	CO4	GEE WIZ
CL1	SEAHAWK	CN67	ACCORD III	CO452	STEEL VENTURE
CL12	NEW VENTURE	CN689	LYNN LOUISE	CO484	ST NICHOLAS II
CL2	TREBLA	CN690	AVALON II	CO5	TRACY LOUISE
CL26	SOLWAY PROVIDER	CN691	SPRAY	CO511	JACQUELINE
CL4	JOLANDA	CN699	CEOL NA MARA	CO517	EVELYN
CL7	THREE SISTERS	CN7	A MAIREACH	CO519	ANNE
CN1	BROTHERS K	CN70	SEA NYMPH	CO53	JOE'S GIRL
CN104	GIRL LINDA	CN707	TWO BOYS	CO530	OSPREY A
CN11	JENNRHI K	CN712	MARY ANNE	CO532	GLADYS B
CN111	FREEDOM II	CN714	LASS	CO538	KATIE LOU
CN114	SEREN-Y-MOR	CN717	HIGHLANDER	CO555	JACQUELINE ANNE
CN117	LADY GAIL	CN722	THREE GIRLS	CO577	LARA B
CN12	REWARD	CN73	BLUE LAGOON	CO585	BIBIEN
CN131	GIRL ERRIN	CN746	EMMY LEIGH	CO592	HYDROMYS
CN14	JURABLE	CN750	KESTRAL	CO60	CREST
CN140	DIGNITY JAY	CN758	FLINT PHOENIX	CO68	GIRL HELEN
CN15	SEA SPRAY	CN777	GLEANER II	CO7	SEA QUEST
CN16	ASPIRE II	CN778	RONA	CO73	MARIANNE
CN17	PERSEVERANCE	CN779	SEA VENTURE	CO734	KARMA BAY
CN18	PRIMROSE	CN78	ADORATION II	CO74	SARAH LOUISE
CN199	SOLSTICE	CN8	DELIVERANCE	CO75	ANN
CN2	LYNSAY LOU	CN87	INCENTIVE	CO77	CEINWEN
CN20	CRYSTAL DAWN	CN89	MARONA	CO791	CWIN MERI

221

FISHING VESSELS CODE/NAME INDEX

CODE	NAME	CODE	NAME	CODE	NAME
CO796	PEBBLE	CT14	LIBRA	CY250	STELLA MARIS
CO797	MARI WYN	CT140	MANX PRIDE	CY254	CHEERFULL
CO798	CELT	CT141	OUR SARAH JANE	CY26	DUNAN STAR
CO803	UPHILL STRUGGLE	CT142	SPAVEN MOR II	CY263	FAIR LASS
CO807	ANASTASIA II	CT145	ALENA	CY27	TRERYN CASTLE
CO81	LITTLE WONDER	CT151	ALWAYS OUT	CY272	SEA BREEZE
CO810	CIAN	CT18	SARAH LENA	CY29	GIRL CATHERINE
CO813	SUN CHASER	CT20	FRIENDLY SHORE	CY3	AMELIA
CO814	WILLIAM STANLEY	CT21	MICHAEL J	CY303	MY AMBER
CO815	MORFRAN III	CT25	AUK	CY312	FRUITION
CO816	NATALIE H	CT3	SHEARWATER	CY34	AQUARIUS
CO817	FISHY BUSINESS II	CT32	JULIE M	CY340	NORDIC WAY
CO818	EHEDYDD	CT5	WHISKY GALORE	CY341	LAUREL
CO820	MASCARAID	CT52	ORCA	CY359	ST ALOYSIUS
CO829	CHLOE BETH	CT58	NANCY ELLEN	CY37	BOY GARY
CO83	PEDRYN	CT74	GIMMAGH	CY38	SANTA MARIA IIII
CO830	INTEGRITY	CT76	MAUREEN PATRICIA	CY4	SAPPHIRE
CO9	SKUA	CT77	SPAVEN MOR	CY40	SPRAY I
CO92	REBECCA	CT8	SCRAAYL	CY42	VENUS
CS119	STORMALONG	CT81	HEATHER MAID	CY43	CATHERINE ANNE
CS121	GET THIS	CT88	BEACHCOMBER	CY433	MARY-KAY
CS144	SAMUEL JAY	CY1	ANNIE T	CY436	SERENE II
CS154	ALBATROSS	CY10	LILY I	CY441	SINE BHAN I
CS177	H R K	CY100	GIRL FIONA	CY445	FRANCES
CS2	DOUBLE OR NOTHING	CY103	CHRISTINE ANN	CY449	NIPPY
CS295	KATY	CY11	AZALEA	CY45	HEATHER BELLE
CS30	DOVE	CY110	GANNET II	CY452	GENTOO
CS361	SPIRIT OF THE WHITE WOLF	CY111	HAZYMOL	CY453	BARRAMUNDI
		CY113	OCEAN SPRAY	CY457	MORENA
CS41	SNOWMAN	CY120	SON DE MER	CY458	MISTY MORN
CS434	SIRENE	CY121	MYSTICAL ROSE	CY464	ISABELLA
CS451	MY WAY	CY127	GUIDING LIGHT	CY468	RESTLESS WAVE II
CS5	TEEGAN LOUISE	CY130	LORIS ELLIE	CY5	FLORA
CS611	KIRSTY GIRL	CY131	GIRL JOSIE	CY52	KENDORA
CS628	JOHN EDWARD	CY136	LUCKY LOUISE	CY550	PRUE ESTHER II
CS632	SCARLET PRIVATEER	CY137	SPARKLING STAR	CY57	ROSIE B
CS635	J & B	CY141	LIZANNA	CY6	IONA LOUISE
CS64	STEPHANIE R	CY145	MIZPAH	CY62	ANNA ROSE
CS644	VENTNOR PRIDE II	CY147	BOY JOHN	CY64	GRIMSAY ISLE
CS645	EMMA-JAY	CY149	GOLDEN PROMISE	CY67	FRAOCH GEAL
CS646	GAIRM NA MARA II	CY150	JOY	CY7	TRUST
CS649	LEESON LADY	CY156	ANNITA	CY70	MAGDALENE
CS658	HORIZON	CY157	GIRL SUSAN	CY701	JOANNA
CS659	VIOLET EVA	CY16	EILIDH	CY72	TINA
CS661	KISMET	CY163	STELIMAR	CY720	PROWESS
CS665	SAPPHIRE	CY174	STARDUST	CY741	SALTIRE
CS670	JO JO	CY177	ANNIE JANE	CY77	BRIGHTER MORN
CS671	MARDESHAR	CY183	MARIE THERESE	CY777	HARMONY
CS672	VENTNOR BAY	CY189	RELIANCE	CY797	SEONAG
CS673	GEORGIA	CY190	BOY DARREN	CY799	RELIANT
CS679	POT LUCK	CY193	ORKNEY STAR	CY8	KITTYWAKE
CS70	MONKS BAY	CY2	RONA	CY807	REUL-A-CHUAIN
CS73	ENDEAVOUR	CY20	ANN MARIE II	CY815	GOLDEN DAWN
CS79	ANGIE	CY202	SEVEN SISTERS	CY820	CARMISA II
CS8	FLO FAN	CY205	HARVESTER	CY824	MY GIRLS J.L.L
CS81	KESTREL IV	CY208	WHITELINK	CY830	DONNA
CT1	SKATE	CY211	MARCAN SINE	CY832	GEM
CT122	DEJA VU	CY231	MARY LOUISE	CY836	LAUREN KARINE
CT133	YN DREAN	CY233	PRIMROSE	CY837	SHAMROCK
CT137	FREY	CY236	ALISON	CY84	OCEAN MAID
CT139	S'AALIN MADRAN	CY243	SIOLTA	CY85	FAIR MORN

FISHING VESSELS CODE/NAME INDEX

223

FISHING VESSELS CODE/NAME INDEX

CODE	NAME	CODE	NAME	CODE	NAME
E516	ALIBI	FD514	TRINA A	FH145	COPIOUS
E519	RENE	FD515	OUR VALERIE ANN	FH17	NIKI LOU
E52	WAHOO	FD518	AVOCET	FH178	MAGDALENA
E520	MIA B	FD520	MOWGLI	FH18	BEST EVER
E523	GOOD LIFE	FD521	MONTE MAZANTEU	FH187	KON-TIKI
E524	SHAMROCK	FD522	AYR DAWN	FH19	LADY MARGARET OF
E531	PELICAN	FD525	SANAMEDIO		COVERACK
E534	ATTITUDE	FD526	UDRA	FH198	HARVESTER
E538	NINA MAY	FD527	PORT OF AYR	FH2	TREVALLY
E544	OUTCAST	FD528	PIEDRAS	FH20	GIRL LUCY
E549	SOLO	FD529	O GENITA	FH200	JEN LOU II
E556	VICTORIA	FD530	PRAWN STAR	FH207	GOLDEN FLEECE II
E559	RIVER RASCAL	FD535	MAYFLOWER	FH21	MILLIE G
E56	OUTCAST 2	FD547	LAVINIA ROSE	FH214	LADY HAMILTON OF
E563	HOLLIE ROSE	FD61	LADY DI		HELFORD
E564	MANTA RAY	FD630	MAR CORAL	FH22	LITTLE LAUREN
E565	MAVERICK	FD64	SARAH JANE	FH222	SUNDOWNER
E566	AZZURRO	FD7	BOND GIRLS	FH229	NEWLEK-MOR
E569	KINGFISHER	FD71	CRUSADER	FH23	IONA
E6	EVELYN	FD79	NAN	FH24	OCEAN PRIDE
E63	K2	FD85	MAR BLANCO	FH243	ST RUAN
E68	SEA SEEKER	FD9	BRISAN	FH25	SOVEREIGN
E7	NINA	FE137	VIKING PRINCESS	FH258	KENDORE
E73	BECCI	FE142	LADY ROSE	FH280	EVENING STAR
E8	SAMIE 2	FE20	VALENTINE	FH293	GIRL PAULINE
E80	LITTLE SHRUB	FE21	CODONGER TOO	FH3	ROSEN
E81	TRACEY LYNN	FE25	TEDDIE BOY	FH30	AUTUMN ROSE
E82	PETIT BATEAU	FE265	SEA JEWEL	FH300	PAULA ROSE
E83	ANNIE JAYNE	FE268	JACQUELINE ANNE	FH32	BESS
E87	PROVIDER	FE269	STELLA MARIA	FH322	BOBBIE DEE II
E88	LADY OF LADRAM	FE270	AMADEUS	FH324	SILVER QUEEN
E9	STORMY DAWN	FE3	RELENTLESS II	FH33	SEA FOAM II
E92	ESME	FE33	LATNEY STAR	FH339	THREE BOYS
E94	SUNBEAM	FE368	WILLIAM T	FH34	BOY KOBEN
F111	CHARLIE BOY	FE370	COPTIC	FH35	DOROTHY ANN
F140	HECTOR	FE371	DENISE	FH353	JANE LOUISE
F165	CARDIUM II	FE379	BECKY JANE	FH395	TRENEGLOS
F167	HORNET	FE380	JULIE JEAN	FH398	ISABELLE
F172	ANGELINA	FE381	CATCH 22	FH4	ROSE
F177	RUBY	FE382	ANNALOUSION	FH401	GOLDEN PROMISE
F179	FAT CAT	FE385	CHARLES EDWARD	FH414	STARLIGHT
F38	JACKO IV	FE386	PRINCESS KEELY	FH416	EMMA MAY
F44	TICINO	FE4	DOREEN T	FH443	SOLITAIRE
F52	OLY-RAY	FE50	ROYAL CHARLOTTE	FH444	LILY GRACE
F57	MELISSA E	FE58	PALINDRA	FH468	GIRL JAN
FD1	MI AMOR	FE6	OPPORTUNITY	FH484	TELA
FD10	ORION	FE60	BOY BEAU	FH485	LEVIATHAN
FD100	CHRISTINA	FE63	JACQUELINE	FH49	TREGLOWN
FD160	COLINNE	FE69	PROGRESS	FH494	SON-A-MOR
FD163	INSOMNIA	FE74	PETER PAUL	FH5	NEW VENTURE
FD170	ALBION	FE75	ROWENA	FH506	SILVER LANCE
FD177	ISADALE	FE76	DALRIADA	FH508	BRITANNIA IV OF
FD20	ANTURUS	FH1	SULA		FALMOUTH
FD281	KORNELIS JAN	FH10	SEA BIRD	FH51	AMIGO
FD283	TRUI VAN HINTE	FH106	FLYING BREEZE	FH52	STILL WATERS
FD366	PROVIDING STAR	FH109	MARIA Q	FH529	KINGFISHER II
FD399	BAY VENTURE	FH11	SEA FOAM	FH535	GONPEZ I
FD449	CHARLOTTE B	FH119	SEA URCHIN	FH55	PATRICE 11
FD46	INDEPENDENT	FH12	MOREL MARGH	FH57	FOXY LADY
FD507	ENIGMA	FH121	BRITANNIA V	FH58	BILLERIC
FD512	PISCES	FH14	JASPER	FH598	GIRL RACHAEL

FISHING VESSELS CODE/NAME INDEX

CODE	NAME	CODE	NAME	CODE	NAME
FH6	CELESTIAL DAWN	FR101	ATLAS	FR349	OCEAN WAY
FH60	NEW HARMONY OF	FR1017	SANDRA H	FR357	SUSAN BIRD
	HELFORD	FR1026	SEAWOLF	FR359	SUNRISE
FH609	DO MAR	FR11	FREEDOM	FR366	HARVEST MOON
FH610	SEA LASS	FR110	MAGGIE ANN	FR37	BOY HARRY
FH613	KERANY	FR111	ENDURANCE	FR375	OCEAN QUEST
FH614	BOY DANIEL	FR116	STAR 'O' BUCHAN	FR380	KINGS CROSS
FH623	BENEDICTION	FR12	OYSTER CATCHER	FR382	HEATHER BELLE
FH629	KATHRYN LOUISE II	FR121	HELENUS	FR385	DEFIANCE
FH638	ELA-J	FR128	ARGOSY	FR39	NEW VENTURE
FH664	AMETHYST	FR129	FAITHFUL	FR4	GUIDE US
FH665	REBECCA	FR14	CUDDY SHARK	FR403	BOBENA
FH669	MARIA 2	FR141	RADIANT MORN	FR41	GENESIS
FH672	KAISA MARI	FR143	REBECCA	FR416	SILVER FERN
FH683	STORM PETREL	FR147	MINERVA	FR42	GUIDE ME
FH690	PETER JOHN II	FR151	LYNDEN II	FR422	JEANNIE D
FH691	BOB WINNIE	FR152	OCEAN TRUST	FR432	MAIMAI
FH693	LIZY	FR156	ENDEAVOUR	FR44	BOY MARK
FH699	SUNSHINE	FR16	LYMIRAC	FR443	MIA JANE W
FH7	GENEVIEVE	FR162	AVOCET	FR444	ZEPHYR
FH702	CORNISH LASS	FR165	UNITY	FR470	NEW DAWN
FH704	RUBEN LUKE	FR167	GRACIOUS	FR487	SUNBEAM
FH705	HOBBIT	FR17	QUEST	FR5	VICTORY
FH706	VICTORIA ANNE	FR171	ADVANCE	FR50	UBEROUS
FH707	SUSA UNO	FR173	DEMARUS	FR515	DA CALYPSO
FH71	SOUTHERN STAR	FR178	CRYSTAL RIVER	FR52	TIRRICK
FH713	SPICA	FR18	SHAUNKELLY	FR53	OTAKI
FH714	FRANCES B	FR2	ORION	FR54	FISHER BOYS
FH715	KIMBERLEY JO	FR20	MARGARET MARIE	FR558	BERYL II
FH717	CORNISH LASS IV OF	FR21	REBECCA D	FR559	KARENANN II
	COVERACK	FR216	CASTLEWOOD	FR583	STRATHBEG
FH722	PROPHET	FR22	ORCADIS	FR59	GOLDEN GAIN V
FH723	HARVESTER II	FR220	ADORNE II	FR6	REMEMBRANCE
FH725	MANUEL LAURA	FR222	REBECCA MARIE	FR604	BLOOM
FH726	LADY LYNDA	FR224	CHRISTINA S	FR607	MAY LILY
FH728	STERENNYK	FR226	CHALLENGE	FR64	CLAIRE
FH729	JACQUELINE ANNE	FR227	TAITS	FR667	SPECTRUM
FH730	PETITE MEL	FR228	CHRIS ANDRA	FR69	VII LOONS
FH731	TIDOS	FR237	OUR HERITAGE	FR699	KARINYA
FH732	JACQUI A	FR24	HORIZON 11	FR7	LILI MEI
FH733	FLOWER OF THE FAL II	FR243	JACQUELINE ANNE	FR77	OCEAN VENTURE
FH734	PATRICIA ANNE	FR245	SHAMARIAH	FR771	OCEAN CHALLENGE
FH740	REBECCA TOO	FR246	RENOWN	FR776	B ALERT
FH744	MINSTREL	FR248	GRATITUDE	FR777	ALERT
FH745	MORVRAN	FR249	FOREVER GRATEFUL	FR795	RESOLUTE
FH746	MILLY II	FR253	VIRTUOUS	FR8	GOLDEN DAWN
FH747	FLASH HARRY	FR254	DELIVERANCE	FR80	JANN DENISE
FH748	SAPPHIRE	FR26	REWARD	FR821	SILVER STAR
FH75	JASMINE	FR268	VALHALLA	FR83	MILLBURN
FH750	MYGHAL	FR273	OCEAN REAPER IV	FR84	COMPASS ROSE
FH756	EMILY JAYNE	FR280	ADELPHI	FR85	NORTHEASTERN
FH76	GALWAD-Y-MOR	FR285	EL-SHADDAI	FR890	DAVANLIN
FH774	OSPREY	FR287	DUTHIES	FR891	GOOD HOPE
FH8	RHODA MARY	FR29	STILL GAME	FR894	SPARKLING WATERS
FH85	SCATH DU	FR294	CONSTELLATION	FR9	OCEAN SURF
FH88	KARENZA JAYNE	FR296	ANTONIO	FR90	CHALLENGER
FH89	CARIAD	FR3	RUBY SUSAN	FR915	FULMAR
FH9	AMANDA J	FR30	STEPHEN JOHN	FR920	SOMERSET MORN
FH93	IDA MAY	FR307	RYANWOOD	FR925	PATSY B
FR1	RADIANCE	FR327	RESILIENT III	FR928	OCEAN PIONEER
FR100	ACHIEVE	FR33	IOLAIR	FR941	PHOENIX

225

FISHING VESSELS CODE/NAME INDEX

CODE	NAME	CODE	NAME	CODE	NAME
FR961	PITULLIE	FY399	BLUE MARLIN	FY843	LUCY B
FR964	JANALI	FY4	EMI LOU	FY847	CARLEE
FR97	EILIDH	FY400	MAKO	FY848	DEFIANT
FR979	HUNTRESS II	FY43	LENTEN ROSE	FY850	TYPHOON
FR980	JENNY LASS	FY431	LIBERTY	FY851	INDEPENDENT
FR983	CHLOE MAY	FY449	ALLEGIANCE	FY860	CORNISH LASS
FR988	BOY ANDREW	FY46	INNISFALLEN	FY868	CORNISHMAN
FR989	GOLDEN SHEAF	FY47	OUR LIZ	FY869	MYSTIQUE II
FR993	INFINITY	FY470	IMOGEN	FY870	ESTHER JAYNE
FY1	THREE JAYS	FY5	FREYA JAE	FY872	MORGELYN
FY10	CELTIC DAWN	FY509	SUPERB 11	FY875	CRIMSON TIDE
FY10	KESTREL	FY52	C.J.	FY88	BUCCANEER
FY101	EMMA LOUISE II	FY523	MORDROS	FY881	PETREL
FY108	TRUST	FY528	ANDORAY OF LOOE	FY884	TIMMYHAM
FY11	TORRI GWYNT	FY529	VESTA	FY885	SAMUEL JAMES
FY111	RED VIXEN	FY53	DEMELZA	FY886	AVOCET
FY119	RESOLUTE	FY545	JENNY JAMES	FY887	PROVIDENCE
FY12	OCEAN HARVEST	FY555	LYONESSE	FY888	PAMELA JANE
FY120	SIRENE	FY566	KARAN	FY890	MOLLY MAI
FY123	OHIO	FY570	SILVERY SEA	FY892	TAMAHINE
FY124	KATYTU	FY58	VENUS	FY894	HALCYON
FY125	SOUTHERN STAR	FY583	NORTHERN STAR II	FY898	MOOGIE
FY126	HEATHER ANNE	FY588	BOY JOE II	FY9	BREEZE
FY14	SHAKIRA	FY59	SWALLOW	FY902	CATHERINE ANNE
FY149	PALATINE	FY6	DOWNDERRY MAID	FY903	GUNGIR
FY15	FOUR MAIDENS	FY60	ARUM	FY906	BLUEJAY
FY16	NEW DAWN	FY602	NATALIE	FY909	MERMAID
FY167	CORAL REEF	FY606	VESPER II	FY91	MANX RANGER
FY17	KINGFISHER	FY614	CAZADORA	FY913	MARY ANN
FY174	EMBLEM	FY66	LUCY TOO	FY916	EMMA JANE 2
FY180	KATIE LIL	FY7	LITTLE MO	FY917	BLUE MIST
FY182	SHEARWATER	FY74	AQUARIUS	FY918	PANIA
FY19	CHRISTINE	FY755	GIRL AMANDA	FY919	WINIFRED
FY2	MEER	FY759	SURPRISE	FY922	JUBILEE BELLE
FY20	WENNAJO	FY764	BOY WILLIAM	FY926	MADELEINE
FY201	IBIS	FY765	LITTLE ANNE	FY927	LADY M
FY23	LITTLE PEARL	FY767	NEPTUNES PRIDE II	FY929	WILLIAM HENRY
FY239	LUCY MARIANNA	FY773	CARA MOR	FY96	AQUAMANDA
FY24	ELLA	FY777	FLYING SPRAY IV	FY97	GALATEA
FY242	CORNISH MAID OF LOOE	FY778	TANEGAN	GH116	SERINAH
FY25	CEE J	FY781	LINDA B	GK1	PEGASUS
FY26	OCEAN QUEEN	FY787	GRANDAD	GK2	EILIDH ANNE
FY27	MYTILUS	FY798	ENDEAVOUR	GK291	PRIDE OF WALES
FY270	RADJEL	FY8	SEA SPRAY	GK52	DEEP SEA ONE
FY278	PUFFIN	FY803	VERONA	GK6	CHALLENGER
FY28	GUARDIAN	FY804	PHOENIX	GK76	DAWN RISE
FY3	STORM CHILD	FY807	JESSICA GRACE	GK77	GUIDE US
FY303	DISPATCHER	FY81	RUBY	GK8	ABOUT TIME
FY304	NEPTUNES BRIDE	FY811	MARY EILEEN	GU100	GREY HAZE
FY31	RANA	FY817	SAMMY JAYNE	GU101	LISA MARIE
FY32	CHALLENGE	FY820	LUNAR BEAM	GU102	SABU
FY324	AQUILA	FY822	FAIR WIND	GU103	J B P
FY33	CARA LEE	FY823	CONWAY	GU104	HILDER
FY332	TAMARA	FY826	SUNSHINE	GU106	EILIDH BHAN
FY345	LIVER BIRD	FY83	ELISABETH VERONIQUE	GU107	CAROL JUNE
FY35	OUR MAXINE	FY830	ATLANTIS	GU108	PAULINE B
FY367	INVESTOR	FY834	KATIES PRIDE	GU109	JULIA P
FY368	MAJESTIC	FY836	LAUREN KATE	GU11	NEW DAWN
FY369	PARAVEL	FY838	BOY'S OWN II	GU110	GINA LOUISE
FY37	OUR GIRLS	FY841	DEMPER	GU111	LADY HELEN
FY38	MAXINES PRIDE	FY842	JACOB	GU113	HOT PASTY

226

FISHING VESSELS CODE/NAME INDEX

CODE	NAME	CODE	NAME	CODE	NAME
GU114	ANNA J	GU24	RACHEL DAN II	GU46	THREE J'S
GU114	JODIE	GU240	GENESIS	GU47	GOOD VENTURE
GU116	AMY BLUE	GU248	HIGH-RIDER	GU472	ALBATROS II
GU118	BRANDY'S THUNDER	GU25	SEA HUNTER	GU479	AMIE ELLEN
GU119	07 II	GU253	SONIA ST CLAIR	GU48	FISHKEY
GU120	VIKING	GU26	PREVAIL	GU484	JJ
GU121	MAR-ROSE	GU260	WESTERN FISHER	GU489	ANGEL J
GU121	MOON SHINE	GU266	WILLIAM GEORGE	GU49	THOMAS V
GU122	MUNCHKIN MADNESS	GU269	LOUISE II	GU50	BOY JEFF
GU124	ATHENA	GU27	LADY OF LEISURE	GU5072	PEGASUS
GU125	QUENON	GU273	LULWORTH FISHER	GU51	LU-LU
GU126	O.C.A.	GU275	ESPERANCE	GU52	LE SOLEIL ROUGE
GU127	ASILE SUR	GU28	NETTY'S WAY	GU53	JANILO
GU128	HYPNOS	GU29	CERALIA	GU54	SALACIA
GU129	LE MIRAGE	GU295	MARGARET K	GU56	BULLDOG
GU13	OUR LISA	GU3	LUCKY SAM	GU58	MISS PATTIE
GU130	LANDY ELEANOR	GU30	OUT OF THE BLUE	GU58	WHITE OSPREY
GU132	NEVER DESPAIR	GU301	SANDRA J	GU59	WAY TU GO
GU133	BRANDON I	GU302	DELIA MAY	GU60	SEA BREEZE
GU135	MARY J	GU308	KINGFISHER	GU61	MYSTERY
GU136	WESTERN LASS	GU31	BRITANNIA	GU63	PREDATOR
GU138	LITTLE SISTER	GU310	CAPRICE	GU64	GREY DAWN
GU139	LA ROUX	GU312	HOLLYANNA	GU65	NOAH-C
GU140	SARADA	GU315	DIEU TE GARDE	GU66	WILD WILLY
GU141	IRENE M	GU316	Q18	GU67	PRISCILLA ANN
GU142	MORA	GU317	CATCH 23	GU69	ALPHA
GU143	MISTY	GU32	SHIRLEY	GU70	BLUE LADY
GU144	PAVALINE G	GU33	JOLIE M	GU71	BUBBLES TOO
GU145	STAR	GU33	LADY HELEN - S	GU72	SEAMOUSE
GU147	STORMDRIFT	GU331	SYLVIA K	GU73	ORCA
GU148	CORMORANT	GU334	JO JO	GU74	KATIE C
GU151	DORADO	GU336	ANDURIL	GU75	SEA SCAMP
GU154	JO JO LOUISE	GU338	INSPIRATION	GU76	NORTHWESTERN
GU155	HANDY MAN	GU34	WISHERMAN	GU77	JUST RIGHT
GU157	LADY LOUISE	GU344	PETIT FLEUR	GU78	JENNY D
GU161	SABAI-DEE	GU35	MISTY MORN	GU79	FLEUR DE BRAYE
GU166	PROSPECT	GU351	RED DRAGON	GU80	ODIN
GU168	DEFIANCE	GU355	HAYLEY B	GU81	CHEVERTON
GU168	LADY PATRICIA	GU36	BLUE MOON	GU82	MOL
GU17	HAZEY DAWN	GU362	MAYFAIR	GU83	EMMA-MAY
GU170	GUIDING STAR	GU366	ROUSSE RAIDER	GU84	ASHLEIGH-LEAH
GU174	R.E.M.	GU37	FIRST PRIORITY	GU85	MISS CONNIE
GU179	ZOEY	GU38	COMPASS ROSE	GU87	PETIT MICHELLE
GU180	SARAH LOU	GU388	ODILIA	GU88	OUR JACK
GU181	SAMANTHA JAYNE	GU39	JANET V	GU89	SEARIDER
GU182	SOUTHERN VENTURE	GU39	JANET V	GU90	CYGNET
GU19	REBECCA	GU396	THREE SISTERS	GU91	TULNA
GU192	TWINS II	GU399	SARAH-P	GU91	TULNA TOO
GU199	PEADAR MARIE	GU40	L'ETOILE DU NORD	GU92	TOOBOYS
GU20	TANAMERA	GU400	HAPPY HOOKER	GU93	FREE SPIRIT
GU203	OLIVIA J	GU41	DISCOVERY	GU94	DAWN TILL DUSK
GU21	JEAN YVONNE	GU417	OUR PORTLAND FISHER	GU95	FIRST LIGHT
GU210	SEA TREK	GU42	WILD WAVE	GU97	PIMPERNEL II
GU214	HANNAH COLLEEN	GU429	SEASTAR	GU98	AMBER-DAWN
GU218	WAVE ON	GU43	BLUE BELLE	GU99	ODESSA
GU219	D-IMMP	GU437	HUNTRESS	GW42	ENDURANCE
GU22	J C D	GU44	COBO MAID	GY127	HENDRIKA JACOBA
GU222	CHEETAH	GU449	APOMORPH	GY1428	HANNAH-CHARLOTTE
GU226	MOLLIE ANN	GU45	LILLIAN R	GY1476	WILD CHORUS
GU23	CACHE-CACHE	GU451	SURPRISE	GY1477	NORDSTJERNEN
GU237	IMAGINE	GU453	DRIFTWOOD	GY1492	HORIZON

FISHING VESSELS CODE/NAME INDEX

CODE	NAME	CODE	NAME	CODE	NAME
GY15	HUNTRESS OF GRIMSBY	H144	PROVIDENCE	HL1085	GYPSY GIRL
GY150	ANNE SCOTT	H145	SWIFT	HL11	J.J.
GY152	SANRENE	H166	HOLLIE J	HL12	PISCES
GY165	PACEMAKER	H171	CORNELIS VROLIJK FZN	HL122	SARAH LYNN
GY189	SORRENTO	H176	ARCTIC WARRIOR	HL125	BONNY LASS
GY199	KRISTENBORG	H2	PROVIDER	HL14	POPPY
GY2	GUSTO	H22	SPURN LIGHT	HL15	SAGITTARIUS
GY25	JUBILEE SPIRIT	H232	TRADITION	HL16	LADY PATRICIA
GY3	SUKAT II	H25	CHRISTINE CLAIRE	HL17	SARAH LYNN R
GY305	RACHAEL S	H291	J KADASS II	HL198	WAVE CREST
GY34	FASTLINE	H292	COURAGEOUS III	HL2	SARAH LYNN II
GY341	IYSHA	H347	OCEAN DAWN	HL208	LA ZENIA
GY356	PANDION	H357	GOOD HOPE	HL238	JUELAN
GY368	HUNTER	H358	SUMMER ROSE	HL257	ACHIEVE
GY388	KESTREL	H360	GUIDING STAR	HL283	LITTLE JOE
GY4	PREDATOR	H41	MADASHELL	HL3	ENDURANCE
GY41	LONG SHOT	H426	NEELTJE	HL321	WILLIAM AND MOLLY
GY450	INGER LIS	H483	PROSPERITY	HL35	MARIE M
GY451	STORMY C	H488	SILVER LINE	HL4	CAROLYN
GY455	EDLEI	H5	K II	HL41	ADAPTABLE
GY480	MYSTERY	H56	CHRISTEL STAR	HL46	SWAN DANCER
GY5	ANNETTE	H59	AQUAGEM	HL5	EARLY ON
GY53	GYO	H600	TRI CAT	HL7	SEA BREEZE
GY563	ALISHA	H67	LISA JAYNE	HL705	STELLA MARIS
GY57	EBEN HAEZER	H77	SIWRENGALE	HL707	WILD ROVER
GY60	ULTIMATE	H771	MARBELLA	HL787	ASGARD
GY900	JUBILEE QUEST	H79	JOANNE T	HL8	ALICEAMELIA
GY903	JUBILEE PRIDE	H8	STARBANK	HL81	JESSIE ALICE
GY991	FRUITFUL HARVEST 111	H80	VIOLET EILEEN	HL9	SOPHIE LEIGH
H1	POPEYE	HH10	JOAN E	IE3	WICKED WENDY
H10	RIPTIDE	HH107	ELOS	IH1	WILLSBRY
H105	EXCELSIOR	HH11	SYLVIA	IH105	LEONIE JANE
H106	JASON A	HH118	YVONNE ANNE	IH2	RENE B
H1063	KATY ANNE	HH120	DOROTHY ELLEN	IH212	REUBEN WILLIAM
H1066	TRI STAR II	HH15	CONDOR	IH219	ODD TIMES
H1069	MAVERICK	HH150	EOS	IH225	GREY GULL
H1070	MISTY BLUE	HH154	BONNIE LASS II	IH234	DORIS LIZZIE
H1073	MADASHELL IV	HH16	LIBERATOR	IH263	WILLY BOY
H1075	MIRAGE II	HH163	R. LAURA	IH290	JUBILEE JOY
H1077	NIC NAT	HH182	APRYL LOUISE	IH3	LADY K
H1094	JORDAN I	HH32	BOY LUKE B	IH311	SILVER HARVEST
H11	PERSEVERANCE II	HH35	INGRID MELISSA	IH314	OUR BESS
H110	NORMA MARY	HH40	BOY ANDREW	IH319	ROCKY
H1101	MARY ANNE II	HH512	SEA HUNTER II	IH320	ENTERPRISE
H1103	PAUL PATRICK	HH55	ONWARD	IH322	VALERIE ANN
H1109	SHELANG	HH56	ANNA LOUISE	IH325	BLACK PEARL
H1117	FERRIBY II	HH62	TRUE TO THE CORE	IH327	RELENTLESS
H1121	CRAZY CAT	HH661	SEA FOX	IH330	FARNOID FARNWORTH
H1122	FLUKE	HH984	MAVERICK	IH36	LOU-ANNIE
H1123	KARMALOR	HH986	STUMARK II	IH38	MARGARET ANN
H1128	DEBRA JAYNE	HH988	ALISON	IH4	HOBBIT
H1134	SEA CAT	HL1	MIZPAH	IH47	MI JENNY
H1135	PROFIT	HL10	LAUREN LU	IH5	AUDREY M
H1136	SUNRISE	HL1054	SUVERA	IH51	THREE BROTHERS
H116	CRYSTAL DAWN	HL1059	CYCLONE	IH68	LAURA ANNE
H119	FALCON	HL106	CRYSTAL SEA	IH89	JOSEPH WILLIAM
H129	SHEILA L	HL1063	VENTURER	INS1	OCEANA
H131	KIMBERLEY	HL1065	GENESIS	INS10	ROCMOR
H132	SILVERWOOD	HL1067	LUCIA	INS1023	SEA MARINER
H135	FARNELLA	HL1081	HOW ABOUT IT	INS1035	JEMONA
H141	LIAM D	HL1082	ELEANOR MAY	INS1037	CARISMA

228

FISHING VESSELS CODE/NAME INDEX

CODE	NAME	CODE	NAME	CODE	NAME
INS104	MAC II	J114	AIGRETTE	J292	JESSIE
INS1040	GIZZEN BRIGGS	J115	SUNSTRIKER	J296	EXCALIBUR
INS11	BONNIE LASS	J116	LUCKY DOLPHIN	J3	WHITE LADY
INS110	BOY JOHN	J121	MASTER B	J300	LUSTY LISA
INS111	PORTIA OF POOLE	J122	KONI	J307	AQUARIUS II
INS12	FALCON	J125	BASS HUNTER	J308	DAWN LADY
INS123	ISABELLA	J127	T J ROCKHOPPER	J316	SUSAN II
INS127	ARDENT II	J13	BRAMA	J317	JILLMAR
INS135	DEEP HARMONY IV	J130	SUSIE TOO	J32	YANUCA
INS140	GEORGIA DAWN	J132	AVALETTE	J321	ANNE LOUISE
INS146	STROMA	J135	DUSTY BIN	J323	SHALLOW WATERS
INS151	CORDELIA K	J136	IMPALA	J325	GEMINI
INS157	NO 8 WILLING HANDS	J145	RIPTIDE OF ST HELIER	J33	BELLE BIRD
INS16	STEADFAST	J148	DAWN LIGHT	J342	TICKETY TWO
INS167	ARCTURUS	J15	SEA HUNTER	J35	FOU DE BASSAN
INS17	DONNA MARIE	J150	BLUEBELLE	J350	JUCLO
INS172	NEREUS	J152	RISKY	J357	BANANA SPLIT
INS178	KEELEY B	J154	CORENTINE	J365	THESEUS II
INS179	APOLLO	J156	SCALLY	J368	DAS BOAT
INS19	DARAMORE	J158	L'ECUME II	J37	ANGIE M
INS2	KALA	J159	MY JEM	J38	CYNTHIA MARY
INS20	KINGFISHER	J163	BLUE PEARL	J38	MERLIN
INS237	ACORN	J164	THE SHILLING	J388	SHYLOCK
INS238	SMIFFYS	J165	SHARKY	J389	SHARNIC
INS24	WESTERLY WARRIOR	J167	LOUIS MARIE	J393	LINGFIELD
INS240	RADIANCE	J17	SYLVIES DAWN	J396	WANDERER
INS241	MARIGOLD	J171	BALLISTIC	J399	PETIT MOUSSE II
INS29	INVERDALE	J173	LE BULOTIER	J4	CONTENDER
INS291	MARACESTINA	J174	R.E.M.	J401	JADE S
INS296	ARGOSY II	J180	JASON II	J404	ROCKY
INS3	ENSIS	J188	CERALIA	J405	ANNA II
INS31	BLUEFIN	J189	PROSPECTOR	J407	ABBA II
INS32	RYAN AMY	J19	TRITON	J41	BONNE PECHE
INS329	DAYBREAK	J194	SEA KING	J418	MARSH MAID
INS35	OSPREY	J2	MINUIT	J419	SEABASS
INS353	ROSEBLOOM	J20	BLUEY	J437	MARIA
INS354	CATRIONA M	J200	GRIZZLY	J444	PROGRESS
INS37	FIONAGHAL	J204	ANN VIRGINIA	J445	STORMBRINGER
INS38	FAITHFUL	J208	GREY DAWN	J45	MATAURI BAY
INS383	CATALINA	J209	ZEBEC	J455	LOUP DE MER
INS384	KIEORRAN	J21	TIME 'N' TIDE	J479	WAVE RIDER
INS386	SEA SPRAY	J211	SHIRALEE	J482	SHEARWATER
INS4	AVISTA	J214	BRETTANE	J485	GOLDEN GRAIN
INS5	BOY BRYAN	J216	EMILY MAY	J486	MARIE GALANTE
INS52	LILY MAE	J22	QUEQUEG	J49	CAROLE G
INS564	ARTEMIS	J227	BENBECULA	J490	SKYE
INS6	ROSMARA	J228	MY YACHT	J494	SACRE BLEU
INS64	BOY DAVID	J229	LOUISE MAY	J499	STARGAZER
INS7	TIZ	J238	OUTRAGE	J50	SEA IMP TOO
INS74	IONA	J25	PIERETTE	J51	INSOMNIA
INS8	ADVENTURER II	J252	DAWN HUNTER	J525	ALLOETTE
INS9	AWA	J268	BANTAC	J53	SYLVIES JOY
INS94	ANT IASGAIR	J27	JUBILEE GIRL	J531	BLACK KNIGHT
J10	CAT 'A' TAC	J273	KESTREL II	J54	SANDUKY
J100	WHITE WATERS	J274	MARGARET WILLIAM II	J55	FULLBORE II
J101	FORCE FOUR	J275	SALTEE II	J559	CAROL ANN
J104	HANNAH LOUISE	J279	LUCIUS	J569	SHARKIE TOO
J107	TIME BANDIT	J28	THE GAMBLER	J57	EMMAJEN
J109	PETER MICHAEL	J280	SARAH ANN	J58	SEAFORTH
J11	SYLVIES GRACE	J283	MARLU	J59	ISLE JERSEY
J112	SAUCY SUE	J284	SEASHELL	J6	JAN FISHER

FISHING VESSELS CODE/NAME INDEX

230

FISHING VESSELS CODE/NAME INDEX

CODE	NAME	CODE	NAME	CODE	NAME
KY1	DILIGENT	KY442	PEGASUS	LA46	ALL JS
KY10	BARNEY C	KY445	OSPREY	LA462	DRIFTER
KY1000	ASPIRE II	KY446	RABBIE B	LA47	JACKY-AN
KY1003	ELLIE A	KY449	KYLIE S	LA48	JOSIE AN
KY1004	ROSSNESS FALCON	KY454	NIGHT OWL	LA5	SHADWELL
KY1009	CAROL ANN	KY455	COMELY III	LA51	POACHER
KY1013	SOLO II	KY458	JANE I	LA572	ODIN
KY1015	HOMELAND	KY459	SANELA	LA575	SAMMY I
KY1019	CATRIONA ANNE	KY5	WESTHAVEN III	LA579	JEAN
KY1021	AKELA	KY505	K2	LA580	LADY ELIZABETH
KY1026	OOR SAUND	KY54	SEAJAY	LA581	SARAH LEE
KY1030	MOLLY	KY58	GUESS AGAIN	LA588	JUMBO I
KY1035	FULMAR	KY6	ARCTIC TERN	LA59	SEA SHANTY
KY1036	BOLD VENTURE	KY61	GROUSE III	LA591	EMMA LOUISE
KY1042	ELENA LOUISA	KY7	TRUE VINE	LA593	ETHANS WAY
KY11	SEASPRAY II	KY70	CORDELIA	LA60	FAIR MAIDEN
KY110	SHEARWATER II	KY71	VIGILANT	LA602	SENNA
KY12	VALAHOPE	KY75	ROYAL SOVEREIGN	LA606	REBEL
KY130	SHIRLEY II	KY783	AMPHITRITE II	LA607	COBRA
KY14	BONNIE	KY79	FORTUNE BOUND	LA608	THREE NIECES II
KY16	MAGGIE MAE	KY8	LAUREN ANN	LA618	CARLY ROSE
KY160	FINE PAIR	KY82	LEA RIG	LA619	PREDITOR
KY17	TINA LOUISE	KY9	KATIE NA MARA	LA620	ANNA BELL
KY18	GENESIS	KY91	ASPIRE III	LA636	JOHN DOE
KY180	ARIANNA	KY981	FIONA S	LA639	ALISA M
KY19	PROVIDER	KY982	REBECCA	LA643	BLACK VELVET
KY196	GEMINI	KY984	MACE	LA644	APOLLO
KY198	JUST REWARD	KY985	CHALLENGER	LA65	CHEETAH IV
KY2	MOLLY C	KY987	LEARIG 111	LA7	LILY ROSE
KY20	GENESIS T	KY989	SHALIMAR	LA73	GUZBERT II
KY204	MARKEV	KY99	CONCORD	LA8	HEATHER D
KY207	BETTY SMITH	KY990	FORTH HARVESTER	LA9	ANNA D
KY21	ZULU	KY992	NORLAND WIND	LH1	WHITE HEATHER VI
KY22	VENUS	KY995	CRUSADER	LH10	LIZZIE M
KY221	DEFIANT	KY996	QUANTAS	LH107	SPITFIRE
KY222	MICHANNDA	LA1	EMMA'S TERN	LH109	SUPREME
KY227	GUIDE ME 1	LA10	JACK OLLIE	LH11	REBECCA
KY23	ANTARES	LA106	JOSHUA B	LH111	BONAVENTURE
KY239	VENTURE AGAIN II	LA11	CABIN BOY	LH112	LONA M
KY25	ELLEN K	LA13	SAFIA ROSE	LH12	SEA SPRAY
KY250	EV	LA15	EMMA DEE	LH126	JAN
KY269	AYEGANTY	LA177	KATE H	LH13	HOMARUS
KY279	WINAWAY	LA19	LUCKY THIRTEEN	LH133	SPEEDWELL
KY28	UBIQUE	LA2	SUSIE J	LH137	KINGHORN
KY3	GUESS AGAIN II	LA21	GIRL EILEEN II	LH138	ROCKHOPPER OF
KY31	CHATERS	LA210	TOP CAT		PERCUEL
KY32	ROB ROY	LA22	QUO VADIS	LH14	LONESTAR
KY322	GUIDING STAR	LA24	HALIMA	LH142	FAIRNIES
KY338	PURSUIT	LA26	COURTNEY REBECCA	LH145	TRITON
KY34	VENUS II	LA27	BENBOW 11	LH147	CRYSTAL STREAM
KY35	ARTEMIS	LA272	SHAUNAD	LH15	CHLOE ROSE
KY36	SOLARIS	LA279	AMOUR II	LH16	WEE BESS
KY360	ST ADRIAN	LA281	EMMA R	LH163	BRIGHT RAY
KY37	EVANDA	LA285	KYDABRA	LH169	ENDEAVOUR
KY374	LAUNCH OUT	LA30	CAROLINA	LH17	GIRL LAUREN
KY38	SEASCAPE	LA37	SAIL AWAY	LH179	ROBINA INGLIS
KY4	BAHATI	LA38	ABBIE SHANAY	LH18	STACEY JAYNE
KY40	FRUITFUL	LA39	CARLIAN	LH183	SCORPION
KY41	SOUTHERN GIRL	LA4	ONTARIO	LH19	SILVER CREST II
KY43	SATURNUS	LA44	DANNY BOY	LH2	BOY LIAM
KY434	BAY HUNTER	LA441	WILZY LOU	LH20	KEYTE

FISHING VESSELS CODE/NAME INDEX

FISHING VESSELS CODE/NAME INDEX

CODE	NAME	CODE	NAME	CODE	NAME
LK20	ANNIE B	LK38	JUNA	LK783	LEONA JANE
LK206	SIGMA	LK394	ZEPHYR	LK79	PLANET
LK207	OCEAN WAY	LK395	RESOLUTE	LK801	DEVOTION
LK209	OPPORTUNE	LK40	ARCTIC SOLITAIRE	LK803	SHALIMAR L.M
LK21	VALENTIA	LK400	SURMOUNT	LK806	OLIVIA ROSE
LK219	CORVUS	LK406	AMAZING GRACE	LK809	MAREA B
LK22	LAEBRAK	LK41	SUD AYRE	LK836	CRYSTAL ANN
LK23	DELTA DAWN	LK419	ANTARES	LK84	GUIDING LIGHT
LK244	FAITH EMILY	LK423	WINDERMERE	LK850	STAR
LK250	SHARYN LOUISE	LK424	BLOSSOM	LK86	CAPELLA
LK257	TREASURE	LK429	ALTAIRE	LK889	EXCALIBUR
LK26	HARVESTER	LK431	PATHFINDER	LK891	SMILING MORN
LK268	KESTREL	LK443	SCEPTRE	LK897	SELINA MAY
LK27	SHEMARA II	LK45	FIDELITAS	LK901	SEA GULL
LK270	FAIRWAY II	LK466	RESTLESS WAVE	LK946	BRAVEHEART
LK272	GUARDIAN ANGELL	LK467	HALCYON	LK95	QUEEN OF HEARTS
LK273	SEA STAR	LK472	ARDENT	LK96	BROTHERS
LK277	STAR OF HOPE	LK497	MIZPAH	LK968	RELIEF
LK280	BOUNTIFUL	LK5	FIDWAY	LK969	HARMONY JB
LK287	ECLIPSE	LK502	ATLANTIA II	LK97	BOY STAN
LK29	NORWASTERN	LK52	RENOWN J W	LK973	BE READY
LK292	JULIE-ANN	LK520	PEGASUS A	LK980	JANMAR
LK297	SERENE	LK537	GIRL LIZZIE	LK983	ALANA JANE
LK298	VERANIA II	LK54	ADORN	LK985	COPIOUS
LK3	UTILISE	LK540	GOLDEN SHORE	LK986	PROLIFIC
LK301	GIRL LYNNE	LK56	GANNET	LK987	SADIE JOAN
LK31	ACCORD	LK57	ALISON KAY	LK989	EMERITUS
LK315	LUSTRE	LK570	GINA C	LK991	ST KILDA
LK318	ARANATHA	LK59	ARCTURUS	LL1	EAST BAR
LK321	OSPREY JA	LK6	DIAMOND	LL12	BOY BLUE
LK325	COMRADES	LK605	MARI DAWN	LL120	UNITY
LK326	COMET	LK61	SWALLOW	LL174	CAROL
LK33	KARANNA	LK617	JASPER	LL179	HOPEFUL I
LK331	CRAIGNAIR	LK62	RESEARCH W	LL231	GRACE II
LK332	UTSKER	LK624	DIVINE STAR	LL272	JENNA LEA
LK3369	ACTIVE	LK626	HOPE	LL273	VICKY LEIGH
LK3374	MARANDA MAY	LK63	TRANQUILITY	LL307	EARLY DAWN
LK3376	JOANNE CLAIRE	LK64	KATHLEEN	LL500	LIZANN
LK339	IVY LEAF	LK641	VENTURE	LL503	GINNY
LK3395	SPRIGHTLY	LK655	SEDNA	LL506	SARAHS SPIRIT
LK3398	ONWARD	LK657	CONCORD	LL57	UNITY.
LK341	SILVER STAR	LK67	ORION	LN1	TWO BROTHERS
LK3412	ALTAIR	LK678	MAJESTIC	LN110	JAYNE
LK3423	BLUE OSPREY	LK68	SCOTTIES PRIDE	LN119	JUSTINE MARIE
LK3430	KIA-ORA	LK686	ENTERPRISE	LN122	LIBERTY
LK3433	KEIRA	LK687	VALHALLA	LN123	LORD CHAD
LK3440	NYUGGEL	LK696	CORAL	LN125	MELITA
LK3447	REBEL	LK7	HOPEFUL	LN126	BOY NEIL
LK345	VERA	LK70	CONTEST	LN129	BOY STEVEN
LK3452	LESLEY A	LK703	NORDIC BRIDE	LN134	EIDER
LK3463	SEASPRAY	LK707	JOSIE ANNE	LN158	MARIE
LK347	MELISSA LOUISE	LK71	RADIANT STAR	LN161	WASH PRINCESS
LK35	AQUARIUS	LK712	VENTURE JH	LN175	LYNN PRINCESS
LK353	INTREPID	LK714	SPRINGTIDE	LN177	OUR LASSIE
LK356	VICTORY II	LK72	DONNA ROSE	LN179	ALISON CHRISTINE
LK362	CHARISMA	LK73	CURLEW	LN182	M & J T
LK365	SONDRA	LK75	VENTUROUS	LN2	SILVER STAR
LK369	LIBERTY	LK755	DOLPHIN	LN20	SEA SWALLOW
LK371	DEFIANT	LK76	SIRIUS RP	LN22	SEAGULL
LK372	CORNUCOPIA	LK779	JUNE ROSE	LN237	BOY CRAIG
LK375	ALERT II	LK780	MERLIN	LN244	CRACK O DAWN

233

FISHING VESSELS CODE/NAME INDEX

CODE	NAME	CODE	NAME	CODE	NAME
LN26	KRYSTLE DAWN	LO583	JAMIE M	LT266	ANN LOUISE
LN266	SOVEREIGN	LO586	RED	LT278	ROSE DAWN
LN271	BOY TIM	LO61	ANN ISABELLA	LT3	RADIANCE
LN449	STARFISH	LO66	RAINBOW CHASER	LT317	EILEENA ANNE
LN453	OUT RIGGER	LO70	OPTIMIST	LT320	ELSIE MAY
LN454	ABBIE JAYNE	LO78	DOGFISH	LT336	RACHAEL LINDA
LN456	SHEILA JOYCE	LO86	MARY AMELIA	LT36	MARGRIET
LN458	TWO MARKS	LO88	RENOWN	LT372	SUFFOLK CHIEFTAIN
LN463	LORD SAM II	LO89	BOY LUKIE	LT399	NORFOLK GIRL
LN464	SEA ROVER	LO92	BOY MICHAEL	LT4	GIRL LUCY
LN465	JOHN WILLY	LR116	DELLA	LT413	AWAKE
LN466	CHARLOTTE	LR173	WILLIAM ARNOLD	LT442	EMMA RAITCH
LN468	JOLENE	LR191	HOPE	LT446	G AND E
LN47	ONWARD	LR204	SEA GOOSE	LT539	NICOLA DAWN
LN471	PAMELA MARY	LR205	SAMYORK	LT546	JULIA HELEN
LN474	GEORGIE FISHER	LR209	HOPEFUL	LT60	WILHELMINA
LN475	SUNNY MORN	LR212	PEGGY II	LT601	FOUR DAUGHTERS
LN476	CATHERINE ANNE	LR22	CAROLINE DIANE	LT603	MARLYN
LN477	SPEEDWELL	LR225	MARJORIE M	LT61	SEA SPRAY
LN478	ANA MARIA	LR226	SAMANTO	LT63	Y PRIS
LN479	FIRECREST	LR33	SIRIUS	LT7	SERENE DAWN
LN481	SOPHIE B	LR38	LINDA LOUISE	LT711	GANNET
LN483	AUDRINA	LR448	JAYNE	LT74	CLANSMAN
LN486	AUDREY PATRICIA	LR455	LINDA	LT87	GERT JAN
LN5	MARY JANE	LR459	WANNY LOU	LT972	OUR BOYS
LN6	LUCKY LUKE	LR53	MARY	LT974	LAURA K
LN69	COMRADE	LR57	EDITH MARY	LT978	LEE-N
LN73	FLIXIE	LR66	BERNADET	LT98	JILL ANNE
LN74	ISABELLE KATHLEEN	LR73	AMY JANE	LT987	JUBILEE GIRL
LN8	BLUCHER	LR76	ELEANOR B	M10	KIMBERLY JAYNE
LN84	ELIZABETH MARY	LR9	KARENJO	M100	AMANDA JANE
LN86	LORD SAM	LR90	MOSS ROSE	M1016	SHELTIE TWO
LN88	CAROLE ANNE	LT1	BOY LEVI	M1020	LADY DI
LN91	PORTUNUS	LT10	JULIE EM	M1033	BAFFIN BAY
LO1	CHARLOTTE JOAN	LT1001	JOSEPH WILLIAM II	M1034	STEPHEN WILLIAM
LO106	SOPHIE JAYNE	LT1002	FAITHFULL STAR	M1039	BELTANE
LO13	TWO SUNS	LT1018	SPRING TIDE	M1041	ABIGALE
LO2	REVENGE	LT1020	JOLENE	M1045	LESHAH
LO20	LEWIS ANDREW	LT1022	ORKNEY DOLPHIN	M105	PERSEUS
LO243	JOBERT	LT1028	ROCKLEY	M1050	LYDON
LO3	XERCES	LT1033	SOUTHERN CROSS	M1060	MAGGIE G
LO324	ELVEN HUNTER	LT1039	CARLEEN FRANCES	M1075	CLYDE
LO33	RELIANCE 111	LT104	GABRIELLA	M1085	DRIFTER I
LO345	SEA MOON	LT1042	GEORGIE GIRL	M109	SPRINGER
LO4	INDIANNA	LT11	BE ON TIME	M1090	MAMOUNA
LO406	ANTON SCOTT	LT15	ORION	M1096	SEAHAWK
LO47	LIBERATOR	LT16	AVRIL ROSE	M1098	LITTLE GEM
LO50	RENOWN IV	LT162	HENDRIK BRANDS	M1099	HELEN C
LO51	KATHLEEN ELLEN	LT163	OUR CAROLINE	M11	DEJAVU
LO524	HAVEN LAD	LT17	GIRL FIONA	M1102	REBECCA JAYNE II
LO526	MARGARET BERYL	LT171	ZULU	M1110	CRAZY HORSE
LO540	BANANA SPLIT	LT175	ICENE	M1116	DYLAN
LO541	MATTY JAY	LT182	MORNINGTON BAY	M1117	REDEMPTION
LO544	LILLEY G	LT199	TERRY WILLIAM	M1122	KOREYJO
LO548	MARLI J	LT2	MISTRESS OF	M1131	GAYLE FORCE
LO552	MAGIE EVELYN		SOUTHWOLD	M1133	MERLIN
LO574	ABBIE LOU	LT22	SOPHIE DAWN	M1134	WAVE DANCER
LO578	SEATRACTOR	LT220	ORTHELES	M1149	LARA
LO58	KATHERINE	LT230	TRADE WINDS	M1152	ENDLESS SUMMER
LO580	MARCUS J	LT231	MIA BLUE	M116	LADY JANET
LO582	WILLIAM WALTER	LT25	KINGFISHER	M1163	KESI G

234

FISHING VESSELS CODE/NAME INDEX

FISHING VESSELS CODE/NAME INDEX

CODE	NAME	CODE	NAME	CODE	NAME
ML384	OUR CARRIE	N15	SEA SPRAY II	N5	NICOLA-JOANNE
ML4	HARVEST REAPER	N162	LAURA	N50	PRISCILLA JEAN
ML445	HUNTER	N17	SHARON ANN	N51	WATERLILY
ML6	NEREUS	N179	BOY ANDREW	N511	MAGGIE B
MN1	BOY MICHAEL II	N18	BOY JACK	N52	DIVINE WIND
MN103	TROJAN	N180	SUPREME	N53	DON VALLEY
MN182	LAUWERSZEE	N182	DAY DAWN	N57	SPINDRIFT
MN200	CERI	N183	SPARKLING SEA	N588	TWO BROTHERS
MN204	JAWS	N189	BONA FIDE	N59	GALENA
MN39	OSPREY	N191	GLENRAVEL	N6	C AND C
MN46	GIRL BARBARA	N193	SPES MARIS	N60	WILLIAM JOHN
MN6	ALI T	N2	BROTHERS	N611	WINSOME
MN60	SAXON	N20	RIAN JOHN	N627	MOREN-DEK
MR1	INNOVATOR	N203	ZEPHYR	N63	VALDEZ
MR3	NIL DESPERANDUM	N209	DARCIE GIRL	N65	LEANA
MT100	ONWARD	N227	STARDUST	N66	CROWDED HOUR
MT105	JALETO	N23	GOELAND	N69	ELIZABETH JANE
MT107	YELLOWHAMMER	N236	MINCH HUNTER	N7	FREE SPIRIT
MT113	LADY PRIMROSE V.C.	N252	MORNING DAWN	N70	VICTORIA LEIGH
MT115	SARAH LOUISE	N258	ATLANTIC	N708	ZOE ANN
MT118	GRACIE GEORGE	N263	LADY ISLE	N714	RAINBOW
MT119	BILLIRIS	N264	LYNNMARIE	N72	CHAMELEON
MT120	BALCARY	N265	STEFANIE - M	N727	ANNA
MT123	SAM LEWETTE II	N268	CONCORDE	N737	STARWARD
MT126	BONNIE LASS III	N27	EVARA	N74	NORTHERN VIKING
MT188	SINCERITY II	N273	OCEAN HARVESTER	N75	GERTRUDE ANN
MT23	CHELARIS	N277	KESTEVEN	N754	ARRIVAL
MT3	ARGO	N28	SILVER STRAND	N77	NORTHERN VENTURE
MT421	DESTINY	N286	MEDINA MIST	N777	NORTHERN QUEST
MT49	SOLWAY PROSPECTOR	N29	SANCTA MARIA	N793	BOY JOSEPH
MT55	ALAUNA	N294	ABILITY	N8	SAME DIFFERENCE
MT66	OUR JAMES	N295	SILVER DAWN	N804	EASTERN STAR
MT72	KINGFISHER	N298	TRUE TOKEN	N806	GOLDEN SHORE
MT79	CORMORANT	N3	MARY ELIZABETH	N808	HARVEST LIGHT
MT99	GOLDEN FLEECE	N300	IRISH ENTERPRISE	N809	LINAN
N1	JOHN BOY	N304	NEW VENTURE	N813	EILEEN ROSE
N10	NORTHERN DAWN	N306	ARLANDA	N818	SAN MIGUEL
N100	RIAINNE	N308	ALISON MARY	N822	SEA HARVESTER
N1013	OCEAN SPIRIT	N31	LUCKY STAR	N829	HEATHER VALLEY
N1015	TRISHA JAMES	N310	BEN THOMAS	N845	VALHALLA
N1016	MARY JAYNE	N312	GIRL BETH II	N850	TEMERAIRE
N102	WILLING LAD	N313	REBENA BELLE	N862	FAIRWAY TWO
N1024	PAPAS BOYS	N32	CHRISTINE	N9	SHANNON BHAN
N1030	ELENOR	N325	BONAVENTURE	N902	OSPREY
N104	EASTERN TIDE	N33	MARTINA ROSE	N904	SOUTHERN STAR
N1042	MICHELLE NA MARA	N345	TELESIS	N905	VOYAGER
N1043	BRANDON JOHN	N347	WELCOME HOME	N906	CLARIN
N105	ST BRENDAN	N368	CATHY ANN	N907	ARCANE
N106	FRANCES ROSE	N370	AARON	N911	COWRIE BAY
N108	RAMBLING ROSE	N38	KATYS PRIDE	N922	BOY PAUL II
N109	ACHILLES	N39	DETERMINATION	N924	OCEANUS
N11	GRATITUDE	N396	BRIGHTER MORN	N929	ELLEN M
N111	STALKA VIKING	N4	GIRL EMMA	N93	MARIE T
N112	EVENTIDE	N40	DUN LIR	N931	SILVER BREEZE
N114	MISS DARCIE K	N411	SPEEDWELL II	N934	SARDIUS
N12	KELLY	N434	PROVIDER	N936	DINGENIS JAN
N120	AMELIA	N444	AMITY	N938	MOYUNA
N123	AMETHYST	N455	MIZPAH	N942	BOUNTEOUS
N136	GOLDEN BOW	N46	SCOTSMAN	N948	MARIA LENA
N14	GWYLAN	N464	OUR GRACE	N950	BLUE MARLIN
N147	THREE SISTERS	N470	ANDRIAS	N954	INISFAIL

236

CODE	NAME	CODE	NAME	CODE	NAME
N955	FOUR WINDS	NN712	SARAH LENA	OB127	URCHIN
N956	LEEWARD	NN722	CERULEAN	OB128	CRIMSON ARROW IV
N96	KARIMA	NN725	CASTRIES	OB129	WESTON BAY
N963	BOY EOIN	NN727	DAWN TIDE	OB134	KITTYFISHER
N964	CAAREEN	NN729	WILLIAM MARY	OB139	MARSALI
N968	EMMA T	NN73	REMUS	OB14	ELENA
N970	HIGHLAND QUEEN	NN732	CLAR INNIS	OB140	SILVER SPRAY
N971	HONEY-BEE	NN733	LE BELHARA	OB141	HARVEST MOON
N973	KEALINCHA DAWN	NN736	DANNY BOY	OB145	JASTLO C
N974	MARY MARIA	NN737	HOPE GAP	OB147	JEAN-FRANCES
N976	RESTLESS WAVE	NN740	PAULA'S FOLLY II	OB149	J AND A
N978	CELTIC HARVESTER	NN743	OLWEN GEORGE	OB15	KAYLEIGH M
N98	BONNY & KELLY	NN745	RELIENCE	OB150	OUR MARIA
N987	IMOAN	NN747	DOT	OB151	ORION
N99	BE READY	NN748	BEACHY HEAD	OB156	BERLEWEN
N998	NIAROO	NN749	HAVANA	OB158	HOLLY ROSE
NN1	TWILIGHT	NN750	LIONEL THOMAS	OB16	KINTRA LASS
NN10	WILD WEST	NN752	VIOLET MAY	OB162	DANNY BOY
NN105	RHIANNON	NN753	FREEDOM	OB164	MAIREAD M
NN111	CHARISMA	NN755	MESMERIST	OB17	MAIRI BHEAG
NN114	HALCYON	NN756	ROSIE MAE	OB175	MAGNUS
NN12	RICHARD HEAD	NN757	MERIDIAN	OB18	LARA
NN130	PRINCESS	NN759	AURORA	OB181	PATHFINDER
NN135	BREAKING DAWN	NN760	SEAQUEST	OB182	GEM
NN137	JOANNA	NN763	BOUT TIME	OB187	CREST
NN15	PISCES	NN766	SUNRISE	OB19	MARY MANSON
NN182	ANYA JAIDYN	NN768	ADRENALINE	OB192	GOLDEN BELLS 11
NN184	FAIR MORN	NN769	ANDERIDA	OB196	INDEPENDENCE
NN2	OCEANS GIFT	NN770	MAYHEM	OB2	JACKY J
NN200	PIONEER	NN777	IZZY MAD	OB20	LILLY
NN201	FREDERICK ROSE	NN779	SPIRIT OF NAVAN	OB211	DODGER
NN227	SAIR ANNE	NN780	TICKETY BOO	OB216	PEGASUS
NN241	OLWEN MAY	NN781	ELLA	OB22	CHARMEL
NN243	LADY CINDERELLA	NN782	MAD CAT	OB227	RAFIKI
NN267	BIRLING GAP	NN784	BEN MANZ	OB235	REBEKAH JAYNE
NN3	PHOENIX	NN785	SPRING TIDE	OB237	JESSICA LOUISE
NN311	PAULINE CLAIRE	NN786	SALUTE	OB24	CLAYTONIA
NN324	TOMENNA	NN790	CARRIE R	OB247	CONDOR
NN359	POSEIDON	NN84	JAYLEE	OB26	CREACHAN MHOR
NN384	HARD GRAFT	NN85	AVANTI	OB262	DOLPHIN
NN4	JANET	NN92	NEW AQUARIUS	OB268	FLIPPER
NN404	TOBY ROC	NN94	SEMPER FIDELIS	OB272	SHEARWATER
NN444	SAJENN	NN96	SEA JAY	OB274	MAIREAD
NN470	SOLE FISH	NN99	SOUTHERN HEAD	OB278	STAR OF JURA
NN48	HAHNEN KAMM	NT28	SEAPIE	OB28	VENTURE 11
NN483	MOONRAKER	NT5	CHERYL ANN	OB284	GANGWARILY
NN485	NOMAD	OB1	HELEN FREYA	OB285	VIKINGBORG
NN491	DRIFTER	OB10	LEX FERENDA	OB287	CATCH 22
NN5	LADY SOVEREIGN	OB1004	ENSIS	OB295	SILVER RAY
NN50	DAVE	OB1015	FEITIZO	OB299	WHITE ROSE
NN500	WIN	OB1024	TOMALI	OB3	SONSIE
NN51	JAMBO	OB1030	TAYMOR ONE	OB316	BOY NIALL
NN56	JOHANNA	OB1040	SGIATHAN	OB321	HUSTLER
NN57	CORINA II	OB1043	NICOLA JANE	OB33	BELLE ISLE II
NN576	LADY ROSE	OB1045	PROTERA	OB330	QUIET WATERS
NN60	ICE	OB107	EMMA-MARIA	OB333	SILVER DAWN
NN7	SERIATIM	OB108	CURLEW	OB34	PATSY DEE
NN70	VALKYRIE	OB11	PIONEER	OB345	KIMBERLY
NN702	MOA	OB113	PATRICIA MARTA	OB349	LADY JANE
NN710	OUR SARAH JANE	OB12	JOLA	OB350	SGIAN
NN711	WILLIAM HENRY	OB120	EDWARD J	OB353	FIVE SISTERS

237

FISHING VESSELS CODE/NAME INDEX

FISHING VESSELS CODE/NAME INDEX

CODE	NAME	CODE	NAME	CODE	NAME
P958	PEGASUS	PD320	MADDY MARIE	PE1048	FRESH START
P960	LADY CHRISTINA	PD323	DIANE MARIE	PE1049	EDGE ON
P968	HERON	PD33	ELEGANCE	PE107	ZAC B
P970	VIVERRINA	PD332	ATTAIN II	PE1078	JAMIE LOUISE
P975	VENTURA	PD34	BUCCANEER	PE1086	GEM
P976	JOHN EDWARD	PD340	OCEAN VENTURE II	PE1087	CARALAN
P977	JODIE B	PD342	ASHLYN	PE1090	SARAH B
P981	WAHOO	PD347	GLENUGIE	PE1094	Y NOT
P987	JENNY G	PD349	ONWARD	PE1098	MIKAL
P989	LITTLE JEM	PD35	TRANQUILITY	PE11	LITTLE OSCAR
P993	OLIVIA N	PD354	FEAR NOT II	PE1105	AMELIA JO
PD1	SPINDRIFT	PD359	MORNING DAWN	PE111	EVE
PD1018	FAST LADY	PD365	ACADIA	PE1111	LILYBEL
PD1021	VIRTUE	PD368	SURMOUNT	PE1119	SHERI LOUISE
PD1022	EVENING STAR	PD378	SUSTAIN	PE112	JOHNATHAN SEAGULL
PD1024	STELLANOVA	PD379	QUANTUS	PE1123	MABEL
PD1025	STATELY	PD38	FAYRO	PE1124	SHANIA
PD1026	NAVADA	PD4	FERTILITY	PE1125	OSIRIS
PD1032	HAPPY HOOKER	PD400	BENARKLE	PE1127	ESPERANCE
PD1054	SEA SPRAY	PD416	ELYSIAN	PE113	IVY
PD1056	FALCON	PD418	BUDDING ROSE	PE1130	GOLDEN GIRL
PD1059	KIND OF BLUE	PD43	ANNEGINA	PE1135	EMILY
PD109	FRUITFUL BOUGH	PD48	BOY JOHN	PE1141	RAPIDO
PD11	ELONA	PD5	VICHANA	PE1151	SCALLY
PD110	KINGFISHER II	PD50	GOLDEN SCEPTRE	PE1155	MACIE LOUIS
PD120	HARVEST HOPE	PD52	MIANN	PE1157	HAPPY HOOKER II
PD135	MOREMMA	PD57	SCARLET THREAD	PE1158	JULIE ANNE
PD142	IVY ROSE	PD6	DANNY BOY	PE1159	TIME AND TIDE
PD146	SUSAN K	PD65	VIGILANT	PE1164	HUMBLE
PD147	ENTERPRISE	PD67	ANITRA	PE1167	JENNIFER ANNE
PD150	STARLITE	PD707	COMPASS ROSE	PE1170	CARLY BETH
PD152	PIONEER	PD76	TERN	PE1176	ELLE JAY
PD154	SHAMROCK	PD77	OUR PRIDE	PE1181	FOX
PD158	ORION	PD776	BREN JEAN	PE1184	HARRY TOM
PD16	AURORA	PD777	SCRATCHER	PE1187	MANATEE
PD165	PATHWAY	PD780	NATASHA A	PE1188	OBSESSION
PD17	FAVONIUS	PD786	STARLIGHT	PE1193	KINDRED SPIRIT
PD175	CAROL ANN	PD787	OCEAN TRUST	PE1199	SOPHIE ROSE
PD177	AMITY II	PD8	KIWI	PE12	LEXI MICHELLE
PD178	TWO BOYS	PD83	CONSTANT FRIEND	PE1211	FAE SILVIE
PD181	GIRL MORAG	PD85	SEA WITCH	PE1212	SEA STRIKER
PD182	OCEAN BOUNTY	PD901	CONSORT	PE1218	ELMAY
PD184	ALBATROSS	PD902	BE READY	PE1219	QUO VADIS
PD19	LAUREN	PD905	HONEYBOURNE III	PE1221	LILY MAE
PD194	SHALOM	PD911	LILY	PE13	JENNIFER ANNE II
PD197	ATLANTIC CHALLENGE	PD92	MIRANDA FAYE	PE14	GREEN AND BUOYS
PD198	OCEAN HARVEST	PD96	OPPORTUNUS IV	PE144	LADY ANGELA
PD2	GUIDING LIGHT	PD965	BRITTANY JAMES	PE16	THERESA
PD202	GRATITUDE	PD97	SUMMER DAWN	PE163	HORNBLOWER
PD220	JESSICA	PD972	LAPWING	PE167	SUE
PD23	KIROAN	PD98	HARVESTER	PE169	KIM
PD235	CALISHA	PD987	PROSPERITY	PE17	ELLA GRACE
PD245	DAISY II	PD991	AGNES	PE19	AUGUST MIST
PD26	KATH B	PD996	BOY JOHN B	PE2	RADIANT STAR
PD265	LUNAR BOW	PE1	WHITE HEATHER	PE20	BIT LATE
PD294	WAKEFUL	PE10	EMMA	PE21	LYCHETT LADY
PD298	WILLIAM JOHN	PE1000	LEDA	PE219	LADY JEN
PD3	DAYBREAK	PE1038	MELANIE DAWN	PE227	PREVAIL
PD30	RUTH R	PE1042	BLUE MOON	PE229	SNAPPER
PD303	SHALIMAR II	PE1043	LITTLE JOSH	PE237	NER E NOUGH
PD313	ROSEMOUNT	PE1044	JESSICA LYNN	PE25	MOXIE

239

FISHING VESSELS CODE/NAME INDEX

FISHING VESSELS CODE/NAME INDEX

CODE	NAME	CODE	NAME	CODE	NAME
PO15	LADY HELEN	PZ1200	CELTIC SUNRISE	PZ4	CORMORAN
PO16	RACHEL ANNE	PZ1202	GEMINI TWO	PZ40	GEMMA
PO17	NORTHERN LIGHTS II	PZ1209	ROSEBUD	PZ410	SEA HUNTER
PO19	ALI B	PZ1218	SARAH STEVE	PZ428	STERGAN
PO2	VALETTA	PZ1228	TRENOW GIRL	PZ437	FRANCES ROSE
PO21	SPIRIT OF PORTLAND	PZ124	REMY D	PZ439	ELLEN
PO29	RAE OF HOPE	PZ1247	LADY JACQUELINE	PZ453	LAURIE JEAN
PO3	DODGER TOO	PZ125	PATRICE	PZ454	SUZIE
PO4	ALEXANDRA JANE	PZ127	OSPREY.	PZ462	GINGER WAVE
PO5	LUCKY DIP	PZ130	HARTLEY	PZ47	LOWENA - MOR
PO7	PORTLAND FISHER	PZ137	TWILIGHT III	PZ476	LISA JACQUELINE
PO8	SOPHIE 1	PZ14	LITTLE LAUREN		STEVENSON
PO9	FREYA MAY	PZ140	PAUL ARRAN	PZ477	MARY ROSE
PT9	FFYON MARIE	PZ146	ANNA CATHERINE	PZ478	LYONESSE OF CAPE
PT90	SKINT	PZ15	CAPRIOLE	PZ48	LORRAINE RUTH
PW1	BERLEWEN	PZ155	SARAH JANE T	PZ480	KELYN MOR
PW10	BLUE DIAMOND	PZ159	GIRL RUTH	PZ481	VIPA
PW100	OUR BELLE ANN	PZ16	SPITFIRE	PZ49	ATHENA FAY
PW104	SHARICMAR	PZ166	VENTURE	PZ490	BARRY ANN
PW105	PISCES 11	PZ17	CARISSA ANN	PZ495	JACKIE MARIE
PW11	MORE	PZ179	MERBREEZE	PZ498	STELISSA
PW473	VIDDY	PZ18	KATY	PZ499	TWILIGHT
PW474	JACQUELINE	PZ182	ASTHORE	PZ5	SOUWESTER
PW479	ANN KATHLEEN	PZ187	NOVA SPERO	PZ50	ENNIS LADY
PW485	SPINDRIFT	PZ191	WILLIAM SAMPSON	PZ51	GOVENEK OF LADRAM
PW493	SQUIDSIN		STEVENSON	PZ512	CORNISHMAN
PW494	BEENY	PZ193	TREVESSA 1V	PZ527	BASS BOY
PW496	KISS MY BASS	PZ195	WILLIAM STEVENSON	PZ53	SUNRISE
PW5	HELEN CLARE	PZ198	AALTJE ADRIAANTJE	PZ532	BILLY ROWNEY
PW56	DARING	PZ199	ALGRIE	PZ536	GAZELLE
PW6	SHANMAR	PZ2	JSW	PZ54	MILLENNIA
PW60	LITTLE PEARL	PZ20	JENNY	PZ540	GREY SEAL
PW64	TREVOSE	PZ209	TARA	PZ542	FILADELFIA
PW7	THREE WISHES	PZ21	LADY OF ENNIS	PZ557	CELTIC BREEZE
PW72	BOY REGGIE	PZ218	SPRIGS OF HEATHER	PZ564	TAMARA
PW75	PALORES	PZ22	SARAH - M	PZ574	FLOWING TIDE
PW77	GIRL RACHEL	PZ23	TREEN	PZ580	AQUILA
PW81	JULIE GIRL	PZ24	JEST	PZ584	BUTTS
PW82	ATLANTA II	PZ244	KENAVO	PZ585	CURLEW
PW85	LACY GRACE	PZ26	MAGLER-MOR	PZ592	ALICE LOUISE
PW95	ELINOR ROGET	PZ260	OUR KATIE	PZ594	STORM PETREL
PW99	VERONICA ANN	PZ27	BONNIE GRACE	PZ6	GIRL PAMELA
PZ1	SARAH BETH	PZ272	WHITE HEATHER	PZ601	FULMAR
PZ10	KAREN N	PZ28	L OGIEN	PZ609	DANDA
PZ100	ELIZABETH N	PZ291	MY LASS	PZ61	GUIDING STAR
PZ1001	RESURGAM	PZ3	ORCA	PZ611	NIK NAK
PZ101	LOUISA N	PZ3	WE-RE HERE	PZ612	RACHEL & PAUL
PZ1052	SEA MAIDEN	PZ30	LOYAL PARTNER	PZ62	SEA FOX
PZ1053	ST GEORGES	PZ302	BOY ADAM	PZ620	CAROL & DAVID
PZ11	BOY DYLAN	PZ307	JACOBA	PZ63	GOLDEN HARVEST
PZ110	IMOGEN III	PZ315	TAMSIN T	PZ631	PENVER
PZ111	JOSEPHINE	PZ317	SEA SPIRIT	PZ638	RO-MI-CHRIS
PZ115	SAPPHIRE II	PZ32	CATHRYN	PZ64	ST ELVAN
PZ118	PENDOWER	PZ329	HARVEST REAPER	PZ641	MARK & JAMES
PZ1184	CLAIRVOYANT	PZ336	NAZARENE	PZ642	SERENE
PZ1187	GIRL STELLA	PZ339	CORNISH LASS	PZ643	GARY M
PZ1191	SALLY ROSE OF NAVAX	PZ343	RUBY MAE	PZ654	HICCA
PZ1196	SILVER DAWN	PZ353	GIRL PENNY	PZ657	OUR ANNA
PZ1197	BOY JAMES	PZ379	BOY HARVEY	PZ66	SAPPHIRE
PZ1198	GOLDEN FLEECE	PZ39	FATHER BOB	PZ660	NICOLA MAY
PZ1199	SEA GOBLIN	PZ395	LISA	PZ663	CYNTHIA

241

FISHING VESSELS CODE/NAME INDEX

FISHING VESSELS CODE/NAME INDEX

FISHING VESSELS CODE/NAME INDEX

244

FISHING VESSELS CODE/NAME INDEX

CODE	NAME	CODE	NAME	CODE	NAME
SS1	BOY JAKE	SS65	HOPE	SU413	CAROLINA
SS10	GIRL CHERRY	SS66	PHRA - NANG	SU421	RYE BABY
SS11	CHARISMA	SS665	BRISSONS	SU432	GRAYLIN
SS118	CRYSTAL SEA	SS67	TRACEY CLARE	SU437	JAY-R
SS12	WAVEDANCER	SS673	MAID MEL	SU438	L'AVENTURIER
SS120	BOTE	SS681	REBECCA GRACE	SU450	LADY LINDA
SS126	NIKKI LOUISE	SS683	MARLIN G	SU461	PURBECK 11
SS13	SWEET AS	SS685	FOU DE BASSAN	SU463	ANNIES SONG
SS134	HUERS	SS694	MIDGE	SU465	I DUNNO
SS136	CYNTHIA	SS697	ELLE V	SU50	KITTIWAKE
SS138	PETER PAN	SS699	OUR LADS III	SU507	CARLOTTA
SS14	MEGWYN	SS7	DIANA	SU512	HOLLY JO
SS144	TORRI BEE	SS707	ORCA	SU513	CHALLENGE
SS149	MARANATHA	SS711	BONITO	SU514	HOPE
SS15	BROGAN	SS713	LYONESSE	SU516	SPIRITED LADY III
SS151	HAWK	SS716	SHIKARI	SU529	RALPH CLEGG
SS16	MYROSS MIST	SS717	BOY DANIEL	SU6	NO MORE
SS161	DIGNITY	SS723	SIR JACK	SU7	SOUTHERN BELLE
SS17	OSPREY	SS738	PROPER JOB	SU71	OSPREY
SS170	JEN	SS739	AUTUMN SILVER	SU916	SAM-TORI
SS173	RHIANNON JANE	SS744	SEA MAIDEN II	SU927	MUDDY WATERS
SS19	RIPPLE	SS748	RAVEN	SU949	FLORENCE
SS2	BLUE BELLE	SS759	MAXINE CHARLOTTE	SU950	ISLAND LASS
SS209	STILL WATERS	SS76	TILLERMAN	SU952	TENDER TO
SS21	TIGER	SS762	KELLY MARIE	SY1	SUNNY JIM
SS22	INSPIRATION	SS769	ROCK HOPPER	SY10	DUNAN
SS224	MARINER	SS8	ASPER	SY101	SILVER CHORD
SS225	AGAN PROVIYAS	SS80	LITTLE CHRISTINA	SY11	NORTHERN STAR
SS226	DAPHNE ROSE	SS84	THREE JAYS	SY118	RAONAID
SS227	AGAN DEVEDHEK	SS87	PRIDE OF CORNWALL	SY123	GIRL HANNAH
SS229	AGAN BORLOWEN	SS88	TEGEN MOR	SY128	SPINDRIFT
SS233	TRYPHENA	SS9	CADOR	SY13	MISTLETOE
SS24	JODA	SS92	ELISHIA	SY132	SEALGAIR MARA
SS247	WINKLE	SSS49	REBECCA JAYNE A	SY135	SHEILA II
SS25	KELLY GIRL	SSS677	LAUREN G	SY136	VIGILANT B
SS252	BETHSHAN	SSS680	ENA DOLAN	SY137	SEABREEZE
SS258	TUDOR ROSE	SSS682	MANHAVEN LAD	SY14	ISA
SS261	AMMO	SSS7	GUIDING STAR	SY144	LEAD US
SS262	ANNA MARIA	ST1	ENTERPRISE	SY148	FAMILY FRIEND
SS266	BELLE BETTINA	ST2	SEAGLORY TT	SY15	BOY ANGUS
SS268	RAZORBILL	ST5	DREAM CATCHER	SY153	ASTRA III
SS270	ZARA	ST7	VIRGO	SY16	JACAMAR II
SS273	ORION	SU1	EXTREME	SY172	REDEEMED
SS276	BOY CHRIS	SU10	INSPIRATION	SY18	IRIS
SS28	LAMORNA	SU116	GALWAD-Y-MOR OF	SY190	SHARON ROSE
SS284	JOHN WESLEY		LYMINGTON	SY192	SEA DART
SS3	GUIDE ME	SU135	SHOOTING STAR	SY197	VALIANT
SS30	ROSEBUD	SU156	AUDACITY	SY2	OCEAN SPIRIT
SS32	SEA BREEZE	SU177	BENJAMIN GUY	SY201	ATHENA M
SS324	BRODI SEA	SU20	COASTAL FLYER	SY203	DAWN
SS33	WHITE HEATHER	SU206	SHEARWATER II	SY205	STRENUOUS
SS35	MAGGIE	SU21	DEJA VU	SY21	KAYLANA
SS4	LUCY	SU233	ANGELLE MARIE	SY212	HARMONY
SS40	TOL BAR	SU3	AT LAST	SY213	MAY C
SS41	SANDPIPER	SU301	SOUTHWEST ISLE	SY22	ORION
SS45	SHANNON	SU302	BOY DAVID	SY23	MAIRI
SS46	MARY MO	SU349	SEA CREST	SY248	SEMPER VIGILO
SS5	KLONDYKE	SU370	SANDIE ANN	SY26	CATRIONA I
SS53	NORAH-T	SU388	NIGHTRIDER OF	SY27	TRACY K
SS6	MOLLIE DAWN		KEYHAVEN	SY274	RIVAL II
SS61	KEIRA	SU412	EIYEEN	SY276	CATHERINE ANN

245

FISHING VESSELS CODE/NAME INDEX

CODE	NAME	CODE	NAME	CODE	NAME
SY28	SOVEREIGN	SY830	QUANTUS	TN101	MAR DE CRETA
SY3	WAVECREST	SY839	CASHFLO	TN102	DAWN MAID
SY30	LOUISA	SY840	SELKIE	TN104	BON AMY
SY300	OSPREY	SY841	SAPPHIRE	TN16	NATHALIE
SY303	GRATITUDE II	SY842	WESTERN CHIEF	TN18	CONCHRA
SY304	INTEGRITY	SY843	EMMA	TN2	TOBRACH N
SY305	AMETHYST	SY85	SIARACH III	TN20	SEA LADY
SY307	ELIZABETH M	SY854	ALINE	TN30	NOORDZEE
SY309	DELTA DAWN A	SY861	CHIEFTAIN	TN35	OLIVIA JEAN
SY337	COMRADE	SY862	MATT DEE	TN36	MATTANJA
SY340	GUIDE US	SY864	RHODA	TN37	PHILOMENA
SY345	REBEKAH ERIN	SY868	BOY ANDREW	TN38	GEORGELOU - N
SY35	PHOENIX	SY869	PEARL	TN40	MAR DE BENS
SY37	RANGER A	SY872	LUAIREAG	TN45	RACHEL STAR
SY378	WANDERER II	SY873	CARLSBAY	TN98	FRIENDLY ISLE
SY38	JUNE-ANNE	SY874	ZENITH	TO10	SARAH JANE
SY4	CESCA	SY882	BOY ARRAN	TO11	LEWIS
SY400	CEOL NA MARA	SY883	MADKATLIZ	TO2	MOLLY T
SY41	FULMAR	SY884	NEW DAWN	TO23	BEN LOYAL
SY412	SPEEDWELL	SY886	POLARIS	TO3	LILYS PRIDE
SY46	FRAOCH GEAL	SY888	QUEENIE	TO32	AJAX
SY47	HEATHER ISLE M	SY889	LANTIC BOW	TO4	ZONA
SY474	MAIRI BHAN	SY890	KITTIWAKE	TO40	INTUITION
SY48	JANINE	SY891	MAYBE	TO41	BOY RYAN
SY5	WINDY ISLE	SY892	SALTIRE	TO46	SHAMROCK
SY50	GIRL RONA II	SY969	BOY GRANT III	TO48	GOOD FORTUNE
SY503	OCEAN HUNTER	SY99	JUNE ROSE	TO5	MARINA II
SY524	SEA OTTER	TH1	MARLIN	TO50	HARRIET EVE
SY532	KITTIWAKE	TH115	SANTOY	TO60	EMMA LOUISE
SY540	FAITHFUL	TH117	GIRL RONA	TO62	FIONA ROSE
SY559	SILVER SPRAY	TH135	ROCK HOPPER	TO64	WHITE MARLIN II
SY564	ISABEL ANNE	TH155	DAWN HUNTER II	TO7	COSMOS MARINER
SY571	SOLUIS	TH156	BIG BEAR	TT1	DOLPHIN
SY573	MARION	TH169	GERRY ANN	TT10	GWALCH-Y-MOR
SY6	SERENE	TH177	ICHTHUS	TT100	NANCY GLEN
SY606	ST CLAIR	TH181	PROPITIOUS	TT101	TARKA
SY64	MARANATHA	TH19	HENRY	TT104	FIONNAGHAL
SY659	PROCEED	TH2	PISCES	TT105	HIGHLANDER
SY670	FIONA	TH20	MARGARET	TT137	FRIGATE BIRD
SY678	SOAY II	TH21	EYECATCHER	TT159	RHIANNON
SY69	MANG	TH24	MIDNIGHT SUN	TT183	STELLA MARIS
SY7	SHEIGRA	TH257	GERRY ANN C	TT2	BOY JONATHAN
SY70	SINCERITY	TH276	ROSIE	TT237	NIGHEAN DONN
SY720	CRUSADER	TH288	GOLDEN LANCER	TT242	WEEMARA
SY73	KESTREL	TH3	OUR GRACE	TT244	SAIL FREE
SY75	ACHIEVE	TH37	ALICE	TT25	VILLAGE MAID
SY756	GANNET	TH377	EQUITY	TT251	SUNBEAM
SY76	KERISTUM	TH4	BOYS OWN	TT252	GOLDEN WEST
SY788	DELTA DAWN III	TH417	VALKYRIE	TT255	HEATHER III
SY79	GOOD INTENT	TH420	AMANDA JANE	TT26	MARGARITA
SY799	ONWARD	TH424	KAY LARIE	TT262	KINGFISHER
SY8	WHINIVER	TH436	GIRL SCOUT	TT267	SCOTIA STAR
SY801	PROVIDER	TH5	HOPE	TT270	SEA DART II
SY807	ZEPHYR	TH6	DAY DREAMER	TT272	FLYING FISH OF TARBERT
SY808	THREE SISTERS	TH7	AMADEUS	TT273	WHITE HEATHER
SY816	MARDELL	TH74	BRONCO	TT276	PRIDE N JOY
SY818	SCALPAY ISLE	TH77	EUROCLYDON	TT277	ELLA M
SY819	GOLDEN DAWN	TH8	MARIAN	TT278	BLUEBELL
SY823	JEMET III	TH82	MOIRA F	TT279	DESTINY
SY828	SHARATAN	TH86	SAMMY B	TT280	BLACK KNIGHT
SY829	AN CUANTACH	TH90	DIRE STRAITS	TT282	SEMPER VICTORIA

246

FISHING VESSELS CODE/NAME INDEX

CODE	NAME	CODE	NAME	CODE	NAME
TT34	CALEDONIA	UL45	FRANCHISE	WA72	TEDDERA
TT35	WENDY LIAM	UL48	FORTITUDE	WA73	RADIANT STAR
TT37	SILVER LINING III	UL5	SEA SPRAY	WA8	HEADWAY
TT5	KATHLEEN	UL50	SILVER FJORD	WA85	CRYSTAL STAR
TT56	VENTURE	UL52	QUEST	WH1	PHOSPHORESCENT
TT57	MARYEARED	UL54	HIGHLAND SEABIRD	WH10	ROCK N ROLLER
TT7	CINTRA	UL541	MARGARET	WH103	DELTA BARBARA
TT7	CINTRA	UL543	OUR HAZEL	WH11	SHONALEE
TT71	POLARLYS	UL545	TRUE VINE II	WH111	BETHANY J
TT75	GALLOPER	UL548	GUNNERS GLORY	WH118	DUSTY
TT77	SILVER SPRAY 111	UL551	RANGER	WH12	SKINDEEPER
TT87	MO MHAIRI	UL554	AUK	WH1236	UTSKER
TT89	CYGNET	UL56	INTREPID	WH13	BLACK PEARL
TT93	SEA SPRAY	UL560	SOLO	WH14	SPIRIT
UL1	ONWARD	UL562	SERENE	WH148	RAMPANT
UL100	PHOENIX	UL564	ANNA MAIRI	WH15	SWORDFISH
UL105	BORERAY ISLE	UL565	SARAH	WH16	BELIVIA
UL107	KATIE LOU	UL572	VIKING III	WH166	GILLIAN S
UL12	BOY ANDREW	UL573	MAIRI ANNA	WH17	BIT ON THE SIDE
UL121	TARA LOUISE	UL574	CELTIC PRIDE	WH181	ATHENA
UL128	KITTIWAKE	UL576	BROSME	WH19	LAUREN
UL137	HARMONY	UL577	DASU	WH197	FISH EAGLE
UL138	NORTHERN LIGHTS	UL578	CHRISTIAN M	WH2	SEALG BRIGH
UL14	FREEBIRD	UL584	LADY NICOLA	WH20	ALANDA
UL142	TWO SISTERS	UL588	SCOOBY DOO	WH22	MARAUDER
UL144	KYRENE	UL59	PROMISE	WH233	ROUGET
UL145	KILDONAN	UL590	TRUST	WH251	THATS IT
UL16	KATIE	UL591	MAREIXON	WH256	SARAH LOUISE
UL176	FULMAR	UL594	MADADH CUAIN	WH264	PROSPECTOR
UL18	DOROTHY ANN	UL595	COURAGE	WH282	GIBSONS CHOICE
UL181	MICHELLE WISEMAN	UL610	ISLAND - PRINCESS	WH29	STELLA ANN
UL193	BOUNTIFULL	UL62	ATLANTIA	WH296	PORTLAND ISLE
UL198	KAY WYE	UL63	CASPIAN III	WH3	MOLLY JAYNE
UL210	SUPREME	UL666	TAHUME	WH311	MALIBU
UL214	GOLDEN ISLES	UL7	JULIE D	WH321	EVENTIDE
UL222	ZENITH	UL72	CEANOTHUS	WH324	LIKELY LAD
UL23	VAGABOND	UL77	TAURUS	WH326	DELLA M
UL231	VIKING	UL78	GLEN COUL	WH332	MOONSHINE
UL24	LOUANDRIC	UL8	ISABELLA	WH336	JIMMY JOE
UL240	LADY VAL II	UL81	FREYA	WH34	PORTLAND PREFECT
UL25	WALRUS	UL82	LAURSCOTT	WH347	IONA
UL251	CHALICE II	UL85	NETTA	WH36	FEARLESS
UL256	ALBATROSS	UL98	BRIGHT HORIZON	WH368	FREYA
UL257	EDER SANDS	WA1	DAYBREAK	WH370	RAINBOW
UL26	MAJESTIC	WA14	HORACE WRIGHT	WH4	MARY J
UL27	CHALLENGER	WA2	SYRINEN	WH401	AUDREY
UL28	BAY OF PLENTY	WA22	JOKER OF NAVAX	WH407	KAREN LYNN
UL29	OPPORTUNE	WA223	MY LADS	WH425	QUARTER BELL
UL298	DUNBYIN	WA224	RACHEL CLAIRE	WH442	PAM
UL300	ARCTURUS	WA256	KBJ	WH445	JOCELYN
UL32	HARVEST LILY	WA257	SEA HAWK	WH448	RITA JOYCE
UL33	EXCELSIOR	WA258	SHELLY	WH452	SUNDANCE
UL335	EXODUS	WA261	KERRY MARIA	WH457	BOY LIAM
UL34	ISLE RISTOL	WA265	HOLLY JANE	WH477	MALACCA
UL341	SKUA	WA31	STJERNEN	WH478	NIMBLE
UL343	AQUARIUS	WA32	ARKTOS	WH48	ARETHUSA
UL347	GOLDEN DAWN	WA35	KINLOCH	WH481	SEABIRD
UL348	AVOCET	WA37	SCOTIA	WH5	KELSEY JANE
UL37	BRISCA	WA38	BARBARA ANNE	WH511	WAIKIKI
UL4	SEA VENTURE	WA39	REVENGE	WH515	MASADA
UL44	LOCH INCHARD II	WA5	PATSY ANNE	WH57	NEW DAWN

247

FISHING VESSELS CODE/NAME INDEX

CODE	NAME	CODE	NAME	CODE	NAME
WH578	BOY BRAX	WK126	DIPPER	WK673	BOY SHANE
WH582	HAYLEY GRACE	WK129	ELLA	WK674	GIRL BETH
WH584	KALUGER	WK13	RAMBLIN ROSE	WK676	LOYAL FRIEND
WH586	SUPERSTAR	WK14	OSPREY	WK677	ROCK
WH587	TRY AGAIN	WK148	SKUA	WK680	KATIE MAREE
WH588	HAVEN	WK15	CALYPSO	WK699	CHOTI
WH589	KING QUIDDLE	WK158	SANS PEUR	WK7	RHEA
WH590	JEMMA T	WK16	C LOUISE	WK70	SHEIGRA
WH6	DAISY T	WK17	PEBBLES	WK71	SAMAR
WH606	LITTLE LAUREN	WK170	BOY ANDREW	WK72	GUNNHILDA
WH66	ALLYCAT	WK171	OPPORTUNE	WK73	ARUN DIVER II
WH684	ALMORAH	WK18	GIRL EVIE	WK8	OCEAN BRIDE
WH685	SKUA	WK181	COMRADES	WK80	SILVER CLOUD II
WH686	STARGAZER	WK19	SANS PEUR II	WK803	BOY ALAN
WH69	TELMAR	WK190	YUNG DHAL	WK806	TAMMIE NORRIE
WH695	ALMORAH TOO	WK191	BONNIE LASS	WK810	BOY RICHIE II
WH700	LIDDL'UN	WK2	GIRL ELLIE	WK811	SPRAY
WH704	SOLE VENTURE	WK20	MAYFLOWER	WK814	KEMARVIN
WH707	ZARANATHAX	WK209	GOOD HOPE	WK818	STRATHDONAN
WH709	RUM RUNNER	WK21	ORION II	WK820	GIRL MILLIE
WH71	LA SERIME	WK22	AQUARIUS	WK822	GIRL ERICA
WH715	ROCKHOPPER	WK24	GIRL JUSTINE	WK823	MAGGIE ANNE
WH717	CHRISTINE	WK241	ERIN	WK825	ISABEL
WH719	SILVER SPIRIT	WK242	INCENTIVE I	WK826	BOY JORDON
WH729	BRUISER	WK26	ANGELA	WK827	BLOSSOM
WH736	BLUE DART III	WK27	DAWN MIST 11	WK828	NORTHERN STAR
WH737	MOJO	WK28	NORSE COURAGE	WK832	AIMEE J
WH741	CHELSEA	WK29	BOY KIAN	WK833	DAWN STAR
WH744	WAHOO	WK30	NAOMI M	WK835	ANNA MARIE
WH75	CHARLOTTE LILY	WK301	DAISY	WK837	TEGAN
WH755	OBI I	WK302	SPINDRIFT	WK838	MA-RONA
WH757	FREELINER	WK306	MHAIRI KIRSTEEN	WK839	RAMBLING ROSE
WH758	KATHLEEN II	WK32	KELVIN STAR	WK84	VALHALLA II
WH760	BOUDICCA	WK338	CELTIC STAR	WK856	ABBYJACK
WH763	GORDEANO STAR	WK341	SEAJAY V	WK858	MOLLY
WH764	GROWLER	WK350	SARDONYX II	WK859	BOY JOHN
WH768	ROYAL ESCAPE	WK36	KAREN JANE	WK86	ELIZA DOT
WH769	BETHANY MILLICENT	WK377	CORMORANT	WK860	CLAIRE LOUISE
WH775	CHRISSIE JEAN	WK4	CARINA	WK862	CHARLIE JACK
WH777	SHAMAN	WK40	KINGFISHER	WK864	WEST COASTER
WH783	HELENA J	WK407	KITTIWAKE	WK867	GIRL ABBELL
WH785	LIZZY JANE	WK41	KESTREL	WK868	MAREA B II
WH786	CLEAR HORIZON	WK42	IONA	WK874	BOY PETER
WH8	DREAM CATCHER	WK45	STEPHANIE	WK875	ANNA MARIE II
WH856	VALIRON	WK456	VITAL SPARK II	WK876	DORIS ANNE
WH9	DAWN MIST	WK46	LILY V	WK9	SERENE
WH90	IAN LLOYD	WK47	SUNBEAM	WK91	DRIFT FISHER
WH95	FLYING FISHER	WK477	LULU	WK914	BOY LIAM
WH97	DRAGUN-AN-MOAR	WK479	BOY JAMES	WK98	DOLPHIN
WH99	KINGFISHER	WK48	SCOTIA	WO1	WE LIKE IT
WI3	FREYA	WK498	VENTURE	WO115	NIGHTHAWK
WK1	BARBARA	WK5	DRIFT FISHER 11	WO130	WENDY II
WK10	WEST WINDS	WK52	CHUSAN	WO148	BOUNTY
WK104	MARGARET ELLEN	WK53	KAYLEIGH	WO15	OLLY
WK106	WANDERER	WK54	CAROL ANNE	WO270	JAYDEE
WK108	LORRINE	WK6	STAR O' STAXIGOE	WO370	CHALLENGER
WK115	ORCADIA	WK62	PANDORA	WO4	BOY CALLUM
WK118	HOPE III	WK66	COMPANION	WO41	MISCHIEF
WK12	KATIE	WK664	RARA AVIS	WO5	NEW VENTURE
WK120	VAR LISA	WK668	AZURE	WO51	SHE-D-LEA
WK122	MAPLE LEAF	WK669	SARAH LOUISE	WO664	JILL

248

FISHING VESSELS CODE/NAME INDEX

CODE	NAME	CODE	NAME	CODE	NAME
WO668	AMETHYST	WY809	ARTEMIS	YH320	NORTHERN LIGHTS
WY1	GOLDEN DAYS	WY81	OCEAN PEARL	YH33	AURORA
WY100	ANNIE	WY810	BAY JOE	YH333	SARA NAOMI
WY102	SAXON LADY	WY812	MARGARET ELIZABETH	YH34	SEA VENTURE
WY115	SEA HARVEST	WY818	STORMY C	YH350	CHARLOTTE MARIE
WY126	IRENE	WY819	BOY MITCHELL	YH363	BLUE BOY
WY127	PATRIOT	WY820	EASTER MORN	YH365	SURF DANCER
WY133	CHALLENGE A	WY821	LUCY ANN	YH394	SHETLAND SUN
WY143	QUEST	WY825	PHEOBE	YH4	ALEXI ROSE
WY144	JANE ELIZABETH	WY830	CHUTNEY	YH401	LUCKY STAR
WY150	KATIE H	WY833	WILD CAT	YH432	SUNSHINE II
WY151	COURAGE	WY836	FRENCHIE	YH438	BOY DANIEL
WY157	CRIMOND	WY837	LUCY	YH45	GRACE ELIZABETH
WY160	LEON	WY839	ROBBYN	YH458	JONATHAN JAMES
WY168	SOPHIE LOUISE	YH1	LOLA KATE	YH46	EARLY ROSE
WY17	GENTLE BARBARA II	YH10	ELLIE JANE	YH48	EARLY ROSE II
WY170	COPIOUS	YH1044	YOUNG LAUREN	YH481	SOLAR STAR
WY173	EMMA JANE	YH11	BOY CHARLIE	YH488	DANIELLE
WY177	BOY ANDREW	YH115	NORTHERN PRIDE	YH497	HEIDI
WY191	FULMAR	YH116	TOMKIT	YH5	SILVER SPRAY
WY209	ELLEN	YH119	ANN MARIE	YH529	SHIPMATES
WY210	CHARLOTTE	YH1245	IF ONLY II	YH533	WILLING BOYS
WY212	SUCCESS III	YH15	ACHIEVABLE	YH537	POCO LOCO
WY218	PRIDE AND JOY	YH16	SEAQUEST	YH563	HIGHLIGHT
WY224	BRIGHTER HOPE	YH2	INDAVA	YH585	CRYSTAL WATERS
WY232	PEARL III	YH206	METEOR	YH6	KIRSTY LEE
WY237	MAYFLOWER A	YH212	IRENE D II	YH7	FIRST LIGHT
WY245	PRUSAK.K	YH213	MARY ANN	YH71	VICTORIA
WY251	FLORA JANE	YH214	REAP	YH776	CHARLIE JOHN
WY261	OUR LASS III	YH238	COMET	YH78	CLAIRE MARIE
WY268	SILVER JUBILEE	YH239	CLAIRE ANN	YH79	LADY IRIS
WY28	NORTHERN ISLE	YH2413	ANNA GAIL	YH845	ALISON KATHERINE
WY304	JENNIFER MARGARET	YH2442	CHARLES WILLIAM	YH86	LADY LAURA
WY318	WHITBY CREST	YH2447	BOY CLIVE	YH9	LISA DIANE
WY319	AURELIA	YH2450	EKEDE	YH909	JAYNE MARIE
WY321	WENDY G	YH2454	JANE ANNE I	YH927	MA FREEN
WY333	DOMINATOR A	YH2460	EVELYN JANE	YH966	CHARLOTTE
WY335	SARDIA LOUISE	YH2462	LEAH		
WY341	NEVER CAN TELL A	YH2466	DONT KNOW		
WY366	J.T. GANNET	YH2470	CARA MARIE		
WY369	BOX-A-DAY	YH2472	TANMAR II		
WY37	NICOLA L	YH2473	RORY JAMES		
WY372	ANDIGEE	YH2474	IMPULSIVE		
WY38	PAMELA S	YH2476	CANDY		
WY4	BRYONY	YH2478	TRADEWINDS 2		
WY50	ANNIE BAINBRIDGE	YH2483	GIRL GUCCI		
WY53	PATRICIA CHRISTINE	YH2484	JESSICA BETH		
WY57	J C L	YH2485	SYLVIA MAY		
WY60	PROSPERITY	YH2487	IRENE D		
WY68	SILVER LINE W	YH2489	HAPPY DAYS		
WY71	B G	YH2490	PREDATOR		
WY77	ADVANCE	YH2502	HAPPISBURGH BUOY		
WY779	MARY ANN	YH26	STAR		
WY78	RESOLUTION	YH27	SAMARA		
WY780	NAZANNA	YH273	TOMKAT		
WY789	WHITBY LASS	YH281	HANNAH LOUISE		
WY79	C LADY	YH29	MANDY KIM		
WY793	ROSS	YH293	MY GIRLS II		
WY803	RAN	YH294	ALICIA		
WY805	OUR JOE	YH299	MARY D		
WY806	OLIVIA ROSE	YH3	RICHARD WILLIAM		

10699201R10140

Printed in Great Britain
by Amazon.co.uk, Ltd.,
Marston Gate.